To:

HqzEE
AND KEN

FROM JOHN G, SCHROEDER

Also by John G. Schroeder

History 1946-52, Headquarters
Army Security Agency, Pacific
(HQ ASAPAC)

Winning In Spite Of

Jeri and Jack's Adventures

By John G. (Jack) Schroeder

ISBN 978-0-692-22760-2

Printed in the United States of America

Printed by Edwards Brothers Malloy
Ann Arbor, Michigan 48104

Accepting our loss of Jeri with no realistic thoughts of what to do next—my thoughts turned later to tell our children about our travels for something to say with them. As I continued doing this off and on, one of our daughters said, "Dad can't you write these stories down for our memories of mom!" At first I had no intention of doing this but as time went on "why not."

Early thoughts were perhaps it would be better to write what I remember and let it go at that. As my stories became interesting, humorous, meaningful, etc, I began talking to them more and more even to the point of when they asked if I had a title to use—"Winning in Spite Of" was my first and only title—it fit so very well!

A few early stories led to many stories almost unbelievable. We were on our way!

How could Jeri smile and seemingly ignore MS?

We did it, even with a wheelchair. We were moving on!

It was quite a ride—doing things our way!

A close friend of ours once said to us, "How can this be!"

John (Jack) Schroeder
November 30, 2013

Our Family

Jeri, Jack, Jodi, Jami, Jeff, Bob, Katie, Jenny, Kelly, Craig, Dylan, Chloe, Niki, Sierra, Sophia

"WINNING IN SPITE OF"

JACK AND JERI 2009

THE SMILE TELLS IT ALL - The story of Jeri, her funs and triumphs.

The fun, adventures, disappointments and triumphs of some of Jack and Jeri Schroeder and family over a period of time when we all grew up with Jeri and her smile. What a fantastic wife, mother and "gram."

The subtitle "JACK AND JERI 2009" of our book was actually created many years ago when our Jami gave us a beautiful hard cover double section red scrapbook entitled in gold "The Adventures of Jack & Jeri." We never used it. The name we based our subtitle on.

JERI AND A FEW FAMILY TIMES

5/10/09 - A song and words made up by two of our granddaughters, Sierra and Chloe, and presented to our family "Christmas in May" gathering at Craig and Jami Baker's home.

To: Gram: The best Gram in the world.
     Wish you were here.
By: Sierra Schroeder and Chloe Baker

We never knew what you went through.
But all of our dreams did come true.
With you by our side everything will be all right.

Wish you were here for us to say.
How much we miss you every day.
Wish you were here so we wouldn't shed our tears

Our theme "traveling song" to Churchill

Jack and Jeri, we're on our way
    into the north
    into the sun.
Jack and Jeri, we'll be back
    another day
    another nite.

Jeri's book – nicknames for our grandchildren who helped Jeri and her book:

Dylan - "Ginza"	Famous Tokyo street	
Sierra - "Fujio"	From Japanese Mt. Fuji	
Chloe - "Sunshine"	From what Jeri called Jami	
Katie - "Ojio"	Town (Oji) in Tokyo (ASA located)	
Jenny - "Watashi"	Japanese for "me" (Jeri used when signing letters to Jack)	
Kelly - "Idake"	Adak – an Alaska Aleutian Island	
Sophia - "Menobabyson" from Japanese "babyson"		

AN INTRODUCTION...This is a story about Geraldine Elaine Schroeder, better known as Jeri Schroeder and best known as simply Jeri. It is not intended to be a biography. It is intended, and we believe it is, to be a happy story, one that our family and friends will enjoy. It is also intended to assist persons who might be facing a long term stay with illness, especially confined to a wheelchair. It is intended to relate how Jeri, with the help of family and friends, overcame the difficulty she had with Multiple Sclerosis (MS) and the problems it brought in affecting her life.

We always seemed to have fun together as a family. We never kept things from Jeri, good or bad news, especially reference MS. We decided early on that the MS cure was out there and that someone would find it. Meanwhile, we lived our life our way.

This story is made up of "stories" and "incidents." Incidents refer to so-called problems Jeri faced primarily because of her MS and how she and we were able to solve most of them. To solve all the problems was simply not possible, but we tried. Reference incidents, no names are included. Names are not important. The incidents are. Many of the stories and incidents are ended without a conclusion. These are deliberate for the reader to decide a conclusion.

Humor was the needed ingredient of our life for and with Jeri. Some of my humor included may sound somewhat mean. Ignore the meanness. Jeri and I knew each other well and always knew neither one would hurt the other. So laugh with us. She said her share of funny things in such a way, I never did find out which one of us was the comedian and which one was the straight guy.

The entire story is centered around Jeri with some areas including family stories and even a few with family friends Jeri and I "adopted" along the way.

"Jeri's Life As She Made It"

All Boy

All Girl-Prom   All "Saint"

GETTING TO KNOW JERI.........by way of myself, our family, friends and unexpected strangers **- even a kiss from President Bill Clinton.**

Talking with a priest we knew about our family and about the strange things we always seemed to get involved with, he remarked, "You are a unique family, you know." Never ever knew what was meant by that but it sounded interesting.

We kind of put our family together one by one with nothing really in mind except we knew we would have a good one.

I was born in Wheeling WV, Jeri in Sewickley PA, Jodi in Akron, Jami in Youngstown and Jeff in Akron. One unfortunate miscarriage by Jeri, for unknown reasons, happened before Jodi.

Jami was Jeri's "Sunshine," Jeff was Jeri's "Little Drummer Boy," Jodi was our "Jodio." After the miscarriage, Jodi saved us and become our first born and later, because of Jeri's MS, often stood in as the big sister and sometimes filling in for Jeri, as mother.

Jodi had a "ton" of food allergies for her first seven years. She was allergic to all foods. Jeri had to bake bread etc and buy from special stores all of Jodi's food. Jeri even got a recipe from a pancake house which showed her how to bake for her. Jodi would break out severely behind her knees and elbows. We had medicine to put on these but the pain was such that we would often do it at night when she was asleep.

I'm not sure how they did it but Jodi's doctor was able to test Jodi for a food and if she was allergic to it, they prepared drops, of what, I don't know. Jeri was our nurse, doctor and scientist among other titles. For additional other food tests showing Jodi being allergic to, the drops prepared for that food could be mixed together. Jeri took Jodi there for constant testing. After so many selected foods were covered, Jeri would be able to give Jodi the drops and the foods that were covered. It worked. Drops were easy to take, there were no adverse reactions.

At seven years, Jodi, as predicted by the doctor, outgrew almost all of this and enjoyed her first taste of chocolate.

Jami and Jeff were our precious baby adoptions. Jami was such a pretty baby that the Akron newspaper wanted to show her picture. We were afraid that someone might recognize her and want her back. When we picked Jami up at Catholic Charities, their dog came after me. I was wearing a suit and it grabbed my pants leg and ripped a hole in it. When we received the call from Catholic Charities that they had Jeff ready for us, they thought about not calling yet because they knew we had reservations at "Disney World" in Florida and didn't want to spoil our trip. We told them that we would gladly give up our trip for Jeff and were happy they called us now. Jeff was all "boy" and grew up nicely with his two sisters. He became a very good drummer in a band.

In both adoptions, Jeri would take new clothes for them and change them right then and there. They were only able to give us a little verbal history about them. We didn't care. We got what we came for. Eventually, we had to appear in court to make it final. One judge said, "It was the only occasion that I enjoyed doing."

Jeri was a delight to know for many reasons. She rarely cried, a few tears mostly from MS pain. She was rarely angry - would feel bad when someone let her down - it's hard to believe that anyone would give Jeri a hard time. With three small children, there were a few occasions when she would give each a slight slap on their leg as needed. The slap did not hurt them, the noise did. She would never threaten them with, "I'll tell your father when he comes home." My grown children informed me that she had to chase them a few times to give them her slap. Shame on them, telling on their mother like that! It's a wonder she didn't slap me also.

She would get them settled down to go to sleep and I would go in and do something funny and get them laughing. I never did understand why that bothered her? It never bothered me.

There were other times when the children needed a little more than a pep talk. I was afraid I would hurt them. Passing my "blessing" on to Jeri to do what she had to do (or was it the three on one odds that I wasn't about to face) to settle a problem, this time she used her shoe on Jodi and tried soap in the mouth on Jami. The soap didn't work as Jami laughed and said that she liked eating it. Jeri reached for her handy hot pepper. "Stick out your tongue" brought fast results. Meanwhile I left the room. No way did I want Jeri coming after me with her hot pepper.

Then there was the time I handled a problem with one of our crew all by myself. It was Jodi. One day she was telling me something that happened. In explaining her story a bit excited, I was listening quietly, probably half asleep, when she used a certain word that not only caught my ear but I almost hit the ceiling. I yelled at her something fierce, "Don't you ever use that word again." In a state of complete surprise, she asked, "What word?" I said, "You know what word I mean." Frightened, Jodi said, "Dad, What does that word mean?" Then I realized that she really did not know the meaning of the word. I scared her and felt bad. It was a case of jumping to the wrong conclusion. She really did not know what it meant.

Jeri always saw to it that there was always enough money and time for the children to do things they would want to do such as baton, dancing, scouting, football, swimming etc. All three became excellent swimmers.

As every mother knows, getting the children to these activities generally falls on them, Jeri was no exception. At dancing classes for Jodi, the teacher's pianist quit. The teacher said she would have to cancel dancing without a pianist. Jeri told her that she knew a little piano and possibly enough to fill in. By glory, she did it. She fooled me completely. Actually she was very good.

Other activities Jeri got involved in on "her" time included volunteering to work with the children's program in the Home Economics Department at Kent State (Jeri was enrolled there). She loved doing this and did it for quite some time until the Department decided to make it a paying job and wanted to begin paying Jeri. Believe it or not, Jeri was actually insulted that they would offer money to help these children. She resigned.

As time moved on and we came slowly into our MS era, it became important to our family that we understand Jeri more so we would be able to help her more. This was not a planned program, just one that we would learn as we went.

As specialist after specialist could not find anything wrong with Jeri, we knew it was going to be up to us to help her and ourselves live a normal happy life. When we found out she was reluctantly treated as having a mystery ailment of MS, we were more determined to live our family way even with some adjustments. Our slogan became, "We will wait for the cure but meanwhile, let's be ourselves." It wasn't a case of being brave. It was just that "we can do it." This "familyship" at this time helped Jeri feel that she was not alone.

By now, we knew a lot about Jeri, and she knew a lot about us. We knew we would have to distract her from thinking too much about MS. Of course, she would see doctors and, we would keep up with learning about MS etc. Meanwhile, we would begin doing more things. She had a great so called sense of humor. I began making fun comments out of situations which perhaps were not considered funny by some people or perhaps that I was offending Jeri. No way would this happen. I would tell these little stories usually in front of Jeri. She never wanted anyone to feel sorry for her and she enjoyed these situation stories - these were our means of entertaining ourselves and others. I would always try to watch her as I told a story to see if she were smiling which, I think, was always. These were our fun times we remembered.

A few examples which worked and were used many times:

People would ask me, if I was frightened when I had to go out on a highway with Jeri and her wheelchair? I would answer, "No, Jeri was in front."

Other times, when wheeling down a steep hill on a sidewalk, someone would offer to help me hold back the wheelchair. As we would start down with our helper holding the wheelchair on a front side, I would ask them if they could run. They weren't sure of what to say. I would continue by saying, "In case I let go, you'll have to run after it." After a brief pause, they would realize I was joking and we would laugh. Jeri would laugh also (I think).

With the travel we were doing, I would often be asked, "Why do you make Jeri take all of these trips when she could be resting?" "I don't. Jeri makes me take her."

Top this off when one time at my Army reunion, one of our members came up to me as everyone was preparing to leave.

He asked me, "Jack, are you coming again next year?"

I said, "Yes" that I would be here.

He then asked, "Is Jeri coming next year?"

I told him, "Yes, Jeri is coming next year."

He said, "Good, If Jeri comes, you don't have to come."

I liked that one. I thought it was precious.

For Jeri "even a kiss from President Bill Clinton"

Running for reelection for president, on August 26, 1996, President Clinton's campaign train made a scheduled stop in our city of Bowling Green, Ohio. Jeri and I, along with our daughter Jami went to the downtown area where his train was to stop. The area was roped off and a crowd of over 20,000 on a warm evening was gathered. With Jeri in a wheelchair, someone told us where they were letting people in wheelchairs watch - right up front. President Clinton appeared and addressed the crowd from the rear train's platform for about 30 minutes. When he was finished, he came down from the train and started shaking hands. It had just started getting dark and was somewhat hard to see him as walked along behind the rope set up. As he walked along shaking as many hands as he could at face level, we figured he would walk right by Jeri since she was sitting low in her wheelchair covered by faceless arms and hands over and around her by by faceless arms and hands over and around her by people doing their best to get to the President's handshake. When President Clinton got in front of Jeri, he stopped, looked down, hesitated and took both her hands and placed them in his. Concentrating and looking only at Jeri, he said, "Thanks for coming, God bless you" and raised her hands and kissed them. He looked at me, I said, "She has MS." He answered "Oh" hesitated and then continued shaking other hands.

Senator John Glenn also shook Jeri's hands as well as Representative Marcy Kaptur. President Clinton's daughter Chelsea was also there and was a big hit with the college students present.

Sometime later, Jeri and I decided to send President Clinton a letter telling him about his evening in Bowling Green. With thousands surrounding you and holding out their arms to shake your hand, you stopped in front of Jeri, looked down at her, slowly picked up both her hands (which she cannot move), kissed them and said, "God bless you," a very solemn and sincere moment. This did more for Jeri than any medicine has been able to do for her. "God bless you this time!"

SAYINGS

Jeri, in buying or doing something, was a person of few words. She knew what she wanted. Sometimes I would disagree with her but after she explained herself, she was always right. Her favorite words were: "Let's" - like let's do it, let's go there, etc. Other words were: "Why?" or "Why not?" as:

11

1. The electric wheelchair we were able to get approved was assembled, part by part, in Cleveland. It was close enough to be called custom built. This was a chair well built in which I had to take Jeri periodically to Cleveland for a sitting to be measured. This took several trips. On one visit for a sitting, Jeri had a question. I, knowing Jeri well by then, stayed out of this one. It went like this:

Jeri: I have an idea on something I would like you to add on the chair.
She explained it to the Engineer.
Engineer: It can't be done.
Jeri: Why not?
Engineer: It just can't be done.

This continued for a while and the Engineer was showing frustration signs. Jeri was as calm as can be. I'm thinking, Jeri, if he can't do it, he can't do it. Suddenly, a higher Official came along and saw the discussion. The Engineer explained what Jeri's request was to this Official and that he was explaining to Jeri why it could not be done. The Official agreed and turned to Jeri.

Official: Jeri, it can't be done.
Jeri: Why?
Finally the Official told the Engineer to go with him into his office. Five minutes later, they returned to Jeri.
Official: We think we can do it!

There is a brief story about this wheelchair under **WHEELCHAIRS – Electric wheelchairs.**

2. At a car dealer, we found a new station wagon demonstrator, fully equipped with a sticker price of around $9,000. Their price to us was $9,000. I offered $8,500. They said they would not go that low. Actually, I thought $9,000 was probably a pretty good price but too much for us. So I'm ready to walk away when Jeri decided to give it her "Why not?" approach and yelled out $7,000. I was embarrassed - I think the two salesmen and myself about fainted! They did not agree on that offer but Jeri insisted. They finally hesitated and then went into their office, came out and said "OK!"

Actually, it was strange the way we bought it. It was about ten at night when we saw this showroom with someone in it. We had never dealt with this dealer before but we were out looking. The sales person, after listening to what we were after (we didn't know ourselves) and that we were not looking to buy an expensive car, said that he had a station wagon demonstrator he could show us. Great, we want to see it. It was parked way up on top of a hill. We knew it was ours. He tried to open the doors but did not have the car key. No matter we said we liked it. So we walked back to the office without looking at this car or even getting in it before buying it. So we bought it at $7,000, practically sight unseen. Not very smart but Jeri did it and we had probably the best car we ever did have.

3. Another related example was a tough one. It was a green wheelchair sold to us that Jeri named the "Green Monster." It never worked right for her and she hated it. It always amazed me that, over the years, how sales people always knew what Jeri needed without asking her. We told the company we wanted to return it. They said OK but there would be a restocking

fee, whatever that was, of $3,000 that we would have to pay. We argued with the company and said we never used the wheelchair. I told Jeri, we may have to keep the wheelchair. She said if we keep it put it up in the attic.

We asked a local TV station, who would get involved in cases like this, if they could help us. They thought we had a strong case and approached the wheelchair company to no avail.

Jeri and I then went back to the company and argued with the owner. Jeri did her best but the owner ignored her and showed no respect for Jeri, his customer. He then refused to discuss this with us anymore and suggested we get an attorney. We did. The attorney too thought we had a good case.

To try to sum this up, we ended up in court and the results were, we returned the wheelchair without paying the $3,000 and we were awarded something like $10,000. However, the court and other costs were $11,000. Our attorney who got to liking Jeri very much deducted his bill by $1,000 to at least let us break even. He did a superb job handling our case and became a lasting friend of our family. The case took four years.

STEUBENVILLE

When Jeri, right out of high school, came to work at our College of Steubenville July 8, 1958, I was on the Administration and hardly noticed her - she was just another nice girl on her first real job. She must have volunteered to be the one to go around our offices and take snack orders in the morning and then in the afternoon and then scoot around the corner to Islay's to fill the orders. She was always so pleasant that everyone soon got to know Jeri. I liked stopping work and getting up to pay her for coffee and whatever else I ordered. I would grab my coffee and take it to my desk. I should have grabbed her - but that came later.

Jeri was secretary to the dean of the college. Later, after the dean got to know her, he mentioned to me that he had Jeri in mind to eventually name her registrar. I made it a point not to tell Jeri that until we were married. The reason is obvious. In those days, Steubenville College, being Catholic, would not allow married women to work there. Would Jeri have chosen being registrar? I wasn't taking any chances.

Just about every day, Jeri could be seen going next door to the Bishop's Chapel for noon Mass. Now, how in the world would I know that (I could see her from my office window) and why would I care?

On picnics, skating, basketball games etc, I would use my car to help take our office staff around to our different events and then take them home afterwards. As time went on, it seemed somehow Jeri would be the last one I dropped off at their homes. I wonder... nah, that couldn't be.

Jeri and I loved to go skating - roller and ice. We did pretty good and were able to skate backwards together, not great but we did it. We especially liked it when there was old fashioned organ playing skating music that you could skate to.

Then there was the time when I began noticing Jeri was not using her left leg to skate with. I told her that you are supposed to be using both skates. Her left leg was just coasting. I later realized that, once again, it must have been the MS beginning.

So we were together quite often this way. We were both confused as to, when we did go out together, whether we were friends or on a date? We don't remember who proposed either but it didn't really matter. I think we knew it would happen. Another time together was at a College of Steubenville Prom held at Oglebay Park in Wheeling. Jeri and I were invited to attend as chaperones. I take it that you didn't have to be married to do so. It was a beautiful prom.

Our college had a good basketball team and one night they were to travel to Youngstown to play. I asked Jeri if she would like to go to the game. As she and I went alone, on our way up it began to snow. After the game, when we started home, it had really snowed a lot. There were hills in this area and winding roads. I slid off the road and we found ourselves in a ditch. No, I did not plan this to be alone with Jeri. We were still good friends, becoming better. Anyway, we were unable to get ourselves out. I said no problem. Our basketball team traveling in a bus will be coming along shortly. I'll stop them to help get us out. As the bus approached in now a bit of a blizzard, I waved my arms to stop them. They waved back and kept going. Finally another car stopped and helped us get back on the road. The next day, I went to see the basketball coaches and asked them why they didn't stop for us. "Oh, we thought you were just waving at us."

I was involved with the students a lot and in one case, I was teaching tennis to those who wanted to learn. Of course, one of them was you know who, Jeri. Teaching Jeri was not easy. I finally told her that she was the worse tennis player I had ever taught. On the other hand, I told her, she was also my greatest challenge. She never did learn, she was not able to keep her eye on the ball. She could only return a tennis ball by an accidental swing, no matter how slow

I would position and throw the ball. Strange, she played badminton very well. I compared this with her playing badminton. Playing and watching her play this game, my goodness, she hardly ever missed hitting the shuttlecock back and forth over a net with a light racquet! She was good.

Looking back, I now believe it was the MS beginning to affect her eyes. Jeri had been having eye problems late in high school and spent about two weeks at Ohio State Hospital about this. They could not determine what the problem was (MS had not been "invented" yet). I could not find this out as to who told her but she was told that whatever problem she had would probably surface later at an early age and she would probably be an invalid. When I heard this, I then knew for sure I wanted to marry Jeri.

Later, when we moved to Kent, a MD eye doctor checked Jeri's eyes. He said they seemed fine. I asked him if he saw any scars on her eyes. He was surprised, said he did not but he would look again. He returned and said, "You're right, there are some." This was an early identification of MS. Could these scars have been with Jeri in her two weeks hospital stay when she was in high school when the hospital could not tell what Jeri's problem was? The scars possibly were there. It would have been helpful to know. If so, then Jeri may have already had MS at that earlier time.

I had planned going to Duquesne University but changed to Steubenville College at a last moment. I don't know how Jeri got there but since her family had moved to Weirton, she was just across the river.

After my graduation from Steubenville, I had plans to join the Boy Scouts. I had received an offer from them but I had also received a call from Fr. Joe to visit him in Steubenville. They had an offer for me to come back to The College of Steubenville. I visited and I accepted. So now I find myself quickly back at Steubenville and, without realizing it, now awaiting Jeri to come along.

We both liked The College of Steubenville and always enjoyed social affairs there including office picnics that we would often be joined by the priests whom we found to be very likeable, many of whom we were able to get to know well. Jeri was a favorite especially with her smile.

Fr. Joe became acting president for almost a year but was transferred to their monastery in Pennsylvania. He was to Jeri and I, a super priest, well liked in the community. We hated to see him leave. We learned later that he became a chaplain in the Air Force. This did not surprise us. Anyone who spent time in Steubenville might have a problem adjusting to a quiet living in a monastery.

Moving on from Steubie U to Kent State U

KENT

Jeri had resigned from Steubenville College about three months before our marriage to get ready for our wedding in Weirton, West Virginia. At the time, I had received two offers, one from a well known college in Pennsylvania and one from Kent State

University. I asked her where she wanted to go. She said, "I don't know where Kent State is but I don't want to go to Pennsylvania." So we went to Kent State.

We knew Kent was a little different from Steubenville. In fact, we had never been to Kent before and I even had to look on a map to see where Kent was to keep an appointment there for an interview.

As we left the hills of Pennsylvania and West Virginia and settled in the flatlands of northern Ohio as newlyweds, I realized it was really great to have Jeri and now be part of a very large exciting University, Kent State. This we would enjoy for the next 18 years with three great children.

Coming from work (at KSU) for the first time to Jeri at our home, Jeri welcomed me with "How was your day? Do you want to rest? Can I get you something special for supper, etc?" This continued for a week. I thought, I don't think I can handle it. I finally told Jeri, "I don't know what book you are reading, but throw it away!" She was trying to be the perfect wife! We've had a perfect marriage since!

It was a thrilling new experience for her, coming from a small college atmosphere to become part of a large university. It did not take her long to be welcomed. The "University Women of Kent State University" cordially invited her to a "Tea and Reception" honoring new members at the "President's House on Campus."

Later, 1965, Jeri was elected president of the "Kent Welcome Wagon Club."

Jeri showed no signs of going back to work in Kent. This was fine with me. It turned out to be that she had a full time job preparing our family to be and helping me.

I was working at KSU a few months before we were married. My first week there was interesting aside from actually working at such a large university. I was in an office right across from the president's huge office in the Administration Building. President Bowman was the president. I decided to go over to his office, introduce myself and thank him for the contract he had signed for me. When I told our secretary where I was going, she almost fainted. "You just can't walk in like that, besides you'll never get past his secretary." She was almost right. The secretary greeted me with, "Do you have an appointment?" I told her that I just wanted to say hi and thank him for my contract. The president must have heard our conversation because he peeked around the corner and motioned me in. I introduced myself and thanked him for my contract. He said, "I believe you are from Steubenville. I want to tell you something about Steubenville. I knew President Fr. Dan there very well. The state wanted me to establish a KSU branch there. I said, No, that Fr. Dan was struggling to get Steubenville College established and I do not want to hurt him." What a nice gesture! I doubt if Steubenville College ever heard of this. He thanked me for coming and welcomed me to Kent State.

Another time, Jeri and I were invited to meet a new president, Dr. Olds. Tradition among colleges having a new president was to have a semi-formal welcoming of faculty and administration where introductions are presented to the president by the individuals themselves and what they did at the, in this case, university. Kent State, being large, the lineup would be quite long. In some respects, it can be an honor and also be boring. It was exciting to Jeri.

As the president and his wife made their way along the line, I decided to do it a little differently. It went like this. "Hello President Olds, we are Jack and Jeri Schroeder. I'm supposed to be your chief accountant." It actually alerted him with a surprise smile. Still smiling, he asked, "What are you in fact?" We both laughed and he moved on.

I let Jeri do the buying and handle our money. She would give me thirty dollars a month whether I needed it or not. The only time I ever questioned her on spending was when I would see a bill from a fabric store - all long cuts of rolls and rolls of various styles of material. She reminded me that they always were discounted prices and that she was making clothes for the children. I lived with this answer and dropped my questioning. Later the local newspaper showed a picture of Jeri and the three children in their new clothes at the Junior Mothers Club's annual style show. She actually was making clothes. She even made me a tie.

Jeri had full use of the car since I liked to walk to work both ways every day about two miles each way. I would often walk the children to school making them take funny steps in our walking. They always seemed to like us doing things differently, like making puzzles out of toast and letting them put the pieces together to eat.

Jeri was a good driver. I only remember twice when something went astray. One day with me in the front seat with her, she turned the motor on in our driveway. Wow! Fur was flying out from under the hood. We didn't know what happened. Looking under the hood, there was more fur. Over behind our bushes we saw the funniest skinned cat we ever saw. It was our neighbor's cat well skinned but unhurt.

One other time Jeri was picking me up at work, pulled into a small parking area near my office and hit a parked bicycle. She managed a reverse goose egg design in our fender but did not hurt the bike.

Obviously, our crew growing up was to be smarter than Jeri and me. I think they worked on me the most - Jeri was pretty hard to outsmart. I punished Jodi once by making her sit at a desk where I had put a cooking timer. I told her she had to sit there until it went off. I had set the timer for three hours. Within about 30 minutes, it went off and off she went. Now how did that happen?

Another time, I received a call from a grade school teacher who seemed upset. She said, "Jodi brought a mouse to school." Having a little problem trying to get myself upset, I asked the teacher if Jodi said why she did this. The teacher said, "She bought it for her mother." Now I am lost on how am I going to get upset? I didn't but the teacher was now upset with me.

One more "normal" story was when Jeff and Jami found our secret hiding place for their Christmas presents. Jami refused to see them while Jeff must have had a ball. Somehow that didn't surprise us.

It was in Kent when one evening when we were in the car coming back from Akron on the back road. Jeri would always ride in the front with me while the three children would ride in the back seat, with Jami seemingly always ending up in the middle. It was a cold night with a little snow on the roads. On the route coming into Kent from that direction, there is a fairly steep hill right before the business district. With my expert driving, the snow on the road didn't bother me. This time, however, there was ice under the snow. As we started down this block long hill on Main Street, we spun around skidding. Jeri yelled to the kids to lie down on the floor. We came out of the spin but we were facing the wrong direction. We headed down backwards, all the way down the hill to near the business district. I turned us around and we went home.

Another time on that same street going into downtown Kent, we were coming home about midnight from Cedar Point. Turning onto another street leading to our home several blocks away, we passed a man laying on the grass next to the street, not moving when I saw him. The kids were asleep. Jeri was not. I turned around and came back and yes someone was laying there. I knew that at that time of night on a Saturday in our college town, a police car would be patrolling downtown. Sure enough we could see it about a block in front of us. I speeded up to catch him, flashing my lights and honking my horn for him to stop. He not only did not stop, he speeded up. Here we were, in the middle of the night in Kent chasing a Police Car! He reached the center of downtown and stopped for a red light. We pulled up right along side of him. I think we really scared him by now. I opened our car window, motioned him to do likewise and explained that a person was laying near the street either asleep or something. The officer looked very relieved. We went home a different way.

Jeri and I plus Jodi (4 years old) were at Kent State during the time of the "shooting" of May 4, 1970. We lived about three blocks from the campus. There had been several demonstrations before May 4, 1970 concerned generally with the Vietnam War. News stories seemed to look at it as a "one weekend" demonstration. Not so. Other demonstrations prior to this one on campus went back almost two years before this so called "final" one. Friday, May 1, demonstrations began again. On Saturday evening, an old military barracks was set afire and burned quickly. Ohio National Guard came in during the night and occupied the grade school right behind where we lived.

Sunday became visitor day on campus as people came to see the damage. They were surprised to find the National Guard there guarding entrances but letting people freely go on campus. We only had Jodi at the time and the three of us walked over to campus to sightsee also. It was a nice sunny day to be out and the campus was quiet. Too still for us, it was spooky. We saw the completely destroyed building and decided to get off campus. Something felt wrong.

Monday, May 4, Jeri had taken Jodi into Akron to shop. At noon a student gathering took place which developed into a confrontation with the Guard and ended with the shooting of four students.

After the shooting, all roads into Kent were closed. Jeri and Jodi could not get back into Kent and spent the night with a friend. Other than that, we were not directly involved except I had to appear in a Cleveland court later to explain how a refund of room and board was computed for those residents who were forced to leave on that day of the shooting. Kent State University was closed that day to students and most employees. All outside doors in all buildings were chained shut. But the whole Kent State story is another story in itself.

One of our biggest disappointments in leaving Kent (later on) was that when Jeri was first told she had MS, several of her close girl friends told me, "Do not worry about Jeri. We will take care of her." They were later very disappointed when we left Kent. They tried to keep in touch with us in Bowling Green and would come to visit us. In turn we made several trips back to Kent to see them. While that was about all we could do, it was precious to know and do this. Later, after we began our traveling by train and car, one of these girls wrote a letter to us saying, "With Jeri's having MS and all that goes with it, when you travel, you always seem to have such a good time. How can this be?"

More stories about Jeri and our family is included in **"A LITTLE BIT ABOUT US"** later in the book.

JERI'S "COLLEGE CAREER"

Jeri finished 6 in a class of 180 at her Steubenville Central Catholic High School.

Working at The College of Steubenville, she was able to begin attending classes and earned:

Semester Credits	56
Quality Points	159
Point Average	2.84

At Kent State University, Jeri earned:

Quarter Hours	38
Total Points	116
Point Average	3.05

Total hours accepted at Bowling Green State University: 105.29

When we later moved to Bowling Green, Jeri's next step in her college career was what she was all excited about. She was going to officially enroll at Bowling Green State University (BGSU) to finally get her degree. Sounded easy enough, BGSU had all the records they needed, even had her preset to start in the summer of 1991 with senior status. She only needed about 20 credits to get her degree. She actually received a document from Bowling Green State University that read Certificate of Admission. It also read, "This is to certify that Geraldine Vidmar Schroeder has been admitted as a summer transfer to the Bowling Green State University, Bowling Green campus Apr. 9, 1991." This was signed by the President and Director of Admissions.

The last step for her was to meet with the University, discuss what program and courses they already had chosen for her and complete the enrollment application.

But, hold on.

Meeting with the university advisor assigned to her in person, they did not seem to realize that she was in a wheelchair until now when Jeri appeared. So where is the problem? Perhaps we should excuse them because it was 1991 and I guess the word on helping handicapped students get an education hadn't reached them yet.

What happened next was that she was told by her advisor that they had no one who could help her to class nor take notes for her. Jeri, of course, could do neither and I was working full time. The next question asked Jeri was, "Why do you want to get your degree anyway? It won't do you any good."

I believe that kind of thinking was prevalent for the times. In fact I had heard one story at one college where the director of handicapped services was, indirectly, suggested not to overdue any more than you had to in helping others. This person told another about this and said that they got the message and went and played basketball every afternoon.

As expected, Jeri did not give up.

One professor offered to come to Jeri's home and teach her a course. He tried hard and Jeri tried hard. The course was a difficult one, in my opinion, and Jeri was not doing too well. I noticed that but I also noticed, too late, where the problem may have been. Her home class was, of course, directly to her, no other students were present to share questions and answers. Not being able to ask questions (speech etc problems), like "can you explain or would you repeat etc?" She was at a difficult disadvantage. Add trying to take a test verbally was near impossible. I don't believe that teachers really knew how to teach someone so very handicapped. It is very difficult for one person to face a teacher alone and far worse when you are handicapped. Jeri belonged in a classroom of students. In Jeri's case, we did thank the teacher for trying.

At this point, the teacher was also very disappointed. He felt it was best to stop the class then while he could still have her withdraw passing from the course before he had to give a final grade. He withdrew her as passing but neither a grade nor credit was awarded. This was good because it protected Jeri's scholastic record for future use.

As expected, again, Jeri did not give up. Neither did her family.

Jeri's last futile attempt to get her college degree..........we were really surprised that from what we read, at least as early as 1990, many colleges were offering credit to adults based on their lifetime experiences on the job or at home and what they had accomplished. Wow, a real possible surprise. Jeri was prepared to show all her experiences. This system was called a portfolio approach and could contain hundreds of pages which in total would be judged by faculty.

We decided to make one more try by using the portfolio method and see if we could find a college that would accept Jeri that way. It was 2008. We decided to see if we could surprise Jeri. We put together a draft of what lifetime experiences etc Jeri had. It was a proven list of many activities. It seemed a perfect fit with what was described as needed in the information we had.

Rather than chose a college we did not know, we chose Kent State where she had a lot of credits from and who had a complete record of. They came up with her needing 28 semester hours for her degree. Oh, they wanted her all right. They planned eliminating certain requirements so she could get through to her degree. However, what was left, they required her to be present. "Kent State University does not allow credit for life experience to substitute for courses," we learned.

End of trail. No degree. It was time to move on. No rewards but a very good "successful" try. She and we learned a lot. I think Jeri may have left her mark at three colleges.

JERI'S "MEDICAL CAREER" ALBEIT WITH HER MS

Jeri's introduction to Multiple Sclerosis – Jeri's symptoms began to show when we were in Kent. We began seeing specialists who could find nothing wrong with her even though she was having problems walking. It was finally suggested that we visit the Cleveland Clinic. We eventually did.

It was 1978 and we still lived in Kent when we were able to set up an appointment with the Cleveland Clinic. It was an all day evaluation of Jeri. At the end of the day in an interview with them, they said she definitely had a problem but nothing was conclusive. They felt that Jeri came to them for some kind of answer. In lieu of this and "by process of elimination, we are treating this as Multiple Sclerosis (MS)." They went on to say to not blame everything on MS when pain or sickness occurs, a sound advice. They did not know enough of just what was this MS?

We appreciated the answer they gave us and how they said it, right to the point. A few other points also helped us as far as a name went. They really had no medical name to go by when they called it MS. I don't think it ever did get its own name. No matter. This adopted name from the meaning of "multiple" and "sclerosis" served well for us. When people would ask Jeri what was wrong or what do doctors say she would simply say, "I have MS." I think one would agree that this was much better than saying, "I don't know and doctors don't know." So MS still doesn't have its own created name but it is working and does have a meaningful name as far is an identification of its own.

As Jeri and I began facing the eventual reality for some home nursing care, we began reviewing our thoughts about this new method of living without it affecting our way. We would have to maintain as much control as we could not knowing this was to be a long term stay or a quick medical solution. As it turned out, it was long term with large and small problems. In a nursing home, reality is you have no control. Home health care, you better adjust quickly. We did maintain our control pretty well throughout all of this except the MS slowly worsened. Our control was maintained by way of knowing more about MS, what Jeri needed (nursing, supplies, equipment etc) and carefully challenging procedures, services, equipment etc as we learned while we were practicing until we felt comfortable. At that point, Jeri wasn't the only one asking "Why?" and "Why not?" We joined and supported her, sometimes taking the lead. It actually was a joy to watch her challenge people, no matter what their status. She knew what she needed. She did a lot of our controlling.

We soon realized that questioning people who did not know answers would be very negative. We were not interested in listening to negative answers. We looked for the positive person and usually found them. They were the persons getting things done. That is where your problem is solved. Remember, while MS itself is the biggest problem, many problems associated with MS have to be also solved to live one's life as best as possible.

Facing a problem, we once wrote a letter to the person we thought could help us. We explained the problem and how it could be fixed. We concluded our letter saying, "No" is not an acceptable answer. We never received an answer.

The main ingredient of control and success was to keep doing what we were doing best, only a little bit differently. This meant Girl Scouts, Avon, picnics, swimming, raising our children (keeping our family intact was most precious}. Throw in traveling and we couldn't lose.

Something interesting about MS – Jeri was not sick. She had MS. This fact, I think, was not understood by medical personnel, especially with home health care. Sick people do not always smile. Nurses all too often would treat Jeri like they would any sick person. Be quiet, rest yourself, take your medicine (what medicine?), let me read (as opposed to talk) to you etc.

Jeri was pretty easy to get her to laugh. So nurses soon learned this and applied their own ways of getting to Jeri.

Talk with Jeri to see if you can make her laugh. One night with a very cheerful nurse here to help Jeri, I said something funny to the nurse right in front of Jeri. The nurse picked up a pillow and threw it across the room at me. I picked it up and threw it back at her. Jeri was the first to laugh when we all joined in. I wonder which one was sick? Jeri? I don't think so. This nurse was one of our better nurses – she could do her nursing and could also talk with Jeri. She would often stay over, on her own time, just to talk (not to) but with Jeri.

One visit, this same nurse had her son along. Now Jeri never had a problem with a nurse bringing a child with them. This never happened a lot, but it did happen. The son, in this case, quickly made friends with Jeri and also vice versa. A few visits later, the 12 year old boy became to idolize Jeri. She was helping him, he was helping her.

He once picked out a certain watch he liked so well out of Jeri's Avon book but could not afford it. Jeri gave it to him as a present. He was thrilled. A few weeks later, his mother told Jeri that the watch no longer worked. The son was very disappointed but did not want to tell Jeri. She acted anyway and bought him another watch and gave it to him. Again he was thrilled. He was always welcomed to visit Jeri. Did Jeri break some rules allowing him to visit her even while his mother was on duty? This was Jeri's home!

Another time a nurse brought a granddaughter to see Jeri. The granddaughter quickly liked Jeri and vice versa. This is a perfect example of "Jeri was not sick." When any of our granddaughters happened to be present, the nurse's granddaughter was so excited playing with her new friends (and vice versa), she never wanted to leave. Now, in front of Jeri and me, this really made us feel good. We definitely were living a normal life. The children never looked at Jeri as being sick because Jeri watched, listened and helped them. They only knew Jeri could not walk was why she was in bed. What MS?

Jeri was not sick very often. She rarely had a fever, a cold, feeling sick etc. Not very pleasant perhaps in my story here, but I don't remember Jeri ever vomiting. She had been very active and kept being active. When at first the instructions were to get rest, do not overdue etc, we soon learned it was going to be up to us ourselves to do whatever was needed to make things work. Actually, Jeri was our biggest helper. We soon learned that no matter how busy she was, MS never seemed to bother her, like she had other things to do more important. When she was on her computer, she would sit 2-3 hours at a time enjoying the little bit she knew. "Go for it" became our slogan. We let Jeri work her own schedule. If she was tired, she would tell us. Getting tired never seemed to have any lasting effect on her. Under difficult conditions, Jeri was controlling her own life.

We were careful as to what medicines she might take, from what we heard from others with MS, even what doctors might say. Books available never did seem to help us much. Accepting selective suggestions worked somewhat as we always appreciated anyone trying to help Jeri. Our own exploring was basically our foundation. What we read about MS in so called "News Releases" seemed at first, great. A new discovery hit the presses often. We never heard about them again and after a rather long period of time, these sudden flashes of success rarely appeared. By that time, they, to us, became a wait and see news story.

With MS medicines, there were very few available. These few seemed to be just simply from other sicknesses that were not intended for MS but in the absence of legitimate MS medicines, they fit the bill but we thought with little success.

Jeri's MS doctor became very fond of her and felt determined to help her. He would ask Jeri, "How are you today?" Jeri would answer, "Fine." He would say, "Jeri, you always say that. I have to know how you really are." Every visit with him went about the same. There was nothing more to do. Then at one visit, the doctor was really excited. "I want to save your right arm." It was the only limb working but losing ground. He continued. "I found a medicine that might work for you. It is called Methotrexate. I would like to try it on you. If you agree, I will call the Cleveland Clinic to see if they would agree to see you if they thought it might work for you." (Methotrexate was an oral giving medicine that was thought to possibly slow progressive MS especially in upper extremities).

"Yes" for going to Cleveland Clinic. The doctors agreed and an appointment was set for February 20, 1995. We were both excited. We even celebrated the rest of the day about it. This was Jeri's first time to be put on medicine that might really help her.

Testing was done by two doctors. After review, they felt it was worth trying Jeri on the drug. They also decided that the drug should be orally given at home through her doctor with monitoring effects etc. Blood tests were to be done monthly. Jeri was to go back to Mellon Center (Cleveland Clinic) July 24, 1995.

Jeri, March 16, 1995, began taking 3 tablets (2.5 mg each) once a week, total weekly being 7.5 mg. She was also to take Folic Acid, 1 mg daily and have a monthly blood test. There were other medications that she was not to take, such as aspirin, sulfa drugs etc. Tylenol, if needed, was ok to take. A few side effects were expected around the day she took the medication but, other than "stomach burning", none appeared. On August 14, 1995, her medication was increased by one pill to 4 pills every week. On August 26, 1996 it was increased to 5 pills. This is when it seemed her speech was getting worse while not choking seemed pretty good. One of our family doctors thought this sounded like the Methotrexate was loosening the throat but may be causing her speech problems.

On January 28, 1997, it was determined that Jeri was doing so well that blood tests were to be done every two months.

On November 19, 1997, Jeri was taken off Methotrexate but was to stay on Folic Acid until end of December, then have blood drawn and a throat X-Ray taken. She was never put back on Methotrexate again. This was the first and only real drug test attempted on Jeri for MS.

This introduction to Jeri's MS leads us to the next stage of our getting ready to handle the MS and other medical problems. MS has many hidden secrets. We had to know our way quickly. The best way turned out to be asking questions and making mistakes. We had Jeri to lead the way, not in front but from behind us. As we began our way down and up the MS road, it was like a maze. We found we had many ways to go. As we would try a way, we would watch Jeri. If she smiled, we were going the right way. We had to think paths to take would be helpful. One try would be to keep MS separate from other sickness. Trial and error would help. I did a lot of my own testing just by watching Jeri's eyes when asking questions or making remarks. Those knowing someone with MS — a husband, friend, children, wife — often will know more about their patient than a doctor. They in turn can help a doctor with what they know and more so if the patient cannot talk, you may be the doctor's only hope to do something. Does the patient cry, is in pain etc. I remember one visit to our children's baby doctor when Jeri took them in to see, he quickly would ask Jeri what she thought was wrong. My listening in on this surprised me. I thought to myself that he was the one we came to tell us! He furthered explained that the mother knows her children better than we do. We want to hear her first. A very good answer, I liked that one. We used that for Jeri when seeing a doctor. I think we did know enough about Jeri to help the doctors. This easily applies to someone with MS as we know MS has no respect for age.

It was several years later when Jeri did become hard to communicate with. **One doctor asked me how did we communicate? My answer then was:**

How do we communicate with each other?

We had a few signals we would use and of course Jeri nodding her head helped. I soon realized there was a better way. Jeri's thoughts went through her eyes while her love went through her smile! You could read them!

What other ways do we or will we be able to communicate more to and with Jeri? I think we had more answers than we expected. I made a simple unfinished list to go by:

Communicating with Jeri –
Let Jeri talk or demonstrate first.
Watch her eyes – are they moving? Small watering tears?
Does blinking mean anything? Any movement at all?
Get to know her and ways to communicate will develop.
Certain looks she makes – looking down, up, away, hungry, sleepy, pain etc signs.
Computer for communicating?

Writing questions for yes or no answers.

Perhaps best of all was her smile while a NO smile may mean something's wrong.

Best of all – trial and error, keeping what works best.

Worse of all – giving up and walking away – nurses especially seemed to come to me too quickly to tell me they could not understand Jeri. Actually Jeri often could not understand them either. It takes patience on each side of the fence.

WE MUST LEARN HOW TO TALK TO EACH OTHER and pass our findings on to the next person. I was always proud when a nurse or whomever found a way to converse or help Jeri and passed this on to the next person instead of keeping something important secret. It seems to happen too often in nursing, business or whatever, where a person discovers something helpful will keep it to themselves so as to look, guess, more important. This is done but I disagree with that approach. It happened to me several times when I needed something done but did not have the answer. Months later, I would learn that someone had known the answer but never said anything. So if you found a good way to talk to Jeri, it should have been passed on and be proud of what you did.

There is more about this communication problem under section **EQUIPMENT – ALERT ALARMS.**

So as we delay further introductions to MS, we look at introductions of learning our future needs. Welcome to the routes we went on

At our early arrival at Bowling Green State University Employee Self Insured Medical Program being used was a unique coverage which could also cover families. The premiums seemed in order and the coverage was good for normal medical expenses. The University established a health office and would "farm" out the primary operation of running the program. A committee was appointed to oversee the program including handling any appeals from employees for denied payments of claims. This really worked nice because it became personal between the needy and the approvals - both sides worked for the same employer - BGSU. Jeri did have some appeals. Some were approved, others still denied.

Medicare – While we had normal family health coverage, we knew that we were in for a possible long term medical environment where bills would often warn of the financial responsibility of the patient. Our early plans showed that our current insurance was not going to do the job. Next, checking with Social Security personnel, Jeri was told that she was "not eligible for Handicap Social Security under Medicare long tern medical insurance coverage."

While our insurance showed some of her expenses would be covered, it would not be nearly enough.

I was getting a lot of mail reference "long term insurance programs" companies were selling. I would tell them we were very much interested. After answering several of their questions, I would say, "Great, sounds good. My wife will be glad to hear this." Of course, I spoiled the whole conversation when I would say, "You know she has MS, don't you?" Of course, I knew the answer. The person's voice changed from sweet to sour and a hang up. So why can't Jeri pay for long term insurance? Now that was a big "up" for the insurance company and a big "down" for Jeri and us.

For Social Security coverage under early payment benefits, we met with Social Security and they explained that while Jeri had enough earnings credit, too many of the credits were too old to count under early payments. They told Jeri she would have to get a job and earn enough current credits to qualify. Now what kind of meaningful work could she possibly get in her condition? The family said, "Avon!" This is discussed later.

Medicare Gymnastics – Under Medicare, Jeri was covered with so many hours in a hospital and any unused hours could be used for home nursing care hours. When her hours at home were used up, we would get her readmitted to a hospital again to build up more home health care nursing hours. Good news for Jeri? Yes and No. She knew she needed the hospital hours or neither Medicare nor insurance would pay for nursing hours at home. Getting Jeri to agree was somewhat easy, not only because of financial reasons to get home health services but also to get her additional legitimate medical treatment for MS.

An approved order from a doctor was required to get an admission. Obviously, he had to have a medical reason. With MS, this was easy. You had many treatments to choose from. Jeri would choose one that she thought would help her, even to the extent as to which hospital she should go to. It's not too often one wants to go to a hospital but these visits had a double effect. She never rejected the idea. It was very important to her.

We weren't through yet however. We had to keep a record of her unused hospital hours to know just when she would run out. The hours used at home were kept by each visit by a nurse. The nursing agency then would keep track of the number of hours remaining, warning us when the available hours were nearing the end of approved hours. Jeri and I would then take time to meet with a doctor to see what MS medical treatment would be acceptable to have Jeri readmitted to a hospital. Our choices we used were Rehab (rehabilitate), medical treatments already approved and in use (certain drugs etc) – all related to MS treatments. Jeri would be admitted, to whatever treatment she was there for, hope for good results and come home with additional hours for nursing care. We chose "Rehab." Sort of a hard way to run a business but someone had to make home health care systems work. We were able to use this method at least once when later she qualified to be put on Medicaid which covered home health care services.

Medicaid – So where else do we turn to for immediate additional medical coverage? I was still working and felt that my earnings would be too much to qualify for Medicaid so why bother? We did know that Jeri was going to need some kind of help to cover at least extended nursing home services. We knew nothing about Medicaid. Jeri suggested we try anyway and we arranged for an appointment. Jeri went with me in her wheelchair. We sat down with a case manager analyst and introduced ourselves. Within a few minutes after this person met and talked with Jeri, I spoke up, feeling embarrassed that we were even there and said, "I don't think we really qualify for Medicaid." She looked at me and said, "Let me be the judge of that. I want to find a way to help Jeri!" Wow. I was happily put down. This person did find a way by searching for a waiver that would qualify Jeri.

With our Medicaid case manager helping us prepare a long application for Medicaid, Jeri was approved for Medicaid. Her help to Jeri and our family was excellent and appreciated. It included a thorough review of what Jeri had and what we had in total. We were advised as to what we had to get rid of by spending for needs for Jeri. Included were some bonds and stocks and, unfortunately, her Avon life insurance. This was a so-called spend down approach in order to bring Jeri to an acceptable level of her assets to qualify. Without this case manager's determination to help Jeri, we would not have even tried to get covered. Approval of Medicaid allowed Jeri to be covered for home care services, something which was severely limited with Medicare and private insurance.

Jeri was now covered by this priority order of coverage by Medicare, Private Insurance, Medicaid and Medicaid-Waiver.

We learned the hard way how important the order of coverage was when Jeri was discharged from a hospital stay. Somehow, the order of coverage was given out wrong. This was a fine mess that took a long time to correct with bills going out wrong.

Medicaid Face to Face Annual Reviews – After filling out the application and attending to all the name changes, sale of assets and adjusting to

Medicaid itself, we were then instructed in the fine art of an annual review, Medicaid style.

This was primarily a financial and medical status update. It generally lasted one hour with the purpose being whether to renew Medicaid or not. It was difficult but until you learned what you had to bring in the way of spending proofs and medical progress, it was more nervous than anything because your renewal depended on the information you supplied and your cooperation. From their standpoint, we recognized this necessity and freely shared this information with them. We often would question the reviewer to explain their question and to explain our answers. Over the years, it worked pretty consistently well. Jeri must have done well because she never failed a renewal. They really wanted to help her.

To comment on some of these reviews, the following selections may explain a few situations:

We had on hand two life insurance policies, face value each $500, given to Jeri years ago. A reviewer questioned "why she was allowed to keep them?" "Because the face value of each was only $500," Jeri answered. The reviewer did not accept this answer and went to a supervisor who said, "It was all right for Jeri to keep them."

Another time, the reviewer insisted we open a new checking account with only Jeri's name on it. This was primarily for direct depositing of Jeri's Social Security check so they could trace her spending. This seemed unnecessary for several reasons including, she could not write. I established a checking account for Jeri and also added my name. We were told by the reviewer that this account was not allowed to have more than $1500 dollars in it at any one time. At a future review, the reviewer found there was more than $1500 in the account. I told them that the accompanying reconciliation of the bank statement with her checking account shows that the account is under $1500. Good, that's settled. Well not quite. The reviewer said, "We have to look at the bank statement only. This is required by the State. Jeri is overdrawn."

This next review, we could not handle. Early in the review, we were uncomfortable. Jeri was trying to follow the line of questioning and was trying to answer by nodding her head, yes or no. Remember, Jeri had excellent memory and could think very clearly. Talking was the problem in expressing herself. As the questioning went along, it seemed to become meaningless. Then it happened. The reviewer, sitting at her computer recording apparently everything to go to Columbus, asked Jeri, "Are you a parole violator?" That caught my ear and Jeri's attention quickly. I looked at Jeri thinking, don't you dare nod your head "Yes." I asked the reviewer, "What did you ask her?" She repeated her question. At that point, I spoke up and said, "I don't think we can continue this."

I then decided we would leave. I asked the reviewer if we could have someone else sit in for us on these reviews? She answered, "Yes." I asked, "An attorney?" She said, "Yes, but why do you want to hire an attorney?" I answered, "I don't but I don't think we can go through this anymore." On the way out of the building, Jeri told me I was right that she didn't think she could go through this anymore either. The following year, we hired an attorney. By the way, Jeri was not a "parole violator." On second thought, I never asked her.

By this time in our career, we were also faced with updated computer data being installed quickly. The reviewer could enter data information quite fast. I believe it was going to Columbus because when the reviewer was finished, the computer could pretty well indicate whether Jeri qualified or not. Actually this was good because we knew right then where we stood.

It's kind of interesting but during the last several years of our annual visit, they not only went pretty good, but Jeri was also told that they thought she qualified for several other financial benefits under Medicaid. This surprised us. They explained what they were and would we like them to request them for Jeri? We told them we appreciated this but we really didn't feel we needed them. We said just continue letting us have what she is currently getting. This is all we need. We can take care of the rest ourselves.

We had been paying her insurance under my University insurance for her even though she did not need my insurance since Medicaid covered her. People would ask me why I was paying for Jeri on my insurance when she was covered by Medicaid. Jeri always told me that she knew this but felt better to at least pay some ourselves.

Medicaid Terminology versus Entitlement

Another area that always bothered Jeri and me was about Medicaid's reference that it was not an "entitlement" program.

Because Jeri and I always felt better when we could pay our own way, we were disturbed to be told this was not an entitlement, while we thought it was. Several times we were reminded by Medicaid personnel that what we were getting was not an entitlement. Sometimes I would simply ask:

Where does the money come from to pay for this program?
Reply: From taxes.
Jack: I am a tax payer.
Reply: No response.

It's strange because shortly after this, they stopped telling us that it was not an entitlement program. While Medicare is built into the framework of it being a Federal entitlement program, Medicaid follows this same policy but it is not clearly specified in the framework of it being Federal.

To clarify our definition of "entitlement" reference need and that we do pay taxes, it seems obvious that it means "While one does pay taxes to pay for Medicaid, one would expect to be helped by Medicaid as needed when medical bills become beyond one's fortune."

Medicaid-Waiver – Getting approval for Medicaid was a real blessing. On top of this, Jeri was put on Medicaid-Waiver.

We did not fully understand the difference. We thought Medicaid was Medicaid, period. As time went on, we learned that there was a large difference. The waiver given her (there were several types) meant that her assets and earnings requirement limits and approvals would be keyed on Jeri's earnings and spending and that Medicaid-Waiver could approve services, equipment, supplies etc not approved by Medicaid. It could also override a Medicaid denial.

Home nursing care – Referring to nursing care, I find no need to mention whether the person is an RN, an Aide, etc male or female, good or bad - this is an attempt to explore realistically the ups and downs and allow one reading this to help come to their own learning and conclusion. We therefore are using the term "nurse" to include everyone giving nursing care to Jeri.

It would have been nice to say that this home nursing care for Jeri was to be hands on learning and getting experience. Since she lost use of her hands fairly early, one of the first things she would tell her nurse was, "You are my hands." I don't think the nurses really understood her in the way she intended. I think they interpret it to mean, "You need me to help you, period." Jeri was, in a pleasant meaningful way, saying, "I can't do some things but my hands are so important to me because I want to do a lot of things that need my hands. How about eating? Holding? Pulling the covers up over me?"

As Jeri and I (and family) faced the need for home nursing care, it came slow at first, like all we needed for a long time was one nurse four hours one day a week. Over the years and changing scenery, like Jeri getting worse, we would have to decide as to type of service and at what level.

All those early years and all the years after, Jeri had the best nursing care one could hope for, her family, who else. Even her grandchildren all helped her in so many ways.

During our time period, nursing agencies did have problems of staffing, finding qualified and dependable nurses. When we only needed one nurse once a week, we went one period of eight months without any service. I had told the nursing service not to take the first person off the street to send us. I would handle Jeri until you found one good and dependable. I wasn't exactly thinking eight months.

It did not take long for us to see nursing and our problems, both medical and operational. We found we were both in a new modern environment, meaning home health care.

I guess we were quite naïve when we advanced from a single nurse for several years to realizing that we better start thinking whether we need more nursing care or not. Our favorite case manager was constantly encouraging us to get more help that we were entitled to. I would thank her and tell her we were fine but if we ever thought we would need more, we will let you know. We did this for probably several years until we finally listened to our case manager.

As we progressed in increasing our nurses, we learned don't count on backups and be patient until a nurse was found for Jeri. A nursing shortage existed to the point where it did no good to switch to another agency they were having the same problems. In some cases, our agency would direct a new nurse, when they applied, to go directly to the Schroeders. They would tell you what to do. Too often, however, many of the nurses were not trained it seemed, for home health care procedures. We would train them the best we could. One nurse, who became one of our best, was sent over to us directly from applying at our agency. Jami trained her how to change Jeri's trach. We finally reached the point that we called the agency and said, "We can't keep training the nurses you send."

We made special effort to help nurses get breaks from just staying in our home taking care of Jeri. We thought one good way was to invite the nurse to go with Jeri and me to get out and do something to break the routine. Three examples we tried included:

1. Inviting the nurse to go with us to have coffee. Where we went was not a restaurant, just a coffee shop with a few tables. You ordered from their counter, not your table. You clean up afterwards. The coffee was hot, it was suppose to be. Let it cool. Our nurse went to the counter and told them, "Jeri's coffee was too hot, I need some ice." The employee said "We don't have any." When asked by the nurse for cold water, the employee went in the back to find some. The nurse took it back to Jeri. A mistake: The nurse should have asked me what to do. I would have said, leave it cool. I did not want a store thinking badly of Jeri. This particular coffee shop, we used often.

2. We tried shopping, which Jeri loved to do (surprise?). In a big store we went to, I thought sure the nurse would enjoy taking Jeri through the aisles shopping. She did. I went my own way just looking around. I came back to them. The shopping was done. The nurse was all excited. She really enjoyed doing this with Jeri. A mistake: I looked in the buggy. It was half filled. I asked, "Did Jeri want all of these items?" The nurse said, "Yes. Every time I held something up to her and asked if she wanted it, she nodded her head yes." I let it go at that. Jeri did not need any item they took. I learned a lesson but paid for this one.

3. Now I knew at home, we should be careful of serving meals to nurses. As a special treat to this nurse who liked Jeri a lot and was doing a good job, I invited her to go to a restaurant Jeri enjoyed for lunch. A mistake: We were in a booth. Jeri needed to

be fed. The nurse hurried and finished her lunch and moved herself out into the aisle to feed Jeri. There are several mistakes here. The waitresses were busy, do not eat or feed from the aisle. We do not want guests feeding Jeri especially in a restaurant. With MS, feeding a person in public is an art. Don't spoil meals for other people eating. Don't spoil ours either. It can be done properly and enjoyable for people in wheelchairs.

My mistake was not taking the nurses out like this. It was my fault not explaining what to do and not to do.

As we moved along gaining our own experience in home nursing, we learned that each agency set their own rules as to when a nurse could leave a patient, for example, when they have completed their work. Some were told to stay right to the hour approved. Sometimes it seemed the nurse made that decision. We finally gave up trying to set a standard time for leaving. We did make one attempt to see if the nurse could be put on a job time schedule. We got nowhere with that one so we bowed out and let it up to the nurse.

To greet new nurses coming to help Jeri, we asked the agency if we could meet and interview a new person before they would start to make sure Jeri and family would like them. Agencies claimed that they would have to pay that person. Since when do employers have to pay someone being interviewed for a new job? We did try it a couple of times but it wasn't working. New nurses looked at the agency more than us as to who was doing the hiring. It wasn't Jeri.

So to greet the new nurse, it would begin at our front door. Actually it was difficult to open the door not knowing who our new employee was. On the other side, neither did the new employee know who was opening the door. This is why a pre-interview is needed. No surprises.

Now the person coming in was already employed. Our approach was to explain to them a little about Jeri and what we needed them for. Jeri would always smile but she was listening very closely to what the nurse had to say. I was listening closely myself.

One nurse within a few minutes talked excitingly that, "Oh, Jeri and I will get along just fine." Now this bothered me. How would one know that quick that they would get along fine? We hadn't explained Jeri's situation very much yet. We continued but I don't think this nurse was listening to us. Unfortunately, we did not think she would work out. Jeri agreed. She just came on too strong. This rarely happened. I only remember one other time when the nurse we were to take did not work out. Within a few days, we learned this person needed help herself. Jeri and I were doing more for her then she was doing for Jeri. We liked the person but we were not in the position of helping her. She was here to help Jeri. Again, a pre-interview would have prevented this.

Our intention in welcoming new nurses was planned this way. We tried to explain briefly certain home rules like: We're not a nursing home. We're a private home. I was the host, Jeri the hostess. People coming to our home were still our guests. We intended to treat them as such. Nurses did not always look at this that way. The way they liked was usually one of "I am the nurse, you are my patient." That is correct but it is secondary to our needs. We knew we needed good relationship with those who came and vice versa. Jeri and I liked our way of treating new nurses as friends first. This was our home. It should be done that way.

Nurses were quick to let us know they had nursing home experience. If you haven't done home nursing, the situation is really a new learning experience. It did allow us to teach them our way. On the other side, we could ask questions as to how they did something in nursing homes. This comparison was helpful. Some answers we used nursing home procedures, some we used our methods.

Terminology was important. Ex: Name calling - Jeri had a name, it was Jeri, not honey etc; Diapers - call them briefs, diapers are for babies. Talk to Jeri as an adult — don't kneel down to talk to her.

Greetings when entering - we generally let their entrance door unlocked so they could walk right in - one must sound off, a rather loud hello or "I'm here" to let us know that they are present. Often, the nurse just walked in quietly without a sound. One night, the nurse was very late and we were being a bit critical talking about what to do now? Call them? Just then, the person came into our living room where we were — from our bedroom! How long was she there? Did she overhear a private talk?

Greeting a patient, especially in the morning, is quite difficult to find the correct message. It has to be decided by the nurse as to what works the best. "Did you have a good night?" was not a good question. A sincere greeting coming or going is very important.

Now one nurse that came rushing into Jeri's room in the morning, before any sign of a good morning, had her mind set on one thing. Pull the curtains shut. It darkened the room and closed off any one deciding to look in. In a nice but firm way, I said to her. Jeri loves to watch the sun every morning. Let the sun in. She opened the curtains but added, "I have to change Jeri's trach, I don't want someone looking in." My answer was, look, Jeri likes the curtains open. No one is going to peek. I had tested looking into the room from the outside. No one can see in from a distance. If someone gets right up to the window smile and wave to them. This is a good example of learning to be in another's home. Ask before you act.

Now another nurse that came at night to put Jeri to bed had her own method of getting Jeri not only in bed but towards the middle of the double bed. Once she lifted and put Jeri on the bed, she bounced her to the middle. It worked every time. Was this proper? This nurse was pretty strong and Jeri did not seem to mind the bounce. Not knowing which way to go, I let it be. The old saying, "If it's not broke, don't fix it."

You try different methods entering or leaving a patient. Smile is a must. If Jeri was sleeping, let her rest. If the nurse is leaving, how about leaving a note to her? Or use Jeri's method — "walk through it yourself" to see what you would expect if you were the patient. Try a little hug, it always works.

In meeting new nurses and helping them feel comfortable with us, we found another way to do this that worked quite well. It actually was to entertain our grandchildren but eventually it entertained the nurses. I was giving a suggestion to Jeri to use when the children brought a gift or draw something to show her. Normally Jeri would give them a smile and always showed interest. I told her the next time when one brings something to you, try to look surprise. WOW. I no sooner said that when she opened her eyes so wide staring right at me, she scared me. It was so funny to see this reaction so quickly from Jeri. How was she able to do that so fast without thinking or practice? I laughed harder than I ever did. It was a perfect "surprise look." I started showing our family —

they laughed more than I did. I started showing the nurses and they couldn't believe it. Everyone we showed this to became fascinated by it. We really did make the nurses feel comfortable, I mean Jeri did. The grandchildren loved Jeri's surprise look.

As we got to know the nurses better, there were a few other instructions we tried to pass on to them that would help us. Being trained their way for hospital and nursing home care, these surprised them somewhat. We acknowledged the problem these might cause but we really needed some things done our way. Such as:

Writing reports in English was fine but too many code symbols were used to make the reports almost useless to us. Don't use codes.

Not sure who trained them in writing reports but the ones we received were usually simply too long. Unnecessary words or comments added nothing to the reports. For example: "Jack is sleeping and/or snoring." I didn't realize I was a star in this show.

We urged them not to wear uniforms or name plates. We knew their names. Wearing uniforms according to one agency was up to us. Inexpensive clothing to wear and changed every day had a tender effect on Jeri. Like flowers in her room (which I don't think I ever gave, but others did) pleased her. So did what the nurses wore. It really did make a big difference in helping Jeri every day.

We were glad the nurses did not bring presents to Jeri. Perhaps a single flower from their garden once a while would be fine. Now I didn't give flowers because it meant extra work for me. Call me scrooge. Better yet, do what our secretaries at Kent State did to my office at Christmas. They painted a very large scrooge on my glass window. I thought this was precious also. Did

Jeri like the treatment I sometimes got? She loved it. I think these girls that did this very good drawing were included in Jeri's invitation for lunch at our home in Kent.

Any cleaning we expected would be meant for Jeri's room etc. They were here to help Jeri. I was told "washing windows" was a no no, that nurses were here to do "medical work," whatever that meant. Since all agencies seemed to have their own rules and would use "It's illegal" wording to their pleasure, I pretty well gave up on asking nurses to do something. I would hope they would just see something that needed done, like running the sweeper or straighten Jeri's clothes.

Jeri had always done the laundering for our family for years. When she no longer could do it, I would do it using the same washer settings she used and wanted. This did not apparently appeal to nurses. They had their own way of doing it. Now, wait a second. Can't Jeri have something her way now and then? I posted a note on each setting of the washer where the laundry was to be done, Jeri's way. I don't think a lot of the nurses actually had ever done laundering before, especially when I saw some just washed, especially new, clothes all together.

What about nurses taking their shoes off at the door? Our carpeting quickly became a nurse's trail from entrance to Jeri's room. We had the carpet cleaned several times but it was so dirtied by then, don't look at it. Taking off their shoes, we were told it was "illegal." Here we go again. We lose without a fight.

One fairly new nurse asked me to get a certain type mop and she would clean bare floor areas. This I did. She left us early, never did use the mop and neither did anyone else.

Another time, when a new nurse came for the first time, I hadn't explained some of her duties yet, like giving Jeri a shower. I was very careful of how a nurse would handle Jeri. Sometimes I would be in another room and hear a bump. Oh Oh, they dropped Jeri again. So as I was leaving to do an errand, the nurse asked me, "What she should do for Jeri." I said, "Just give Jeri a sponge bath." She asked, "What's that?"

I didn't really mind her answer. It told me something. She really did not know what a "sponge bath" was. It is a good example of nursing home experience and no home care experience.

Vital signs reports were very important to me especially if anything showed up not so good. Jeri's blood pressure readings were on the low side but very good and were never a problem. They were so consistent that when we took her to her doctor's office and the receiving nurse would take her blood pressure, I, to be funny, would call out her numbers ahead of the nurse taking the reading. I was nearly right on every time. I would kind of get a smart aleck look every time.

Now with her temperature, we looked at it a little differently. Usually her temperature was a steady lower reading than what was considered normal. We were told, because of MS, if her temperature became 99, then watch carefully. A 101 temperature meant ER pronto. When I took Jeri's temperature and it was close to 99, I did two things quickly. One, I began sweating. Two, I would grab the Tylenol quickly and begin charting her temperature. The Tylenol worked fine. I don't remember ever having to rush Jeri to ER because of temperature. Jeri did have a high temperature in the hospital a couple of times. She only had pneumonia once. Actually, she was always considered in good health by the doctors.

Let me add something probably few agencies would agree with. The general rule of agency nurses being in the patient's home is a twofold NO. One is you do not eat their food. Second is you do not talk about your personal problems.

Briefly, One is generally true but exceptions can be unbelievable helpful to patients and family. Partial and full meals are out. Being sociable usually is a must. Don't offend me if I offer you a cup of coffee and a donut. Make it tea and a donut. Second, using Jeri as a good example, she often loved to talk to her nurses. If the discussion included a nurse's little personal problem, Jeri was the one to talk with. She listened and enjoyed being asked questions. She really had answers. Do not disallow this. Be careful but let them help each other. Again, Jeri was not sick. She wanted to help people. She could hear well and nurses relished this association. To top this off, I would suggest some coffee be made and served by our nurse, provided she would join us. So after Jeri would be transferred to her wheelchair and out in our veranda, coffee, at least, would be served, the nurse and me from a coffee cup and the nurse giving Jeri hers through her feeding tube. Can you top this?

Other factors affecting the way we lived our normal life

Do we know now more about MS? We do, of course, but how much more. There is world research going on but, in our 35 years experience with many false alarms, we have learned not to quit believing, just continue to do what we like best. We still believed the cure was "out there." This being the case, there are many distractions to do in the meantime. While there is no known cure yet, there are a number of prescriptions available to help somewhat. However these are primarily for those with the relapsing type of MS and not the progressive type that Jeri had. These recent finds were helping delay the relapsing but were not cures. Jeri's MS doctor at the time did not want her on any of the available prescriptions but said, "If any of them were to develop a liquid type to swallow, he would consider it."

Word was kind of out to encourage your doctor to put you on one of these new prescriptions that were approved. I studied the side effects and did not like what I saw. Jeri was never on any of the prescriptions.

So, did Jeri really have MS? It never bothered us when people would ask or even when they did not ask. We made it a point upon meeting people beyond just an introduction by telling them she had MS. People seem to appreciate that because we made no mystery about it and we certainly were never ashamed of it. They seemed to be relieved. Jeri, like most everyone, did not want people to feel sorry for her. We would not tell people that. We showed people that with her smile and me telling people we do a lot of things like traveling and we always have a good time. Funny, we did.

Don't blame everything on MS..........this was so true. We learned that from Cleveland Clinic in our first lesson with them. We were always on the alert for this and we sometimes had to caution a doctor about this as a reminder. In a nice way, we would say, "We know it could be the MS but we just aren't sure since MS is so difficult to understand." We think doctors appreciated this.

We had one good case on this subject:

Jeri had a really painful toothache that was lasting several days. Now when Jeri asked to go to a doctor, she really was in pain. She could even point to which tooth it was. We went to her favorite dentist. He keyed on the tooth she pointed out very well – there seemed to be no doubt that this was the problem. An x-ray showed nothing wrong. All other teeth seemed all right. Could it be the MS? No proof but a good thought - but remember - don't blame everything on MS. Another good thought. So what to do?

The pain was there in that one spot, she insisted. The dentist said, "We could pull it or do a root canal. I don't like either idea," he said. "Her tooth is too good to pull and the x-ray does not indicate a problem." Before deciding on a root canal, the three of us (Jeri, Jack, her dentist) decided to run this one past her family doctor. He did some checking on his own and found a statement that said one pain in the upper part of the jaw on a certain side was sometimes found in MS! A prescription was issued to Jeri. Contacting her MS doctor, he agreed that this was worth trying and agreed with the prescription given. Jeri took it for a while but soon seemed to be affected by it since it was not helping the pain. The prescription was stopped. A short while later, the pain also stopped. Nothing ever came of it again. Was it the MS? Anyway, success: The good tooth was saved and the pain was gone.

Hospital visits and stays..........

Jeri was admitted to The Cleveland Clinic for five days in 1990 for an exacerbation of her MS and treated with high dose pulse steroids. It did not help her except she did feel that her voice was stronger as well as her right hand.

On March 11, 1991 Jeri returned for another visit with The Cleveland Clinic in which they prepared a history questionnaire and going over many questions and answers with her. For the most part, there were no negative answers and many positive answers except none seemed to help trace MS. No serious medical treatments appeared and on two pages of serious questioning there were 64 answers – 12 yes (negative), 52 no (problems). Nothing apparent came of this as far as MS in which they were after. Jeri was not admitted. We were not surprised that not much came of this because by now we knew MS was going to be a tough one to solve. MS was usually looked at as not being any "end of life" body breakdown. We never called it an illness or an injury. We only had "MS" to call it with brief explanations to others as to what was thought it was. At least this part had worked pretty well.

For several years after that, we continued seeing the Clinic about every year for a while but nothing really good came of it, but nothing very good at other hospital stays worked either. At one of our rounds seeking MS information, we were given a cautious prediction that a cure would be found within five years. That was some 25 years ago. But wait a second. So this cautious prediction did not come true. When told this, we were delighted that someone was really working on a cure. It gave us a happy feeling and HOPE.

We went away from the hospital encouraged. The fear in such acknowledgements of being told "nothing can be done" is devastating. With MS, you never knew nothing could be done because eventually it would be done.

Usually when Jeri was admitted to a hospital or whatever, the standard questions to her were "can you?" or "do you?" walk or dress yourself etc - a long line of mostly negative answers - very discouraging. The Cleveland Clinic made it simple and encouraging by saying, "Tell us what you can do."

When we were at Cleveland Clinic, our doctor there said to keep Jeri active so that when a cure is found, she will be a good candidate. This we did - this was the easy part. Being in Girl Scouts, becoming an Avon Representative, having three children growing up, traveling - throw in learning her computer - I think Jeri kept herself quite active "in spite of MS."

In one stay at a hospital, when we went to visit her, we found her at one end of an almost empty patient floor. This room was way down from the Nurses Station. We learned Jeri was not getting any attention. There was a button to ring for attention. How nice, except, Jeri could not use it. There were about five or six empty rooms between Jeri and the Nurses Station, one right across from them. When we asked the nurses if Jeri was getting attention, they said, "The button is right there for her to ring." But Jeri has MS and cannot press a button. "Oh" was their answer. We asked, "Can she be moved to the empty room right across from you?" They moved her down to that room. Gee, it was good we came along and helped them solve a problem.

As far as other hospital stays for Jeri such as MCO (1989), Mercy (1992), Wood County (1994, 1998, 2002, 2007), we found such stays to be well done.

Jeri's Medical Career goes beyond just MS - known as a peptic ulcer which led to a "Feeding Tube"

While this was not a major problem because we were getting use to the fact that with MS, you better get use to not solving problems quickly. When you do, it is most surprisingly strange.

This is a case where one problem was solved and another one created at the same time. I think one will find this one interesting. Not exciting, but interesting. It covers a period of about 11 years. This one stayed and became difficult and annoying.

Jeri had her first and only what was called a peptic ulcer 3/27/98 in the hospital. Hey, that was my birthday! They even took a picture of it, the ulcer not me. It was not smiling.

The surgeon, looking ahead, talked with our family, had suggested that since he was to go inside, "He might as well put a feeding tube in her because, with her MS, she would need one sooner or later." We approved. As usual, I didn't follow him very closely. I agreed with putting the tube in. However, a few days later when Jeri was being discharged and I was being instructed by the discharge nurses, I told them they forgot to take the feeding tube out! I thought the doctor meant it was in Jeri while she was in the hospital. They looked at me and with a funny laugh said, "The tube stays in Jeri to take home." I didn't faint. I just looked at them and said, "What? I don't know how to use it." They replied, "We will teach you." Now I fainted! No, not really. I should have but didn't know how. More like "stunned."

It got worse for me. The nurses started giving me the instructions like I would have to test it often, check the water and on and on. I finally said to them, "I could say OK but I would be kidding you." I found the doctor before we left. He briefed me a little differently telling me just to make sure the tube does not get stopped up by testing it at least once a day. Now that sounded like one I could handle. Let's go home.

Jeri took all of this in good strides. She never flinched once about the tube and, strangely enough, seemed to trust me using it. I'll say one thing. I spent a lot of time reading instructions about it and had a lot of selective questions to ask. A few nervous questions:

What if the tube comes out?
It won't. Don't think about it.
If it does, what comes out the little hole?
A little bit of liquid.
How do I test the balloon in it?
Leave it alone, it will be ok.
Is there really a little balloon there?
Yes, full of water, keeping the balloon in.
What if the tube becomes clogged?
Use carbonated soda pop.

I had more but decided to learn by trial and error. There seemed to be little that could go wrong and we did have nurses at home to do this and help me. I felt comfortable the more I learned about it. I know Jeri did too. So, go for it.

The amazing part about this was the so many individual questions with different answers.

The tube did come out. We were told, no problem for a day or two but Jeri should be taken to a surgeon to replace it as soon as possible, otherwise the little opening over her stomach would close. What happens if it did? Surgeon would have to go in again to reopen it. Great, now it's becoming clearer. I'm going to tape it not to fall out. How then could I feed her through the tube, I asked myself. You have to hold the tube straight up to get into her stomach. I felt like I'm talking to myself and giving myself wrong answers. OK then, I will tape it in such a way it will stay and I can still hold it up.

Much learning about this was still on the horizon. I was determined to learn all I could about it. Heck it's only one little gastrostomy tube. It has a single opening on one end and a double one on the other. That's all. Now the instructions read a little different like "Check tube placement before each intermittent feeding."

I was beginning to ask better questions in which I found others didn't have solid answers either. I asked one medical person who seemed to know feeding tubes just where does Jeri's tube really go to once it enters through the opening? His answer was, "The fluid would go into an intestine." I was confused on that answer. If you had to replace a feeding tube, how could you put it in to go through the skin opening and into an intestine? Talking to another doctor later, I said I understand Jeri's food goes into an intestine from the feeding tube. He answered, "No, Jeri's goes right into her stomach."

Especially since Jeri and I were already taking long train trips alone, I intended to know all about feeding tubes and suction machines – these would be with us on these trips and we were not about to stop the trips for little things.

We were learning. Jeri's feeding tube was way too long. I had to fold it around and kind of tape it on her somewhere. We were able to exchange the size for a much shorter tube.

We learn to carry a spare feeding tube with us

On one of our first visits to the surgeon to replace the tube, his office said he was away, that we should go to the emergency room. We went to the hospital but, while they had different size feeding tubes, none would fit Jeri. Rather than waiting to order one, they put in a temporary one and suggested we get to our regular doctor to change it to the size that was used.

To avoid this problem in the future, especially traveling, we decided to ask our doctor for a prescription to buy a spare. He thought this was a good idea, gave us a prescription which worked for the supplier and would be covered by insurance. From now on, the word was out. If we called to have Jeri's tube changed, they would say, "Don't forget to bring your spare." When we would go to have it changed, we would hold out our spare and say, "Here it is but we want a new prescription to buy a new spare." This often brought a surprise or a laugh when other people found out we had to bring our own "medical supply." It did sound funny but it worked. We thought it was a great way to make a problem not a problem.

Another time when we went to the doctor (with our spare, of course), I was allowed to watch him change the tube. Jeri was placed on a bed and he began. I said, "I bet you don't find any water in the balloon." He answered, "You're probably right." There was no water. It took him 15 minutes to change the tube.

Another time with another doctor (with our spare, of course), I again watched. The doctor changed Jeri right in her wheelchair, easy on Jeri, easy on the doctor, done quickly within a few minutes. This was the best way to do it.

We were told different things like reference water in the opening – a little won't hurt, shower is ok, no plastic patch is needed. If swimming, a lot underwater - use a small plastic patch, cut a hold in it or a slot to cover the opening, the whole tube doesn't have to be covered, just make sure it's supported.

The company making these tubes insisted that patches were not to be used. Well we found out several things about that. First of all, if Jeri had an arm spasm, she could easily pull the tube out. Another reason, traveling was no place to have a tube come out. Finally, while I had seen many put in, I had never put one in myself.

The tube had a lot of play that we had to get use to. In traveling, I always put a patch over it. In Halifax once, the tube seemed out a little too far. I usually knew how much play was safe on the outside. This time it came out further than I expected. It was still in but was anything holding it in? I was certain it was barely hanging in. I patched it extra strong to not let it come out any further. When we got home and went to the doctor, we took the tape off. The tube came right out with the tape. So the tape held it in enough to get us home.

We watched a nurse open Jeri's clogged tube by forcing the air through enough to do so. It opened it easily. We followed this method. It worked very well especially in traveling and saved many trips to a doctor or ER. I still wasn't satisfied. I called the company that made our tube and asked them about clearing a clog tube by blowing air into it. They said better be careful, you may explode the tube.

This was one time when nurses who had nursing home experience would tell us that the nurses changed feeding tubes all the time. Great, this was good news. Hurrah for the nursing homes. Pretty soon we were letting an experienced nurse change the tube for Jeri.

Our tube had a plug attached to open for liquids and then close it. Being opened and closed a lot would stretch to where it would not stay closed tightly. Force of pressure would open it and liquids would come out. We tried many ways of trying to keep it tight without success. Even one doctor gave us a long plastic plug to try. Sounded and felt like the answer. Tried it that night and, within a couple of minutes, pressure blew the plug up, out and away.

Our nurse learned that there actually was a plug to be used for this purpose. She had our regular supplier send us one that they thought we were talking about. It was perfect. A little plastic plug about 2-3 inches long that fit perfectly into the tube. It had a little on/off switch. We ordered a couple of these to have on hand. After using it with liquids we always had to close the switch to "off" on the lid. Why was this important? If you left it on, the next hour or so, you would learn quickly. Jeri and her clothing and bed would be wet with liquids that came out. I left it open once, never again. Sometimes you do learn fast. Why didn't our supplier tell us about this switch a few years ago?

So the feeding tube stayed with Jeri and us for over ten years. We never had any emergency with it. It was inconvenient for Jeri but we stood together with it and never let it get us down. On with our train trips and the feeding tube.

Solving our medical problems ourselves.... One method that seemed to work well in trying to get our problems solved ourselves, like a insurance denial, was to meet people whom we thought could help by an unannounced visit without an appointment. This usually disturbed them but nevertheless they would see us. We are not talking about a problem needing immediate medical attention - just simple problems of MS affecting us that we might be able to get answers or suggestions for plus an override of a denial. While a bit rude, it would work for us.

Another method that helped us was when an insurance company assigned a nurse to handle any calls from us about Jeri directly. They gave us a direct phone number to this nurse. This really was an excellent procedure.

Getting our own medical supplies............ dealing with various suppliers, one would think we would get good attention since we were a continuous buyer. Often we did not feel like a customer.

Our nurse whom we had from day one when we brought Jeri home from Rehab agreed to take on the rather large job of ordering, receiving and checking supplies we needed. She had her hands full and, in spite of problems, did a nice job for Jeri. I could tell when she was having a bad time on the phone and would step in to help her.

On one order for supplies, the nurse had just called in our monthly order. Included in the order were some single swivel elbows for trach care. These were very important for suctioning attached to Jeri's trach. We had a call from the manufacturing company that they thought the double swivel elbows were much safer and that we should use them rather than the single. The nurse had just sent in her order but called right away to cancel the single and order the double swivel elbows. The supplier said, "Too late. Your order is being processed. You'll have to wait a month to order the double unless you want to pay for the double." How's that for "no cooperation?" That's all they said, no offer to check with someone higher up. Now they certainly knew we were talking expensive medical supplies needed for someone on a ventilator. Or did they care? Wait for a month? Or pay yourself? We should have gone to someone else there. We waited, a mistake on my part.

Getting "limited" supplies..........now who thought this one up without providing for authentic exceptions or even consulting with people engrossed on the medical front?

While we often never knew which of Jeri's four medical services were paying for what, this really didn't bother us because our concern was to get Jeri the needed equipment, supplies etc, primarily medical. Medicaid began limiting the number of some supplies one could order. It was like so many each month.

Now, in itself, this was ok. Controls were necessary especially when insurance etc was paying it and not the patient directly. It would make no sense to ask a vendor to send me all you have. However, good rules have to bend. Example:

There was a one inch wide cloth neck band Jeri had to wear around her neck to keep her neck dry and for other medical reasons. Moving her head started causing band friction and the band was causing red areas causing fears of infection. If one did not check her entire band and neck closely, her neck would become dark red and sore. If she had a shirt collar on, it would be hard to find. It needed to be changed often to prevent this. How about every day with a new dry cloth? I think these bands were four dollars each and there was a limit of four a month, one a week. It had to be changed, perhaps more than once a day.

We contacted the supplier and explained what was happening and that we needed to at least double our monthly order to eight of these bands. Our phone call went like this:

Jack: If you are in charge of this supply, Jeri needs at least two bands a week. Can you override the limit?
Reply: No.
Jack: Who can override it?
Reply: No one.
Jack: How do I get these items?
Reply: Buy them yourself.
Jack: But that is why Jeri has Medicaid etc.

I contacted Medicaid's hot line. After some delay, the answer was "see your case manager." We talked to Jeri's case manager. She said she was not the one that could override the limits, no other comments. We only had one other so called case manager and that person was our Medicaid case manager who handled our annual approval for Medicaid visits. Even if I could contact that person, who usually was hard to get especially without a delayed appointment, I don't think they were in charge of issuing supplies.

Sometimes, getting to the right person, the supplier would just send us what we needed but in this "supply case," the rule was being enforced.

I did call one other supplier who was kind enough to send us one free - they were not allowed to bill Medicare. This person told us that this "limited" supply program had become hard to handle. They were in business to make sales based on orders received, that they did not know how to make exceptions. It put them in a spot to reject customers they worked with.

It was also suggested we see our doctor to override this. Our doctor to override it, I don't think so. A doctor's job is certainly not to override supply limits, is it?

This was one of the few times I think we kind of gave up on. Somehow we worked with what we had by washing the bands and drying them and continue getting four new ones each month to increase our little "inventory" by laundering the bands. I suppose this was sanitary. I think if the package containing these bands came marked "washable," there would not have been a problem.

Attitude, "untrained" or "simply not caring" judgments, remarks etc, not realizing that they may be hurting someone they are trying to help.

A conversation I once had with a medical insurance executive was telling me how he couldn't believe what he had just seen at a Rehab. These adults were just stacking blocks and positioning different objects. "What a waste of time and our insurance money."

Another time, out taking a walk, we came across a person we knew and stopped to chat with her. Talking about Jeri and how she is doing, and for something different to say, I said, "Jeri still believes a cure will be found." The person looked at Jeri and responded with, "Jeri, you're just dreaming." I answered, "That's a terrible thing to say to Jeri." A few days later, we were in a group having coffee when this same person was present. I remarked to her that she hurt Jeri that day. She said, "Oh, I did not." I said to go over to her and ask her. This she did. "Jeri, did I hurt you that day?" Jeri, "Yes."

Some everyday medical concerns are often too easily overlooked...until something happens...caring for Jeri's daily routine needed to prevent problems ....washing, changing, dressing, feeding, exercising (not the "Professional Kind" – our own nurses and family who did a good job mostly their and our way), getting her out of bed, brushing her hair and just talking to her.

But wait, what about bed sores? The one horrible skin problem that every patient, nurse, doctor etc fear are the little sores that appear and, if not treated quickly, become large blisters and where the big problem begins.

We were pretty fortunate early on, probably because Jeri's room and care was kept clean. I never realized myself why this could be a big problem. Once when the first serious large blister was discovered on Jeri, naturally where one would not easily find it, I watched the nurse begin caring for it right away. She was able to correct it within a few days. I became a believer. How do we prevent this?

At first we would watch for blisters more. Not many appeared. Apparently everyone was doing well, only casually, did one appear, but when one did, there was concern. Our procedure was to be sure to pass this on to the next nurse. I think I learned to watch and due pretty good when no nurse was present (with help of family, of course). But this to our family wasn't good enough. What else can we do? Jeri wasn't exactly thrilled with this either especially since there was no way she could help.

The best date I can determine was when one of our nurses found out about a mattress pad that would possibly correct the blister problem and even turn Jeri little by little periodically. The date was February 19, 2008. This is when an air mattress was delivered. It was a plastic pad that was power regulated to circulate air slowly through connecting air pockets at timely intervals (as needed) and would eventually move air through the entire pad and keep repeating this. All of this was controlled by a pump usually placed on the bed frame at the foot of the user. The less covering between the user and the mattress, the better it worked. I was not a believer. I was asked to lay on it and they would turn it on. I couldn't believe it. I expected to lay on a piece of plastic full of air, which would be an uncomfortable mattress to sleep on. It actually was very comfortable. It was even giving me a gentle massage. We learned that this was actually for controlling bed sores. We found our answer. It worked beautifully. I don't think Jeri ever had a blister again. It also helped move her periodically as we controlled the pump. If only we had learned about this sooner.

Our own research..........

     Over the future years, we tried to keep up with the MS especially in research, support groups etc. However with many false alarms about cures, Jeri wanted to wait and see, rather than keep making hospital visits or trying the new cures. We did a lot of our own research by trying to keep up with where the research was being done. It seemed difficult to really get a reliable status report on MS from anyone, despite magazine and newspaper articles about MS. You may see one article about a potential cure and never see any progress report.

This is why we started doing some of our own research. For example, with our own research once, we found out that there were 18 MS research centers in the US. We were unable to find any public indication of any coordination. Other times, if you asked for financial information, you would be offered a financial report. Reality is that financial reports given out are usually of little help. You really need to know what's behind all the information!

Jeri did volunteer to help one group doing research. It was one of the few times Jeri was ever asked to offer her experiences to help.

     When she was asked by MedStar Research Institute in Washington, DC to participate in their research study entitled "Evaluating the Health care Experiences of People with Spinal Cord Injury, Cerebral Palsy, and Multiple Sclerosis," she joyfully agreed. This study included 530 participants and lasted three years. When it was finished, Jeri received a letter thanking her and saying the results would be distributed to the disability community including disability advocates, researchers etc.

Jeri, in filling out one of MedStar's medical survey questionnaires found one question being asked that she disliked:

Question: In general do you feel depressed?
Jeri's answer was checked "none of the time."

Jeri wrote a footnote to this and sent it MedStar saying: "Depressed" implies mental problems. MS people prefer "Discouraged."

In our own way, we were doing research for MS and what went with it from the first day it became "official" that Jeri had MS. How does this sound for unprofessional research:

One way - Come to the table..........

In an edition of one of the State of Ohio's publications reference disabilities, an article written had a section that claimed that they could not get disabled people to "come to the table." I said to Jeri, that's the person we want to talk with. After several phone calls trying to locate the person who wrote it, we located them. I introduced Jeri and myself and said, "We want to come to your table." After our apparent surprise, there was hesitation on their part with a few "ahs, well, ah." They really were not prepared to know what to say, like "great." I always tried to make my calls like this on our speaker phone at a time when Jeri could listen. She was always interested. So were the answers. Anyway, this person asked where we lived. I gave them our Bowling Green address and phone number and explained that Jeri had MS. They then said, "I know someone in Toledo that I will give this information to and have them get in touch with you." End of conversation. End of going to the table. We never heard from either one.

Another way – We wrote to the Editor of the MS Society's Monthly Magazine saying we found an important part of the magazine which was the biggest help to us - letters to the editor. We were always disappointed, however, to find it was limited to two pages. We always learned from those that have been there (with MS) and probably still are. Their letters were very meaningful to us. We asked them if they could add more pages to the letters. I think there are still only two pages.

Our joining a MS Society support group was one more good way of learning to solve our medical problems, learn research going on and have a good time also. This, even with some turnover, was a good group that MSers felt comfortable with and all would generally get into discussions about MS, what one was doing about it, what medicine they were taking etc. No one was prying. Everyone was looking for ideas. Everyone knew each person's MS was always a little different with each person, so what was that suppose to mean? It meant learn but don't necessarily copy. With MS, all information given by those with MS was useful in one way or another. Sometimes experienced speakers would be brought in to speak on MS. I think we learned more from each other than from any speaker. So, in effect, we were at the table.

Before one meeting began one night and in front of several people in wheelchairs, a person whose office was near where we met attracted attention with something they wanted to tell the group, even though they were not part of it. Everyone became quite. They said they realized all those present especially in wheelchairs were living a difficult life. They continued and said, "I want you to know I understand. I spent an entire day in a wheelchair to see what it was like." Just then Jeri, of course, yelled out, "Try it for a week!"

As for having a good time, every meeting there would be laughter and people feeling relieved that others were listening to them with equal feelings. To top it off, every Christmas we would have a Christmas Party with everyone including spouses and friends, receiving gifts, compliments of area businesses. Each Christmas, for many years, after the gifts were distributed, an announcement was made that there was a truck load of whole hams waiting for everyone outside. There was no panic. There was enough for everyone. Wow. Now that was a party. Did we talk MS? Heck no. This was Christmas.

WHAT ABOUT MS AND PAIN? WAS THIS FORGOTTEN AND LEFT OUT?

A good point – not forgotten but almost left out. There doesn't seem to be very much mail on what has been happening with MS pain over the years, even recently. It seems that a reasonable solution has not been solved yet. One of the last things we did not want was Jeri to have pain. Now early on with MS if Jeri did claim she had pain, we would give her some Tylenol without concern. She seemed to point out her pain fairly easy. Later years when the pain did increase was when we found out that there was not much you could do about it. Where was the pain and how painful was it? MS pain could be everywhere in her. So what do you do? Of course, we tried the "numbers and pictures game." That was a waste of effort. Show your pain from one to ten Jeri – come now, she can't do it. The nurses could not make it work either. They would point to a number, and ask Jeri if that was where the pain was. I think Jeri tired of this system and even probably shook her head yes just to satisfy the nurses. Guessing by Jeri was not the answer.

We decided to trace the history of Jeri's pain. Actually, as far as we could tell, she had little pain in her early going. She rarely had a headache etc in which it was "easy" to give medicine to her. Trying to identify just when Jeri did begin having real MS pain was hard to establish. I reviewed a large number of our home nursing report copies left with us to see if these reports showed Jeri having pain.

The reports I scanned for 1988 showed nothing for pain. One report said she had a headache, another that she had blisters on her toes.

Reports scanned for 1992 showed only some spasms and blisters but no mention of pain.

Reviewing the beginning log we had maintained for Jeri reference the Methotrexate showed her starting March 16, 1995 indicated a lot of "stomach burning" which ceased as she adjusted to the medicine. Some minor pain came next which was treated with Tylenol as needed. Even with increased dosages of Methotrexate, Jeri seemed unaffected by all of this. She was not showing any signs of improving, hence the stoppage.

The next date might best tell us when her pain became more painful. On March 29, 2002, we purchased an electric Heating Pad. This she used a lot. It worked pretty well but then after perhaps a couple of years, her pain became worse and the heating pad was not helping too well. Bean bags did not work either. One more interesting note I found on this subject was when I was checking out a train trip, I found in my listing of what we took with us to DC in 2005 was "Tylenol pills + 1 bottle." Strange, I do not remember ever giving Jeri Tylenol on a train.

So from 2005 on seems to be when she suffered the most and there was not much we could do about it except go with what we knew and had.

One article about Tylenol indicated if you cannot locate where the pain is, Tylenol is a good choice. However, use it appropriately not excessively. Tylenol is an over-the-counter medicine but their warning is do not give an overdose. I like the warning. I stood by this with Jeri. Now we know Tylenol 2 is a prescription but I found it to be carefully allowed by a doctor. It worked the best of what we had but was to be used for excessive pain.

The nurses wanted to give Jeri Tylenol every time they said she was in pain. This became difficult to explain to all the nurses. When asked if she had pain, Jeri would say "Yes" usually shaking her head. She undoubtedly had some pain, but she didn't want to say no if asked. I would tell the nurses to be careful asking Jeri if she had pain. Observe her, don't ask. If she had pain, let me know. I knew Jeri better than anyone and usually could tell if she was in pain or not. Remember she could rarely talk and when the "trach" was installed in her throat, she no longer could talk at all. As I was told, this trach covered her vocal cords

I tried to instruct the nurses what to do about the pain by leaving written notes. These notes did no good. I think they thought my notes always were to someone else, not them. So I left very few notes.

I then decided to use our methods based on how I handled Jeri. I recommended that the nurses try them. At the same time I told them that I would start being the person to give Jeri Tylenol. I was hoping the nurses would understand what I wanted to try and would help me find the best way to solve Jeri's pain. I think they did good considering most nurses seemed to want to do it their way. I think often nurses feel they are not wanted or not able to contribute their suggestions unless asked in situations like this. They should always speak up with a suggestion and accept a no answer if given. Remember, it may be accepted.

Our methods were if Jeri had pain: Take her temperature. Does she have a fever? Look into her eyes. Are there tears? Jeri rarely cried or had tears. Tears were what I always looked for. One night I beat Jeri to the draw. I saw tears in her eyes. I told her, you're in pain aren't you? She nodded yes. I gave her Tylenol.

Other ways were: try the heating pad again; distract her – get her to smile or laughing. What else? If she's ready to take a nap or to sleep for the night, stall with her for a few minutes. I mentioned early in this book how we had to apply medicine on our Jodi at night for allergies – while she slept. It worked every time. Another way to identify pain was to observe Jeri without her knowing it like when talking to her. Her expressions, movements, being discouraged anything one can think of. Would giving her a little food or liquid help? Asking her if she would like some coffee (she would prefer tea)? How about some Dr. Pepper or wine? A train ride worked the best. Funny but if you would ask her that last comment, her eyes would light up. Forget the pain.

Granted, the nurses did not like me telling them that I would give the Tylenol. This would be temporary until we had it under control.

A couple of examples of happenings:

One night the nurse got upset when she wanted to give Jeri Tylenol. I said not to give it to her. The nurse answered, "But I asked Jeri if she needed it and she said yes." The nurse started crying and left the room. I thought she just went to our ladies room. I waited to try to explain to her more. She actually had left our house, got in her car and drove away. It was about two in the morning. We never saw her again.

While I'm on Tylenol, I find this one interesting and I'm kind of proud of it:

I was really trying to test Tylenol and the only way one can test something is to do it yourself. My way was to be the one to give Jeri Tylenol, then I had a good record to keep track. This was not deliberate but to save myself one more step to the store, I bought five bottles of regular Tylenol and put them in our bathroom medical shelf. One day I went for Tylenol and looked twice. There were only four bottles there. I knew I had five. On another shelf covered, I found the other bottle, half used. I had to think about this one. If someone took a bottle, I did not know who. A first reaction would be to question the nurses. I didn't like that one. I assumed that someone was giving Jeri doses without my knowing it. I had a better idea. I thought if I were in their position and knowing it was only Tylenol and that, in this case Jeri, needed help, I think I would have done the same thing.

MEDICAL PHONE CALLS

These are phone calls I made trying to get medical etc answers for Jeri reference equipment, insurance etc in cases where original answers were negative and simply not answered well:

A call to Medicare – Why were we unable to get some financial coverage for a "travel" wheelchair?

We already had a regular heavy wheelchair for use in our home covered by Medicare etc but needed a "travel" wheelchair for Jeri for doctor visits, traveling, even walks downtown with a stop for tea and coffee, anything to get outside, even to go swimming.

Our first regular wheelchair was purchased in 1985. Our first "travel" wheelchair was purchased in 1992. As we learned from getting a "travel" wheelchair, we really needed both chairs, nothing more, nothing less. Our car was used for either but after a few "problems" with using a wheelchair in and out of a car, we learned that the regular wheelchair belonged at home our travel wheelchair was needed outside the home. Now it is on to our prime question of using and paying for two completely different wheelchairs.

Our insurance denied our request for a "travel" wheelchair, saying Medicare will not pay for it and since Medicare will not pay for it, neither will we.

Calling Medicare March 10, 2000, I told them that I had called Medicare July 28, 1999 in which they said, "Medicare WILL pay for it if the person cannot self propel her own wheelchair." My current call person then told me, "..this was correct that Medicare would pay for a travel (light weight) wheelchair as long as the person could not self propel her wheelchair."

I said, "That's no problem. Jeri can't propel any wheelchair."

The person then said that − "Oh, if that is the case then NO we cannot approve a travel wheelchair for her."

I asked, "Why not?"

Answer: "She doesn't fit the criterion. We thought you meant she could not self propel a heavy wheelchair, in which case, YES we would pay for a self propel wheelchair."

Now I was confused. The person refused to answer any more questions.

I asked the last person I talked with (a supervisor, I believe) and asked her if the lightweight travel chair was covered or not? She began talking and I asked her if she was reading something or making it up as she went along. She said she was reading from something and was answering me as she went along. I asked her if she could write notes for me from what she was reading. She said she was reading from a manual but was not allowed to let me see it. I would have to write to the Freedom of Information Office to get it. I wrote for such a manual because I wanted to see what it said in cases where the person CANNOT self propel. I received a copy of a manual but there was no explanation in it to answer my question.

I called this number back the next day and got another person on the phone who said they would review this with the people there and get back to me. She never got back to me.

This was becoming ridiculous. It was more ridiculous when you realize we have been working on this now for almost two years!

To try to solve this question so I can go on with the book, I did my own research and found out that, while we had NEVER heard of it, a certain different type "travel" wheelchair entered the scene and became a "second" travel wheelchair (lightweight?) that allowed a person to "self propel" and if they did so, Medicare would pay for it! Now we think this was fine for persons that could manually do this but, while they were receiving payment for the chair, it meant other handicapped wheelchairers were "on their own." Something seems wrong here.

More about wheelchairs is covered under **WHEELCHAIRS** later.

Enough was more than enough. No answer and it is time to be on our way. We kept paying for our "travel" wheelchairs.

Phone calls about denials – I liked my questions I used several times when I was getting a denial about insurance, equipment etc. Reference one call to an insurance executive where we were denied a claim and after talking for a while and getting nowhere, I asked him, "Why don't you come and meet Jeri? It just might look a little different to you." He answered, "You know, you're probably right, but I can't do that." I made this invitation to others too. It should work but it didn't. No one would come.

Another call to Medicare -- Wheelchairs always seemed to have problems connected with trying to get approvals, not with sellers but with financial approvals.

One problem was Medicare's policy on approving wheelchairs. The wheelchair had to be for in-house only use. I decided to question the meaning of this to be sure I was not breaking any rules. All the wheelchairs we ever had were used in and out of the home. I decided to call Medicare - I would get different answers no matter who I talked with. It would go like this:

If we get approval, does the W/C have to be used in the home only? Reply: "Yes."

Can we walk someone around the block? Reply: "How far?"

Can we go to a restaurant? Reply: "How often?" Reply: Once a week? Reply: "Probably OK". How about twice a week? "NO." It continued like this until one person saw my point and didn't want to discuss it. They nicely said, "Look, in six months the wheelchair will be yours, you can then do whatever you want with it." I got my answer and stopped calling.

A call to State Nursing Services in Columbus about trimming a patient's nails – now why would this have to be a problem large enough to call Columbus?

Reference Jeri's all her nails – first, no problems. I would cut them but soon a nurse said she would do it for me. For a time, a new nurse would come and would cut them. But soon, it started. One nurse said she wasn't allowed to cut them. Why not? "I was told I wasn't allowed to do it." Another nurse came, said she wasn't allowed to do it. Why not? "It's against the law." Another nurse would come and say, "Oh, I can cut Jeri's nails. No problem." This went on for probably a year or longer with the same answers.

Enough is enough. Is it Illegal? Who tells them, they can't do it etc? Who is telling nurses that it is or not ok? I think most nurses who would do it simply didn't ask their Agency and did it out of feeling (1) it was part of their job and (2) they did it with patients all the time. So I kind of let it alone and would just ask the nurse who came when they asked me what to do, I would ask them if they were allowed to cut Jeri's nails? If I got a "yes" answer, great. If I got a "No" answer, I would do it myself and let go at that. In time, I tired of doing this "their" way.

Since nurses had to pass certain state tests to get a license, why not call the state, even though it sounded pretty minor to go to the state for a routine answer.

I could not locate an office that had a stated answer to the question especially if it was legal or not what to do. Finally, I was directed to call the Department of Nursing. The person gave me a simple answer within 10 seconds. "It's up to each agency." I got my answer.

To add one more thought to this, I had been told that a certified nail specialist (doctor or whoever) would be covered under insurance to come to our home to cut Jeri's nails. That indeed would be great. I'll find one. Need I tell you I could not find a single professional to come to our home to cut Jeri's nails? They were going to Nursing Homes only. So we lived by what we knew. If the nurse said her agency would not allow it, then Jack gets the job.

A similar situation existed with cutting Jeri's hair

I was getting a pretty good training on my phone calls to know what to expect so I skipped a phone call on this one. I wanted to handle this one myself and start building a little more self confidence in this medical world in which I did not expect to be so full of needed answers.

Our homemade procedure for getting Jeri's hair cut at least every three months took a lot of luck. Three months? Why not monthly?

At first we had no nurse volunteer to cut Jeri's hair but some did agree to shave her where necessary. For cutting, I would take Jeri to a woman's shop, or whatever it went by, and usually tried to stay with the same one. My first time to take Jeri, I gave the first chair our name and sat with Jeri. They were busy but we were in no hurry. Not paying much attention, we waited and waited. When I saw other people coming in after us were getting their hair done ahead of us, I went to the girl by the door and asked why they hadn't taken Jeri yet? "Oh, you haven't signed in? Did you want a cut? Then sign in and you'll have to wait your turn." I saw no sign there and the person in charge had no mercy. We waited but never went back there again.

Now that I'm learning how to play my new role, our next stop, I made it a point to sign in. It was a bit difficult to get Jeri in position to have her hair cut being in a wheelchair. By the way, I used our travel wheelchair any time we were not home. Our regular w/c would never have worked. This is a good example of why a second w/c is always needed. I would move Jeri to a sink where they could wash her hair. I would back her to the sink and tilt the w/c to fit her arm rests under the sink and at the same time plant my foot behind the back wheels to keep the chair from moving. They would put a towel around Jeri to keep the rinse water within the sink while they washed. This worked fairly well except there was a lot of water on the floor when finished. The hair dresser never complained about that. Of course, the tip was a little higher.

Hair cutting at home saved us a lot time and work. We found it difficult to find someone to come to our home to do it so when this one nurse said she could do it, we gave her a chance. She did well. We tipped her too. Was she allowed to accept tips? At times, it's better not to ask questions. Just do what is best and, if necessary, fight it later. We would have fought this one if our nurse was told not to do it. If we were to have to fight this one, I would say then you get on the phone and do the calling.

DISCOVERING WHAT'S WRONG

An introduction to what went well – many things went well as you will read herein throughout this book.

An introduction to what went wrong – minor problems were easily solved or ignored.

Some minor problems

We had several minor questions to ask our nursing agency so we asked for a meeting in our house so Jeri could listen. We had heard about a free advocate agency that would help people with disabilities. We invited them to send someone to attend our meeting. This they did. We discussed several topics about helping Jeri more. It seemed everything we brought up to the agency, they did not agree with us. I shortly realized the advocate person was agreeing with our agency. Hey, whose side are you on? I decided to throw in a good one. During the winter especially, nurses would come in with muddy shoes on etc. Our carpeting left their trail from door to Jeri. It was a mess. I had been thinking about making them take their shoes off but I was told this would be illegal. Who thought this up? I let it go at that. I then asked, "Can we get Medicaid or whoever to pay to clean our carpeting?" A loud laughter shook our house. At least I got the group laughing.

If a night nurse didn't show up at all, sometimes we said, "good we get the evening off." It would do no good to call the agency involved, they never had a backup. I would put Jeri to bed and we would watch one of our videos on TV. Sometimes the next day I wouldn't even report them not showing up. It really wasn't our responsibility to keep track of nurses coming and going. We learned to live with it and surprisingly it often worked well. It took us quite a while to live with late or no shows and learned that it wasn't that bad after all.

We got taken one night. We were having a nurse come at 11 PM for an 8 hour shift. Jeri had been put to bed by the evening nurse and we were waiting for the night nurse to come. At 11 PM not only did a night nurse show up but within a few minutes, a second nurse turned up. This caught us really off guard. What do we do at midnight? Call the agency? Which one? I'm still in the room with Jeri. I overheard the two questioning each other not very nicely with, "What are you doing here?" I said to Jeri, "I think we have a problem. I think I have to go out there."

Well there were two nurses out there, one from one agency, the other one from another agency. They both said they were the one scheduled to be there, do something. Now I had no idea who was wrong and what schedule they were on. That definitely was not my job. Only one answer, call one of the agencies. Call at midnight? So, what else is new? I picked the one I thought was wrong, oops, I mean would be more apt to call for me. It's now near midnight. I knew if they were lucky, they would connect with a person hired just to answer the phone. Then that person would try to get hold of someone to help. I'm really getting good. I was right. One called their agency and was told they would call someone to call us. Now everyone waits. They knew one of them was not going to get paid – not my idea. Within an hour, the one calling their agency received a call that she was not suppose to be there, to leave. Not a sound from her, she put her coat on and left fast, obviously upset. Who won? Not me. How in the world did we get mixed up in an error like that in the middle of the night in our own home?

Call a doctor at midnight? Not if there is no emergency. One night around midnight Jeri was having a problem over something I don't remember. It was not an emergency. I would always observe Jeri if any problem developed and go from there. The night nurse said, "We should call the doctor." I answered no need to yet unless something develops. We just can't call the doctor unless it really is necessary. Their answer was, "Oh, but it is and that is why he carries a phone to be paged." "I said no, do not disturb him." The nurse called anyway and had him paged. Nothing happened. There was no problem and no doctor.

Another time happened on a Sunday. Jeri was on a prescription, of perhaps an infection, which our nurses were giving to her without any problems. This day, a substitute nurse arrived to take care of Jeri, I told her to also give Jeri her medicine, which she would find in the bathroom. Well, this nurse insisted to see the original doctor's prescription. I said well just follow what's on the medicine bottle. I wasn't about to go searching for a doctor's prescription because all of our nurses followed me, the primary caregiver, without question. She insisted. I said, "Never mind, I'll do it myself."

Another time, I was trying to wean Jeri off the ventilator a little by little, day by day when the nurse sat down to watch. I was putting the tubing back to connect on Jeri's trach. While still holding the tubing the nurse grabbed the tubing from me. I said, "Why did you do that?" In panic, she said, "Look at the ventilator, the numbers are too high, do something!" I said to her, nice and calmly, "Give me the tubing back," which she did. I connected it to the trach and told her, "Now, watch the numbers." She said, "Oh, there're going down." I didn't have to say anymore. She was really frightened. She frightened me too.

How about drug stores prescriptions – any problems? Getting prescriptions filled for supplies taught us another tricky way if we were turned down by a pharmacy. We would take a prescription to them which would be paid by Medicaid. They would look at the prescription and tell us that what we wanted was not approved by Medicaid. We asked them, "How do you know?" Answer was, "We keep a record of what's approved." We asked, "Would you mind sending this prescription in anyway?" We had learned that Medicaid had a habit of changing what was approved by them. The pharmacy wasn't happy but sent it in anyway. It was approved.

For an intermediate problem, we have one we decided to try to work out ourselves. I had an idea to try but needed Jeri and the nurses to help with it. They agreed.

When we brought Jeri home from a rather long stay at Rehab, we found two problems. One was she had gained too much weight. The second was she had no control over having a solid as opposed to runny bowel movement. We found ourselves letting her go in bed or giving her a laxative as needed or doing a digital. There was a better way. We would find the right combination of food, cranberry juice, prune juice and timing. This would all be liquid fed through her feeding tube. We had a nutritionist, would you believe in Connecticut, that had been working with Jeri about her food feeding. We explained what our team wanted to do. She was excited. She said she had also been working with Jeri's doctor on how much to feed her. I asked her if this would be ok? Yes, of course, a very excellent idea. Now we are ready to experiment.

I think I can sum the rest up. We stayed with what we proposed. No drugs or medicine. Trying different combinations different ways, keeping track of our testing – which was easy. I would mark in a log the time and what we gave Jeri every day. It took a while but it began to work. We kept in touch with the nutritionist and she kept in touch with the doctor. After three months, it was working beautifully. Her bowel movements were her own. Rarely a laxative was needed. Rarely a digital was needed. She had her bowels moving daily with a formed soft texture. It was so much easier for Jeri. We were all excited and surprised. I say, we had a wonderful team. Were we really able to do this? We were also able to reduce her weight with this and with weighing her just about every day on her new scales which we fought so hard to get.

Jeri turned from losing weight, down to perhaps 80#, to overweight too quickly to about 120#. Why? We didn't pay too much attention to this at first as we had brought Jeri home from Rehab and continued feeding her through her feeding tube by hanging Ensure, which we liked, in a proper sack, on a portable "hanging rack." The nurses on duty generally watched this and would change to a new bag as each drained through Jeri's feeding tube. The schedule was four cans of Ensure each day. We thought this was working well. We had all questions answered and kept in touch with Jeri's nutritionist who in turn kept in touch with her doctor. We were getting the Ensure with our regular needed supplies from a larger company who would deliver to us. But wait. Her weight kept increasing. A little "soul" searching was needed. I could come up with nothing except I did see a can of Ensure we were using. It was Ensure alright and it was in the same size can we were using. However it had a different cover on its can! So they put a new cover on the can, so what. I kept thinking about this and called the company who made it and asked for a nutritionist to talk to. My question: "Would there be any difference in this can and the one we have been using?" Ah, there was. She said, "This can would have more vitamins etc in it! You should decrease your dosage!"

It obviously was too late to go back but we changed the four cans to three cans. It worked much better. We were now reducing Jeri's weight. It is difficult to keep track this way on eating, medicine etc and also when many people including nurses, doctors etc are involved. I would guess this is why one person, the primary caregiver, is given this authority and should be recognized by other people helping, that, like it or not, this person is in charge and not, for example, an agency that they might work for. I had very little problems with this but found out you have to "respect" others helping to listen to them at times. Our changing from four cans to three cans of Ensure was a good example especially since it took me a while to discover the problem.

We were able to reduce Jeri down to about 115 pounds and counting. Her normal weight was about 100 pounds based on her height of about 5 feet 2 inches.

Let's look at some of Jeri's major problems in which we had little or no control over.

Personal physical involvement where very limited time approvals stopped the sessions based on "not improving." We fought this one many times but never won. Why, when we were so right!

Swimming (water therapy)

We believed, by experience, that one of the very best treatments for Jeri's MS was swimming. The more times in the water for her, the better it was. As her MS became worse, we tried to take her to as many pools as time permitted. When she stopped walking, one of the first things she said, when in swimming was, "It feels so good to walk again." The water actually helped her to walk. It seemed unbelievable. We were excited about that. Since heat was devastating, cool water worked the best. Of course, buoyancy in water helped her to float and walk. This walking ability stayed with her for a little while after getting out of the water, but not enough to continue walking, but definitely she was able to move her legs for a while.

At one time, reference MS swimming did not seemed important for patients. Doctors knew water on the cool side could affect moving arms etc a little bit but had no lasting effect. But wouldn't that give a little clue to follow, especially since research was just really getting started?

Scanning through our Archives, I came across a few interesting letters etc relating to Jeri's swimming therapy. By now, I think our whole family – me, Jeri, Jodi, Jami, Jeff and the kid's dog Pete – realized that swimming was the answer for Jeri. Actually, it turned out to be the only medicine that ever worked for Jeri's MS. It, indeed, became important to us.

We had a few ideas and with help from doctors, nurses and a few "swimming holes," we began another journey, led by our own Jeri, to where she could go for the swimming.

We found an early perfect place to go, The University of Toledo Kinesiotherapy Center. Beginning in 1987, she was enrolled in their aquatic exercise program. We would take her there weekly, park right at their indoor campus pool and manually lift her into the pool from her wheelchair. This continued through 1991.

This four year period of excellent therapy was not without problems. The problem was insurance companies and Medicare (and perhaps Medicaid). It always was about no improvement. UT's Center worked hard to show that there was improvement. We strongly argued that decreasing the worsening was an improvement. We used and showed this many times but could never sell this to insurance etc.

Jeri's final initial ending of therapy at UT reads from an insurance company: "....treatment will end December I, 1991. Since the patient's condition does not appear to be improving we will not be able to consider charges beyond the above date. Maintenance therapy or supportive care is specifically excluded...."

UT had set the stage for Jeri and other swimming locations followed closer to our home which helped a lot. After a lapse of time, we would again apply for water therapy. It again would be approved and again, after several months, it would be denied by insurance etc. This rule must have been built in stone. Everyone we tried had the same answer - not improving - end of therapy.

This one was our last attempt to get water swimming approval for Jeri. Oh, we got the approval OK, no problem there. But watch this one which worked like this:

The swimming therapy, this time, had a new twist. After 2 thirty minute swimming sessions, Jeri's swimming was stopped for not improving. AFTER 2 THIRTY MINUTE SESSIONS, IT WAS STOPPED! WOW, this swimming instructor must have been really good to be able to analyze someone that quickly! Well, we couldn't let that one get away. The questioning began and went like this:

Jack: Why did you stop Jeri?

Reply: She wasn't improving.

Jack: Jeri, do you think you were improving?

Jeri: Yes.

Jack: So after two sessions, you called it not improving?

Reply: Yes.

Jack: But Jeri thinks she was.

Reply: Jeri, how were you improving?

Jack: Now you know she can't talk. She knows if she is improving or not.

Reply: No reply.

Jack: We feel that if worsening is slowed up by swimming, then it is an improvement. Do you think decreasing the worsening is an improvement?

Reply: No.

Jack: We want to talk to your supervisor.

Reply: Go ahead.

Jack: To myself quietly. It always bothered me when I would have to tell someone that I was going to tell their boss and their reaction would be, "I don't care" or "Go ahead."

We immediately went to the supervisor and discussed this. The supervisor supported the instructor.

About all we could do was to leave. No more swimming therapy.

Physical Therapy

This therapy seemed a little more complicated than the swimming therapy. Obviously, there was a difference but that was not a problem. Each had a different mission. While swimming would have a fixed location (a pool) in which we would go to them, physical therapy was done either in nursing homes, hospitals, or private homes. It seemed that therapists preferred going to nursing homes, probably because they could do it where they could see more patients with one stop. We found it difficult finding anyone to come to our home.

I was surprised to see at hospitals, their physical therapy sessions would last only about 20 minutes as we learned from watching them with Jeri.

We were finally able to find someone to come to our home. To our surprise, they would take only about 30 minutes. Were these short visits adequate?

I called physical therapy simply exercise. I guess I knew what exercise was but did not fully understand this physical therapy. What's the difference? This "time and motion" method also threw me a loss. I saw it done. To me, it was still exercise. Why confuse home patients and primary caregivers? We had enough problems with codes etc. When a therapist would try to teach me, it didn't take long for me to end up with a mixed up method. I saw nothing wrong with giving ordinary exercises to home patients where one would know the patient much better than a visiting therapist. I gave Jeri many hours of exercise in the middle of the night and could tell which ones were working. Our MS doctor would check Jeri for how we were doing and would correct me and show me movements that even the therapists didn't tell me about.

Our family knew that this therapy was critical because of the MS, especially as Jeri became worse. We wanted Jeri to get this therapy as often as possible. I intended to supplement their coming with my giving her additional exercise even trying to do it the way they showed me. I was not too successful in following their many directions. It was too exactness. I did want them to be able to continue doing this with Jeri. They informed me that they were limited, that they were to teach the primary caregiver. I wonder how many primary caregivers were able to follow these many therapy directions. I believe physical therapists were licensed to be able to get that title. So why would Medicare, or whomever, approve this therapy to be done by an unlicensed person?

Jeri's first experience at our home with the therapist turned into a rather quick exit, for the therapist, that is. Jeri stayed. During the therapy, this person soon came to Jeri's left arm. She worked a few minutes on it and finally told Jeri, "I'm not going to do this arm anymore." Jeri asked, "Why not?" Response: "It's dead." Jeri, "What do you want me to do, cut it off?" Dead silence except I heard from another room what happened and I told the therapist to leave. One point for Jeri! I was proud of her. Sometimes, you have to stand up. Jeri had to stand up often.

By the way, Jeri did have off and on a little movement in her left arm. MS is tricky!

Following is the last story on Physical Therapy. This is a truly good story that got nowhere.

One physical therapist that came to help Jeri turned out to really be good. We were very impressed and excited by what they accomplished. Neither of Jeri's legs moved except very slightly when we or the nurses were exercising her. After a few visits, this therapist had Jeri moving her legs herself up about a foot at a time. This had not happened for many years. When Jeri's time was up after the number of approved visits were finished and the company handling this physical therapy had to move on, the person in charge paid us a visit. This person was very pleased that there was progress in moving her legs and had a plan. They were very optimistic. Jeri and I were also. In fact, I signed a paper to agree with this plan. They suggested that if we could continue the therapy with Jeri's legs as good as it was then or better, they would come back to see Jeri again in a couple of months. If she worsens, we were to let this person know. They would want to start therapy again before the couple of months were up. If it looked like we maintained the gain or better, they would try to apply for another approval to return again to Jeri. We did kept her legs moving pretty well and then, we tried to reach this company to see if they were coming back as planned. It appears that they were now working in another area and it seemed they forgot about us. They did not return − a good story that never finished.

Our title for this section being "Discovering What's Wrong," I would put these two therapies (swimming and physical therapy) at the head of their class for being so difficult to make them work. Seems there was no need not to make them work. Jeri did her best. We did to. I still think the decreasing the worsening is an improvement. Perhaps someone will agree and get that thinking corrected.

Other "Discovering What's Wrong"

What no Dr. Pepper?

This is a strange one you may not believe or maybe will prove it yourself.

Jeri and I learned early on that her medical needs would not be available to the degree she needed. Could we try different simple ways of finding aids by ourselves? This we tried many times, from lifting her, changing her clothes, etc with a lot of success. What about eating and drinking? Anything we can improve? One item we overlooked and had never been suggested by anyone to try was right in front of us one day. Dr. Pepper, the drink.

Let's try it and see if it has any value to us. Jeri drank it. My goodness, she raised her arm several inches up. We were amazed and began buying more to let her drink it to see what happens. Raising one arm seemed to work best – one at a time. Now this was on an earlier side of her having MS. It continued helping her, the best I can remember, for several years. Later on as the MS progressed, it wasn't helping her. Her arms were no longer to move – but look what it did for a pretty long period.

What else seemed wrong?

Everything was not wrong. Jeri, among many things, had wonderful hearing. She could hear very well from a distance people talking. One time swimming in our condo pool, I was talking to someone about Jeri. Now, Jeri was out of the water in her wheelchair in the sun and sleeping, I thought. We were on the other side of the pool away from her. I always tried to keep an eye on Jeri and said to this person, "I can tell Jeri is listening to everything I say. Right now she could probably be arrested for what she's thinking about me." Just then Jeri opened her eyes with a very large smile. See, she is listening! That rascal!

Jeri and I learned early in her MS journey how to entertain ourselves, especially since we never would have guessed it would be so long. It had sounded to us that science was on an early fast track to find the cure. In the meantime, we began realizing our social life was changing and there were things Jeri could not do. We knew that to live normally at home or traveling, we would have to entertain ourselves our way without depending on others all the time. In other words, when things seemed wrong, we would have to correct what we could and live with what we could not correct. We spent a lot of time correcting what could have been a life time of waiting.

At first, the teaching of MS patients seemed to emphasize rest as much as you can since you will become tired easily. We practiced this but soon, by observing Jeri, we did away with that thinking and let her be the judge. She enjoyed this freedom and did it her way. This activity (exercise, whatever you want to call it) did not seem to hurt her MS. Mentally it helped her. I think the big help came after I retired, was with her more and when real traveling entered our life, we found the right road to take. We found that it was no use waiting for a cure. None was in sight. Doctors could not help Jeri very much. A doctor once told us, "If you find anything promising that might help Jeri, let me know." They too were waiting for research that could come at any time to help them help people like Jeri. We still kept six months appointment with Jeri's MS doctor. She felt comfortable with him and it helped keep her (our) hopes up by maintaining these appointments. We wanted to be right there available quickly if something good developed. Actually, I think Jeri helped the doctors by her smile and patience and their not calling it quits. When we would keep our appointments, we were at least able to ask a few questions. Her doctor showed me some good ways of improving the exercise I was giving Jeri. The doctor was amazed at Jeri's traveling trips and when we would tell any recent trips, which were often. Jeri enjoyed my telling them with her listening. I think she was amazed herself. They really worked because trips were great on ignoring MS. I think too, especially Jeri, we were trying to impress the doctors not to give up on Jeri. I think this helped a little. If anyone could do this, it would be Jeri.

MS research and financial support...... In trying to keep up with research being done and not being done, I don't recall receiving much financial information about MS research being given to patients etc other than a lot of solicitation, money raisers etc. It always sounded like money being raised, spent and raised some more. Money definitely was needed. But what good is it if the research is not making much progress? Or was it making progress? It was difficult to tell.

Just recently scanning some news reports about the progress being made by research, I felt like I was reading the same reports I read 30 years ago. Where are we in fact with any MS progress? I was really surprised and disappointed.

I think people with MS now, more than ever, have to see what they can do to help. Start with going to the table. Our people with MS know more about MS than they get credit for. Their MS knowledge is the best, I think, available. I think MSers would be thrilled to be invited to the table.

After many years reading into MS we learned more about MS but, unfortunately, not enough. There were quite a few MS books and magazine articles to read. Such articles became outdated quickly. The unknown MS secret was not about to be solved so easily. I would suspect not many people with MS asked or cared about receiving financial information. I was interested but was not able to get any worthwhile information plus working and helping Jeri was my first priority.

Jeri and I did try to sit in on a meeting about MS held by the MS Society. We asked if we could be invited to one, assuming it would be one we would be interesting in and could take part in. We received a thank you note and were told they would invite us to a meeting. This they did. We were thrilled. Now maybe we can finally contribute a little something towards a long sought cure.

We were notified when and where to come to the meeting. We didn't know the subject except that it was about MS. Anyway, we would be there. The meeting started. We learned what this was about. It was basically how to file a request to the government for a grant for MS! This was a real major disappointment for Jeri and me. How to apply for a grant? Not that this wasn't important. It just wasn't important to us. It was about government money. We wanted to be involved with MS research by way of someone (Jeri) who had it for many years. Anyone can file for a grant. Not many are willing or able to contribute on the line information or are even asked! We did not say anything and just sat through the meeting listening. We were not invited to speak. When it was over, I mentioned to the person in charge that we were disappointed that we were not asked to speak. They said, "Oh. I didn't know that. Can you tell me what it was you wanted to say?" Everyone was leaving so I said, "No. That's OK. Thanks anyway." We left. Well, we tried.

Another lesson learned by us the hard way......there were two types of MS......we were Jack and Jeri come lately, when we found this out - **PROGRESSIVE** and **RELAPSING**. We learned that Jeri had Progressive. We further learned that 15% had Progressive while Relapsing had 85%. We further learned that very little, if any, money was being spent on Progressive research. WHOA. What gives here? It seems this was a well kept secret, intentional or not. When we raised questions about this, we further learned that Relapsing MS was easier to research and the one most likely where they will find a cure. Then when they find a cure for Relapsing, it should be easier to find a cure for Progressive. There seemed something very wrong with this logic and fairness. We thought that money donated for MS research would go to MS research period. When was this distinction ever made? Jeri and I were sure others with Progressive MS were stunned with this news that is, if they even ever heard about it. Where were we when this was decided? Who decided? Shouldn't we have been notified about this step? How long had this been in effect? Could not the key to the cure be found just as likely in the Progressive MS?

Another way of looking at this decision......I would tend to think a cure would be more likely found in someone with Progressive MS. Relapsing MS meant it went dormant for how long, days or months? During the relapsing period, could research actually be done on that person? With Progressive, MS was continuous, uninterrupted research!

The well known statement that backfired "But you look so good"....... was intended not to hurt. We doubt that anyone with MS took it that way. How were friends expected to talk to people with MS? This is something gone wrong. You have to put yourself in the place of the one with MS and act out what you would like to hear. One certainly doesn't want a friend to avoid them. Think ahead of what you say to someone who has MS. It will work.

Jeri had many wrong comments like that happen. She did her part usually by smiling and let it go at that. It is difficult to just walk away.

People in a position to help or who simply wanted to help Jeri...a difficult statement to explain how in the world could this be wrong?

Many people did help Jeri. She and family appreciated this very much. We tried to always thank them, even if it wasn't what she needed. Compliments and little things like a smile, opening doors for her in her wheelchair always went a long way. The best help of all was a simple hello or better yet, if they knew Jeri, a "Hi Jeri" with a smile. She would always return a smile.
So how can you help someone in a wheelchair? Simple answer is to find out by asking and meaning it. Think if you were in their place. Here is one thought. If you are going to help someone in a wheelchair, be sure they want your help. Once on a train, this girl we

met in the handicapped section had her scooter with her and used it on the train herself. When it was her station to get off, I assumed there would be someone to meet her. Without thinking and wanting to be helpful in getting her off, I said, "I guess you will have someone meeting you to help you." She answered firmly, "No. I don't need anyone helping me."

The next part is a question. How do you tell someone that what they brought you was not what you needed? Items received by Jeri that she did not need and probably would not use, were accepted with the normal smile and thank you. We know the intent is important and people not only were happy to bring Jeri something but would actually be excited about it. They have made someone happy.

But what Jeri needed she needed. If the person bringing something, outside of a small gift, had only asked Jeri first, it would have worked better. One is not made happy getting a wheelchair that doesn't work, nor is one happy getting one that does work. Happiness would be getting rid of it.

Some examples of "ask a person first" should help to understand this – think if you were Jeri:

1. Bathroom faucet in our new condo – workmen, in putting in the faucet for Jeri, knew she would not be able to use the handle of the faucet being inserted, so they put in one with a long handle. Jeri could not use her hands so she could not use that one either. Besides Jeri not using it, no one else could use it either. We found out later you could not turn it on very far because it hit the back wall.

2. Wheelchair for walk-in shower. The chair worked fine in the shower but it had no headrest. Jeri could not hold her head up. We knew our case

manager worked hard to get this for Jeri and was excited to surprise Jeri. We let it go as was and made the best of it. It made each shower for Jeri a little more difficult.

3. When Jeri eventually was put on a ventilator, the shower wheelchair was of no value. Jeri would get a sponge bath which meant her hair would be washed in bed. The nurse that was helping Jeri had been with us for a year or so and was doing well with Jeri including washing her hair. A case manager decided to see if she could get approval for an inflatable vinyl under head hair wash basin with hose which she did. Excited, of course, to bring it as a surprise, she gave it to Jeri to use. The nurse started to use it on Jeri and Jeri soon said she did not like this basin type and wanted to go back to the other way. This was fine with us. It was up to her. When the person that gave her this new washer, came back, she was surprised and asked Jeri why she didn't like it. Jeri just nodded that she didn't like it. To me, if Jeri didn't like it, she didn't like it. Let it be. Actually, I didn't like it either.

4. When we moved into our new Condo, we found we had a step into the garage that would need a ramp for the wheelchair. Asking if Medicaid would cover this, they said yes, to get a contractor to measure the ramp needed and send in his request. A contractor came and measured what would be needed. Listening to the contractor, the ramp sounded like it would have to stick way out to the middle of the garage. My goodness, it was only one step. Why such a long ramp? Where would we park the car? Besides, Jeri could not propel a wheelchair. She would be using the ramp but not driving up or down it herself. The contractor said, "The law requires this measurement for us to install it." Is this another law without exceptions again? Or were there exceptions but never

used? I never saw the contractor again and I never asked a case manager or Medicaid again – I built one myself that worked fine. If we would have let the contractor get approval from the case manager, we would have a nice long unworkable ramp. This is why we had to consistently watch over what we were receiving or being made. Spying? No. Avoiding problems! Ask us first - Advice not often taken.

Other Discovering What Went Wrong incidents......a special section for incidents that didn't mean much but on the other side, didn't make sense either......Reference MS, we were always watching for news items that occasionally showed people involved and doing a lot for solving, in this case, MS problems. We found a good one, a member of Congress:

We had a good idea or two which we were sure would interest them. We wrote a letter to the Congress person we heard about who was showing a lot of interest in MS. These were MS comments hoping for help in solving them. These were not political. It had nothing to do with politics. We thought we could help each other. Jeri was real glad to do this because by now, she knew a lot about MS. This person was in the news. This was the one we wanted to alert. We finally found someone influential that might be interested in what we had to say. We sent our letter.
No answer!
We called the office where we had sent it. We think it was clear that this was not political. Why, we didn't even know what party they belonged to. The person we talked with answered quickly, "Oh, we have an agreement with a certain member of Congress that we send them their mail that belongs to them and they

send us our mail that belongs to us. We sent your letter to them."

But this mail was intended for a stated person. What gives here?

We never heard from the other member of Congress either.

Why can't we pay the difference to get what we need........... With our variety of needed wheelchairs, Medicare agreed to pay a portion of one's wheelchair but limited their choice to just a few approved wheelchairs. Does this method actually allow the patient to choose the right wheelchair they need? We always felt a better way would have been to allow us an allowance towards our selection of what we needed. This could apply to other equipment needs also. No allowance was ever allowed to be given.

A similar case involved a bed provided by Medicare for Jeri.

As Jeri worsened and could not move around in bed, nurses would periodically move her by turning her over to one side etc. When no nurses were here, I did all the turning. We had always used a double bed. Since at night I was where I belonged, next to her, I was able to move her periodically during the night. I could turn her over with my legs and arms from where I slept. I could help her during the night because I could tell when she needed something. How? I would ask her and being right next to her it worked every time from nodding her head, the little way of her answering me or a smile or no smile to my question.

When Jeri was brought home from a stay at Rehab, a single bed was provided by Medicare. I don't know who ordered this bed but if they had asked me, I would have asked for a double bed as we were use to and which worked well and would have kept our system intact. Too late, the bed was already here. Do I think I could have talked them into sending a double bed? Can you jump over a house? I certainly would have tried even using Jeri's method of "Why not." I ended up having to buy another single bed and at night move it next to Jeri. My bed, when I moved it next to Jeri at night, did not fit evenly with hers. This did not help matters.

We learned that there is no way you can put two separate beds together (unless bought that way or rebuild etc) because they would never fit properly and even sometimes spread apart leaving a nice big hole in the center for one of us to see how far it was to the floor.

This next one is kind of on the funny side — depends on how you look at it. Here goes:

One night, in our one double bed (before the single bed came), I was turning her over but she went too far, right on out the bed. I heard the hit and thought it sounded like Jeri. I got up turned the light on. She was right on the floor. I asked if she was ok. She said yes but my nose hurts. I said I would check her in the morning. I put her back in bed. The next morning she said her nose still hurt. I put her in the car and drove to the hospital emergency room. She had a broken nose.

Now one could say that the above double bed was part of the problem (her falling out) would be correct but the double bed allowed me to be near her CLOSER while two single beds cost me to be further from her. Besides, I learned not to push Jeri out of bed any more using just my legs!

Back to our very dull brown ugly bed delivered for Jeri, It looked like another Smithsonian relic taken out of display and put back into action. We soon found, it would not raise Jeri up at all. But give it a chance. What was this piece of metal at the foot of the bed? Call the nurse. It was what? It was a crank to move the bed up and down. We and the nurses were not very happy about this. It was difficult to use and raise a person especially when someone was in it. We finally got approval to put a remote for the bed to raise it. It worked but the bed was still ugly.

Medicare never did reclaim it back.

I like to think I invented the following but it did not seem to impress many nurses or their bosses in charge. It was my way of transferring Jeri from bed, wheelchair, car etc to another position like a chair, bed etc.

Actually I used it whenever needed. It was safe and much easier for Jeri and me. What's wrong with that if it worked?

This happened in a hospital. I was visiting Jeri and she dirtied the bed pretty good or should I say pretty awful. Nurses were kept busy with Jeri. I asked a nurse why they didn't take her to the bathroom. They said it was too much trouble transferring her back and forth. Well the bathroom was in her room. I said I could get her there easily. The nurse questioned me how. I explained to her that Jeri had good strength in both legs which actually would hold her. You move her to the bed's edge, move her legs over towards the floor, lift her under her arms holding your own legs around hers, then a little swivel from her bed (resting on her both legs briefly) to the wheelchair. There was very little lifting to this. It worked for us for years.

To continue, I thought the nurse had followed me because sitting a person on a toilet without a back, needs to be balanced and held. I looked around, no one was with me. I did it alone. I always used the digital method to help move her bowels. Back to bed was simply a reverse. It worked and was easier and cleaner for Jeri and nurses. I don't think they liked the idea. I don't think they used it. They seemed to just let Jeri go in bed and let others clean up. I didn't agree with that for Jeri but they made the call.

Another time, this one at Jeri's Rehab: I saw two nurses lifting Jeri into bed from her wheelchair. This time they were using a (yak!) lift. I tried again, "Would you like me to show you an easy way to do it?" They watched and it worked nicely. No lift, little lifting, safe. One person could do it. (I was always one person.) They liked it and said they were going to use it.

The next day when I went in, they were using their old method. "What happened?" I asked? "We were told we were not to use your method." I wasn't surprised. Sometimes people look at rules as not to be broken. I always felt good rules were those that could be bent.

I continued using my method for a long time.

Case Managers – very important people for us – but, unfortunately, almost never lived up to their capabilities and authority.

When we were assigned to our first case manager, we were both thrilled. Jeri was to get first hand attention from an RN whose mission was to help her. They had other patients too, perhaps too many and perhaps was their downfall.

Their mission was to see that Jeri would get needed nursing care, proper equipment and supplies and work with agencies serving Jeri. At first they would listen to Jeri's concerns and said they could and would help her. That was terrific. They generally did real well at first but then potential success turned to no shows. The turnover was high. One small period, we had three different case managers. When at first they were to physically visit Jeri in person every month or so (depending on need), it soon turned into a rather hasty phone call (possibly had many patients to call). They would ask if everything was going ok. They usually sounded relieved when we would say everything is fine. Sometimes I think we said it that way because we just didn't want to discus minor problems by phone. The personal visit value was lost. Obviously, cost was involved in this and it was cheaper to phone than visit. In the medical world I think the correct procedure would be visit or forget it.

We had high hopes for this and never turned a case manager away. We were long believers that this would work.

I think a better approach would have been, whether calling or visiting, to ask, "How can I help you?"

Now some case managers seemed more optimistic in getting problems, some very difficult, solved. We had one for several years who started with Jeri that didn't either seem too interested or did not know how to help. Over perhaps a year, they become our favorite and most helpful case manager we ever had. We could always count on this person who almost seemed part of the family. One time she did one of several things for us and we thanked her. She said politely, "You don't have to thank me, it's my job." Wasn't this the way it was meant to work?

When we brought Jeri home from Rehab, we found out that there still was a nursing shortage and also that most agencies would not take someone on a ventilator. We knew there was a nursing shortage but learning that only a few agencies would take someone on a ventilator really surprised us. When we tried to get an agency that we had before, we were told by a case manager that the agency we wanted did not take ventilator patients. We later found out that this was not true, that this agency would have taken her. Meanwhile, Jodi had done all the finding of nursing care herself. Where was the case manager? Why we could not use any nursing agency, we found out, if this is correct, that the agencies had insurance problems with accepting vent patients. Could this really be true? Now we know Ohio is in favor of patients going back to their homes. This was a complete surprise to us that it took a lot of effort finding nursing care in spite of Jeri being covered with four different medical coverages. Seems something's wrong here. Who helped us? Our family did.

Reference setting up the Ohio Home Care Program by case managers, we understood there was always to be a back-up plan. I don't know of any ever existing.

Finales for this important section of "Discovering What's Wrong."

I would think anyone having experienced what Jeri many times had to go through and had no control over would understand this ending discussion. Waiting and waiting and wondering. A never ending series of no shows, lateness and getting needed services from nursing agencies. Now, we're talking Home Health Care – the best way to go.

No shows. When we easily chose to have Jeri at home always, if possible, it became an entirely new experience. The first time we had a no show I simply called the agency and told them. What do you mean you have no one to send? This would continue to be the case for many years. Adjust to it. When a nurse would be late, adjust to it. We thought we could change these practices but learned that, at best, agencies would try to correct these happenings with little success. Some nurses were very dependable. Others would have excuses, some very good. Jeri and I spent a heck of a lot of time looking out the window waiting for the nurse to come, especially the night 7-9 o'clock schedule. Change that statement to: Jack spent a lot of time. Jeri, while never really adjusting to people being late or not coming as planned, just kind of dozed off and waited. She seemed long resigned that, if we could not control it, live with it. This was unfair.

Because there always seemed to be a shortage of home health care nurses, I learned and rarely called the agency to tell them another no show. In spite of these situations, we learned to be patient and usually would not question a nurse as to why they didn't come or were late. We learned, especially if they were good and we liked them, we would still welcome them. We needed them. We knew if they had a good reason, they would tell us. If they didn't have a good reason, we just let it pass. We would try to correct tardiness but our methods never seemed to work. For example, I would tell them, if you're running late for whatever reason, don't bother calling us if you will be here within an hour of being late. This helped us a lot. Of course, when the hour was up, I became concerned. Jeri took it much better than I.

We also had to realize that nurses coming to help Jeri actually had two "bosses," the Primary Caregiver and the agency boss. No one should have two bosses. Regardless, it was always a relief when we saw car lights show up in our driveway at night. I don't think we ever yelled at someone being late or not coming at all. We tried to give them the benefit of the doubt. Actually when one would show up late and we welcomed them this way, they felt better and we did too.

Agencies finding nurses..... Besides keeping track of employees and turnovers, agencies had other related problems with providing nursing care, finding them. I always thought they were not giving prospective employees enough incentives to come and stay. They never asked for our advice.

At times when an agency had no one to send, our case manager was to see that Jeri had nursing coverage and was to find help. In this one occasion, the case manager could not find anyone either and recommended checking with another agency. Now with our current agency, Jeri had some nursing care but another nurse was needed to replace one. The case manager did find another agency that could provide additional services. We didn't realize at first that this could be a problem. Well it became one.

Nurses would often finish one visit with a patient and then proceed to their next case, Jeri, for example. Now this visit to Jeri's would often find the nurse coming late, either because of a delay at their previous case (cannot leave a patient if there's a problem needing the nurse, for example), or a problem getting to their next scheduled visit on time. This happened a lot. Arriving at our home, the nurse could be late and needed one hour or more to take care of Jeri. Along comes another nurse from another agency arriving at their scheduled time but finding the other nurse still working on Jeri. They would help the first nurse by working together. Actually, this worked well. It also helped Jeri knowing that while the first nurse may or may not come, another nurse was scheduled to come shortly. Something so nice was working? Impossible!

Then the bubble broke. The agencies somehow were told that no nurse was to be paid if they came at the same time another nurse was there. Only one nurse could be there to be paid, not two at the same time. Our family argued against this strongly. It was working and services were getting done. What was so wrong? It got a little worse.

Apparently each agency told their nurse not to be at Jeri's home at the same time. Just don't be seen there if another nurse is there, whether they were late or early.

The next time a second nurse came and saw another nurse's car parked in our driveway, she said she stayed in her car out of sight up the street from us and waited until she saw the other car pull out! Was this strategy for real? Is this real nursing? The ruling was confirmed to us, "No two nurses were allowed to be there at the same time, even if from different agencies."

One more for this section and on to the next.........supervisors often would drop in unannounced to question Jeri about her nurses. This time, with pen and notepad in hand, they questioned Jeri on one particular nurse by asking her:

Question: Would you say the nurse was "excellent?"
Jeri: No.
Question: No? Why not?
Jeri: No.
Question: Can I put down "excellent?"
Jeri: No.

The person questioning Jeri was becoming quite upset. Obviously, they wanted Jeri to say "yes" and did not want to leave without getting the excellent mark. Jeri gave her honest opinion, what more can one do? Jeri held her ground. It ended. What was written in the notepad? We didn't know, Jeri didn't ask and they never told us. They just left.

I could follow this from across the room. Once again I was so proud of Jeri. She knew her mind, she knew her nurse. She was not about to change.

After the person left, I complimented Jeri. I also said to Jeri that, from now on, we would not answer any questions that required a grade or opinion of someone working with her.

ADD A BEAUTY FOR THE ROAD TO DISCOVER WHAT'S "RIGHT"......A Star arises or "How to become a professional in one day!"......the making of a video presentation called, "Caring Program for Caring Professionals."

As with many medical problems, incontinence has no favorites. One easiest way to control this problem for Jeri meant getting the right brief to wear. With many brands on the market, we found most to be unreliable, especially cheaper ones. After testing many brands, she found the one she liked, one that fit well and absorbed well, a Tranquility brand. Surprisingly, the company producing this one was near Bowling Green where we lived.

One day, Jeri received a letter from this company's President asking Jeri to be part of a commercial video about this brief. Jeri was excited and quickly answered "Yes" and soon found herself signing a contract. I don't remember much about the details because we were too excited for Jeri.

A few days later, Jeri received a phone call from the company's script writer who asked Jeri questions in developing her script. There were three other women who were also to be in the video.

When filming day came, we drove to a Country Club in Perrysburg. Rehearsal was in the morning, then lunch followed by an afternoon of camera action.

Jeri was nicely dressed and carefully was given (it had to be Avon) appearance makeup etc. by her daughters. She looked like a Star, humble style with her smile.

The script was pretty well followed — I don't remember any of the four women reading their part. They were all prepared.

At the beginning of the program the four were part of a general discussion. They were each introduced and told a little about themselves.

One was a private nurse and was always on the go and had this problem until Tranquility made a big difference for her.

Another said she goes out a lot and I like to play cards with my friends. I probably wouldn't do any of this if it weren't for Tranquility.

The third was a grade school principal who said with Tranquility, she is much freer to do things.

We have added more of Jeri's answers per:

Jeri: I may be a different type of case -- I have MS, Multiple Sclerosis, and being in a wheelchair, that limits me in that I can't transfer to the toilet when I'm home by myself during the day.

Question: Are you at home most of the time?

Jeri: Mostly I stay at home, but I go out to church on Sunday or to graduations or things like that. But when I'm going to be home all day, I have the nurse or someone put the Tranquility pants on the wheelchair and I just pull them up to sit on them for the day. I like the idea of the gel absorbing rather than clumping up. Tranquility feels softer, it's more absorbent and it feels dryer. It's not uncomfortable and that's a big improvement to the quality of life for me.

I suspect all four of these women were first time Stars in a film. The only difference was they were not acting. They did a remarkable professional performance.

When we were about to leave, Jeri was handed an honorarium for $50.00. This really surprised her and us too. I think if Jeri knew she was going to get paid for this, she may have refused to do it.

We later saw the video. Jeri looked nice, spoke well and did not seem nervous. This was something she could do and she did it.

JERI'S "OTHER CAREERS" OF GIRL SCOUTS, AVON AND COMPUTERS

GIRL SCOUTS

Girl Scouts of the USA was established in 1912 incorporated under DC laws and established National Headquarters in New York City. They are still located there. In 1917 they established the first troop for handicapped girls. The first local council charter issued by the National Organization was to Toledo, Ohio. Camp Edith Macy opened as a national training center in 1926. The first Girl Scout Cookie Sale was in 1936. In 1950, GS of the USA reincorporated under Congressional Charter.

Jeri was a natural to lead Girl Scouts. She came along at the right time and the right place, becoming involved with Girl Scouting in 1973 in Kent, Ohio.

Scouting was changing from the days of women doing women things to the days of women doing all things. History never left scouting but scouting certainly changed history. Uniforms became modern though remaining traditional green. The scouting logo was changed to portraying a sketched live image of three girl faces behind one another. Trails in the woods remained but added were modern life styles for the modern girl to learn and grow gracefully into womanhood.

Their Girl Scout manual became a restated approach to the modern Girl Scout still following the rules that meant a lot to the past and to future scouts. It kept helping others, pledging our flag and following the religious beliefs that still exist. The older girls found themselves in a completely new scouting environment.

Somewhere in all of this was Jeri who wanted Jodi and Jami to become scouts. The three of them would learn together.

Jeri establishes a Girl Scout Troop plus two. Surprising us, Jeri had already established her rules of leading a troop. First she organized a troop that did not exist at St. Patrick's Grade School in Kent. So as not to interfere with their school day, she scheduled scout meetings to be held during early evening hours in our home. Our son Jeff and I were volunteer evictors from our own home during scout night. We were allowed to listen to their singing, laughing etc from outside but inside was off limits. We hadn't realized yet that Jeri had other scouting plans for us.

As the girls grew and advanced to the next level, Jeri found out that it was difficult to get Girl Scout troop leaders. Facing no troop nearby for her girls to join, Jeri solved the problem. She would also lead a new troop that she would establish and register as an official new scout troop. This happened again when the girls were ready for this next level. Jeri established a new troop. She was now the official leader of three troops all registered at St. Patrick's School and all active at the same time. Jeri's troops:

1974 Organized "Junior Troop 318" with 10 girls
1976 Organized "Cadette Troop 779" with 8 girls
1979 Organized "Senior Troop 189" with 4 girls

Meanwhile, Jeff and I were beginning to see which part we might be assigned to by our three star leader, aka mother and wife. I was appointed to be Assistant Scout Leader and soon was wearing the official man's green Girl Scout blazer plus an official man's tie. My job description, which I never received, included, among other surprises, setting up chairs etc at formal promotional receptions held at schools and elsewhere.

Actually Jeff and I did not mind helping Jeri such as with badge work. When the girls were working on learning the compass we would set up a compass problem around the neighborhood to solve. They liked doing meaningful projects leading to their scout badges and advancements.

The girls become real troopers...each troop would meet separately in our home on different nights for meetings, working on badges, planning trips and never ending activities as planned by Scouting Councils and rendered by Troop Leaders. Jeri kept countless records of each girl's achievements and promotions and always kept on hand a large supply of many badges that she would eventually award to each scout. She was always at Akron's Girl Scout Headquarters getting badges and other awards to issue.

Camping...by a day or several days were highlight experiences where they would earn badges the fun way. While the modern badges were for modern living, the traditional badges for camping were what they could enjoy more as a troop. Jeri taught them well setting up tents, cooking, campfires and above all, the so many Girl Scout songs they learned and remembered. My favorite was "On My Honor."

One strange trick Jeri had me help her with was teaching the girls how to build a wet fire. It sounds contradictory. However, when camping, just how do you start a fire if it rained all night? To show them, we would have them find proper size tree wood lying on the ground and build a campfire ready to be lit. We would take water and pour it on their dry wood. Surprised, they would say, "Now we can't light it."

To solve the problem if rain was expected, they were to gather small sticks of dry wood and put them in their tent. After a rain, use the small sticks to get a fire started, adding them to the wet wood as the flames developed.

Now that the fireplace they had just built was soaking in water, they could easily find dry sticks to light and begin adding them to their wet ones. Did it work?

Jeri took her troops camping at several locations but primarily to Akron's "Ledgewood," a large Girl Scout camp with lots of activities, workshops, wooden trails and short and long term camping sites. It was a very safe camp with gates being closed at night. There were rules. Included were only one car could be kept at your camp site. Another was "bring what you need – you carry what you bring."

One trip, Jeri invited their troop Chaplain, Fr. Anthony, to say Mass at camp. On a clear Sunday morning deep in the woods of Ledgewood, he had Mass for the girls and some 20 family members/friends who attended. After distributing Communion to the girls, he looked towards the wooden bleachers where the visitors were seated and invited everyone there to come join their Girl Scouts in receiving Communion. Everyone did.

Parades...they would pride themselves – in their uniforms, their flags – before their hometown and their families. How nice they looked and acted. They attended the annual Memorial Day parade which was 1-2 miles long. Jeri was right with them in her uniform walking stride by stride. Only in the last parade she participated in was she bothered. Half way through, she was limping quite a bit and was seated in a parade truck for the rest of the parade. It took the MS to stop her.

 In one parade, our Jodi was carrying the American Flag. At a pause in the parade, a picture was taken of her holding the flag. She looked like she had fallen asleep and the flag pole was holding her up. A large size picture of this appeared in the Kent State University newspaper on the front page. With her in full scout uniform, she looked neat. She had both hands holding the flag pole, it was not about to be dropped. This American Flag was the flag we were able to receive from the US Capitol. We had requested this one because it had flown over the Capitol itself for a brief period. We still have the flag.

Awards to the scouts...Award Night...was held at St. Patrick's school in front of parents and friends. Jeri would have all badges and other performance patches ready to distribute to the girls mixed in with a little Girl Scout singing, a salute to our flag and even taps.

When it was time for the scouts to advance to the next level, this was called bridging and would be held on an award night. This was their favorite time. It took a lot of camping, singing, fun times and badges to get there. A bridge of scouts not bridging would hold hands and form a bridge where the advancing girls would go under and through to be met by others already in an advanced troop to be welcomed. One occasion, their Chaplain, Fr. Anthony, was present. The girls made him go through the bridge.

Other scouting awards...Churches... There were other awards often given to the Scouts by respective Churches, even those who did not have Girl Scout troops. These were usually supported and encouraged by Scout Councils, in our case, Western Reserve Girl Scout Council in Akron.

In 1977, two girls (Jodi Schroeder from Jeri's Cadette Troop 779 and Mary Beth Burns of Troop 504, Kent) were awarded the I Live My Faith medal, presented at St. Patrick Church in Kent. Jeri also sent a medal to Charlene Morris who participated in the program as an individual.

April 22, 1979 four girls (Mary Duffy, Elayne Rogers, Laurel Sawyer and Jodi Schroeder) from Jeri's Cadette Troop 779, earned, and were presented with, the "Marian Award" medal by the Bishop of Youngstown at Columba Cathedral in Youngstown, Ohio. It took almost two years of work to earn. These were for young women ages 12-15.

March 9, 1980 the I Live My Faith medal (for girls ages 9-11), a recognition of how each girl found ways each lived her faith and as a reminder of her growth as a Christian person, was awarded at Scout Sunday Mass. Nine girls (Tammie Davies, Danielle Grunenwald, Kathy Hostetler, Elaine Kunka, Theresa Leiher, Sheri Sabol, Jami Schroeder, Gretchen Wood and Lisa Woodman) from Jeri's Junior Troop 318 earned this medal. It took them four months to earn and was presented to each at St. Patrick Church in Kent.

Awards like the preceding required a lot of hours to earn. Jeri would ask and delegate a parent or whoever qualified to help lead these girls to enjoy and succeed. Scouting could only succeed with the help of parents etc under the guidance of a qualified dedicated leader. Jeri led, I followed.

Highest Girl Scout Award...51 Cadette Girl Scouts of Western Reserve Council were honored October 14, 1979 at a First Class recognition reception. This was the highest award for girls in Girl Scouting. Included from Jeri's Senior Troop 779 were Prerna Kaul, Kathy Martin, Elayne Rogers and Jodi Schroeder. (Katie)

Bronze Pelican Award...this surprise of Jeri's participating in Girl Scout programs - the presenting to Jeri unannounced and unexpected, this Catholic Scouting Award. This was given to her at Scout Sunday Mass at St. Patrick Church in Kent on March 9, 1980. She was the first woman in Portage County to win this award. The purpose of this award was for outstanding contribution to the spiritual development of Catholic Youth in Scouting. (Kelly)

One more Girl Scout award I almost left out which was either the ultimate or the introduction to special Girl Scout awards – ORDER OF THE GREAT GREEN ANGEL.

The award read: "This is to certify that Jeri Schroeder has proven beyond all doubt her dedication to the Girl Scout movement and is hereby awarded honors of entrance to the ORDER OF THE GREAT

GREEN ANGEL, awarded this day May 27, 1981 with justifiable excitement & delight. Western Reserve Girl Scout Council."

John Schroeder also received a Green Angel award in his name; the same form was used but the "her" was changed to "his."

Scout Sunday...a traditional Girl Scout day in which troops, each year, would be invited to another church to attend services. It was very impressive to see all troops together and in their scout uniforms. Scouting was long in recognizing the importance of religious activities. Many different  Churches sponsored troops and you were welcomed to join any of your choice, especially if a Church did not have any scout troops.

Jeri's first holding of Scout Sunday was written up in the Church bulletin for Sunday March 9, 1980 announcing guest troops from Brimfield and Kent joining St. Patrick Girl Scout Troop in celebrating "the founding of Girl Scouts in the US and carrying out the Girl Scout Promise."

The following year other troop leaders were not stepping forward to take their turn. When it seemed there would not be a Scout Sunday in our area, Jeri volunteered to hold it again with our troop being the host. The question arose as to why her troop was given the right to hold Scout Sunday every year? When it was discovered that Jeri was the only volunteer leader willing to hold it because she did not want it to cease, all became quiet.

Girl Scout Cookies...this needs no introduction - always good cookies and always a lot of work for the girls and families. This was a mixture of fun and energy. It was the prime source of money for the troops for daily activities and scout trips. The money collected was divided between the troop and national scouting administration. The troop's money was meant to be used wisely and for the girls who earned it. It also meant Jeri had to make a superb effort to collect, control and spend all of this wisely to carry out their goals every year.

While Girl Scout Cookies have a long history of selling cookies successfully, it took additional work and selling other activities to support their Scouting goals. They would take on just about any type of work or selling to meet their goals and usually had fun in doing so, like washing cars together. Money making projects always needed the approval of their Council with the idea that most of any profit was to be spent in the period earned with little carryover into a new year unless an approved trip or goal had been planned. Of course, all of this money earned put a lot of responsibility on the leader to account for.

Pipestem State Park – a park located in southern West Virginia with an average elevation of 2,300 feet above sea level and within the mountains of West Virginia. Our family made this our vacation location several times. It became for Jeri to select it as a future Girl Scout camping trip, in which she did in March, 1979.

A Girl Scout ultimate fun goal is usually a major trip, one that will remain a long time memory. Organizing such trips are often overwhelming to someone putting one together to secure the necessary assistance needed and all that goes with it. Jeri's local camping and educational etc trips with her three troops gave her experience of preparations needed. Included with this trip was Scout Council approval, family and doctor permissions, safety concerns, money, transportation, equipment, supplies and responsibility. As part of Council's approval, the Scouts had to be directly involved in the planning and there had to be badges, patches etc available to earn. It was not unusual to cancel a trip. It can be difficult to go through with one. Probably the most important part of preparing such trips is "will they enjoy and have fun?"

Jeri's planning for this trip left little out. Being in Ohio and going to West Virginia, she wrote to West Virginia and applied for a tax exemption. She received one.

Jeri's Cadette Troop 779 was the one going to Pipestem. There were fifteen members expected but only five were able to go after two years of planning and raising money through car washes, flea markets etc. One flea market: Earned $26.00 – lot of work, not too successful but they were trying and learning. Donuts sold? 257 dozen ordered and delivered at a profit of 59 cents per dozen, showing a profit for the troop of $152.31. Way to go Girl Scouts!

Prerna Kaul, Kathy Martin, Elayne Rogers, Laurel Sawyer and Jodi Schroeder were the five Girl Scouts able to go. Jeri also had to have an emergency plan required by Council. This was rather easy. The mother of one of the Scouts going was a Kent Police Dispatcher. She became a contact.

Jeri had one more written report to make to their Girl Scout Council before final permission could be given. The questions were centered on having earned enough money to go, what they would do with any leftover and did the girls learn anything.

Her report showed how they made enough money, what they would do with any leftover (they would continue troop activities) and did they learn anything? Her written answer was:

> They learned to cooperate & work together to get a job done. How much people appreciate good honest service and a good job well done. They also learned to "be independent" and earn money for a trip so they don't have to ask Mom & Dad, takes cooperation,

planning, and hard work, but it can be done, can be a learning experience and can be fun also. (JS 3/19/79)

Let the adventure begin. We needed two cars. Jeri's assistant, Joan Rogers, drove one, I, the other car.

Arriving at Pipestem March 22, 1979 for a four night stay, we were able to show the girls not only Pipestem's layout but also a rare type entrance to a hotel. We parked our cars in the hotel parking lot and entered the lobby of "McKeever Lodge" to report the arrival of Girl Scouts, present and accounted for. A

little surprise to the girls when they learned that to register and go to a room on the elevator, you would go **DOWN** to the rooms! The seven floor Lodge was built on the side of the mountain, the Lobby was on the fifth floor and that's how you entered it from the parking area. From the outside, you could not tell you were on the fifth floor!

For this trip, we had reserved a large cabin with four rooms, fireplace, dining etc included. Since there were eleven in our party, it worked fine. Actually, we had one more Girl Scout with us. This was our Jami who was in Jeri's Junior Troop 318 – she was with us as a family member since Troop 318 was not on this trip.

The days that followed allowed them everything they expected and unexpected. There was horseback riding through trails, swimming, tennis, archery, an amphitheatre and all the other little attractions that pleased what you liked.

When we went on a hayride pulled by a tractor which took us throughout the park, of course all eleven of us climbed aboard which meant about twenty were there. One thing was missing in this hayride. No one was singing. Jeri to the rescue - she started our group singing Girl Scout songs. Now everyone aboard began having a real "Hayride ride." Our tractor driver, who was funny and played his part well, took us to an open area in the woods and lo and behold, there was a big campfire burning with hot dogs, buns, pop and marshmallows for a help yourself treat waiting for us.

I think the biggest surprise came later which I think even surprised the Park.

Within Pipestem, there are two lodges. One of which we were in often for snacks, gift shop etc. The other, called Mountain Creek Lodge was located at the bottom of Bluestone Gorge near the Bluestone River.

The Mountain Creek Lodge was accessible only by an Aerial Tramway. A Canyon Rim Center housed a gift shop, snack bar, craft shop and an upper Tram Station that carries you down 3600 feet and crosses over the Bluestone River to the lodge. The Tram had 18 gondolas that carried four at a time and rode about 90 feet above ground, taking 12-15 minutes to make the trip. The girls were excited about riding the Tram all the way down to the other lodge. This was a surprise. However another surprise surfaced when they went to see about riding the Tram. It was off season. The Tram was not in operation. They came back to tell Jeri the disappointing news. Jeri wasn't through yet. She and the girls tracked down whoever told them the Tram was closed and talked with them. She said her girls were a Girl Scout Troop camping here at a Pipestem cabin. Apparently this moved the person to think about it. He got back to Jeri and the girls and said, "We are going  to open it up for the Scouts and take them down to the lodge on the Tram." Now they were excited. Down the mountain they went.

After doing their own cooking in their cabin, Jeri had one more activity planned. They would end their stay with a reserved table at the main lodge and have dinner there. One more little item the girls had to do, including herself - they were to wear their Girl Scout uniform. This they did and the eleven of us had a nice

dinner together. They really looked nice and behaved well in front of all the other people having dinner there. They surely had some memories to take home.

The ending of the Pipestem Saga, brought about by Jeri should only end with hand written remarks by the Scouts themselves. I found the following most interesting unnamed and unscreened written on paper that is now brown and old and in no order:

Cadette Troop 779 of St. Patricks in Kent went on a 4 day trip to Pipestem state park in West Va. during spring break. The trip was packed full of fun! The troop went horseback riding, swimming, tennis, hiking, a tram ride down the mountain and sightseeing. There were many beautiful sights to see. They found out what a road runner is (roads going along mountains).

On the tram, we saw a white lightning still hidden in a cave in the mountain side. We saw the sunrise, mountain ranges and foot bridges over streams covered because of high waters.

Saw deer, had breakfast (yuk), saw shacks (or so called houses), saw water coming out of rocks (like Moses did), climbed rocks for pictures, lunch, tennis, swam, game room, supper. game room again. Laurel and Kathy jogged and locked themselves out of cabin, stable (rode horses, Mrs. Schroeder rode Nonic), Laurel's horse jumped the water, gift shop (went shopping), hiked 3 miles, swimming, game room, went to lobby to watch TV.

Went to black bear lounge for pizza, back to cottage and fire place, hot chocolate, played cards.

Saturday, breakfast, horseback riding (rained-sore butts) saw baby colt, gift shop, pool for swimming but didn't go to game room – went instead to explore hotel (without leaders).

All drove to Bluestone Dam, saw water coming out of mountains, walked around town of Hinton and went to St. Patrick church greeted by an "in style" priest. Mrs. Rogers drove her car here and parked. Mr. Schroeder put money in the meter for Mrs. Rogers but put it in the wrong meter. Mrs. Rogers had to move her car to that meter!

Sunday, dinner at Bluestone (actually "McKeever") Lodge (20% discount).

We ate all the oranges.

We ate all the time.

The trip was a great success.

A COSI Camp-In...an overnight camping trip to the "Center of Science & Industry" in Columbus, Ohio. It is where Jeri took her scouts to experience the fun of indoor camping and personally press the buttons and lights of exhibits, witness demonstrations of learning, such as to construct a volcano and grow crystals and all that the museum had to offer.

This was all under the permission and encouragement of Western Reserve Girl Scouts to venture to Columbus to experience this overnighter. Many Girl Scout troops took advantage of doing this including choosing certain dates scheduled for visits by troops.

As a St. Patrick's Girl Scout troop, Jeri scheduled their troop to go on a Friday May 1-May 2, 1981. Other troops joined them, enough to fill a charter bus.

I was not aware of too much of what was going on or what Jeri was up to. Whatever it was, it seemed worthwhile to watch. I was outside just watching scouts come to our front yard with luggage and sleeping bags. My eyes opened wide when I looked up and saw a Kent State University bus coming down our street and stopping at our house. By now I remembered what Jeri had been working on. She even signed me a position to be responsible for a while. I was to hold the fort down. In her typed trip schedule she passed out, it read "Emergency Contact" Jack Schroeder 673-2395.

In this typed trip schedule of what to bring, there was one paragraph that read, "Change for vending machines for snacks, beverages, etc, if desired...(A Fri. evening snack is provided... and machines are locked during meals)."

Arriving home, it sounded like they had a great time. All meals were in place, sleeping (on the floor) in their sleeping bags was at a recreational building next to the museum and activities were very active.

They arrived back at our house in the same bus that Saturday and everyone unloaded in our front yard. It was a sight to see with scouts, luggage, souvenirs and parents or whoever was to pick them up - obviously a happy time.

Many other activities for the girls to choose from...these are the ones that Jeri chose:

All Ohio Leaders Conference – Ohio's first Girl Scout leader conference at Columbus was held in 1981. Forty-four persons from Western Reserve Council was their allocation. Workshops ranged from arts and computers to human relations and communication skills. "Strict leadership criteria" was followed to approve applications. Jeri and Joan Rogers were both accepted.

Dolly Derby – Girl Scouts and Goodwill Industries working together collecting discarded dolls. Goodwill's handicapped employees would clean them up to be given to Girl Scouts to dress the dolls which would be entered in the Dolly Derby. Winners would be announced and then the dolls would be returned to Goodwill Industries to be sold in time for Christmas giving.

Life Style 80 – Sponsored by Western Reserve Girl Scout Council and held at the Hilton Inn, Akron, this was a three day opportunity for high school girls to study the mechanics of living and expectations of the future. This was planned by the girls themselves and included meeting role models one day and spending time with them the next. The role models were local women and included from a "dog breeder" to a "social worker" to a "medical technologist" to a "teacher" and to many more. Attending were 152 young women including several from Jeri's scouts and 20 advisers including Jeri and Joan Rogers. A nine-member Senior Girl Scout planning committee prepared a tentative schedule of events based on what girls want. Included on the planning committee were Debbie Clawson and Jodi Schroeder from Jeri's scouts.

New Citizens Ceremony – held in Ravenna, Ohio Court, troop would attend in uniform to observe and present the flag ceremony. This was interesting experience for her scouts and Jeri.

Sea World – Located about fifteen miles north of Kent, Western Reserve Council took part and encouraged their Girl Scouts to attend Sea World's special fall and winter programs for which they would earn patches. The girls were exposed to both land and sea species of fish and land animals related to the sea, such as snakes, jelly fish, even octopus etc. The only one missing was the large whale that Sea World always used in their summer shows. The whale had to be transferred to warmer winter weather. This was done by special airplane. Being a favorite of summer tourists, the whale would be back.

This location was great for Jeri and the girls to attend, including families. Our prize was that everyone in attendance received complimentary admission tickets for the following summer season.

"Incomparable Macy"...this Edith Macy Training Center for girls was turned over to the Girl Scouts in 1925 for the teaching of Girl Scout leaders. Located in the Adirondacks in upstate New York, Macy and eventually Camp Andree Clark, on land next to Macy, became the camping and training centers for national Girl Scout training. To train in these two camps, which were both used together, was considered the "ultimate" in high level Girl Scouting and the precious "Macy Pin" that came with it. Jeri was even able to take part in Macy's 50th anniversary.

In 1976 Jeri decided she wanted to go to Macy and we were going to take her. We knew Macy was a Scout Camp but this meant little to us because by now we knew of many Scout Camps. "But what is a Macy?" We liked the idea. Jeri received her approval to attend so, on June 18, 1976, the five of us (our family) packed our car and headed to the Adirondacks Mountains somewhere in New York. We headed straight to the camp by way of several side roads after we got off the New York Thruway. We found it about noon the next day and we went straight to the camp for Jeri to check in. Jeri was told she was to camp with the rest of the girls she would be with, in their own camp area in Camp Andree Clark, which was right across the road from Macy. Camp Macy was temporary closed and no one was camping there.

We had assumed that we would be together. Jeri asked if her family could camp at one of the tent sites. With a little hesitation, they agreed. They said they would let us stay in Andree Clark but a bit away from where the Girl Scouts were. We would be on our own and were not to disturb them. We would be allowed to visit their campfire once but only briefly. We were assigned a camp site higher up the mountain. We had to park our car in their lot and walk to the camp site. No cars allowed. Jeri came prepared because she had brought camping food and supplies except she thought she would be with us. She walked up the hill with us to get us settled in. There were platform tents already set up so after we put our food away and became oriented, she abandoned us. Before she left us, she gave me a clear order. "Every morning carry each child over to the washroom, have them take a shower and get dressed. Do not let their bare feet touch the ground."

This was the 50th Anniversary of Macy. Over two hundred scout leaders from the United States attended, including nine (including Jeri) from Akron's "Western Reserve Girl Scout Council." At the first evening's campfire, all those who attended were awarded a special gold "Macy Pin."

Jeri did come to visit us when she could which wasn't too often. Watching her one morning coming into our camp after hiking up, she looked like a true trooper with her Scout green jacket tied around her waist. I did notice her limping a little but other than that, she looked great.

The kids were beginning to miss seeing Jeri. After a couple of days of not seeing her, they began writing her notes for her to pick up on her next visit. Their handwritten notes were all printed on scrap pieces of paper and read:

"Come tonight please, if you can."
"We've got a surprise to tell you. You'll never believe it! (So come tonight)"

"Got your note mommy. Miss you a lot, and guess what? Racoon got into half our food in the green cabinet. See you tonite (hope you can come). Love xxxxxx Jodi, Jami, Jeff, Jack."

"Racoon came in tent. Jami's tick in stomach. Racoon unlocked and ate half our food. Then we went into hardware store, we came out and a DOG was in OUR car!"

"Got your note mommy. Miss you a lot and guess what? Racoon got into the green cabinet and it was locked! The racoon ate half our food. See you TONITE (Hope you can make it). Found a trail down from Lone Pine to the road by Cedar Cove, also found a trail that we think is the trail you were talking about. Lots of love, Character Jeffrey – Sunshine Jami – Pumpkin Jodi – Jack Dade."

"MOMMY. NO RACOON. Love, Jami Schroeder."

To Jami with all my love (drawing of sunshine), Mommy.

One note from Jeri to Jodi, Jami, Jeffrey: "Enjoy your Ice Cream – Have Fun – and don't give Daddy a hard time." Love xxxx Mommy

Well, there was a Raccoon, two or three of them, and they did eat half of our food. The other half was all over the floor. There was a hand lock on the green door but it never bothered the raccoons. We did go to town to a hardware store to buy patching plaster to "capture" their hand and footprints the next night if they came back. They came back and we watched them in the dark walk right through our laid out plaster. We still have the prints.

And yes, there was a large red color dog sitting in the driver's seat of our car. He was not about to move. A crowd had gathered to enjoy this. We could not get the dog to come out. Along came a police car that pulled up right beside our car. They got out, looked at me and asked, "Is that your dog?" "The car is mine, the dog is not." They could not get him out either. Finally a man came along, walked to the car, opened the door – the dog came out. We suspected he was the owner.

Jami's tick

Yes, Jami had a tick. She tells me that she had it all night and it scared her but I apparently, as usual, did not pay any attention. We were sleeping in our tent in the morning when Jeri arrived to see how we were doing. Jami cried out, "Mommy, a bug is eating me." She was right. Right in her stomach! I had remembered reading how to remove a tick. It sounded logical and easy. Just light a match, hold it near the tick and the heat will force the tick to back out. I did so and killed the tick! It remained embedded in Jami. Jeri had other ideas. With her Girl Scout training she apparently knew that mountain ticks can be poisonous. Checking with the Macy staff, they agreed with Jeri and suggested Jami should be taken to the hospital to get the tick out. Directed to North Tarrytown about 12 miles away, where the hospital was, we got in the car to go there. It took us about thirty minutes. Jeri, who was missing her training, came with us, of course. A little while later Jeri and Jami came out of the emergency room, with all smiles. Jami was wearing a "Hero Badge" awarded her by the hospital staff. (Chloe)

As things settled down for us and Jeri now was busy training, the three children and myself spent the week on a routine daily schedule of morning bath, breakfast and heading to the Village of Pleasantville NY (not far from Macy) to play at a nice playground we found and then had supper at a Friendly's Restaurant. Then it was back to our tent before dark. Being the only ones, ·it seemed, in Macy, it was a bit lonely and scary but we managed and had fun, especially when Jeri would come see us for a little while.

When we checked out of Macy June 24, 1976, we headed for New York City, which was only about an hour away (30 miles). With our family once more intact with Jeri, we spent time at the Girl Scout's National Headquarters in New York. This was unexpected and we enjoyed visiting there. After a few days visiting the UN building and seeing other NYC attractions, we headed for Pipestem and checked in July 5 for a week's stay then home. But wait! We were not quite finished with Macy. Jeri was already planning to come back next summer, which we did. Twice to Macy! In Jeri's words "Why not, Let's."

Visiting Macy a second time, a real experience repeated….. We knew our way and routines of Macy quite well this time. Jeri's Macy's approval came and we were again welcomed. This really was an unexpected adventure for our family, especially a repeat at Macy.

It was Sunday, June 19, 1977 (would you believe 4:25 PM?) when we pulled into Macy, a day ahead of schedule. Jeri checked in, they again assigned her to a new group. This allowed us to again camp up the mountain in a camp site within Camp Andree Clark. This time they allowed us to drive our car up there. This was not exactly a road – more of a bumpy path. It was easier hauling supplies and the three children up and down and Jeri's training was closer this time.

Being ahead of schedule, we were able to roam around a bit. The next day as other women began checking in we were at the parking area just watching. One woman saw us and asked how things were there. I said "Great, if you don't mind the raccoons." She said, "That does it. I'm going to a Holiday Inn."

 "World of Well-Being" was the training subject for this class of 27 women, who came from around the US. Jeri was the only one from Ohio. She stayed with this group the first night but she felt uncomfortable with one person and decided to stay with us the rest of the time at night. The Scout program was again held in Andree Clark.

Our routine was generally the same. Jeri would be training all day with campfires at night. However after her first night, she was allowed to stay with us.

Our tents at Macy (Andree Clark) were medium size "4-man" tents with wooden floors raised about a foot off the ground. Platform tents, they were called. Tents were set up on "level ground" as well as possible. At least the entrances to each were on a level. Behind the tent was still the mountain, some tents with backs facing downhill. One evening when the children were exploring, I was sitting at the entrance of our tent when Jeff came in to go to his "room" in the tent. He walked right by me to go to his section in the back of the tent. Within a few minutes, Jeff again came into the tent at the front entrance, passing me again, and went right to his area. Surprised, I asked Jeff, "How did you do that?" He answered, "I fell out of the tent." (Sierra)

This time we kept our food locked up and this time we could eat it in our camp our way.

Apparently Andree Clark became the primary camping area. No matter, the entire Girl Scout camp grounds were still referred to as Macy.

As Jeri would end her Macy career she would leave with a bag of ashes taken from her last campfire at Macy. A long tradition of Girl Scouting was that at the last camping campfire, each scout was to gather ashes from the cold remaining ashes, take them home with her and sprinkle them on their next home campfire, referred to as a Friendship Campfire Ceremony.

Jeri would also leave with her gold and silver Macy pins.

Camp Edith Macy with some 400 acres had several different named areas, one of which was Andree Clark. It was common to refer to each area as Macy. As times changed, Macy proper rebuilt its training center into a modern conference center where small and large groups of Girl Scout leaders could gather and live while attending training. It was renamed Edith Macy Conference Center and was dedicated in 1982.

From Jeri's Macy notebook and written in her own handwriting, we found a passage (not sure if she wrote or copied it, no matter) we think may have been her guide in teaching the girls. It read:

I cannot learn to decide, if you make my decisions.

I cannot learn to be myself, if you tell me what to be.

Let me choose what I must learn.

Looking through Jeri's notebook, we found many ways, ideas and suggestions to choose from that she apparently used in teaching these girls to grow and say "I am me."

Leaving Macy for the last time...we did not think about this being the last time. We probably considered it like all of our major destinations – "Bye. We'll be back."

Checking out of Macy on June 25, 1977 we again headed for New York City and a four day stay at Loews Summit Hotel which included going to the Statue of Liberty. Jami decided to bring some Chicken Pox with her stay at Loews. Checking out of the hotel on June 29 we headed for our favorite Pipestem Lodge in West Virginia arriving there where we checked in July 3. Jodi decided to bring some Chicken Pox (July 8) which, after one horseback ride, cost her no more rides. We checked out of Pipestem on July 9, 1977 to continue our vacation. Jeff was not left out. He joined his two older sisters on July 14 with his own Chicken Pox. A fine time was had by all! We never had a bad vacation!

All good things just don't come to an end, they just change position...it became this way with our family when I accepted (with family reluctance approval) a position at Bowling Green State University. This move would affect Jodi, Jami and Jeff to have to attend school in BG. It possibly affected Jeri the most. She would have to give up her three Girl Scout troops. We did not realize that it was going to take us almost three years to sell our home in Kent. My contract with BGSU called for me to start on September 14, 1981, only three days after I had resigned from Kent State. It was impossible to find proper facilities in BG that quick. We decided that I would take Jami and Jeff with me to BG while Jeri and Jodi stayed in Kent. We commuted every weekend to Kent. This allowed Jeri to stay with our house to sell and with her Girl Scout troops longer. During this period, Jeri would go back to BG with us for a week at a time to help us get along there. We had rented a small two-room section of a house. She would first clean our place and then serve our meals on a card table and help Jami and Jeff with school or whatever.

Jeri, knowing we would move permanently to BG when we sold our house, began thinking how to eventually phase out her troops. This was not easy for her though she never showed it. So what happens to her three troops? She found another girl to take over Junior Troop 318. She could find no one to assume command of her other two troops. On June 28, 1982, Jeri closed her last troop's bank account.

Jeri did not enjoy ending her eight year plus career with Western Reserve Girl Scout Council of which she belonged and worked closely with. She knew them well and they knew her. Between them, this was an active aggressive girls group that I would think was one of the best Girl Scout Councils in the country and Jeri was part of them. She trained hard and taught all she could give. What MS? I think she often forgot she had it. There were more important things for her to do and Scouting was one of them.

On May 19, 1982, a Western Reserve Girl Scout Council "Thank you Card" was sent to Jeri from Sara Kennedy, Jeri's Evergreen Kent Neighborhood Field Manager. Sara wrote:

Dear Jeri and John,
Thank you for all your time and dedication which you gave to Girl Scouts in Kent. Your working with a troop this year while maintaining two households and commuting between them was above and beyond the call of duty.

I hope your Kent house sells soon so that can can build in your new location.

Thank you for all your support and help. We'll miss you!
Sara Kennedy

Once settled in Bowling Green, Jeri still had intentions of getting reregistered with Girl Scouts in the Toledo area. It took a while before she could do so because of the MS and our own children growing up. Finally it was June 4, 1990 when she made contact with Maumee Valley Girl Scout Council in Toledo. A meeting was set up with the Council's "Director of Program Services/Facilities" to meet with Jeri. The director was very pleased to meet Jeri and thanked her for coming. She found that Jeri could keep her same ID number and so she became registered as a Girl Scout leader once again. When asked her interests, Jeri said she would like to offer her services helping handicapped Girl Scouts. The director said, "she would have the service director for Bowling Green call Jeri about being an advisor." No one came. Jeri did maintain her

Girl Scout membership for many years but never was active again.

AVON

When we moved to Bowling Green little by little, we lived at several locations starting with a Howard Johnson motel. Our first real experience of Bowling Green was when this girl on a horse came riding to where we were at Howard Johnson. Getting off her horse she introduced herself. She had already met Jodi and was an early friend. This would never have happened in Steubenville or Kent arriving by horse! It turned out, though we never realized it then, that "Karen" would eventually become a "member" of our family. What a sweet way to meet our new "family" member.

We still had not sold our house. In effect we ended up living both in Bowling Green and Kent. To our children's delight, we continued commuting back to Kent just about every weekend, primarily to check our house. Many times when we arrived, there would be lights on and our children's friends, whom Jeri and I always enjoyed as family, were in our house waiting for us. What nice receptions!

In Bowling Green meanwhile, we were living in an apartment. With Jeri walking less with her MS, we met with the Social Security office to see if Jeri qualified for Disability Social Security. Needing at least 40 hours of work related credit, it was determined that she did, indeed, have that. However, the credits were too old, that she would need so many current credits to qualify. They suggested Jeri get a job.

So now our family had another one of our many "family hall" meetings. Avon won. We became an Avon family which was to last over 25 years and still counting.

It was exciting. Our own business and Jeri was named the official Avon Representative (Rep) while I was named assistant. We were assigned an Avon territory which was ours to build customers within. One by one, we did this.

After completing our first Avon campaign and having actually earned a tidy profit of $18.00, we gathered around and divided it by 5, our family number. Each one received the exact amount.

It took 2-3 years to earn enough credit for Jeri to qualify for Disability Social Security. This was about the same length of time to begin achieving Avon's President Club status which would warrant higher discount earnings the following whole year. Jeri met this every year thereafter. Two or three times she was able to sell more in a year which gave her an additional discount – this was because she was able to secure, for example, schools to use our Avon for fund drives of their own. I think we always gave such students full discount for what they sold. While it gave us no profit, it did allow us to get more sales to reach a higher discount level. In addition to sales, it also awarded Jeri each year with an Albee, a porcelain doll representing an Avon representative, each year being made differently showing the Rep selling Avon.

Many years later, because of the changing way of living, door to door sales slowly were disappearing and becoming more of selling to customers who worked and were no longer available at their homes.

With this change, the restricted territories also changed by elimination of this practice. One could now sell anywhere.

Did Jeri help Avon? Of course
Did Avon help Jeri? Of course

Avon began helping Jeri about as soon as they met or heard about her

Jeri and I for years attended many Avon meetings and met the different district managers who were in charge of our district. They always gave Jeri a lot of help. They never put undue pressure on us to sell more etc. At meetings, the district manager would often pass out standings to the Reps to show each one how they were doing. An example of Jeri's ranking:

Volume of sales, Jeri was 10th of 20; Increase, Jeri was 4th of 20 and in Sales for Year to Date, she was 20th out of 50! Not bad for someone with MS.

A couple more statistics at random included was one during 1998 when 19 Avon Reps met President's Club Goal and Jeri was one of them. Minimum sales to reach this goal were $9,100. Now that was a lot of "lipstick." Jeri's total sales in 1991 were $16,631; in 1992 they were $15,539. The 1991 and 1992 sales were at a level called "Star President's Club."

Training for Reps was done at the monthly meetings and at special training sessions which Jeri would attend. Actually the training never ended because new products were always being introduced. Jeri liked all of this and we took her to as many meetings etc as we could.

Once on "President's Club" level, we never missed that level again. The best Jeri could do on reaching higher levels was two or three times on the next level through school sales. Higher levels were simply impossible because of her MS and not being able to meet potential customers in person. We were happy and satisfied that she did so great on what she did do. Jeri was part of our family and our family made it work. Further higher, future success was not in our plans. Jeri, herself, was. Even after several more years with MS and having to spend time at a Rehab for a choking problem, Jeri returned home where our family was carrying on with Avon, she still took part in our Avon family business. She was our leader and knew it. Our family still continues having and selling her Avon. Needless to say, it is not quite the same.

Somewhere in this time period, the state would not renew Jeri's driver's license, because of the MS. Having giving up already so much because of MS, now there was little left. Though she never complained, it was tough on her to have to give up her last realistic identity. She was eligible for an ID, but that was a poor replacement. From then on, I became Jeri's chauffeur. About this time also, Jodi was able to get her driver's license which helped delivering Avon orders.

Every year an Avon president's reception would be held for Reps that had attained President Club status.

One year it was in Detroit. They provided busses for that trip which included a Christmas review of new Christmas gifts. Jeri was there.

At these receptions, awards would also be given out. Twice, Jeri received the Spirit of Avon award (I think these were ours and Jeri's most precious awards of all awards she received from Avon). Among other rewards she received was an "Avon Products Inc. proudly honors Geraldine Schroeder upon the successful completion of Personal Sales Success Training" dated September 15, 1987 and signed by James E. Preston, President, Avon Division.

At the beginning of our Avon escape from MS, Jeri and I would work together every campaign (every two weeks) putting sales in an order book manually. She would call the names etc out to me while I would write them into the order form and price them to mail to Avon. Jeri was not able to write them any longer. We often did this while listening to the radio. What was on the radio so important? Jeri loved listening to BGSU sports especially football, basketball and hockey. When a team wasn't doing very good, you could hear Jeri speak out "Go BG!" She understood and loved BGSU sports because we attended many of the games in person. At Kent State, she loved the sports there also and we attended many football games. Unfortunately, it was a tough era for Kent as they lost a lot more games than they won. At Kent, I did not like Bowling Green's mascot "Falcon" coming there and always beating Kent. As the world changed and we moved to BGSU, I became a fan of the Falcon. I still liked Kent and their "monster" mascot, a very heavy creature that everyone liked. I forget its name and they don't have this one anymore.

A note about Jeri listening to sports on the radio: I never realized until many years later why Jeri would rather listen to the sports on radio rather than to watch them on TV. She never needed glasses (per testing) and rarely used them when issued for whatever reason. I finally decided to watch her eyes very closely as someone once told me to do. Sure enough, there was a slight drag difference if you followed her eyes closely across the screen. I called them "lazy eyes" although the medical world never agreed with us. They called something else that but not Jeri's eyes. Her eyes were never corrected, perhaps because it could not be. It was eerie to watch.

We were slowly learning to use the computer for Avon instead of manually writing and sending orders. Eventually, Avon converted the entire system to computers. This systems change would not work at all on our computer.

It was probably Jeri's district manager who alerted Avon about this. Avon called Jeri, said they had found in their storage all the necessary equipment that Jeri would need. Within days, the equipment came - monitor, computer, keyboard, modem and a mouse. All of it was in excellent condition, some even looked new. They said it was on loan to us. They never asked for it back even when I once talked to them about returning "their" equipment. We were back in business. They always told Jeri whenever she needed help, or if someone was installing computer equipment for her and needed help, to call them or their computer help desk. I think by now, most of Avon knew or heard of Jeri. If they didn't, they would eventually. It seemed that whenever we went to an Avon meeting, awards, social, training or whatever, Jeri always felt comfortable and was treated as such. Like Scouting, Jeri was in the right place at the right time – something she could handle – what MS?

Another change in Avon's system of receiving credit card charges by Reps was that the representative themselves had to call the payment in for their Avon bill. The computer could identify the caller by voice and approve the call. Since Jeri could no longer talk, I had been doing all the calling. Now what?

Rather than change their system, Avon had a better idea. They gave Jeri a very restrictive phone number to use that I could use to continue calling in our payments. The first time I used this number, the person answering in an excited tone asked, "How did you get this number? This number is limited to very few important persons. You must have known someone way up to get it." We have been using that number ever since, probably over 10 or 15 years.

The day Avon stood still...the day the Avon Reps celebrated...a day spouses will never miss. It was time for the annual Avon shindig for our District 4181 and other districts. This was awards day!

The elite of Avon Reps were to be entertained with praises galore, table gifts for everyone and very good door prizes for just about everyone in sight. There were probably some 200 women there (a few men perhaps but I don't remember any) dressed as nice as any Avon Lady you have ever met. No wonder Jeri wanted to go. Not only was Avon important to her, she was important to Avon.

Tables dressed for a Queen greeted each rep with their reservation name on THEIR group table. A formal luncheon was served. No alcohol. Jeri was seated with her group and looked as nice as anyone there all dressed up. I was dressed up a little bit and, being needed by Jeri, began to enjoy this. I managed to stay out of the way to sit quietly with some clapping and smiling. Did I feel out of place? Well, it seemed like "no man's land" but this was their well deserved party. Let it be. They, including Jeri, just ignored me – she had a beautiful time.

It didn't take Avon cheerleaders long to make some noise. All the women put on quite a show especially when going up for their rewards or prizes. Dancing, singing, clapping all unrehearsed, hit the ballroom. I don't remember ever hearing a more spirited group of women and Jeri was one of them. How proud I was of her. What MS? What wheelchair?

It was nice that spouses were not there. They either would have fainted or laughed – actually, many would have been proud of them.

While this was going on, I decided to sneak out into the hall of this very large hotel and find the men's room. The first restrooms were women. Then as I walked down the hall, I found all the restrooms were women. They had covered up the men with women. I smiled and continued down the hall. I then realized there were no men restrooms in sight. I don't remember what I did next. I think I just gave up and went back to Jeri. I'm sure that if she could have gotten up, she would have taken my hand and said, "Come, I'll take you to the little boy's room."

Other little Avon incidents

Another of my Avon duties I qualified for was delivering Avon campaign brochures. Jeri appointed me delivery boy for Avon books. I probably was not eligible yet to deliver Avon orders. Books, I should be able to handle.

On this particular delivery, it was going to take me walking about three miles which would take me about one and a half hours to read each address and place the books inside doors. No mail boxes. For this long walk, I decided to put something soft in my shoes. I saw Jeri's latex medical gloves and, without telling her, took two gloves and put one in each shoe. Nice and soft they were. It was a nice sunny day to do my work. The neighborhood was quiet and I saw no one. As I was about half way finished, I heard a loud BANG, sounded for sure like a gun shot. I stopped quickly, feeling ok, looked around, saw no one, waited, still no one in sight. Took about five more steps, BANG! Again I stopped quickly, still no one around. I thought sure it was another gun shot. It sounded exactly like the first one. Oh Oh! I think I know what it was. Jeri's latex gloves were popping one by one as I walked pumping air into the fingers. I figured at that point, I still had eight shots coming!

Another time in our Avon career overlapping into Jeri's computer career, Jeri was in her wheelchair practicing on her computer with me sitting in a chair that was next to her. Since I was the one answering the phone, I had to be careful not to hang up too soon. I had to be sure it was one of our Avon customers placing an order. By now I was having some hearing problems and Jeri had been losing her voice.

The telephone rang. I answered it on the speaker phone and listened carefully. I could usually recognize one of our Avon customers. So don't hang up. This call was a lady talking which I didn't recognize yet so it went like this:

Jack: Could you repeat that?
She: Repeated.

Me: I'm sorry, I still didn't understand. Could you repeat that?

She: Repeated.

After a couple of more tries, I could tell she was getting frustrated. I still didn't know if it was an Avon call or not.

She: Is there somebody else there I can talk to?

Me: Well, my wife Jeri has been sitting here listening to every word you've said.

She: Good, would you mind putting her on the phone?

Me: No, I would be glad to except I can't hear and she can't talk!

We find Avon in Churchill – Churchill, Canada, that is...in one of our trips there, we decided to take gifts to some of the people we had begun to know there, Avon gifts. We thought they would be surprised. We wondered if anyone way up there would have even heard of Avon. As we began giving our gifts out one by one as we met them, we received a bigger surprise from them than they from us. Not only did they know about Avon, one of our gifts to this one girl said, "I'm an Avon Representative!" What a surprise. We all laughed. We couldn't believe it. We asked her how many customers she had. "She said seven." Yes, we gave our Avon gift to her.

DECEMBER 3, 2007 JERI WAS TOLD, "REPRESENTATIVES LIKE YOU REALLY ARE THE HEART AND SOUL OF AVON."

The letter received from Avon also included another message to Jeri, "Congratulations Geraldine, on your 25th Avon Anniversary...a truly remarkable achievement!" Signed Andrea Slater, Senior Vice President, President, Avon U.S.

With this December 3, 2007 and Jeri being congratulated for 25 years Avon service and our family continuing with Jeri's Avon then and beyond 30 years, what more can we say!

COMPUTERS

Ah! Computers - my definition of a necessary evil. As most computer owners and probably most who are not computer owners are distastefully aware of the ups and downs of trying to become a computer expert, try it with MS. To a great extent, it can be done. To Jeri and other handicapped people, it was not an evil, it was a blessing.

I was going to leave this part out but the grand kids kept telling me it was funny - of course it could only happen to Jeri: Running the word correction on the computer, when I first put Jeri's name in the computer, the correction came up "Jerk." Every time thereafter, I would correct it by hitting skip which left "Jeri" in. This worked until one day THE computer changed her name to "Jerk" everywhere it appeared. Now the kids had a real laugh.

Jeri, Ahead of her time.......... When Jeri received her first computer in 1992, courtesy of "Ohio Bureau of Vocational Rehabilitation" (BVR), she was ready and excited to relive her life by adjusting to a new way of so doing. "I will learn the Computer. I will get back to normal living."

This was the day I had retired from BGSU where we were installing a new accounting computer system and I could finally say, "No more computers for me." Jeri greeted me at the door and said, "Guess what? I'm getting a computer." So Jeri and I joined our own computer age, she was thrilled, I was appalled.

The BVR application for help included goals to be chosen by the applicant. Jeri's were: To communicate and to do her Avon.

Since Jeri was an approved Avon Rep, this helped her get aid from BVR – she was already working, just needed help. I explained to the BVR representative that while Jeri was indeed a Rep she was not showing much of a profit. He answered, "The profit doesn't interest me. It's the fact that she is indeed working. We can help her." He liked her goals. She was on her way.

Now that Jeri was approved by BVR, the local office staff began their part which was to provide equipment and training at home. They mentioned to us that they were to ask if the family could contribute towards any equipment. They were apologetic about this but we agreed and would pay for part of the equipment. We then had to sign an agreement with BVR outlying what was to be done.

In learning a computer, the level of knowledge is the guide as to how far one can succeed. You improve, you move to the next level. Amazingly, Jeri began improving quickly, listening and following an instructor (she had several different ones that taught her) BVR provided. Jeri must have impressed someone in Columbus BVR. They told the local BVR office, "that as soon as Jeri was able, herself, to type an Avon customer invoice on her computer, they would write a story about her to put in their monthly magazine." Wow!

Another time as Avon was slowly converting to being able to use a computer for and by Avon Representatives, they began looking for Reps to do some experimenting with using a computer for recording and sending Avon orders. Out of about 60 Avon Reps they approved for this, one of them was Jeri. We were excited about this. So was BVR.

As Jeri moved along learning and using HER computer, excited and going at it for hours at a time, she forgot about getting tired, she was too busy. A system was chosen where she would move a metal bar up a keyboard to a letter for her to hit and print. Jeri still had movement in her right arm and hand and, at first, she was doing well. Then she began having trouble moving the bar. An engineer assigned to Jeri in addition to her instructor, took the bar several times to have it refined to move easier. Each time, it was failing. He made an interesting remark after seeing Jeri trying the best she could to move this bar. He said, "I never realized Multiple Sclerosis was so devastating."

Next tried were IntelliKeys, a flexible keyboard with overlays, in place of a standard keyboard. It required a switch or a clicking tool and use of her hands. This did not work for Jeri. Losing more use of her right hand, she began using a system called Ke:nx. She used this system on PC Avon software by using her chin to enter data. This looked promising. Working hard on this system, she turned out her first Avon invoice, well almost. I had to help her use the function keys required. We then found out that this system would not handle function keys and they had not found a way yet to do it. To use PC-Avon, you had to use function keys. So much for Ke:nx.

In those days technology was reacting very slowly especially for handicapped systems. A few systems were on the market but they were nothing like the ones to come in the future, so BVR and Jeri had to live with what was available. Along about now, Jeri had lost her movement in her right arm and hand. Her brain message was not getting through to them.

As I understand, the brain system works like an electric wire that has been shorted or disconnected by its insulating covering missing or exposed – the electric may or may not get through to where it is suppose to go. In MS the brain's message is not getting through the nerves because the myelin (the insulating protective covering around the nerves) is wearing or worn off, exposing the nerves. There has been some success in learning that this protective covering might be able to reproduce itself or be replaced by transplanting from somewhere else. This is still being researched. We think it is the closest anyone has come to helping MS with its first cure.

To continue Jeri's wild journey finding a computer system that fits, of all the computer systems she was being tested for, I think the best one was the one that used a headband to move the cursor. This system, called Cyberlink used three small (about ¾" square) plastic pieces (sensors) attached inside the headband and was placed on Jeri's forehead. This related to moving her eyes, head muscles or other places. With this, Jeri could move the cursor very well. I often never knew what she was using to move the cursor.

Sometimes it seemed she had to search to find herself what would work. Was it her eyes alone moving? Blinking? Her facial muscles movements? These were all available movements possible. Really amazing! I couldn't tell which ones she was using. Maybe she was using all of these plus other movements. She was choosing, controlling and typing. She loved this system best of all. The mistake was, I think, not keeping her on it and getting the headband to fit her properly.

This system showed her muscles and other moving body parts being used by color scales moving up and down, each with a different meaning and with a different color. She could bring this up on the computer to see what was happening and what was working the best. The manual also read, "It will not allow you to read her mind." Shucks.

Jeri did well for a headband not fitting her good. The headband censors had to fit flat on Jeri's forehead right above her eyes. They had to stay flat in place at all times to work. Unfortunately, the three pieces, although attached together, were difficult to place correctly. When we would find something to hold the pieces in place (like a swim cap), it worked for a while but not long enough. Somehow with us adjusting this headband off and on, she made it work. She had the headband working well but I think then that the system needed updated especially for her typing.

Reading an article about this, it read that this could be a problem with women. Why? It was claimed that many women's forehead curves inward at the top, therefore the pieces would not maintain proper contact. Her instructor (and we did too) tried many ways to make it work. If you held the headband yourself on Jeri's forehead, it worked well. I made a suggestion to Jeri's teacher. We understood the inventor of this headband system lived in southern Ohio. I would think we could get him to come himself to see Jeri. I don't know if my suggestion got very far or not, but it was never answered. I don't think the BVR appreciated me interfering, they felt they already had their own people to handle problems. I did learn later that the teacher did go to their supervisor and asked about bringing this person here to see Jeri. The answer was that it would depend on finances. Nothing ever came of it. Rattlesnakes!

So, for the time being, we continued making the headband work. Jeri was now doing the "impossible" – moving the cursor herself. "Look, no hands." She was then given computer games to practice on. This was to give her practice on moving the cursor and enjoy the fun that went with it. In between games, she still practiced typing random letters and numbers but still had problems typing names, numbers and words consistently. This was a tiny target to hit each letter to form names etc. She did not need glasses for this. She could see the letters and numbers. The computer had to be good enough to allow her to move slowly and deliberate which I don't think it did. The computer was depending on her as was. She did like her new games and could play them alone and not depend on someone else being nearby helping her. Until she became tired, she would stay at it hours at a time. She knew when to stop.

As Jeri began working the games using her headband to move what was required to move, she quickly found out which ones she liked and could actually play. She loved making  the computer do things – she was in control, whether it was moving "vases" around the "room" or letting them drop accidentally in which case you could see the glass breaking and hearing the noise at the same time. Playing ping pong, the cursor was the paddle in which she could control moving it up and down, right or left, to hit the incoming ping pong ball. The winner was always the computer. Jeri did not like that. This was her computer, time for a change. Her first win brought a loud cheer from the computer game audience. From then on she was able to win her share of the games. With practice, playing with a "maze game" it took Jeri 18-20 minutes to move the arrow (cursor) from one point across the screen to the finish point. Eventually she could do it in 18 seconds. It was exciting watching her.

These were not just games. They were teaching encouragement, confidence and moving the cursor. I generally stayed away from them to save myself from being embarrassed and being easily outplayed by "you know who."

When friends would visit Jeri and see her operating the computer with the cursor moving around, they would watch her hands not moving and ask, "How is she doing this?" It gave us great pleasure to watch Jeri in action. Showing off? I certainly hope so. This was uncanny to watch. I acted like an attendant and when people came, I would say, "Come in and watch Jeri at her computer."

I always had one criticism about computer teachers. When a student would get stuck, say in typing or playing games, the teacher would move too fast to help. They would say, "Here, let me help you" and hit a key that corrected the problem. They would not say which key they used or explain what the student did wrong. My thoughts were always, "Let the person make their own mistakes and correct them or explain to them what they did wrong." Corresponding to this would be when a teacher would say, "Jeri is doing fine." I often watched Jeri and my own thoughts would say, "No she isn't." It was meant to encourage Jeri but she herself knew how she was doing and wanted to hear what the teacher really thought.

When off her games, Jeri practiced typing for real. She was making good progress now after the games helped. She finally learned to move the cursor to the letter but still was unable to align letters with words. We concluded she needed a next level of instruction or a system change. This really never happened so she struggled with what she had and could do and with her teacher helping her as much as they could.

One thing had become notably missing. The MS was interfering with her progress. Furthermore, it being a slow progressive type of MS. Computer technology, while not changing very often for handicapped persons, was becoming outdated for Jeri's use quickly instead of giving Jeri time to use it properly.

Jeri's MS doctor's periodic six months visit with her informed her that he felt her MS had stabilized. This was good news. He was always amazed at what she was doing, in spite of MS, including all of the traveling Jeri was doing. He liked our stories, especially going to Canada near the Arctic Circle so many times. He said, "You're the only couple I know that goes north for a vacation." (Note: this going north for a vacation is mentioned again in our Prince Rupert trip.) We rarely asked him much about MS findings. We followed it closely and there was very little to wave about. Primarily he was checking Jeri's current happenings, including showing us the most important exercises to give Jeri.

I sensed early that BVR was becoming impatient and was questioning how much more time and money would be spent on Jeri. They realized they had a tough case to resolve, that because of MS and lack of updated market equipment, could they ever solve this one? Of course, they loved the easy cases and so publicized them more often in their magazine. Still, they had to prove their existence. To Jeri and me, finding ways to eliminate MS and/or a lot of it was a major challenge. Anyone can solve easy problems.

We were asked to meet with BVR to discuss Jeri's case. I figured they were looking to close her case and were hoping we would do it. We met at our condo September 14, 2005. Jeri was present and there were three from BVR including an executive of BVR. He did the talking at first explaining the difficulty they were having towards finishing the case. After his talk, he looked at me and said, "You know that if you cannot move the cursor, you cannot use the computer." I answered, "You are absolutely correct." Pause. "But Jeri can move the cursor!" Surprised, he turned to one of the other people with him and asked, "Is that correct? Can Jeri move the cursor?" A struggled answer was "Well....Yes." Meeting adjourned! The person in charge told the other person with him to continue to pursue finding the right system for Jeri.

This was fine we are back in business but another wait for Jeri. Whenever we changed systems, it would mean another long period that she would not be at her computer, sometimes over a year. No matter who we talked with about Jeri having to wait so long and losing all that practice, confidence and desire, we could never apparently find the right person to keep equipment and systems moving as needed. MS was not waiting for Jeri.

A new system was found and really did look promising. This was to be Jeri's last attempt of reaching her goals.

This new system (and it was an advanced system) is difficult to explain why it never was set up properly for Jeri to learn. To explain:

The system seemed to be in two parts.

One was to practice on a new monitor, attached to her wheelchair, a word choosing board that Jeri could choose with one touch a word or phrase, one at a time. This seemed similar to what she had started with years before.

When the person selecting which system to get for Jeri, he had this one brought to Jeri to try before BVR would buy it. He had noticed that Jeri could move her head good and tried holding a "clicker" under her chin to see if she could click on it to print a letter from the board. She clicked and printed a letter. I was asked what I thought. I felt if I turn anything down, we will probably be told that there was nothing else available. So I said it looks like she can do it.

The second part of the system was truly a remarkable piece of equipment that looked really promising if we could get it set up properly. From what I could tell, this system included two critical parts. One part included several different sensors that could locate many active body positions to use to move the cursor. The other part was a switch that could choose which sensor you wanted to use that would work the best. These could be attached to eye glasses and the sensor selected could be moved to its best movement selection. The sensors therefore could select eye movements, blinking and any "body" position that had motion.

While the clicker was the first to be set up for Jeri, I failed to ever understand why the several other promising choices were never tried. They were part of the equipment delivered to give Jeri a real chance to be tested as to which would work the best. It seemed that everyone became dependent on the clicker.

This new equipment was delivered to our condo 3/19/08. The original search approval was given on 9/14/05. So Jeri, one more time, had a long wait between computer systems and nothing was set up to practice on in the meantime. I often wondered what ever happened to our "headband" system that she was doing so well with and enjoyed? Anyway, she now has a new system. That was the easy part. Now to get it set up. Not so easy and not because of the equipment. The equipment was here waiting to be set up and then we were to learn it.

There were to be several people involved in this and apparently each had their part, at least that's the way it turned out. The first was a person hired by BVR was to come in to attach the monitor to the wheelchair and then load the monitor with squares of data that Jeri would want to click on to communicate. This was done. We put together messages to load that Jeri would like.

Jeri entered the scene and began making her choice of message she wanted to show by moving the cursor to it and clicking. She did pretty well but I could see eventual problems with her clicking as she became unable to use her chin properly. However, I had a more important question.

I had thought we were to use Jeri's present computer at her desk, that she was to continue typing her letters herself to communicate what messages she wanted to send to advance her to her next level. I asked the person that was doing the installing this. They answered, "Oh that comes later."

To continue, when they were through setting this monitor up and running, I asked them when they would be back? They said they would not be back, that they were only hired for two days to do what they just did. First surprise!

Second surprise! The person arranging this system also said they had done what they were to do, that we no longer needed them.

Now Jeri waits again. What was to be done next and when? She had part of the equipment which she could at least practice on if someone would show her how. I now was not too favorably impressed and I certainly did not know how to use the new equipment, at least yet. If Jeri's original "headband" system were still connected, I would have moved her back to her computer room and put her back on it. I knew at least how to put her back on her games.

In the meantime, the company that supplied Jeri with all this new equipment came to the attention that there was no one to show Jeri how to work it. Right on! Their company assigned a person to help get Jeri a teacher. This person met with BVR and outlined their plans. BVR was to hire someone that they would teach first. That person could then become Jeri's teacher. So far-so good, we thought. No more surprises, at least yet. The strange part here is that everyone working on this thought this was a great way to go, that it would be easy to find someone, with some medical or computer knowledge, to hire. Not so. BVR did a wide search approaching facilities such as

Nursing Services, even hospitals, that could provide help or find someone to help but to no avail. No one was ever found. The system did not get installed.

Jeri really was ahead of her time........... It would seem that reading this section tells you this. Jeri was ready but the technology wasn't available yet. She was a pioneer. She was ahead of the technology. Looking back, what was available was expensive and was designed with the handicapped in mind. Thus, sales were probably at a minimum. The customers were probably few, the profits had to be low.

Now in this new generation, we have modern general public methods for playing games on TV without even using computers as we knew them. New inventions are in demand and people are buying. It was even then discovered that many of these new items can actually be used by the handicapped even though it was not originally intended for them. Sales now favor everyone.

Lest we forget..........while computers played an important part in Jeri's life, it was very far from her "real" life. Her family, church and people were her real life. Being on a computer from 1992 to 2008 (16 years Wow) gave her a lot of comfort and joy – SHE was doing what she wanted to do and was so glad that we were with her and joined her in her computer travel. In other words, she was still part of the family. Heck, anyone can work a computer. Not everyone can do what she did, except perhaps other handicapped persons.

So, Jeri with her computer was successful. Goals were met, maybe not quite what she hoped for, but she did it.

As far as all the delays and waiting by Jeri in getting computer equipment and services, I believe we can learn from Jeri by the way she would get things done by asking "why" or "why not" when something was denied or delayed. BVR was with us all those years and never quit on Jeri. This was remarkable. I think, if anything, they, and others, such as case managers, were just too nice and too lenient with contractors and providers in providing what Jeri needed when she needed. I think everyone learned from Jeri because she too was a teacher.

ARMY SECURITY AGENCY PACIFIC

Long before Jeri was aware of the existence of ASAPAC it eventually became part of our life along with the CFM (Catholic Family Movement) and eventually living the "Churchill Experience." These three probably are at the top of our memory list. All were about "lasting friendships."

CFM (in Kent) was made up of small church related family groups that would meet monthly to talk about family activities. Groups would go to a different home each time where light refreshments would be served and where the friendships would begin. It was the rare time that we would have a baby sitter watch our children. We use to get criticized by people for not using baby sitters more often and get out more ourselves. We would always rather be with the children.

On 15 September 1945, the **Army Security Agency (ASA),** a new US Army unit, was put in control of all Army signal and communications security. It became worldwide and was to be a self sustaining force with its own personnel, equipment etc.

On 25 November 1945, the **Army Security Agency, Pacific, (ASAPAC)** was organized to be able to intercept messages from within the entire Far East.

When I entered the Army in 1950, I eventually was assigned to ASA and then ASAPAC in Japan. ASA was established with headquarters in DC and eventually began establishing posts worldwide in different locations, each with its own title like ASAPAC, all under ASA.

Jeri became aware of ASA when we drove to an ASA alumni picnic in Warrenton, Virginia in August, 1993, which was held at the former ASA camp called, Vint Hill Farms Station. There is more of this later under our car trip August 4, 1993.

REUNIONS

Skipping back to 1963 when Jeri and I were married, she really never asked me about the Army and I really wasn't too interested anyway. Besides, since everyone in ASA was sworn to a life time secrecy oath, we were never allowed to talk about it even to our own family. In the late 1990s, we learned that the oaths were refined to the point where you could talk somewhat about ASA.

In October, 1993, Jodi drove us to the first reunion of ASAPAC, Alumni at Ft. Mitchell, Kentucky. This was the first time Jack LaDove our reunion President met Jeri. Up to her old tricks of smiling, Jeri became a favorite of Jack. He began calling her "giggles."

This is when Jeri became to know and understand for the first time, ASA. We began attending ASAPAC annual alumni reunions, in which other wives and spouses attended. There were mostly men in ASA and the few women seemed to be all officers. We had one fine lady with us, our beloved (by everyone) retired Lt. Colonel, USA WAC, Martha Sachs. Jeri and I became good friends with Martha.

Jeri seemed to be proud to be a part of all of this. I think all the wives were. She mixed in very nicely and, in spite of being in a wheelchair, was very comfortable with everyone and they also became friends with her. Jeri was never left alone.

Headquartered in Tokyo during the Korean War and with subordinate units all over the Far East including Japan, Korea, even one small unit in China, there was a lot to talk about. The women present listened to the stories (all "true" of course, well perhaps a little "stretched") and enjoyed many interesting and sometimes very funny ones. It was a real learning experience for the women hearing first hand from soldiers who were there involved in "Intelligence." I once heard that our ASA unit was known as a "unit that never existed." Gee, I was never told that. I wonder what I did.

The unique part about these reunions was that large tables were set up for this social activity with food and refreshments. The men and women sat together - no men, no women tables. What a nice arrangement to get to know everyone. Jack LaDove, who had developed our alumni from start, had said, "Remember, you are both host (and hostess) and guest, introduce yourself." This is where the lasting friendships began.

We would have about 50 to 90 people at every reunion. Needed breaks from talking included other activities such as bowling, golf and usually a scheduled tour around the area since each reunion was held at a different city for some ten years when it was decided to stay in Kentucky from then on.

Our reunions always ended with a semiformal banquet – for men it was suits, for women, their choice. The women always dressed so very well. They made the reunions the way reunions should be. Now me with Jeri, I usually wore at least a suit jacket. When

 I was alone with Jeri, I did the best I could for her. Now when our girls were with us, Jeri was turned into a well dressed woman. She was dressed in silk stockings, beautiful dresses, shoes, make-up and topped off with a beautiful hair dressing.

Jeri and I would go on some some tours where you could walk to but we were not able to go on any bus tours because there were no handicap busses. However, with Jeri, anything could happen. Here is a good example of Jeri's "never left behind:"

Our reunion in 1998 in Albuquerque included a bus tour to Santa Fe. This was a favorite tour and everyone signed up to go on it except one couple, us. I had walked up to where the bus was loading our group and was watching them board when the bus driver asked me, "Wasn't I coming?" I said, "No, that Jeri was in a wheelchair and we couldn't get her on the bus." He asked where she was and I said back in our room.

He said, "Go get her, I'll stall the bus and I'll help get her on." I ran back to our room and told Jeri, "We were going on the bus, let's go." She was excited and we ran back to the bus. The driver helped get her on and put her by a seat near the front where I could hold her in her wheelchair. So, our first visit to Santa Fe was on! When we got there, the driver helped us get off and then had to help us get back on to return. Meanwhile, the group now was off the bus but on an organized walking tour into buildings etc. This would have been difficult for us so we went our own way with me as tour guide. We visited an old Spanish church on our tour and then I had to remember how to find our way back to the bus. This is when Jeri would usually take over and start praying. I couldn't hear her but I could feel it. We found our way back and enjoyed the bus ride back to Albuquerque.

A more complete summary of ASAPAC Reunions including more ASAPAC history book researches is found under TRAINS – DESTINATIONS .... OTHER DESTINATIONS: JACK AND JERI AMTRAK TRAIN AND CAR TRIPS TO ASAPAC REUNIONS

HISTORY BOOK

At one of our early reunions, our President, Jack LaDove, asked me if I would be historian for our alumni. I agreed. He then showed me a letter he had written **AFTER** he had appointed other officers, in which he said we would also need an historian "providing we could find someone gullible enough to be talked into the job."

Jeri and I were then asked if we would write our unit's history for 1946-1952. We said everything seems to be still classified but we would give it a try.

My very good friend, Vic Grimes and his wife Mary, volunteered to assist Jeri and me with the book. I had been assigned to Vic at our headquarters in Tokyo. Vic was the officer in charge of our S-2 Section. After departing, we never saw each other until this reunion, some 40 years later. Jeri and Mary became good friends while Vic and I resumed our great friendship.

As we began our history book research, Jeri and I realized we would have to travel to get information. Actually it gave us a reason to travel. Mixing vacations and research proved to be just what we needed. It became exciting and fun. Jeri loved it. Little did we realize that she would have a huge part in the making of this ASA book! It distracted us from the MS and led us around the country searching for information that pertained to ASAPAC. We thought we would have some problems getting information especially if it was still classified and was meant to be kept secret. Another surprise appeared when making many visits to military facilities they would say, "We never heard of ASA."

At Fort Belvoir in Virginia, we got to know the Chief Historian pretty well including his assistant. He told us that if we didn't write our history, it would not get written, that there was no intention of the Army doing it. He thought we would have a difficult time getting classified information, that we should probably just get our own troop stories. This sounded like a challenge to Jeri and me.

Other places we visited were MacArthur library in Virginia, Ft. Knox, Kentucky, Army Library in DC, Ft. McNair in DC and other places, finding very little information of value to us. We even visited original ASA camps including Arlington Hall (Virginia), Vent Hill Farms Station (Virginia) and Two Rock Ranch (California) with little success.

At the Army library in DC, Jodi was with us on that trip. After Jodi, Jeri and I cleared security entrance to an upstairs area where some ASA information was, we found the people very busy. The soldier in charge showed us this one area of files which was not classified and if we wanted to look through these files, we could do it ourselves and make copies of what we were looking for. There wasn't much time to do this but we were not about to leave without looking. As Jeri watched us make an assembly line – I would pull out what looked good and hand them to Jodi to make copies – it was a real fast production that gave us a lot of information. We finished with enough information and copies to make our visit worthwhile. We thanked them and left the building.

We made five trips to the National Archives at College Park, Maryland, staying as long as three weeks at a time. Many days there searching, brought little findings. We both and Jodi when she was our driver and with us, had to be "cleared" at entering the Archives and after questioning of what we were there for, we were issued badges that got us to a floor that we were interested in. I was really happy that Jeri not only enjoyed this but what an experience for her, something she never expected. Everywhere we went to do research, she was so very welcomed – I was so proud of her! One staff member, at the Archives, came over to talk with her and told her, "It is so good to see you here."

One time in the Archives Jeri and I found, searching their index folders, a packet that might help us. You had to request documents. This time they said we would have to go to a certain restricted room to search there for it ourselves. To get to this one room, we had to go through 4 or 5 more clearance points, the last being we would be taken to the room by someone and then we would have to wait until someone came to take us back. We found the packet we were looking for. It was of no value to us. I was never disappointed. Watching Jeri doing this and loving it, that's all I needed.

Again, this proved that ASA was indeed secret so we always thought that if we did finish a book, perhaps it would have a lot of meaning to families. We would often search for just ASA information believing that if we found any "good" information, it would lead us to ASAPAC. At the Archives, you pretty well do your own researching. Since we were working on an Army history book, I think they liked helping us as much as they could.

One trip, we found one document that looked good but it was going to take a lot of copying to print copies plus it was still classified. To get it declassified, the Archives would have to check it to see if it could be declassified by their staff. We asked one of the employees in charge about this packet we found but that it was still marked classified on every page. The person took the packet, checked it with someone and came back to us and said, "They could declassify it." How would they do this with so many pages and quickly for us? This person gave us a little sticker marked "DECLASSIFIED, NARA (National Archives and Records Administration) and a date." He gave us one sticker, showed us how and where to place it on the copying machine screen, written side down where the blank sheets of paper would be printed. Each page would then have this message on each page being printed. There were over 100 pages. They allowed us to do it. So our next step was to run our copies as quick as we could since others were waiting to copy. Copies were free but you were only allowed 15 minutes at a time if others were waiting. They did have several copy machines. A staff person saw what I had and said he would try to let me keep copying without interruption. It worked. At last we found something of importance. Once again, Jeri had quite an experience to partner this. "I declassified all these pages?" Good thing Jeri was my witness.

When we left the Archives that day, we were questioned about this as they reviewed what we were taking out. They approved it and we took our packet with us. I believe that Jeri was enjoying a once in a lifetime experience that few people would ever get the opportunity to do. With all of our traveling, researching and meeting people everywhere, it had to be heartwarming for her.

To begin gathering the other puzzle pieces of the book, we began asking for written stories from our group - we ended up with over 60 stories. We also started writing to the Freedom of Information Office at Ft. Meade, Maryland for documents pertaining to ASAPAC. As we began slowly to receive requested documents, most had to be declassified and sanitized. Some took several years to receive. Some we still have not received.

With Vic and Mary Grimes help, we finished and distributed the book in 2006. People started asking us if we were excited about publishing it. We told them that we were pleased but the real pleasure was that we were able to publish enough information, that wasn't classified, to tell families of those who were in ASA as to what ASA was and what did ASA do. I remember getting a letter from a girl that said her father had just died, that he was in ASA – what was ASA and what did he do? I think we answered this in the book.

After all was done but not over, our Reunion Alumni presented plaques to Vic and Mary Grimes, who had help us with the book so very much, and to Jeri and me.

Ours read: **HISTORY - 1946-52, HEADQUARTERS ARMY SECURITY AGENCY, PACIFIC.....**"With special recognition to Jeri for her moral support and tolerance during (this) long endeavor."

After publishing this ASA book, our local newspaper asked Jeri and me if they could write a story about it. At first, we told them no, we didn't think so. After giving several reasons why they wanted to do it, we agreed. Then they sent a photographer to our home to take a picture of Jeri and me holding the book. To our surprise, they published the picture and story on the front page. That is what we didn't want but I was glad for Jeri. She was a real trooper. This had all been

nothing but fun with Jeri. If she had not been with me, I would never have tried to print such a book.

Strange, after the book was finished and distributed some 12 years later, Mary and Jeri both passed away within weeks of each other.

A LITTLE BIT ABOUT US

Before we were married Jeri spent a week in the hospital for some dental surgery. Letters were sent by priests and brothers of Steubie U to Jeri. I liked the card sent by Bro. Sal to Jeri telling her to "get better we want to have another skating party if we can keep Jack from messing it up as usual."

Another little surprise before our marriage and even engagement came when Jeri met my mom & dad at Wheeling's Oglebay Park in a shock to me. My dad was always strict who his children married. Here I was 33 and Jeri was 20. I had avoided taking Jeri to meet them, waiting to be sure this was "it" first. When we turned the corner at the Oglebay Lake there they sat. I was really caught off guard. I introduced them to Jeri – it was obvious they liked her and came to our wedding and forever after always liked her.

Preparing for our wedding day, I think my only instructions were to be on time. I would be driving from Kent, Ohio to Weirton, West Virginia but I almost destroyed the wedding and possible the marriage. I had bought a new Ford Fairlane from the dealer in Kent a few days before. I didn't realize it at the time but they told me the car would be ready and I could pick it up the day of the wedding in the morning. I went to pick it up. It was ready. Later I realized I had assumed that it would be ready. Now I was worried.

Wow, what if it had not been ready and I had a two hours drive to get to my wedding. I almost blew it.

Our wedding was held July 27, 1963 at Jeri's parish church in Weirton. We never did find out which of us proposed and "how?" It was a lovely wedding and, while far from a large crowd, it was nice to see so many friends. I think most had given up on me. We received a lot of congratulations from the Franciscans we knew but by now, most were back at their  monastery in Pennsylvania. An "Apostolic Blessing" was also sent us for our wedding of July 27, 1963 by Pope John XXIII, signed on 18 April 1963. Ironically, the Pope died June 3, 1963. This blessing was secured and mailed by Fr. Leonard Sardo, a College of Steubenville priest stationed in Rome, who knew Jeri well, and surprised us. We remembered this so well that in later years, we asked the Bishop of Wheeling if he could get this Blessing for each of our three children. They were received from Rome as each one was married.

We did receive a Western Union telegram from Loretta, PA from Fr. Felix and Bro. Ben, our former friends at Steubenville College, on our wedding day delivered to our reception with congratulations and best wishes and that Fr. Felix was celebrating a Mass at 5:15 PM that day for us. Another one of our congratulations came, by letter, from Fr. Joe, who now was a Chaplain in the Air Force. He is the one who called and talked me into coming back to Steubenville College as controller. Now if he had not called or if I had not accepted how in the world would I have been able to meet Jeri?

I was told that a close girl friend of Jeri's when she found out Jeri and I was seeing each other asked Jeri if we were planning to be married. She told them, "No, we're just friends." When her girl friend received an invitation to the wedding, she said, "Well, you must have become very good friends in a hurry."

Away we went in our new Ford...leaving Weirton and heading east – to Pittsburgh, 25 miles away. In Pittsburgh which was Jeri's favorite city to shop with her mother, we spent our first night of our honeymoon. We were exhausted. From there, we headed over the mountains in New York State for New York City. I believe this is where our "jinx" started, one that would last throughout our married life and to this day we never found out which one of us was the "jinx?" It didn't matter. We made use of it often and had fun doing it.

Going up a mountain in New York, our brand new water pump in our brand new Ford made the funniest racket I ever heard. We kind of coasted downhill to find a service station. Wherever we were, we had to stay the night to get this fixed.

On to Cape Cod but first, a stop in New York City. As we drove past the Waldorf-Astoria Hotel, we looked at each other – stop there? Jeri, of course, "Lets." I don't think so but we'll park along the street and I'll give it a try. I sure didn't want to pull up to the front door – we would have been faced with all kinds of service that I would have to tip. At the desk, I asked how much for two of us for one night? The clerk said $24 dollars. I knew it would be high. I said it was too high and began to leave. He asked if I had any kind of card that might allow him to give me a discount. I pulled out my Kent State University card. He said, "That'll do it. Your room would be $17." I took it and ran all the way back to the car to tell Jeri the big surprise. "We are staying at the Waldorf." We drove back to the hotel and, this time, pulled up right to the parking garage inside the hotel. The attendant asked for my keys. He would park it. Now I knew I had to give him a tip. How much? I reached in my pocket, found a dollar bill and gave it to him. This was the biggest tip I had ever given someone. To top it off, he thanked me so very nicely. Did I give him too much? No matter. We later had dinner. The only thing I remember, coffee was a dollar a cup. A dollar - coffee was about ten cents from where we came from. I did not complain. Jeri wrote a letter home to her family telling them, "Just a quick note to let you know we made it. Believe it or not – The Waldorf, it's fabulous."

Now it was on to Cape Cod and Provincetown and our honeymoon. We were not disappointed and had a good time. Jeri loved Provincetown. Well there was one disappointment. Our hotel only had one room for us for one night. One night! On the other hand, It was a double room with private bath and television facing the water and only cost $20.00. You can't win them all, even with a jinx. Little did we realize we would still have a good time no matter what might go wrong - we returned several times to Cape Cod in our future.

With our vacation (not our honeymoon) fading away, one of us had to get back to work. Since Jeri had taken an early "retirement" that left only one "bread winner" to head home. I took Jeri with me. We finished our first and only marriage by stopping at Lake George in New York, one that would also get on our future list and where a couple of our children learned to water ski.

Since we were unable to take a longer honeymoon on our first "real" trip together in 1963, we put a "vacation" (what, not another honeymoon?) together in 1964 to see what we missed in 1963.

We headed further north towards Maine. From two earlier trips with Jeri's family, we had visited Maine and we both remembered finding a beach area that we stopped at briefly called Drakes Island. It seemed vacant so we only stayed enough to walk around a little. We stopped a year later again to see this same beach. We never thought of it again until 1964 when  Jeri and I both wondered if we could find it. This time we were alone and married. We knew it was in Maine. We got off the highway we were on and got on a country road. Now that was more like it. It looked familiar. Unbelievably, this country road led us right to Drakes Island. A name and place we never heard of and never forgot – and we never spent a penny there! The road took us right to the beach, end of the line. We got out and couldn't believe it. Right in front of us, a beautiful white sandy beach that extended to never never land it seemed. No one was on the beach. We saw no one anywhere. We took off our shoes and socks. The water was cold but we could go in up to our ankles with no problem. It was delightful. It was "our" beach! In the water and just walking along the beach, we simply enjoyed it and must have walked a couple of miles, with Jeri picking up small pebbles in the water. There were few shells or rocks.

There was still no one to be seen. Funny, Drakes Island was not an island. After spending several hours there, it was time to move on. As usual, we would say to the beach (or wherever we were), "Bye, we'll be back." Jeri taught me that!

We did return - still no people on "our beach."

Many years later, we discovered in one of Jeri's boxes, a tiny plastic bag with I tiny shell, 1 small piece of shell, 1 little rock and eight pebbles in it. On the outside she had printed "Drakes Island Maine and Presque Isle."

Presque Isle would have referred to our favorite beach in Pennsylvania at Erie. We would go to it from Kent often and when traveling in the East, we would always allow time to stop there on our way home.

Our last major stop on this 1964 trip caught us driving north to Bar Harbor, Maine. Now Jeri was the best picnic preparer I had ever met. We were driving along a road near the Atlantic Ocean on a beautiful sunny warm afternoon watching this beautiful view. When we approached a high hill where we could see a picture scene we probably would never see again, what did Jeri do? She said stop and let's have a picnic right here. That was fine with me. There was a picnic table right there. Nobody was using it. In fact, nobody was to be seen nor were there any cars. My magician-turned wife started pulling food out of the car with all the goodies and drinks. She even pulled out a table cloth. If a rabbit came out, I would have fainted. She set the table. We sat down to a surprise feast. But wait - it seemed to be getting windy. No problem. We kept eating. We both noticed the wind did seem to be getting stronger. A few minutes later, there was no doubt about it. We gathered the food etc and got into the car mighty fast. The sun was gone and the wind was strong. It finally slowed up enough for us to drive  on. The next morning reading a local newspaper, we found out we were in the middle of a hurricane - a picnic in a hurricane?

At Bar Harbor, Maine, we discovered this large car ferry boat called Bluenose. Why not? We drove our car on and for seven hours rode this ferry from Bar Harbor, Maine to Yarmouth, Nova Scotia, passing whales in the process. Some passengers became seasick. We did not. We met two men aboard one who was asleep on a bench on the ship's deck. The other man began talking to us laughing a bit. He said the person with him was seasick. We said that was not good but we were almost across. The other man said, "That's correct but we left our car back at Bar Harbor. He will have to go back with me to get it. He doesn't know it yet." Now that was not good either.

This was probably the closest to a sea going ship Jeri was ever on. She loved it. There was more to it besides watching whales. We were on the Bay of Fundy (which connects to the Atlantic Ocean) which was noted for its highest tide range in the world. Several rivers flowed into  this bay, one of which was named Saint John River. At high tide, the river reverses itself.

Arriving by boat no less, this was our first visit to Nova Scotia. We would never have believed it would become one of our favorite places to visit, especially Halifax.

From Yarmouth, we drove north covering most of Nova Scotia. Our homeward trip by way of Maine, Vermont etc took us back to Kent to continue a normal way of living, well almost normal, well maybe not so normal. After all, I did bring Jeri back with me, again. She made the difference in our family in all the things we did. I wasn't about to lose her.

A SECOND BEGINNING..........back in Kent and having three children we eventually added three rooms to our split level home doing a lot of the work ourselves. Jeri had on the job experience in designing. After having a carpenter frame our addition in, we took over and with instructional help from some of our members in CFM, we were able to complete it. Jeri was very good at laying real hardwood floors. We wanted our new addition to follow the design of the original house by split leveling it also. We added three levels to the existing four levels - now it was a seven level house and each child finally had their own room.

As our family grew we enjoyed playing children games with the kids. I never really wanted to beat them and always let them win without their knowing it (or did they know?). But NO, Jeri played to win and would beat them. I wonder which way taught them the best?

Swimming - Jeri was really a poor swimmer. Even I could beat her. She took one or two swimming courses at Kent State - from then on I could never beat her, she really was good. However, I still held one record over her. In Kent we took our family many years to this one small lake for picnics and swimming. So one day I proved to Jeri I was still pretty good because that day I set a swimming record at the lake! It was for the slowest mile. Even the life guard helped me by postponing the hourly safety check (everybody out) so I could finish the mile. One guy from the shore yelled out to me, "Hey, you're walking out there."

I was now finishing fifth in our family play time. Now, I was not letting any of them win. They earned it and I was glad. So Jeri's way, of not letting them win but letting them earn it, was the better way.

Our favorite amusement park we took our family to several years in a row while they were still growing up was not the large amusement parks most children are brought up on. Ours was one that favored the children but also made room for the parents to be part of their growing up. It was called **Fantasy Farm** and was located in Ohio. Everything parents needed were there in a very safe environment with the adults enjoying most of the rides with their children except the restricted ones reserved for the children only.

 **A Birthday Party at Fantasy Farm....**on one annual visit, it was one of our children's birthday when we saw a sign at the "Three Bears House" which read "Have a

children's birthday party here. Just reserve it ahead of time and we will serve your cake free in the bears' house for your party. Minimum number is 10."

Well, we did not know to reserve the Bears House nor did we have 10 people with us. We were disappointed but using one of Jeri's ways of getting things, we went to the Bears' office and explained our situation. Our children would love to have a party here. The "bear" we talked to said "No" but since it was not reserved that day, they said they would see if they had a cake on hand. They came back and said they did have a cake but you need 10 people. You only have 5. I said no problem. Give us five minutes, we'll have our ten. We went to where there were families walking with their children. We waited until we saw a family of five that looked like they were primed for a children's party. We told them our situation and that we needed 5 more to join our family. They were delighted. We went back to the office, said we had 10. Can we have a party? They gave us the cake and we had an unexpected double family happy birthday in the Three Bears House.

Several years later, we happened to be passing Fantasy Farm which seemed closed and run down. We stopped and talked to who seemed to be the caretaker. Closed? We asked, why? He answered, "Our insurance was raised so high, we could no longer afford it." What a terrible loss to children and families.

Speaking about birthdays, children that is, our children loved their birthday celebrations. Jeri gave them the full course - sometimes a surprise party with friends, not unusual, of course, the traditional cake and ice cream and presents. If no presents, there would be no party. Presents were pretty conservative, nothing extra fancy and carefully chosen, each one receiving about the same priced gifts each birthday. We added one step – we always had a small wrapped gift for each of the two children whose birthday it was not.

We tried to be equally fair with all three, especially when they were younger and age didn't mean as much. At Christmas, we would generally have to give each the same number of gifts, no matter what the gifts or sizes were. Why? They would count their gifts and make us accountable if the number was not the same for each.

Christmas time, MS style

Heat being hard on Jeri, we overcame this with our own Winter Wonderland while living in our own Kent and Akron area. Christmas time was family fun time at its best. Into the hills (not mountains) our family went. Christmas meant church, of course, but it also meant picking out your own tree, cutting it down and hauling it home. Everyone had to help with the cutting. While Jeri could not do that, she enjoyed watching and helping pick out "our" tree. It was so muddy one time she insisted we wheel her to still pick out a tree. What mud? Those days, families would go together and even let their children help choose, cut down and help carry the tree back to their car. It seemed to be before the days of electric saws to cut and driving up to carry your tree. This was part of Christmas, especially if it was snowing and it let you wander around a winter wonderland picking out your own tree. These were the things that are remembered. Jeri would walk with us both ways until she no longer could. Everyone, including me, would make their choice of which one was to be our family tree. Who won? I certainly did not.

We, including Jeri, would go ice skating, outside of course. More fun it seemed. She could still do pretty well. The high hills near Akron which were mostly clear of trees were perfect for sledding – your choice of steepness or long slower rides downhill. The hills had hay bundles at the end of the ride for those who liked to stop as to those who liked to see how far they could go before crashing into the trees remaining.

What about Jeri? Are you kidding? Of course she was going to go sled riding. She chose the longest rides. She always went down with one of us either sitting up or laying on our backs. But how would she get back up the hill to come down again? Easy, whoever took her down pulled her back up.

We would do this often during the winter. Then we would head to our favorite spaghetti restaurant to eat and warm up.

Creating our own home entertainment for our children as they grew, Jeri and I had an idea – Welcome to our five bears family stories.

This idea came out of nowhere and our entire family of five helped create and use stories "about five bears and their friends." This was around 1975 in Kent. We knew what they liked to do which was reading and acting out stories they read. If it meant climbing a tree, they would get up on their bed and bounce up and down using their arms and legs. They enjoyed doing this because they not only followed the story but they also added their own thoughts in acting them out. They liked the idea and helped plot the stories with names, situations etc. The beauty of this was that they did most of it, creating many situations as they went along. With us helping them get started, they were able to come up with several separate stories with the same cast and adding to the cast as stories developed. One of their stories, "Grandma Lost in Space," is included under the section **JERI HOLDS UP MORE THAN JUST TRAINS.** The other three stories are shown below under **THE STORIES**.

When we were putting Jeri's book together, our children remembered our 5 Bears Stories and the fun they had acting them out. They always remembered "Peanut Butter Bear" getting into trouble. I found the stories that were written, four of them, and reviewed them to see it they would fit into Jeri's book. I decided that maybe they didn't belong and marked the folder they were in "Not used in Jeri's book." Shortly after that the children came back at me with, "Why not?" I reopened the bears' folder and pre-marked their folder by voiding "not used" with a "used" in Jeri's book

As is said above where one story was put, it was decided the other three stories would be put in this section. A new problem arose, our grandchildren wanted involved in this as they read the stories. We settled this with, since our three children were the creators, the grandchildren would type each story into the book. So be it.

The stories were often crudely but effectively (imagination) acted out with parts for everyone. As stories were repeated, our children began to add or change parts as they saw it. They became the story. The stories as taken when originally prepared are, with minor exceptions, copied as they were back in 1975.

The Five Bears – The series is centered around five bears (children) and a few of their friends (Oink, Oink - the pig, for example) and of course mama bear and papa bear. The favorite is Peanut Butter Bear who is always getting into trouble. His four brothers were Honey Bear, Watermelon Bear, Puff Wheat Bear and Banana Bear. They lived in the country and walked to school.

THE STORIES:

A Bear Christmas Tree

One day before Christmas, Papa Bear said to all the other bears, "Let's go out and cut down our Christmas tree." They all yelled, "Hey that's a great idea" so in the car they went. After driving way out into the country, they found a field of Christmas trees. Watermelon Bear said, "There they are."
Honey Bear ran to one tree and said, "I want this one." Banana Bear ran to another tree and said, "This is mine." Watermelon Bear said, "I want this pretty little one." Puff Wheat Bear said, "I want this great big giant one." Mama Bear said, "I want this bushy one." Papa Bear said, "Hey now, just a minute. We can only choose one tree and I like this one," he said as he pointed to a real tall bushy pine tree.
Honey Bear said, "I don't like that one." Banana Bear said, "I don't either and I'm not going to help cut it down." Puff Wheat Bear said, "Me neither."
Papa Bear said, "Stop that. We came out here to have fun and you are going to have fun whether you want it or not." Papa Bear took out his saw and said, "Ok, let's get to work. By the way, where's Peanut Butter Bear?" Everyone looked around and said, "I don't know." Papa Bear said, "Oh my, here we go again. That bear is missing again. Well we will look for him after we cut the tree down."
They all began sawing and pulling their tree down, then it began to fall. Papa Bear yelled, "Look out, here it comes."
As he yelled and looked up, out of the top of the tree came Peanut Butter Bear right down on top of Papa Bear and all the other bears and saying, "Here I am, Merry Christmas!" (Jenny)

Up the Tree

One day as the five bears were coming home from school, they came across a really tall tree. Watermelon Bear said "Wow, look at that tall tree. I bet no one could climb that!"

Honey Bear said "That's too big. I would be too scared."

Banana Bear said "me too. No one could be that brave."

"I could climb it!" spoke up Peanut Butter Bear.

"No you can't" said Banana Bear, "no one can, you're just saying that."

"Come on, let's go home." said Watermelon Bear.

"No, let me show you." said Peanut Butter Bear.

Watermelon Bear said "Peanut Butter, we have to get home. You know you can't climb it so let's go home before Mama and Papa wonder where we are." But Peanut Butter Bear started up the tree. Up, up, up he went. "Look at me."

"Gee, he's way up there" said Honey Bear, "he sure is brave. Look how high he is."

Up, up, up went Peanut Butter Bear until finally he reached the top. You could hardly see him.

"Look at me." he yelled again. "I did it. I'm at the top."

"That's great Peanut Butter, now come on down" said Puff Wheat Bear.

"Come on Peanut Butter, we have to get home" said Watermelon Bear, "come on down."

Peanut Butter Bear was looking down grinning and enjoying himself sitting on the top of that tree. Suddenly he stopped grinning.

"Come on Peanut Butter" said Watermelon Bear, "what's the matter?"

"I'm scared" said Peanut Butter, "I can't get down."

"Peanut Butter Bear, quit fooling around and get down here. We have to get home, it's getting dark" said Watermelon Bear.

"I'm not fooling around, I can't get down."

Just then Jami, a school friend of theirs came along. "What's going on? Wow, look at Peanut Butter Bear way up there!"

"Yes, but he can't get down." said Watermelon Bear.

"I can get him down" said Jami, "I'll go up and help him."

So up, up, up went Jami all the way to the top. "Come on Peanut Butter, I'll help you down."

So down, down, down they went all the way to the bottom where the other bears cheered them.

"Thanks Jami, I'll never climb that tree again," said Peanut Butter Bear. Then off they went. (Katie)

Asleep in the Right Place

One sunny day as the five bears made their way through the trees to school, Peanut Butter Bear thought it was too nice to go to school that day. It was late fall and winter was just about due to come in with all its snow and cold. Sitting under a tree seemed a lot more fun than sitting at a desk studying.

"Come on everyone, let's get to school before we are late" said Honey Bear.

"I'm not going" answered Peanut Butter Bear, "I'm going to sit right down here and spend the day."

"Peanut Butter, you can't do that, now come on. You're going to get in a lot of trouble if you don't come with us" said Puff Wheat Bear.

They all agreed and yelled at Peanut Butter. But Peanut Butter was not the kind that would scare or would listen if he had other ideas.

"I'll see you later" he said and down he went happily under a tree.

Off the other bears went to school. What will we tell the teacher? What will we tell papa bear? It looks like Peanut Butter Bear is in trouble again. Poor Peanut Butter Bear! Peanut Butter Bear fell asleep and slept all day. When he awoke, he could see nothing - his head was covered with snow. He blinked his eyes several times and the snow fell off. He still couldn't see very well - it was getting dark. He stood up, shook himself from the snow and looked around. All he could see was snow, lots of snow. Oh oh I think I'm in trouble, he thought. I better get home. But which way is home? Which way is school? Oh well, I'll just start walking.

Now how do I know where I'm walking? He leaned over, picked up some snow and made a snowball. He threw it at a tree. Smack! Right on the tree it landed. He made another snowball- smack, right on the next tree. I'll mark my trail with snowballs. He picked up more snow - swish, a miss. Swish, another miss. This time, he built a huge snowball - smack! Right on.

After what seemed like a long time to Peanut Butter Bear, he was wondering why he had not come across anything he would recognize. He kept throwing his snowballs until just when he was ready to let one loose, he saw the tree already had been hit by one! Oh oh. He knew what that meant. He was back where he started. He walked further but was now following the trees he had marked and now it was dark. He was hungry and a little bit scared. He wasn't very cold because he had his fur coat on. Well I can't do anything now until day time. I'll just make me a nice snow castle and go to sleep. He then made a huge pile of snow and dug it out just as he did sand castles when he went swimming. When he was finished, he crawled in and went to sleep.

A bell woke him up and he could hear voices or rather yelling. It sounded like a lot of children. Just then who comes crashing through his snow castle? Why it was Honey Bear.

Peanut Butter Bear stood up, looked around - he was in the middle of their playground!

"Come on Peanut Butter Bear, It's time for school," said Honey Bear.

"Time for school! I'm hungry!" said Peanut Butter.

"Too late" said Honey bear, "you missed supper and breakfast and wait until you get home!"

So off to school he went, ignoring the others who were asking him where he had been.

I wonder what we are having for lunch, he thought!
(Sierra and Sophia)

SINCE WE ARE AMONG STORY TALKING, LET US REVIEW OTHER TRAVEL AND HOME STORIES THAT CAME INTO PLAY AT DIFFERENT TIMES:

Falling in a lake in Wheeling, WV where at one time Jeri and Jack would use for ice skating.

One day at Oglebay Lake Park, Mommy (Jodi), Jenny, and I (Katie) were in a paddle boat, going around the lake. Gram, Kelly, and Grandpap were onshore watching us. When we came onto shore and were getting out of the boat the worker, who was helping us, helped us out of the boat. Mommy and Jenny went first and got out fine. Then I went to get out. He had his foot pressing down on the front of the boat and water was coming up. He instructed me to put my foot on the front of the boat where the water was, then jump up to the dock. Easy. I slipped off the front and went tumbling down into the water. My head went all the way under. They helped me out and got me a towel. At least I got to go swimming with the fishes! (Katie)

Grandpap's Bear Friend

On one family trip to Tennessee, the cabin that we were staying in, the adults went to bed before us. All of a sudden, Grandpap started telling stories. The only ones still up were Chloe, Sierra, Aunt Jami and Katie. Grandpap was drinking lemonade and saying that it made his head itchy. We pretended that there was a bear in the room. As Grandpap was talking we interrupted to tell him, "Pap Pap, you have a friend!" and pointed to the stuffed bear behind his head. Then he saw it with a surprised look on his face. He made his fingers into a finger gun and pointed at it saying, "Imma shoot it! BANG!" We all started laughing. At that point everyone went to bed laughing and we never heard the end of the story. (Katie)

Jeff falls into a hole in our new home

A "storm shelter" built of cement was laid next to the basement crawl space. A put together wood piece was placed loose over this storm shelter, which was next to the door to the kitchen. The shelter wooden cover was to be always covered so you could walk into the kitchen. One day a worker was working in the crawl space and had removed the wood cover over the shelter so he could get into the crawl space. He finished and left but forgot to place the wood cover over the shelter which was about 4' deep. Along about then, Jeff came home, came through the garage and into the kitchen. Well, not quite. Before he got to the kitchen entrance, he fell into the shelter. He didn't know the cover was not there. He bruised his leg enough to need medical attention. We filed a claim with our insurance company which in turn wrote back to us with a question, which was, "Where was Jeff when he fell into the hole?" I wrote back and said "right over it." (Sierra)

Kelly's "Honesty"

This is one about Kelly. She was 9 years old when talking with her, I said, "Kelly, you're the nicest girl I ever saw." Kelly, hesitated and then said, "I think you're mistaking me for someone else."

Going through Jeri's archives recently, I found a rough document written by Jeri dated shortly after she began working at Steubenville. She had listed several departments that were near her office. For each department, she wrote the name or title of the one in charge, obviously so she would be able to address them accordingly. The list consisted of seven offices. The first office was "Office of the President." The last was listed "Office of Picnic Director – Jack." Why that little rascal!

On the other side, I too had written something. On my office desk calendar, I had filled in my July 27, 1963 schedule which read:

10:00 a.m. Wedding – (mine)
11:00 a.m. Court House – Divorce Office
12:00 p.m. Tennis
4:30 p.m. Bachelor Party - "Welcome Back"

NOW, BACK TO THE REAL BOOK WITH JERI and FAMILY "MOVING ON" THE HARD WAY.

As time moved on, a couple of incidents happened. One, Jeri was soon to be in a wheelchair. Second, we had not planned on moving. We began looking all over the area for a house accessible to a wheelchair. In a hilly area like Kent, there seemed to be none to be found. As it turned out, we eventually ended up moving to Bowling Green (BG) Ohio to accept a position with Bowling Green State University (BGSU). We had lived in Kent for over 18 years.

We continued this Christmas time spirit on into Bowling Green. The only thing missing and we could not bring with us were our sled riding hills. We did find one decent hill to sled ride on to keep our "record" intact.

Between 1981 and 1984, we began our ongoing move to BG. We first put our Kent house up for sale. This became a story in itself. Searching for a decent family home, we found no place to stay. Prices were high for apartments. College students and faculty were already in place. There was nothing appropriate available. Having a dog did not help matters and neither did not selling our house yet. Home ownership interest was at 19% as we tried to sell. It took two and a half years to do so.

We were able to find what really wasn't a house or fully qualified "apartments" – a few apparent rebuilt rooms acting as apartments separated by walls. Again, we had little choice.

We decide to separate our family "briefly." Jeri and Jodi would stay in Kent to sell our home and Jodi would also stay in high school there and remain on the swim team. Jeri would be able to stay with her Girl Scouts a little longer. I was to take Jami and Jeff to BG with me.

On September 14, 1981, I took Jami and Jeff to start school at St. Al's in BG and at the same time, I started work at BGSU. They were already two weeks late starting in a new school. Later the teachers told us how exciting each class was when told they were getting a new student, that they were anxious for them to come to meet them. So that part worked well.

The other part to our plan was that Jeri and Jodi would stay in Kent until we could find a real apartment - and it had to allow a dog. We commuted to Kent evey week. Sometimes Jeri would come back with us to help Jami and Jeff in school and clean our "outpost" the best she could. It was difficult for her to do this especially cleaning because she was now limping a bit more. She would serve our meals on a card table. We were girl scouts you know.

It took four months to find a house to rent and would allow a dog. It was small so a little crowded. Water started leaking through the roof to a room but pots and pans worked pretty well. Jodi called it our Dog House. The best part we were once again all together. It was January 1982. It would be 1984 before we moved into our new home.

We were now at least able to begin planning our new stay which including designing a new home for our so called "handicapped" ichiban (meaning number one – the best) member of our family and role model to many, aka Jeri. Our short stay in our new addition 7 level home did not go to waste. From that experience,

Jeri began designing our new home in BG. As part of her "Home Economics" college classes, she learned quite a lot about this designing.

We soon found a nice half acre lot available on the western part of BG facing a wide open flat area with only a few houses. Now we wait. Jeri was to design our home and guess who was suppose to sell our Kent home. Now remember, it only took me two and one/half years to do so.

While waiting for me to sell our Kent house, we still had to make our weekly two-hour trip back and forth between Kent and BG. Now, we had five of us in our station wagon to make the trip, plus one dog. Actually the kids liked this - they could keep their friends in both places. Jeff's best friend in Kent missed Jeff so much he said if he had enough money to buy our house in Kent, he would buy it and make us stay there. To make matters a little worse, we found out later that Jodi, who was a sophomore on Kent Roosevelt's high school swim team and doing very good, "had" to leave with us to move to BG. After leaving, her swimming points were counted towards a letter. She was one point short of earning a letter. No letter was awarded.

Continuing our weekly visit to Kent, it seemed to get easier each time. As mentioned earlier, when we arrived, we would find our house all lit up with neighborhood kids inside waiting for our kids. What a nice way to return home.

We had a routine of how long of a drive it would take and then revert back to our original way of being in Kent. We would see our friends, we would get to church and we would eat at our favorite two restaurants. We had a nice Chevrolet station wagon and by using the Ohio Turnpike, we could make the trip in two hours. On one trip, I couldn't figure out why all the big trailer trucks were blowing their horn at me each time one would pass. I thought I was driving ok. Jeff was riding in the third seat. A truck behind us was starting to pass. Jeff was giving (new to me) to the driver an up and down arm movement which the driver responded with a few honks on his horn. Why that big rascal!

We still made the most of this. One weekend just before Christmas on our way back to BG, we stopped at a small mall in Kent at a large discount store. I'm not sure what I was after but it was not a Christmas tree. As I was leaving the store, I noticed one pretty fully decorated lighted Christmas tree, about three feet tall. I asked a sales girl, "How much were these trees?" She said, "It is the only one left, there aren't any more." I asked her, "How much for that one?" "Oh, I can't sell you that one. It's for display purposes only." "May I talk with your manager?" He came over and I asked him, "How much would he charge me for the tree as is?" He said, "It would certainly help me. I would not have to take all the decorations off to put it away." He gave me a price. "Sold" I said and picked it up as was, paid the cashier and walked out the store carrying this very pretty Christmas tree high in the air with one arm and waving it to Jeri and the kids in the car. This was exciting. It made our Christmas!

Now the three kids all became good swimmers so I never tested them. Jeff finally started beating me in tennis and I had promise if any of them beat me in tennis, I would quit. Jeff was the first and I quit. Jami was on Bowling Green High School's tennis and basketball teams while Jeff was on his grade school basketball and football teams. By high school, he was playing the drums real well. Jeri and I had a family we really loved and were so proud of.

BG's high school track field was near the tennis courts which Jami and I had just finished playing. I asked Jami if she would race me around the track. She said "sure." There was not a doubt in my mind that I could not beat her. Later, she told me there was never a doubt in her mind that she could not beat me. So we raced. So I was left standing at the starting gate. I refused to discuss it thereafter.

In BG, we carried on many of our traditions. Of course, there were no real hills in BG. What do you do here in winter? No outside ice skating? No long hills to sled ride? Certainly there had to be Christmas tree fields to cut our tree down! Ah. We found the perfect one about five miles east of BG. The owner we got to know and with a Santa Clause beard he made our cutting trips realistic. Our first trip to BG's wonderland tree forest found our family of five scouting for several trees. Jeri, with help in her wheelchair, went right up the path to find her tree.

Still trying to keep up with our family in BG, our children were coming into their own (whatever that meant) while we were still playing tag with them. One summer weekend, they had reservations to go to a "Yogi Bear's Jellystone Campground." They politely asked us if we wanted to go with them. When we showed interest – I should say Jeri showed interest, while I was debating – they said come with us, you will not have to stay in a tent. We will take you to a motel. Each day we will bring you back to the campgrounds. So we went camping a new way – in a motel. We stayed there twice but it seemed a lot of trouble making someone come and get us every day.

Jack got stuck in our tent! – When we learned that a spare tent was available, we took it. Our kids put the tent up for us. Then the campfire ritual of marshmallows etc was on. Jeri and I were ready for bed on a blanket covered grassy hard spot, the ground. We were easily able to get Jeri out of her green travel wheelchair and into our tent. She actually was enjoying this. I was next and put myself to bed next to Jeri. She was smiling, I was worn out. The kids pulled the tent flaps together – whoops, I mean a two piece screen that went together with a zipper. How times change, even camping.

It was around four in the morning when I woke up and saw a cold mist outside our tent. Jeri was sleeping away in dreamland. I was standing up in dreamland trying to figure out how to get out of the tent to at least walk around and do what I came out for. The zipper was all the way down, or was it up? Neither way worked. I was stuck in the tent. I dare not cry for help, it was too quiet. Was there a lock on this zipper? Never mind, I gave up and joined Jeri once more, not to sleep but to wait to be released. As our other campers awoke and walked out of their tents, they had early morning entertainment - me being released from our tent. This was probably my last time sleeping in a tent. Jeri? Probably not. Actually we did have a good time and were glad to rough it once again.

After selling our Kent home, Jeri prepared the design well for our new home and worked with bids and potential builders

who were interested in building Jeri's new design. The house was built her way.

We moved into our new home and finished painting all the wood around all the windows. Everyone helped with the painting. Then we purchased new beds so each of the children would have one for their own new bedroom. It was a 4-room one level open space house with wide hallways and no carpeting for Jeri and her new electric wheelchair. Our new home was built on our half acre lot we purchased as mentioned facing open space to the west where you could see "forever."

Jeri became confined to a wheelchair in 1984, the year we moved into our new home. She never walked in it.

Later, Jeri and I designed a real fireplace. We had a company install the inner metal wood burning unit while we took care of framing it with wood and putting dry wall and metal fencing to hold cement. We purchased flat sided heavy stones to be used to form the outside of the fireplace. Jeri would instruct me from her wheelchair where she wanted the stones to be and I would place each stone on the floor how she wanted the design to be. The rest was easy. Take each stone, coat it with cement and put it where the design showed. We finished it off with flat square stones raised above the floor for sitting around the fireplace. Add one piece of red wood to form the mantel and "we did it." Jeri always loved just sitting around a fireplace, poking the wood to keep it going and just dreaming a little.

1998 A Year to Move Once Again – this we did from Jeri's designed home to a condo exactly one mile away. Now whose idea was this? I would guess it was Jeri's but it was probably me. Actually it was neither one. We learned that our Jami and her husband were thinking of getting a larger home because of now having two children and also to a place out a bit from town and with a nice home and yard. Hey, that fit our home. Jeri agreed and since we were the only ones in our home now, perhaps we can sell it to Jami and Craig and move ourselves into a condo. Everyone agreed. So Jeri and I began our look for a new condo. It sounded easy but after some visits, finding high prices and, worse yet, nothing that even came close that Jeri with MS could ever manage was ever found. So anyone have any suggestions? For a few minutes no suggestions. But wait, if one's smart, they would never believe our next move. But then, we always did do some funny "stupid" things. It went like this:

Jeri and I had just finished looking at a beautiful new condo waiting to be sold to us (per seller). It would have been a terrible mistake to buy it, not because it seemed overprice but rather it was unfit for anyone with MS or whatever. The seller assured us that they could make it right for Jeri. Yea! How much? Never mind, we walked away discouraged without any more leads or ideas. As we began heading for our home, we passed a sign on the road that read new condos to be built on this site. Our four eyes met and Jeri's "let's" hit me squarely. We decided to check this out. We walked into a small temporary office near the sign and met the only person sitting at a desk. Are you the one we can talk to about the new condos to be built? Just then a worker walked in who was apparently in charge of the construction that had just started. He introduced himself and inquired if we had any questions. He saw Jeri in her wheelchair who naturally gave him a big smile. He said wait right here, I'll be right back. Within minutes he came back with blueprints of the new condos and began showing us what they would look like. While showing Jeri he pointed to one drawing showing a condo and said, "This is the one I want Jeri to have." Jeri shook her head yes. I agreed. We agreed to buy it then. He knew Jeri would need certain changes, like wider doors, no steps, room to use a wheelchair (in bathroom for example) etc. We never had to tell him much as to what Jeri needed. He knew and eventually changes were made as construction was being done. Our condo was just getting started so there was not much to see yet. Can you imagine buying a house not built yet and not even having a finished drawing yet! Jeri and I signed a "Settlement Date" March 2, 1998. We were never disappointed and Jami and Craig got our house.

Interesting, when our new found construction man, whom we never knew before, began adjusting the construction for Jeri in OUR condo, the other three condos in our one building was being built as originally planned. When new potential buyers heard about Jeri's adjustments such as no front door step and the veranda would not have a step down, they wanted their condos to be the same as Jeri in this respect. The contractor made these adjustments in new condos being built.

Now that we settled in our own home, where did we go from there? That was easy. The three children soon married, we continued with Avon and before long a string of seven grandchildren took the stage, all eventually idolizing Jeri. The only other missing change was the MS refused to give in. So did we. The only other major change was that we would attack MS by way of traveling by car early on and eventually around two countries by train 23 different times. Not bad for someone in a wheelchair and calling the "shots."

TRAVELING

One custom Jeri and I learned quickly that does wonders in traveling was do not use your last name in introductions! Surprise, then listen: We are not talking legal reasons, being unfriendly etc. Now I would say most people, when introducing themselves use full names and vice versa. That's a very correct thing to do, most of the time that is. In traveling and meeting people you don't know, we found that new friends have a hard time remembering your name. We would simply say, we are "Jeri and Jack" or "Jack and Jeri." This always seemed to go over well. You will not remember too many names but a Mary and Bill are pretty easy to remember. Isn't that the idea? Furthermore, if one is older or whatever and they give you their first names, now you know what to call them. Full name, addresses etc can come later. On trains you may sometimes only meet passengers once. Others, we have seen many people leaving the train after meeting someone earlier asking, "Can you give me your full name and address. We would like to keep in touch." Great, you now have a real friend.

BEFORE MS

The traveling herein is mostly with Jeri's parents and brother. I suppose you could say they were chaperoning us. I think Jeri and I both did not need a chaperon, we were a bit naïve (or was it me) and very respected and trusting WITH each other. I think we were both thinking marriage. I know I was concerned she might tell me no marriage.

Jeri and I began traveling together long before our marriage. I would say about four years before. Broken down, it was about one year as new friends, then one year as good friends, (not sure if we were dating or what but we were seeing a lot of each other at the College and at our office picnics) and then two good  years of unofficial dating (dating, not engaged) and traveling with her family. I didn't think we were ever engaged, but our children informed me that Jeri had an engagement ring. Just recently, I found a note in Jeri's "Private Stock" box that read under December 25, 1962 "Jeri and Jack engagement." So I guess we were engaged. Wonder why she never told me?

Jeri was not exactly new at traveling. She had gone with her high school senior class to Washington, DC and New York City. Our traveling included mostly with her family, including her younger brother, on many car trips. We visited New York City, DC and other places in the summer and then in the fall, drove to see the colors in Virginia and wherever fall was decorated with color leaves.

One trip west we took was kind of an unexpected surprise. It was in 1962 when I received a grant to attend the University of Omaha for a week to take part in an accounting class for college business managers. It was a pretty nice cash award that I talked to Jeri about why don't you and family come with me. The grant covered more than I would need so I could pay all expenses. Jeri liked the idea so we did it. I went out to Omaha by bus and a week later they would come to pick me up in Omaha. It turned into a great vacation taking us in the west to see a rodeo, Yellowstone, black bears and everything the West had to offer. Jeri's dad did the driving in their car. When they pulled up to take me aboard, I didn't step up into the car, I stepped down into it. The car was so packed down with clothes and five of us that the step runners to get into the car almost touched the ground. It was this way our whole time — it worked somehow. No problems.

Where there were mountain trails to follow, Jeri and I were "allowed" to take hikes up the trails by ourselves. Well, I guess we were allowed. We didn't ask. On one trail, we found a beautiful view of mountains and rolling valleys in the distance that had few trees and were very barren. We apparently were pretty high up. There were patches of snow in the far distance. There was no one in sight for as far as we could see. One tiny little winding trail of a road, no cars, no animals, just a very serene and quiet view, a delightful spot for our first kiss.

Climbing Pikes Peak in Colorado in 1962 by way of their "Cog Railroad," was exciting and interesting. This peak was reported to be 14,110 feet high. The cars were pushed up the mountain by cog wheeled engines. Coming back down the engines were in front of the cars. It didn't take Jeri long to say we are all going up to the top and we climbed aboard the next car going up. Half way up the cog track, the driver discovered a problem and decided they would have to go back down. Their brakes would not work. No one was to get off as the car pulled into a siding and waited for another car to come to our rescue. When the other car made its slow trip up to us, both cars were hooked together. We did go back down – backwards - using the other car's brakes. We eventually made it up to the summit – the second try - and were awarded a button which said I MADE IT PIKES PEAK alt.14,110 ft.

I wonder if these family trips had anything to do with our marriage. A little before our wedding, I drove Jeri, her brother and her mom on a New England and Cape Cod vacation. The next time to Cape Cod, Jeri and I went alone!

BEFORE MS VS WITH MS – ESTABLISHING A DATE IS NOT NEEDED NOR IS IT POSSIBLE. IT

IS ALSO NEAR IMPOSSIBLE TO SEPARATE MS INTO TWO TIME PERIODS. BUT WAIT – Before MS, you live a certain life. After MS, you live a certain different life. Both ways are important to acknowledge! Let us try.

"Before MS" was an exciting time for Jeri and me and lasted about 20 years free from MS (at least by knowledge). Creating and finding a family, handling the ups and downs as a team etc was pretty normal. We lived a great "Before MS", had no idea of our future and took care of our present with a lot of enjoyment even when Jeri reached for her hot pepper. As mentioned we knew ahead of time that Jeri was going to face a major medical problem. I should say we were going to face a major medical problem. Strange, that did not bother us one iota.

As time moved on and the first indication of our problem to face showed up secretly over a period of a long presence, we really didn't have time to be concerned. It was coming anyway.

Entering the age of "After MS"

Whatever it was affecting Jeri moving her legs etc, no common medical name was known at that time. Possible early signs were in her eyes as a teenager (around 1960) and later when her walking problems (around 1974 or so) took her to see several specialists with no results. Nothing was wrong with Jeri! As mentioned earlier under **JERI'S "MEDICAL CAREER"** our visit to the Cleveland Clinic in 1978 established a starting point for us including calling Jeri's illness (I don't think she was ill) or whatever it was to be, MS! For conversational and other purposes, we then used 31 years as an official identity of how long Jeri had MS. (1978-2009). Actually with our "unofficial" research with Jeri's MS, I think we can show several studies of her having MS several years before our official date. However this is no longer needed. We will leave the official date as is.

Heck, the many years "After MS" were just as exciting. A little different perhaps but we did exciting things together and with our family. What MS? Just remember, we could never forget MS – it was the distractions from MS that worked in our favor!

Now, we are not questioning the name MS or when a reasonable date is used to help identify it – it served our purpose for 31 years. I would suspect researches would rather have more specific findings to identify what this was and when did it happen. I also still feel the researchers, wherever they are would have gained a more practical search from someone like Jeri. She responded they did not. Amen.

As mentioned earlier, there were the many times before and after MS when we went roller and ice skating, rarely falling. I would often ask her why she was not skating on her left foot. I kind of assumed she was tired lifting her left foot. I guess that made sense at the time. But wait. Was it MS causing this? Both of these instances seemed like it was MS – it also gave us the clue that her MS started first in her left leg. It continued around her body ending last when her right arm gave out.

Another situation about Jeri was her preferring to listen to the radio rather than watch TV. Jeri still rarely used her glasses even on her computer. As mentioned, she loved going to BGSU's football, basketball and hockey. She seemed to watch very well. Now hockey was a hard sport to follow but she did well. When we did not attend in person, we would listen on the radio. To throw in another remark, the three sports Jeri loved to go to usually had no seating for wheelchairs. Again, we were once more ahead of our times. But watch this: One day Jeri and I were coming out of a bakery when we ran into the basketball coach. We didn't know him, he didn't know us. He was wearing a basketball jacket. I asked him if he was BGSU's basketball coach. He replied that he was. I decided to ask him a question. I explained that Jeri loved seeing the basketball games but there really was no place to put her being in a wheelchair. He kind of jumped to that question. He kindly said, "The next time you bring Jeri to our basketball game, you call me ahead of time. I'll find a place for her!"

These are just interesting discussions. I was glad to learn that her tennis (prior subject she was not able to do) and skating problems were not her fault.

AFTER MS

Traveling with MS sounds like you brought someone along you didn't like. Well, Jeri certainly didn't like MS but was unable to leave it home. It did sound terrible when someone would say "I have MS." It sounded a little better when Jeri would say, "I have MS but it's not stopping me doing what I want to do." Jeri would feel better and whoever she told this to would feel relaxed with her, even then carry on a normal conversation with her. Jeri would ask them how they were doing. Everyone has ailments to talk about and Jeri was a self made good listener. Her smile would end any further questions about MS. In

217

her own way, Jeri was always helping someone else. Her home nursing care by nurses often included their telling Jeri problems they had. Jeri's listening was a blessing to them. Sometimes on the train, I would leave Jeri by herself for a spell and when I would return, I would find her talking to someone who sat down with her. Jeri would listen, ending with a gentle smile and I think they would always feel better. The attendants were always good with Jeri and often would sit with her. They generally would receive complaints from passengers – not from Jeri. She belonged on the train with or without MS.

Our trips with the MS just became more extensive as time moved on. With her saying "let's go," we would never quit. As we moved into our MS days, we learned that we would have to count on ourselves more. We began more of our own entertaining. Wheelchairs made it unreasonable for us to do things, especially with other people. We tried never to encroach on their having fun. So we would usually be unable to do a lot of normal things like bowling, tennis, skating, socializing etc. Jeri had been a very good dancer. We still could do this with her in her wheelchair. This really didn't bother us. We were together and it became amazing of the new activities that we could and would do. With MS now, we were traveling MS style, in a wheelchair. We began calling all traveling "adventures" – each wheelchair trip was an adventure no matter how short or how far we went. We still went to movies, attended sporting events, went swimming etc. Swimming - try getting a wheelchair through the sand to the actual water on an ocean beach. We did this in California. We got Jeri to the water - what more could you expect? Swimming at home in our condo pool or area pools helped Jeri a lot. Early on, she would be able to swim herself, actually scaring people who watched her because she could stay under water a long time. Later, when her legs were getting the full treatment of MS, the water buoyancy would help her to walk. Since heat was so devastating to MS, Jeri always did better in fairly cold water.

Casinos were no problem. All money is good, no matter who uses it. The few times we visited a casino, Jeri liked it but not enough to go often. I don't know whether it was a lot of fun or not. Jeri would limit me to $5.00. She always won more that she used.

Hotel entrances - When we would stay at an expensive hotel, especially for several days, we often found the main entrance not accessible for wheelchairs. Remember, "handicapped" laws were yet to be "invented." We would be directed to some side entrance by a doorman. The entrance would lead us to "somewhere" in the back confines of the main floor. We would locate the lobby to register but future entrances required us to find our own elevator. One nice thing, I didn't have to tip the doorman each time.

Handicapped (I wish there were a better name) people actually helped "normal" (that's not a good name either) people in unexpected ways. I know Jeri felt normal in a lot of things she did. Riding a train can't be anything but normal! Handicapped – watching Jeri beat a computer almost every time in ping pong was even above being normal. Ha!

Curb cuts - we discovered that in downtown New York City, the curb cuts were the favorite way of crossing the streets easily. Watching the crowds on a busy sidewalk, as people neared a street to cross, they would all form towards the corner where the cuts were, cross the street and up the cut on the other side.

They would do this without breaking a stride and seemingly not even looking down. What a strange blessing! They loved them and I'm glad because they were easier for EVERYONE. They would even move over a little to allow us to walk along side of them. Now the opposite side was when some in the general public would take a little unfair advantage of the situation and we would have to wait and break into the line when we could. We were not bothered with their using curb cuts. It was one more sign of how money used for handicapped people was also available for those not handicapped. In other words, all persons using these curb cuts owe their thanks to handicapped people!

This next little episode I caught in an article which covered a parade of floats and bands in California. Crowds were large and it was difficult to get a good position to watch. One reporter saw a man and lady watching the parade in the front row in their wheelchairs. He interviewed them and said that was a good idea. Then they told him they were not their wheelchairs that they were using them to get to the front row to see. The reporter wrote that this was clever of them. My My Clever??

On the trains, a similar approach is used. When we would see someone in a wheelchair waiting at a station, we would introduce ourselves because we thought we would see them aboard and this was a good time to meet them. However, many times we would see them, once aboard, walking through the train, no problems at all. They found a way to board early to get the best seat and not to have to walk a long platform to get to their car. Now, with health problems, this would seem to be fine, but when you saw one leave the wheelchair, climb the steps, sometimes to go upstairs, and walk through a fast moving train, you would wonder.

As mentioned before, Jeri was not sick. She had MS. Rarely was she sick from other reasons. Her vitals always seemed normal. Her mentality and hearing were fine. Did she have MS when she had Jodi? If so, it never affected either. Doctors rarely gave her a prescription for anything. She was in good health. People were always surprised as she grew older that her skin and body stayed so young looking. (Maybe that was because she used Avon and I washed the dishes!!).
Is this all normal for those with MS? I don't remember reading anything reference this in any research. So is there any connection when people say to someone with MS, "But you look so good!" Perhaps, we should take this as a real compliment.

In Jeri's life, something was always happening

One day I received a call from someone in Connecticut. The girl asked "if this was where Jeri lived?" "Yes." She then said, "My mother also has MS and doesn't get around very much and when she heard about Jeri and how Jeri travels and is so active in trying and doing things, she became so excited that she wanted me to call and tell Jeri that she was her role model." Stunned, I was slow to thank her. I said, "I will gladly tell Jeri who will be pleasantly surprised and grateful."

A LITTLE TOUCH OF RELIGION – always unexpected but not unwelcome.

It seemed most of our touches of religion occurred while we were traveling, hence traveling is where we show it.

An early exposure of this occurred when Jeri became confined to a wheelchair. When communion would be distributed, we would wheel Jeri up to the altar to receive it. I didn't like the idea of squeezing Jeri into a crowd of people in line or making them wait for us. We decided to watch Mass from the back or side. The ushers liked this and would tell us that they would let the priest know to have communion taken back to Jeri. However, we soon found the ushers would forget Jeri. Now, it's too late for communion. One trip into Canada at a church I forget which, the priest, after listening to our story asked, "Why don't you take the communion to Jeri?" So, our first attempt to change the rules of the Catholic Church, we tried it. Jeri and I both liked the idea. I found myself actually honored to take Holy Communion to Jeri.

Now, about a priest or lay person distributing Holy Communion from the altar, there was rarely a problem, many funny looks perhaps but I was always given the communion by holding my hands out and saying, "I need another one." Now we continued our new method all over the US and Canada. One Sunday in Las Vegas, the lay distributor refused to give me Jeri's. He distributed it himself to her. This was fine. I would certainly not argue over who gives it. However, after the Mass, I told the lay distributor that he was the first time any one refused me communion to take to Jeri. I was just curious as to why he refused? He said proudly, "Oh, the Pope would not like me doing that." Good point. I thanked him and moved on. I didn't know he "knew" the Pope.

There was one other time this happened - it has never happen since. While in DC, we went to visit the Basilica of the National Shrine of the Immaculate Conception and stayed there for Mass. Yes, at communion I asked for an extra one. This time it was a priest who refused. I explained she was in a wheelchair. "I will follow you," he said. Well Jeri was way in the back of the church. We found her. I was curious but I did not question him. He didn't question me either.

Jeri is introduced to the Bishop of Wheeling

I grew up in Wheeling with a close school friend and neighbor. When we graduated from high school, he left to become a priest and I went to meet Jeri 13 years later. Bernard Schmitt was his name and in 1989, Fr. Schmitt became Bishop of Wheeling. A few years later, this title became Bishop of Wheeling-Charleston.

Shortly after he became Bishop, Jeri and I were in Wheeling and stopped to see him. I wanted him to meet Jeri and vice versa. They became instant friends to the point he insisted that every time we were in Wheeling, we were to visit him. This we did several times even when his secretaries would try to stop us because he was very busy and we had no appointment scheduled. Sometimes he heard us come in and would come out. Sometimes we said just tell him Jeri and Jack are here. It worked every time.

With Jeri already advanced with MS, Bishop Schmitt become all the more liking to see her because he was always impressed with her and how she was doing so great.

On some visits we had other family members with us. One time we had Jeri's mom, another time we had our Jami and, watch this, we had Jodi with us who was carrying yet to be born Katie. The Bishop would always give us his blessing. This time he not only blessed Jodi but also blessed her baby waiting to be born, Katie. That was a pleasant surprise.

RAIN IN HALIFAX...... Jeri and I had visited Halifax, Canada several times by train. It was at Saint Mary's Basilica where we would visit often.

Jeri's favorite picture of "Mary" was among several pictures hanging on the walls of the church. I never knew why she chose our Lady of Guadalupe as her favorite. At the same time, she lit a candle under the picture, almost giving the church a little fire practice as she held the lighted match to light the candle.

Being rather dark because there were no services on, I came within inches of wheeling Jeri right over a step I didn't see half way up the aisle as we were leaving. The aisle we entered the church though had no steps. Apparently when the church was built on this very steep hill, one floor was built ok but the other side was uneven. Apparently, they had put in a step to even the floor which I did not see until the last second. A close call spelt dangerous.

On another visit to Halifax we planned one evening to go back to the Basilica the next day to go to the 12:15 pm Mass. Our hotel was on a hill away from the church. That evening it was raining pretty hard. There was a steady rain all night.

On the morning when we awoke and found it still raining, I told Jeri, "no problem, the rain should stop by the time we have to leave."

Midmorning, it is still pouring. 10 am, still raining. We dressed for church. 11 am raining hard. I told Jeri, "If it doesn't stop by noon, we cannot go." We had no rain gear. Umbrellas are worthless with a wheelchair, besides we never carried one with us. Noon, we hear the church bells ringing. Rain continues. We are 15 minutes from the church.

Jeri said, "Go."
I said, "What?"
Jeri said, "Go."
I said, "Jeri. I can't let you get soaked that way."
Jeri said, "Go!"
I said, "OK, out we go."

Four steps into the pouring rain - it stopped!

Ten minutes to go by way of down a steep hill, then over a block and a very steep hill to the church. We arrived just as the priest came out to begin Mass. (Chloe)

Still in Halifax – was the Parish Priest sleeping during the Mass while the preaching was being done? .... it sure looked like it. Here's the situation. On another trip to Halifax, Jeri and I were at another noon Mass. By now we knew this priest fairly well getting to know him when in Halifax. At this Mass, we happened to get a pew on the other side of the church with a large pillar blocking us out from where he was sitting during the preaching part. I could see him and he had his head down low. I don't think he could see Jeri. All of a sudden, he lifted his head and looked straight over at Jeri. Did he see Jeri? I thought maybe he did, it looked that way but he didn't even know we were there. When the Mass resumed, he went to the altar to prepare giving communion to the people. Several distributers were to also distribute the communion. The priest, however, kind of beat the others to get to the people. He went straight to Jeri and gave her communion first!

This was one of Jeri's and my favorites.... While our three children were growing up, somewhere along the way, they developed a liking and an association with a near saint called Blessed Kateri Tekakwitha. She was an Indian girl born in New York many years ago and was converted to Christianity and sustained a difficult life. She was recognized as being beatified in the Roman Catholic Church. It seemed we could never find her recognized with her picture hanging up anywhere we went, in the US or Canada. On our only trip to Prince Rupert in western Canada where we spent a week there, one day Jeri and I were taking a walk around town and decided to stop in to just introduce ourselves to the parish priest. The receptionist directed us to his office and told us to wait there. We sat down. Looking up at the wall, it seemed impossible. There was a picture of Kateri Tekakwitha!

Nearly being thrown out of Church.......... now this one was unexpected and unwelcome. In Winnipeg, Canada waiting to catch our train on a Sunday to Churchill, we decided to find a Catholic Church to go to Mass. We found a very large one but we had a hard time finding a way inside, plenty of steps, but we could not find a handicap entrance. After circling the Church, we found an entrance to the Church that I was able to get the wheelchair through and then we found where the Mass was being said. No one offered to help.

Our normal place to watch Mass, as mentioned, was to stay near the back in the middle aisle where I would sit in the end seat and Jeri would be right next to me. It never failed. Well, until now. An usher came over and said we could not stay there, there was a handicapped area up front (I never did see it). I said we usually stayed in a church where Jeri could be out of the way and could see. We did not want to attract attention. People in wheelchairs, making their way up front always drew a lot of curious attention, per our experience. The usher said, "I'm not asking you to go, I'm telling you to go." WOW! Now that bothered us. We said, ok, we will stand over on the side. He said, "You can't stand there because there's a procession coming through there." Along came another usher and joined in, "You can't stand there because the Fire Marshall doesn't allow it. You have to go up to the handicapped section." I saw other people standing in the back so I said ok we will stand in the back. One more word from an usher and we would have left. We stood in the back which was crowded with people standing. By then, I think we had the church audience nervous. They could easily see and hear what was going on. No one would look up at us and they seemed to be in "serious prayer." We stayed put in the back, though Jeri could not see. I got Jeri communion without any problem to take back to her when finally a lady came over and apologized for what happened. I thanked her. By the way, the so called procession was just the priest and a couple of servers and assistants making their way to the altar!

Interesting, when we arrived in Churchill, we happened to meet two women tourists there one being from Winnipeg. In that case I repeated what had just happened to Jeri and me in Winnipeg not only trying to find a means to get into the church in a wheelchair but also to hear Mass. The one lady said, "Oh we never go to that Church. We never liked it. We go to another Catholic Church near the one you went to."

Another interesting story about the ladies was that I sent a Christmas card to each with pictures we had taken with them and telling them we had a nice time meeting and being with them. The one living in Winnipeg returned a Christmas card saying, "Hilda and I had a real good time too." She also said, "Yes. Churchill is special."

So where were we wrong? We have no problems with handicapped seating whether in a church, a football stadium, how about a parade? A lot of facilities do not have handicapped facilities but, if they can, will try to find a place for you, like in a restaurant. Losing one's independence is, like MS itself, devastating. Jeri's car license, her last valued proof that she belongs, was taken from her. So what's left for handicapped persons? Independence. Offer help if you will but do not demand it. It will work. Let the person themselves decide!

How to handle some of our religious concerns - Jeri, just out of high school, told this one about asking our favorite priest, Fr. Joe at Steubie U. how was she suppose to handle going to Mass on one travel trip when she found herself without a hat to wear? (This was the time when women were to wear hats in a Catholic Church). Fr. Joe answered her question with a question. "Which was better, not going to Church or going to Church the way you were? She knew that one quickly and often applied it to other cases.

In my case, when we brought Jeri home from Rehab loaded down with equipment on her, a priest said to me, well if Jeri can't go to Mass, you can still go. I answered that one without pausing. Father, if Jeri can't go to Mass I don't go either. We are one!

Not knowing what to do? Follow the children

At church services, as mentioned, we usually tried to sit in the back with Jeri in the aisle and me next to her in a pew. Church traditions seem now to call for greeting your neighbor by shaking hands or whatever way you decide. Unfortunately and too often, people would miss introducing themselves to Jeri. Was it the wheelchair and they did not know how to greet Jeri? Probably in most cases or because she was in the aisle or possibly being down so low, people shaking hands with others (always standing) would overlook her. So how would you introduce yourself to Jeri? Let's see how a 12 year old boy would do it?

With Jeri sitting quietly waiting for someone to introduce themselves she would just sit with a smile on and wait.

I happened to watch a couple in front of us, who shook my hand, and noticed they had their son with them. When the parents (I assumed), were done shaking hands with people in front and rear of them but not Jeri, they sat down. Still watching the boy, for some unknown reason (we did not know the family), he stood up and climbed past his parents into the aisle. He turned towards Jeri, held out his hand and touched Jeri's arm. Her smile was her thank you. He turned around, reentered his pew, climbed past his parents to sit down. Just before he sat down, I kind of motioned him to get his attention. He looked at me and I gave him a "thumbs up" and lightly moved my lips with a "Good Job." He knew what I meant and smiled, then sat down.

Now, you know what to do.

Coffee breaks, with our own Pastor, Fr. Ed

In Bowling Green, while we were registered at St. Al's, we often went to Mass at the University St. Toms. St. Al's at the time had no ramp to get Jeri in, while St. Toms was all on flat land and needed no ramp. We later got to know Fr. Ed at St Al's quite well and Jeri liked him a lot. Jeri was now homebound. He would bring communion to give to his other stops first, making us last on his monthly schedule. He then would visit Jeri a bit longer. We liked his visits and he seemed to like our traveling trips to the point, I think he sometimes used them in his sermons without naming us. This was a compliment.

On one visit – we liked the way he would come in, especially in cold weather, take his coat off, give us each communion and sit down with us for coffee. If we had nothing much to say, he would say a little prayer with us and perhaps take a few minutes about what was going on in Church doctrine. This time he was on "lying" and how it was always sinful. I couldn't resist this one and said, "Let me give you an example and you tell me if it was lying. In the Army, I had to take a lifetime oath to not talk about our unit ASA to anyone, family included. In uniform I would often be asked, "What unit are you with?" I couldn't say ASA. We did wear Signal Corp brass on our collar. I would simply say Signal Corps which drew no further questions. We were never in the Signal Corps! Was that a sin? Fr. Ed with a surprise look didn't answer but turned to Jeri and asked Jeri, "Was that a sin?" Jeri nodded her head and, without hesitation, said, "No." I knew Jeri would have a simple answer.

These little discussions with others did wonders for Jeri. The key was: Do it with Jeri. She is part of the family and feels it intently. Forget the MS.

On another visit by Fr. Ed, it seemed he maybe overrated Jeri for what she could do. I said to him, "Father, do you realize that if Jeri is alone, and a fly lands on her nose, she cannot brush or move to make that fly get off her?" Actually, I don't ever remember a fly landing on her nose.

We hosted a small group church weekly meeting during lent and advent. About 6-8 would come and discussions would be held plus refreshments. It became common when everyone got to know Jeri, to stop talking if Jeri had something to comment on that was being discussed. They would listen in complete silence to her. She often gave some short excellent comments. One subject being discussed with everyone taking part was about when people died young, had serious illness or bad things happening, how can this be explained? Was it something they did or did not do, why was it them? No one had any decent answer. After they finished their part of the discussion without any conclusion, Jeri drew their attention and said, "God knows why!" Complete silence. An answer was given. She was so excited to take part in things like this. We did this for probably 5 or 6 years.

Fr. Mark, at the time new to our St. Al's Parish in Bowling Green, was the parish priest. It wasn't long before he met Jeri, coming to our home to bring her communion. When we told him she was not to eat or swallow food and liquids, he was mystified as to how would he be able to give her communion. We had solved this with the previous priest, Fr. Ed.

Place the host on her lips. Jeri herself had developed the next step which was to kiss the host with her lips. He was then to give me the host and I would swallow it. We then thought of the wine which we had never given her. We shall use her feeding tube for wine.

The next time Fr. Mark came, he acted a little strange. He said he was mad at himself. At his early Mass that day, he had forgotten to bless a host to take to Jeri. "Then, I thought. I know what to do. I'll say Mass at Jack and Jeri's and I'll bless new hosts there."

From then on he indicated that he would say Mass for Jeri every time he came. He came one more time.

One more star for Jeri or should I say prayer came to Jeri by mail December 9, 1999 from a Brother George, whom we had met in our first visit to Churchill. After spending a couple of days with him, he hated to leave Jeri whom he became so fond of because of her handling MS so well.

A quote from the Brother was, "For you Jeri you could not say very much, but your smile and acceptance spoke much more than words. Even if we may never meet on this earth I am sure I will recognize you in the front row in Heaven."

EQUIPMENT (SCOOTER, WHEELCHAIRS, SCALES, LIFTS, SUCTION MACHINES, ALERT ALARMS AND CAR)

SCOOTER

A rather poorly developed plan to help Jeri move around was tried but our inexperience and those trying to help Jeri were also apparently inexperienced. But we tried. We were living in a small inexpensive apartment complex biding our time until we sold our Kent house. Five of us living there and it was where Jeri became an Avon Rep. A scooter was ordered for Jeri – I think by BVR and delivered to us. Was there room for a scooter? Not in a small apartment. Jeri tried it. As expected, she was not able to maneuver it. We were able to trade it in on Jeri's first wheelchair with the help of BVR.

Winning a scooter... "In Spite Of" ... It took 15 years after Jeri had tried the scooter and we had an opportunity to actually get one by winning one free! How about that? And we didn't even try.

I answered a phone call that asked to speak to Geraldine. I asked the girl, "What was it about?" "We want to congratulate her. She has won a scooter that we raffled off." The person was very excited. It went this way:

Jack: How could we win this when we didn't enter it?
Girl: Well maybe someone else entered her name.
Jack: Who?
Girl: I can't tell. I'm reading it on a computer.
Jack: Well, who sent it in or how did you get her name?
Girl: I don't know.

Jack: Anyway, why would we enter this? Jeri can't use a scooter. She has MS and would not be able to use it.

Girl: Does this mean you don't want the scooter?

Jack: Yes.

Girl: Do you want me to take the ticket out and not use it?

Jack: Yes.

Girl: Well, good luck to you.

We did not get the scooter. I think we also saved by not having to pay taxes on it.

WHEELCHAIRS

This "introduction section to wheelchairs" is a mix of "regular" wheelchairs primarily for in your home and "lightweight" wheelchairs used mostly for outdoors and traveling. Both chairs have similar duties to perform. This following is based on wheelchairs in total because most chairs are of the same purpose for knowing and using. The rules and safety generally apply to both chairs.

Understanding a wheelchair, besides it being a people carrier, it can also be a safety hazard. A wheelchair is only safe when no one is in it. If one is a regular wheelchair, they are made of heavy metal which can cause accidents or damage. In your house, run into a plaster wall accidentally, and you have damage. One is usually not given a safety class in learning how to use a chair. It's enough to learn where the brakes are and how to close and open a wheelchair to put in a car etc seemed to be the way people, or those in need, looked at it.

The safety feature comes through experience, yours and your driver. Do you have a safe driver pushing you? If you can do it yourself, look out for whom you might accidently run into. A wheelchair rider is at the mercy of the driver. In our case, I was a self appointed driver. You try to make the rider comfortable and feeling secure. You also have to face broken sidewalks, curbs, construction detours, crossing streets, even no sidewalks and on and on.

Closing or opening a wheelchair can be painful to fingers getting caught — by metal wheelchair parts. Wheelchairs always open and close differently. Some will fit in car trunks etc which can cause a lot of lifting. If you don't know how to lift a wheelchair, you may find out and once is enough. Since wheelchairs come in all sizes, weights, brake positions etc, you will learn from each accident. Riders have the most serious problems to face, unless they can jump out or watch where they are being taken and do some back seat driving. Chairs are not a comfortable ride, the longer the harder, but they are better than nothing by far. Cushions are usually used and come with the chair as an additional cost. New better ones will cost $250 or more. We never found them much better.

One of our biggest concerns was hidden steps and curbs. Outdoors became the broken sidewalks you tried to avoid. Curbs were also usually bad to cross into streets. Curb cuts? Some fair, most not very good. The law requires them to be smooth to street surface. This is rarely done. It was thought by some that there had to be a "lip" to allow water to flow. Not so. The law meant smooth. The lip could cause a bump to a wheelchair either going off the sidewalk or going on. It really needs to be smooth. When a sidewalk was laid at our condo complex, there were no curb cuts. I reminded the people doing this about the required cuts and the smoothness required at corners of the streets. The next day, I heard cement cutters drilling our sidewalks at the corners. I had to see this for myself. Good grief, they were chopping the cement into small pieces and laying them to meet the street. Our condo corners still show broken curb cuts. When I walked Jeri in her wheelchair, I had to cross over our curb cuts slowly and very carefully to get to the street.

I gave Jeri many scares pushing her and when a step would appear out of nowhere, I would have to stop fast to keep Jeri from going over. Obviously, the driver never went over. Taking your hands off the wheelchair handles could also cause scares. One time waiting for a taxi in DC, I thought Jeri was on a level sidewalk. For an instant I let go, was watching for the taxi, while Jeri was heading for a curb to go over. I moved towards her for a new personal record, reaching her an inch or two before she would be in orbit.

Even at home, one must always be alert for a wheelchair wreck. One day we had been out roaming around when we came back to our condo. Taking Jeri in through the front door (no step, thanks to our builder who eliminated the front step), to unlock our door, I had to use both hands and, for a couple of seconds, had let go of the wheelchair and faced the door. I thought our entryway was flat. The wheelchair began to follow the level of the sidewalk leading away from us. The chair had actually turned completely around by gravity and began drifting 25 feet to the grassy area of our yard. I caught up to her as she hit the grass which stopped her abruptly.

Sidewalks – whoever invented them left out wheelchairs – it's like if you don't like them don't use them.

Now if everybody were in a wheelchair, we wouldn't have this problem. So what can be done? You really aren't too interested until your time comes to have to use one. I think the first thing is don't let it bother to think you will correct all sidewalks. You won't. Once you actually use a sidewalk with a wheelchair, you will realize that you must do something. There is no such city without sidewalk problems, one of the worst being Washington DC. Give them credit for trying even though what they recently did in the monument area was poorly thought out. By whose opinion: Mrs. John G. Schroeder, herself. Their sidewalks were made without separate sections, which was ok but what they used was some type of material that looked pretty, all one section, easily laid and wide and would not crack like cement. Did those responsible for the sidewalks test them by taking a wheelchair ride on them? Assuming they did not, then what was Jeri's problem with them? As best as we could tell, they were made of lots of tiny stones placed flat somehow to stay flat. Riding on these, Jeri found them to give a rough bumpy ride that she could feel so badly from the shaking it gave her. She did not want to use them. You know that your wheelchair seat takes all the roughness it rides over. With you in it you feel this roughness. Now a pillow may reduce this rough ride but wheelchairs usually come with pretty seats with little padding. It's a difficult unappreciated problem everywhere. What about right here in Bowling Green?

As Jeri and I took our walk to downtown one day, the sidewalks did seem to need a little attention. By the time we were almost in town, we decided to stop in the city building and pay a visit. We introduced ourselves to the receptionist and told her we were wondering if there was someone there we could talk to about sidewalks? She directed us to an office where the receptionist there heard our request of inviting some official on an "awareness walk" to observe sidewalks that people in wheelchairs had to use. The receptionist thought that this was a reasonable request but that no one was available right then but she would pass our question on to someone. Fair enough, we left and continued our walk with some good feeling that at least we are trying.

We received a call from someone with some authority in public works to take our walk with us. We agreed on a date to meet and that it would take about two hours to walk from our home, downtown and back.

They met us at our home where I asked them just to follow us to downtown and back another way, no questions or discussions. Comments were ok. They followed us on the way we would use to go downtown. Interesting, our condo sprinkling system was on wetting the sidewalk and we had to use the street part way. When we came to a corner to cross the street, we had to cross over the broken cement pieces. The other side was not smooth to get on to but one of the men said that was for the water to run by. I did not agree but kept my promise and did not say anything. When we came to a side street, we were asked to cut through and not go all the way to downtown that the other person had to get back to work. So we cut through on this side street to reach a street to take us back to our house. This cut through street was a perfect example of broken sidewalks. I had to take Jeri by way of the street, not the sidewalk because of this badly broken sidewalk. When we were walking back on another street, one of the men commented that it was almost impossible to fix sidewalks smooth enough to avoid bumps where they connected. On this next street on our return, I commented them to look at a recent sidewalk installed at how smooth the contractor had made it. Jeri felt little bounce, if any. This sidewalk was what was needed. Nothing came of it.

We arrived home and we thanked them. We thought we did ok, except the one person was on their cell phone talking the whole time to their office about business. At least one listened to us. A couple days later, we wrote a thank you letter to them. I don't remember ever receiving one from them. But they did observe and were friendly. Did it do any good? It certainly did no harm. I'm very sure Jeri appreciated their attention to one lonely wheelchair trying to solve a major problem.

Wheelchairs generally do not come with seat belts. They should and would at your expense. I have observed wheelchairs used in public and have never seen one with a seatbelt except with children chairs. One time we were in DC getting on the train. Jodi and Jami's husband Craig were walking in front of us as I pushed Jeri. I saw this man by himself in his wheelchair pushing hard to get to the train. He missed seeing a badly broken sidewalk and was thrown out of the chair and flat out on the sidewalk on his face. He laid there. Jodi and Craig went to him quickly. He couldn't get up but did not seem hurt. Jodi and Craig needed help from a passerby to get him back in his chair. He said, "I didn't see that broken hole."

Wheelchair drivers are also one waiting for an accident. I was walking in a crowded building and got hit in the heel by a wheelchair and its driver. Crowded areas are dangerous for wheelchairs running into you. I always stayed clear of any if I was walking.

I have never seen a seller actually giving a safety program showing the person buying and the one driving. At present, the theory seems to be, have one accident and you will learn quickly. In our travel section, you will see several experiences.

WHEELCHAIRS – THE SOCIAL SIDE

One's first experience in adjusting to a wheelchair is an early on the job training. It is not only the wheelchair it is also how do you want to use it in society? We learned the answer to this in many ways but it took a lot of our exposure to society. What did Jeri learn and what did she teach our family?

At random, a few ways we did things:

In meeting people, I would introduce Jeri and squeeze in that she had MS. We were not ashamed of MS or the wheelchair. A smile relieved anyone's tension. Eating in restaurants, we often asked to sit in the back – it relaxed Jeri and us in that we could push the wheelchair under the table, well I mean as far as Jeri could also go, and, especially when Jeri could not feed herself, we could do it for her. Jeri never wanted people to feel sorry for her – and she proved this by being seen a lot. I think she felt, "What wheelchair?" Nowadays, in restaurants ones in wheelchairs may feel that they are made to sit in the back simply by showing them to a table in the back. If you know where you want to sit, tell them. We happened to like the back for privacy and would often ask for it. With that in mind, we also seemed to get more attention! Waitresses would get to know Jeri and, since it would take Jeri longer to eat, would enjoy talking with her, especially if they were not busy. In a restaurant, she often became the person they liked a lot and we usually would get extra service, for example, extra napkins for Jeri. If they knew us, they would bring them without our asking. During our travel trips, by the time we would get aboard, we would have a lot of napkins to take with us compliments of our favorite Bob Evans restaurant. Reserve seating for handicapped people in wheelchairs – churches, sports, shows etc is great. We would use them a lot but not always. Sometimes we felt we were forced to sit there. Why couldn't they ask Jeri if she would like to be seated there? Usually we accepted their guidance and sat where we were directed and thanked them. But sometimes, we wanted to do it our way and often did. Ushers, when they saw Jeri, would usually automatically show her to the handicapped section. Now sometimes that would be fine. A movie theater for example usually meant real good seating.

Jeri did have MS. Jeri was in a wheelchair. It was hard to make her unseen. To enter a restaurant, a hotel or even entering a hospital as a patient, I always made sure they talked to Jeri first and ask her their questions. How to do that? I simply would look the other way. "Talk to Jeri." She is still a person. I know Jeri liked that way. Ignoring her in those occasions would have been devastating to her.

An introduction to People Movers aka wheelchairs...I would add to the term People Movers also luggage, groceries etc with or without someone in the wheelchair.

Unlike other equipment, there has been a disappointing progress of improvements in wheelchairs at least in appearance of institutional looks over the last 24 years of our needs. Our first major improvement in style appeared during the last couple years of our needs when a new lightweight wheelchair appeared, as explained later. The day of single wheelchairs which were to satisfy anyone needing a wheelchair is gone. One size fits all doesn't work anymore. In addition, one wheelchair no longer can do all that one needs. Adding new attachments is fine. However, if you try to make one wheelchair do everything, it can defeat the purpose of a wheelchair. We are in the period where almost each wheelchair has its own purpose. It does nothing except seats and moves you. One can climb stairs. One used for the bathroom. Others that can "stand" you up and then lets you back down; lift your legs; that have all kinds of headrests and now a few with your choice of color. Of course prices vary accordingly. On top of that, if you have Medicare, you may find yourself limited to a certain few choices. Early on we believed, when you had Medicare and you owned private insurance, then your insurance would approve or not approve based on their own decision. Not so, insurance companies follow Medicare.

I do think that someday wheelchairs will be developed better and actually will be able to handle more than one job. Wouldn't it be nice if a wheelchair could also lift a person and do away with lifts? Currently handicapped people accept wheelchairs as needed. With lifts, not so welcome.

Referring to attachments to a wheelchair, they can overload a wheelchair and cause problems. Too many overloads can indicate you are using the wrong wheelchair and may need a new wheelchair. You overload a lightweight wheelchair, the weight goes up. We had one chair where a computer seller installed an attachment to Jeri's wheelchair to hold a heavy bar with a monitor on it so Jeri could work right in her wheelchair. I told the person attaching the holder that, where they were putting it, would interfere with a working part of the wheelchair and suggested they should talk with the wheelchair company. They said they didn't have time. It was installed anyway.

For long time expected riders, wheelchairs should be assembled individually, which, because of costs, they usually are not. So, it becomes a guess work of choice. If you need a headrest, a wider armrest, a different size, whatever, you may find yourself needing several different wheelchairs. If one can't self propel? Try using smaller wheels. It is amazing how much less room they take up and look nicer too. Large wheels make it a wheelchair. Small wheels make it look more like a chair.

As MS changed slowly on its own regular schedule (as it seemed), we found that Jeri's body's schedule also changed slowly and could not use some wheelchairs and/or she needed new ones. A wheelchair should fit a person properly and when the person changes, a change in wheelchairs or adjustments to the one you have, would be needed also.

A wider armrest mentioned above leads to another interesting problem. On one new wheelchair, when the sales person delivered it, we saw a problem with the armrests. They were too narrow and short. Remember, Jeri had no use of her arms. Well, in a wheelchair the armrests are part of the wheelchair. No big secret here. They were meant for a person to rest their arms on and keep them on the rests or move them around a bit. One never sits in one position without making adjustments to be more comfortable. OK? Are you still with me? In Jeri's case, not able to move her arms where they were placed did not work. What happens was, if she coughed, her body leaned or an arm spasm would move her arms. This would cause her arms to drop off the armrests. She could not move them back herself. Her armrests had to be wider, longer and a raised border (a lip) around the armrests to keep her hands within and on the rests. At the very least they had to be wider and longer and of course padded. No problem, we thought.

We informed our seller that the two armrests would need to be exchanged. She said she would check with the company. The manufacturer told her, "We only make one size. If you want different sizes, you will have to find someone that makes them. You would have to pay them." So what could she do about it? She said she would get back to us. She called back and said she had someone handy with making things that would make them for us at no charge. Our experience told us that this was not good. If it is not a qualified company, it will not work. Wheelchair armrests are not easy to make and install them on a wheelchair. A few weeks later, we had the armrests. I could have done better. They really weren't very good. I asked our son Jeff who had made us a pair on another wheelchair about this. Our son made the two armrests, for his mother, of course. They were excellent, better than what could be bought, and no charge and no offer of payment by the original company and insurance. Jeff became our official armrest builder.

Another time, we had another new wheelchair that after a while did not fit Jeri right and would not hold her head up at all because she was losing the ability to do so herself. On a visit to her MS doctor, he said he had another patient that could not hold her head up either until they went to a company that fixed her wheelchair. He suggested Jeri go to this company to see if they can help her.

We set up an appointment with this company explaining to them about the chair we had and that it was not helping Jeri hold her head up. Of course, there was a two or three month wait. Jeri and I met with them. After explaining again to them what the problem was, the person asked, "What do you want us to do?" Surprised, I said, "I thought you would tell us." A pause and the person said, "Well there are two choices for you. One is we can make a bean bag for you or we can attach our computer to Jeri and take measurements." Another pause this time, us: "What's a bean bag and the cost? What is the cost of the computer method?" Answer. "You have seen small bean bags holding beans. The one we would make for you would be a very large bean bag with a lot of beans. You can make it fit Jeri wherever you sit her. The charge would be cheaper but insurance will not pay for it. The computer method would be a sitting hooked up with the computer at certain places on Jeri to give us a reading of how we would make a new back for the wheelchair for Jeri." Well, it was obvious we wanted nothing to do with a large bean bag. We were only slightly ready to go with the computer. I couldn't believe this discussion we were having and I think Jeri was very disappointed. Bean bag? What next? But we had to do something. The computer would be covered by insurance. The computer it was. Next, "Bring Jeri back for the computer measurement."

After the sitting and a month or so afterwards, the new back was delivered to us by their delivery man. He brought it in. I asked, "When are they coming to install the back?" The delivery guy said, "Oh, I'm to do that. It's easy." End of story? Not quite.

This expensive back was attached within a few minutes, nicely shaped to fit Jeri. Well someone had to try the fit. "Jeri, come here. We have the new back for your wheelchair. Let's see if it works."

I said, "Great. It looks good. It seems to fit perfectly." Jeri answered, "Oh, it fits perfectly. I can't move." Good grief. It's like a straight jacket. She can't move! End of a success story? We put it in our garage. Sometime later, I took the new back, the old back and the wheelchair and donated it to "Goodwill." End of story.

One early MS meeting Jeri and I attended to discuss MS, there were four or five tables of attendees. Before the meeting started, we were discussing MS within our table. A girl in a wheelchair from another table wheeled herself over to ours and said, "I want to sit at your table. It sounds like the people here know what they are talking about." We welcomed her. I noticed she only had one footrest. I asked her, "Why do you only have one footrest?" She answered, "It was the only wheelchair they had to give me." I said, "My goodness. You are certainly entitled to two footrests."

After the introduction of wheelchairs above, we now explore Jeri's wheelchair career's beginning and ending. We came in weak but left with experience galore. We had no one to teach us. I don't think anyone existed. The persons using them became the teachers. This is in spite of sales people, who tried hard but only the ones who were using them knew the facts.

Jeri's first wheelchair, a loaner for one evening, came while we ate pizza and did shopping at a mall in Toledo. We finished eating, the three children spent their coins (from the pizza) on some game machine and we went shopping, Jeri included. By now, Jeri was limping a lot and had to sit down every so often to rest in this large department store we were in. One of the children said, "This store has wheelchairs for use. Why don't we get one to try?" Jeri made no resistance. They went for the wheelchair. Jeri put herself in it. This may be a poor comparison but it seemed like Jeri broke the horse by riding it. She seemed so relieved to rejoin her family in shopping and not needing help. We had a really nice family evening.

I remember someone saying, "Don't put yourself in a wheelchair you'll never get out of it." Perhaps but for us it was one of the best things Jeri did having MS. Not an exciting moment but the start of a new life style. She was glad to have one. We never realized how much traveling we were going to do in the future. What would we have done? Stay home? That was not what we had in mind.

We became quick learners when it came to equipment. Sickness means you don't want equipment you "need" it, a very important term to use in buying and selecting any equipment from sales personnel. Such sellers knew their product better than us. However, their selling techniques were generally based on want rather than need. Ex. "Oh, you'll love this wheelchair and its soft seat!" How about letting Jeri decide?

Our first purchase of a wheelchair for Jeri came from a want standpoint and not from Jeri's need. This time we were in our new home. By Jeri's design, all floors were linoleum type, hallways and doors were wider than normal. Everything was on one floor.

So Jeri's first owned wheelchair was shipped to her on November 21, 1985.

When the sales person told me the wheelchair she was showing us had a life time warranty, I was sold. It never really worked. From then on, Jeri became the buyer.

Electric wheelchair....... After using this first wheelchair for six years, we had a chance to get an electric (battery operated) wheelchair. This wheelchair came in 1991. We donated the first wheelchair to the MS Society.

Jeri did well at first with this "electric chair" (electric chair?) using a joy stick. Within a few months, it became too difficult for her to guide it around. There is a brief story about this chair under the **SAYINGS** section.

Without our "electric" wheelchair, we reversed back to getting another wheelchair that was standard indoor and a pretty nice red color with nice armrests. At the same time we concentrated on the necessity of having a lightweight outdoor chair for all traveling, by car or walking. So for several years Jeri did very well when it became time to get an indoor wheelchair to suit her computer work. This took time but we had to go this way because there were some improvements on new wheelchairs.

Searching for lightweight wheelchairs especially for local and distant traveling was a different game. We had to do more homework and find the right vendors. We definitely did our own research on this little guy –

not too heavy, easy to get in and out, actually I think more comfortable outside riding around and much easier getting it into a car. Of course, the only insurance, money etc came from us. Amazingly they were well built and never needed repaired. You also had a choice of color. Our first buy was a green chair in 1992. We used this chair for a lot of traveling for some seven years when we were introduced to a "improved" lightweight blue chair which we bought and began using. It did not please us. After a few trips, we switched back to our original green chair and "dumped" this perfect new wheelchair on Goodwill. So our "unbreakable" green wheelchair gave us a total of eleven years service. Using it for all of our local and train travel, this was incredible.

Continuing with wheelchairs that you don't want but need requires patience, some understanding and a lot of experience. It's a difficult call. Better not to read any instructions yet. Look at it, sit in it, hold it, and say nothing. Jeri learned to know what she needed. The right equipment that you choose will help you – this is your call.

Begin with just what is medical equipment? I should use what Medicare and insurance companies live by when it comes to medical equipment. The term is "durable medical equipment." I dare you to define that. We never could. Seems simple enough!

Talking to a Medicare equipment specialist, I asked them, "What is meant by durable medical equipment?" Answering from their rule book, they said "equipment to be used in the home that can withstand repeated use." Actually, not too bad!

We try our hand at buying a new wheelchair, Oops! Wrong time to "practice"...it was January 1999 when Jeri needed a new wheelchair. Jeri and I began a search. We really needed one wheelchair that would be both a travel chair and an indoor chair. We were told that what we were after didn't exist. By March 1999, we had picked two possibilities, one was a travel chair and one was a more expensive heavier chair. Both were sold by the same company. We pursued the heavier chair. Now that we chose one chair we liked, we were told that we would have to buy two wheelchairs to get one. We have to buy **TWO** wheelchairs??? Furthermore, we would have to find a dealer to handle this. We have to also find a **DEALER**? We only want and need one and we already have picked it out. What a time to be an apprentice trying to help Jeri. She was a bit shocked too.

OK, where do we stand? Fortunately, we knew our regular dealer and thought we could count on them. Two wheelchairs whose idea was this? We actually were hoping we could get one of our three government medical providers (Medicare, Medicaid or Medicaid-Waiver) to approve our one chair. Now we have to get approval for two chairs, which was extremely unlikely.

Before approaching Medicare etc, we met with our sales person from the dealer we used. We decided on choosing two wheelchairs and go from there. Well, we had already selected the two we were interested in. Our sales person suggested that we chose which chair we would be willing to pay for if need be. The other chair, their company would request Medicare or Waiver to pay. Since one was a lighter travel chair than the heavy chair, it would be cheaper for us to pay for the travel if we did not get approvals for both chairs. Medicare was more likely to pay for the heavier chair, a regular size indoor wheelchair. Our sales person agreed.

Our sales person did the paper work needed and presented this to the insurance company for approval and told us it was now in process. A few days later, they called us and said, "You're not going to believe this but the heavier wheelchair was denied by the insurance company based on **"not medically needed."**

Jeri and I, once more took things into our own hands, and paid a visit to the insurance company. We got the approval for the heavier chair.

Our dealer then asked us if we would commit to pay for the travel chair within ten days. We agreed and paid $1,796, a rather large price for a lightweight chair. We later tried to get Medicare to reimburse us which they would not. This left the other wheelchair to be paid to our local dealer by Medicare and our insurance company. So we ended with two good wheelchairs for one price. If insurance had not covered the one wheelchair, we might not have gotten either chair. In any case, it "only" took about five months to get what Jeri "needed."

Along our merry way, Our regular wheelchair company approached Jeri about a new tilt wheelchair they had and wanted to show it to Jeri with all its improvements. We said OK. They brought one to show Jeri. It was a nice improved wheelchair, even had color to it. Jeri liked it. While it was large and very heavy, Jeri could use it at her computer. With the sales person showing Jeri this, it was an improvement. We questioned, however, whether Medicare would approve it. I didn't think we had gone the "sacred" five years between chairs that Medicare based their approvals on. We were aware though that if there were sufficient improvements that could help the patient, then Medicare might approve one. Our sales person said they would like to try to get approval if we would agree. I didn't think they would get the approval but they did and surprised us. It eventually was delivered and Jeri began using it. It did work better, no question.

Learning "tricks of the trade"...... sellers who help you......teaching yourself...why didn't we learn more ahead of time? It was because it was trial, error, learn as you go.

Medical equipment is a high price item. Companies sometimes seemed to be in business to sell first and help later, if at all. You have to choose the ones to help you. An example of this is at one time we dealt with a sales girl who really did a great job for Jeri. She helped with selections, securing insurance coverage up front, making sure we received the right service etc. We had her for over ten years.

What did we learn to be self sufficient?

Jeri was covered by Medicare, private insurance, Medicaid and Medicaid-Waiver, A great coverage that everyone should have. It takes a lot of mistakes before you learn how to use this coverage. First and most important, we learned to be sure you told the seller the coverage you have – IN THE ORDER OF COVERAGE. If you don't do it this way, you will have a lot of bills with problems. Second, be sure the seller is a PROVIDER.

In one wheelchair purchase, I thought we had made sure the vendor had our purchase covered by insurance. After receiving the wheelchair, I received a bill for part of the chair that wasn't paid by insurance. What gives? With bill in hand, we went to the vendor quickly, "I thought we were completely covered under Jeri's insurance. Aren't you a provider?" "Well yes. I am a provider for Medicare, private insurance and Medicaid. This is what they paid for. You owe what is left." I asked "aren't you a provider also for Medicaid-Waiver?" He asked, "What's that?" "I told him that it was different from Medicaid, it was a separate coverage." He never knew that and said he was not a provider for that. Now that bit of surprise caused the next problem. Can it be fixed? More "fighting" on our part but somehow we got out of paying.

Jeri's final regular wheelchair came when she was in Rehab when a different equipment company paid Jeri a visit to the Rehab to talk wheelchair. I was present so we listened. They explained they had a new wheelchair they thought would work well for Jeri. It sounded like it was brand new on the market. When there is a chance for major improvement with a new wheelchair, you listen. With our approval, they said they would pay several visits to Jeri while she was in Rehab and do a complete measurement of her with the wheelchair. We approved with the measurement idea but had not approved the wheelchair yet. They said that they would not be able to actually go for an approval for the wheelchair until she would be discharged from Rehab. Again we approved. They did all the measurements they needed and we then waited until Jeri got home.

At home, the company came to begin getting the wheelchair. We knew it was new but had never seen it yet and asked for a picture of it. Good grief. It looked like the same one we had bought a few years ago. I mentioned this to the sales person who said this might be possible but ours is a new one. They asked if they could borrow ours to take with them to compare with the one they are selling. A couple of weeks later, they brought our chair back and said, while they seem similar, ours is an improved chair and we think the one we have is best. OK, we approved, but they might have trouble getting Medicare to approve. Apparently they had no problem. We were delivered a new wheelchair.

As this turned out, it was the last regular wheelchair we would get.

In the meantime, we had kept looking and questioning whoever would listen, why can't new wheelchairs change that institutional look?

We never gave up on that one. Granted, this was a tough question, so? To me, it seemed depressing. Can't something be done? Paint big flowers or something on the wheelchairs but something sooner or later will be done. Let's not wait. But wait. Maybe we are getting close.

The "Institutional Look" is disappearing at least with travel chairs..........at last, after years of searching, we finally found a lightweight wheelchair that was great for taking walks, car and train travel and did not have the institutional look.

Buy it quickly we thought. We'll even pay for it ourselves, if need be. This can't be true. It can't be this easy. Why, Jeri doesn't even have to be measured for it. It's "our" chair. It's beautiful!

I don't remember how we found this wheelchair but as soon as we saw a picture of it that was all it took. This was in 2003. It was a nice looking lightweight wheelchair. The company sent us brochures on this chair and we told them we wanted one. We knew no insurance would pay for it. They told us they could not send it to us direct, that we would have to find a dealer who would accept it and receive payment. So we found a dealer. The dealer agreed to do this but told us that any returns or repairs on this chair would have to be covered by us. We agreed. The chair arrived and we paid the dealer $677.86 for our new lightweight wheelchair.

Jeri chose our new traveling chair color to be burgundy. The padded seat and back were burgundy while the frame and leg rest (only needed one because the one was made wide enough for two legs) were chrome. The chair's wheels were four small double wheels. The ride was smooth and comfortable. Another surprise of our new chair, the armrests were padded, fitted nicely to help keep her within her chair and attached downward onto the chair frame. Another surprise, armrests were positioned so that the wheelchair could easily fit under tables, a real benefit in a restaurant. We picked this chair out ourselves. Our experience finally paid off.

We did find a couple of problems with it and did have to send it back to the company. A short time later they returned a new one to us.

People would ask, "Where did you get that wheelchair?" We explained where and that it was an "adult stroller" that folded down nicely like a child's stroller and it fits nicely in the trunk of our car. It was the best wheelchair we ever had.

Later on and because the brakes on our new find were wearing down, I called the company to see if I could purchase a spare. Like a stroller, the back wheels were double wheels on which one would apply the metal brake to the wheels by stepping on the brakes. My call went to the sales people who shocked me when they told me that they no longer made that type of wheelchair. I told them that they had the best wheelchair we had ever bought, that we found people very interested in it. To no avail, the company said it did not sell well, that they were disappointed. Interesting, I told them that I had called to see if I could buy some replacement wheels because we were using the chair a lot and I wanted to have a spare wheel on hand. They said they now had left over parts that they would send us. This they did, two of the heavy wheel posts with double wheels at no charge. We were very disappointed that the company stopped building them but who could we complain to? We kept using this wheelchair wherever we traveled and even at home. It turned out to be Jeri's last wheelchair she needed – a scant 24 years in a wheelchair.

So how did we move Jeri so many years in her many wheelchairs.......... We had the wheelchairs. How did we use them?

We felt a lot of pressure from advertising and friends that we needed a van that would carry Jeri and the wheelchair. In our case, they were distributed, Jeri to the front seat, wheelchair to the trunk or back, if a station wagon. We agreed that we could use a Van but who was going to pay for it. Seemed prices were like

$30,000+. All auto companies would offer would be a swivel front seat or something like that.

But we didn't want one anyway. Jeri received a lot of exercise, a more comfortable seat and a view she could enjoy. Besides, she felt more normal. We truly were a common family again going for a ride. For about 9 years, we used a Ford Escort Wagon. We built a rack over the spare donut in the trunk even with the tail height so there was no deep lifting out the wheelchair or putting it in. Moving Jeri to the front seat from her chair was easy. Since she could hold weight on her two legs, I would lift her up out of the chair and swivel her around and onto her seat, the reverse to put her back in the chair, just like I explained to nurses without success.

Would you believe that every time we transferred Jeri to the car front seat, two things happened: It was real exercise for her body and the front seat of a car is very comfortable, more so than most home chairs. Besides when I drove, I always wanted her next to me. She also helped me in keeping awake. Jeri rarely slept in the car.

So how many years did Jeri use a wheelchair? Rounding it off in years, let's use (1985 to 2009) = 24 years.

One more surprise remark about wheelchairs and even medical supplies. We have donated several wheelchairs along with supplies to people and welfare companies. Some may have given us an automatic "thank you" but I can't think of anyone showing real thankfulness for our "gifts." I don't remember ever receiving any written "thank you" notes either. Are thank you notes important? No, but they do two things: they make one feel good and they make one want to contribute more. Why did our donations feel like a business transaction? I would suspect that the final person needing such equipment would feel quite thankful in receiving them.

The following is a climax, with no ending, to wheelchairs as Jeri and I experienced them. I give you a ten page copy of a federal "Wheelchair Policy." Actually my thoughts to you will be but a few remarks and a little information about this wheelchair policy document.

I don't remember ordering any "Wheelchair Policy" manual but it was more interesting than valuable. To give credit somewhat to whoever developed it, indeed it was well done – all sizes, measurements exactly stated etc – all covering many types of wheelchairs. It lost me on the first page. Anyway, when I received a letter to me dated 5/12/00, it read, "This is in response to your request for assistance under the Freedom of Information Act. In your letter you requested a copy of the Wheelchair Policy." This came from the Freedom of Information, Medicare.

Comments: I do not ever remember a wheelchair company presenting anything like this. I think it was way too broad to understand and to find exact wheelchairs like shown to be of value in selecting a personal wheelchair. To us, it would have only worked after you found the chair you wanted by seeing the chair in person and then review the manual.

The manual did present answers. There was a time when I could not understand what was meant when the term "self propel" was used to determine if a patient would or would not qualify for a wheelchair. I still do not quite understand it but here is a question in the manual:

Is the patient able to adequately self-propel (without being pushed) in a standard weight manual wheelchair?

If the answer is "No," would the patient be able to adequately self-propel (without being pushed) in the wheelchair which has been ordered?

Note: this is one of the several questions to answer in writing from a form called "Certificate of Medical Necessity." I never saw such a form in all of our travels for wheelchairs and I only remember one time when we learned that an insurance company rejected our new wheelchair based on their **"Not Medically Needed"** statement. It actually caused us problems until we could show that it was a "Medical Necessity." This is briefly covered in an earlier part of this wheelchair section.

Reference wheelchairs "one" more time: Using wheelchairs outside most of the time we learned that's the only way to go when your rider needs a ride. It definitely should be in a "travel" wheelchair. We learned the hard way early by using a regular wheelchair for both needs. They were built separately for their two needs, inside and outside. Using regular wheelchairs before we learned the difference brought on a lot of waste, friction, difficult situations on and on. Regular wheelchairs outside: With a car, very difficult to fold and put somewhere in your car. Don't ride vehicles in a wheelchair. Sit and enjoy your ride. Get out of your wheelchair. On trains, we caused many problems with ourselves and especially the crews trying to handle a heavy wheelchair. They can be difficult for busses, taxis etc also. I don't think Jeri and I could have done what we did or would want to do without BOTH wheelchairs, one at a time. I think we have explained this pretty good in our travels.

I rest my case. It's on to SCALES!

SCALES

Scales has several meanings. Herein we are talking rugged weighing scales that can handle people and wheelchairs. We never paid much attention about weighing Jeri. All we had was a bathroom scales that seemed to decide what weight you would like. We apparently had low priority for scales in our dealing with MS. Jeri never seemed to care and always kept her same weight. We never recognized any changes in her weight until long after we got into more choking and more MS.

As we moved along in time to when Jeri was not walking, she could not get on a scales to be weighed either. Not too important at first but it became a problem when she began to lose weight. How do we weigh her? Some doctor offices had small scales. One said they would estimate and others would ask me. Moving Jeri a lot, I could tell her weight pretty good and it was always pretty consistent, around 90 pounds. We never found any that actually had a wheelchair scales.

At one hospital when Jeri was being admitted, the nurses were not able to weigh her on their scales until one nurse said, "We have a wheelchair scales, I'll get it." She found and brought it to Jeri. It would not work. The wheelchair was too large. It would not fit on the wheelchair's scales.

Our home scales were of little value. It was simply too hard to hold Jeri, any more suggestions? Where can we take Jeri to be weighed? One more and I quit. Someone suggested taking Jeri to a vet to weigh her. An animal vet, that is! I quit.

We decided it was time to get our own wheelchair scales, time to keep a log. We would do it with one large enough to hold a wheelchair and then deduct that weight to get Jeri's weight.

This was August 27, 1998 when we started working on what was to become one more problem we didn't need. We began gathering the prescription, doctors' recommendations, an excellent evaluation report from a nutritionist reference weight loss etc.

We did a little homework and found out there were no specific scales for wheelchairs. I checked with companies supplying freight scales to stores, all sizes, all prices – many companies had to weigh their product they were selling or buying. They did not make or buy medical scales, but what was the difference? We talked to one company, told them what we were after and why. They told us what they sold were scales for weighing – they didn't care who used them. When we told them we needed the scales to weigh Jeri in a wheelchair, they said they had what we were after, even gave us a price. So we had been fishing in the wrong place. Forget the medical community, go to professional scale companies.

With our homework done, I approached our case manager and gave them the request that we needed scales for Jeri. I then had to prove our case as to why Jeri needed this. Would Medicare et al approve payment?

We then began sending this information to where we were told to send it. Now the denials started coming in. "Not medically necessary."

May 28, 1999, Insurance Company was still denying the request.

The Wheelchair Scale Arrives.................
Success at last, but hold up, it did not fit.

On May 5, 2000, an unannounced delivery was made to our home which "lo and behold" it contained a large metal digital platform scale.

The delivery driver wanted me to sign for it and was ready to leave. Whoa now, wait until we try it. I brought Jeri out who happened to be in her wheelchair. The scale (according to their spelling of scale meaning one) was laid down on the driveway. The wheelchair would not fit on it – the scale was too small. We told him to take it back, no wonder he was in a hurry to leave. "What do you want me to do with it?" Take if back from where you got it - another disappointment for us. I think we were loaded with disappointments but this never surprised us. With MS, it is easy to become patient – you haven't much choice.

We were not aware of where the scale came from – what company or who had it sent. It turned out that it was our case manager who, talking to us later, did not realize we had returned it. On September 8, 2000, another scale was delivered to us. This one did fit. In fact, I mentioned in surprise that I thought a horse could be weighed on it. It took two men to carry it. Before they escaped me, I had them take it to our spare bedroom and quickly chose a section of the room that might be used permanently for the scale. We haven't moved it since. This time we won. It was used almost every day to weigh Jeri which allowed us to keep tab on her weight. Jeri's case manager did a good job getting this. But the story continues.

Now what? Jeri started receiving a sizable bill from the scale company telling her they were not receiving payment for the scale. Calling the company and asking them why they were sending Jeri the bill, they told me they were having problems collecting from Medicaid-Waiver and that Jeri was responsible. Adding to "Jeri's bill" was interest each month. This went on for several months. We had told them to send the bills to her case manager. Contacting the case manager, we were told to ignore these bills. Not too easy to do but we tried it. The final bill received by Jeri was dated February 1, 2003, it now totaled $1,297.76. We did not pay it.

This scale was a real help for Jeri. We used it constantly over many years. It was a little inconvenient each time we used it to make sure we knew the wheelchair weight and that Jeri had like clothes on to give us a true Jeri weight figure. We controlled her weight dependent on this. The nurse who handled it and getting Jeri ready each time we used it did a nice job showing a lot of patience and understanding to a rather difficult job. To get Jeri on, we had to push her right up to the scales and then lift the wheelchair front wheels on and then lift the back wheels on. There was no direct way to get on. The height of the entrance was 3 and one-half inches. There was also a 1" lip on the other three sides. It was a well built scale. I wish we had a horse to try it.

Later when Jeri was losing weight and we were trying to find out why, we would weigh her constantly. With the scales (as we called them), we need not guess. We were pretty successful in getting Jeri back to her normal weight, at least for this time period. As you can see, it took a lot of time and effort to get the "scale" but it was worth it.

Curious, how long did it take to get this scale? It was 2 years for delivery, another 3 years for billing settlement. A nice and cozy 5 years.

LIFTS..........Not my favorite subject......like computers a necessary evil. Will a wheelchair that can lift people ever be invented? I hope so. Meanwhile, let's see why Jeri needed them.

Jeri and I were not only related but we shared most secrets. Lifts were not about secrets, it took us little time not to like them. If you wanted us to use the word hate, you've got it.

I think it first started with swimming. Since swimming was our number one source of help for her MS, we had Jeri in the water, I would guess, two hundred+ times. It worked every time to some degree. Because heat was devastating to MS, we would always test the water before putting her in to swim. If it were on the cool side, good show. By now, Jeri was actually a good swimmer. Because she could not move her legs, she did little swimming but did a lot of floating around. When I would be in with her, I would push her underwater several times. She would come up herself but scared everyone around her who probably thought I was trying to.......well not really. When she did go underwater herself, she was unbelievable in holding her breath. I finally got use to it but not people around her. As mentioned earlier in our condo pool, she really could hold her breath under water a long time and could do it ever since I had met her. I would tell people watching her and a little frightened that Jeri was OK. She does this all the time. Swimming was one thing SHE could do herself and enjoy it herself.

Getting Jeri in the water was easy and simple. Use the pool lift? No. Jeri became frightened with lifts. We shared this fear. Whether it was a water lift or a house lift, it was scary. She did not like this idea of floating in the air with a "lift off" and then a "landing." We learned that other "flyers" felt the same way.

We always would lift Jeri into a pool either with help or alone. Usually the lifeguard was glad to help us. They liked it because it was a lot of inconvenience putting someone in a pool lift and then taking them out. So from wheelchair to water in one quick move is a bit faster and easier. It did take two to lift her out but this she liked better than a lift. Can you realize how long it took to go through the lift method of putting one in the seat, cranking it up, swinging it over the water and, well not letting go of your passenger, but dropping them into the water and then unfastening the seat and getting that lift out of there before hurting someone? I think our manual way was not only liked more but was actually safer.

The other type of lift, the home lift.............
Would you care for a ceiling or floor lift?

A floor lift for lifting one out of bed was probably, I would think, the most popular. If you used a ceiling lift between rooms, you would need tracks in the ceiling connecting to other rooms. I asked someone, how they would get to the other room or rooms? They said they would cut a wide space in the wall to get through and lay tracks. Forget that ride. It wasn't for us. In fact neither was the floor lift but, having to choose, we went with the floor lift. Reluctantly, I accepted the idea, Jeri dreaded the idea. It showed in her face every time we had to lift her that way. Looking back, when Jeri's arm was broken by a, we think, nurse, I think I could and should have continued using my way. Her arm mended and I could have put my hands under her differently. The nurse had lifted Jeri with a long lift from wheelchair to bed and then to position her in bed is when under the arm it became hurt. My way, as explained elsewhere, was a light lift from wheelchair to rest on her legs and then a swivel to the bed, nothing ever happened to Jeri this way. I was "warned" not to do it my way. We would never have had to get a lift my way. I should have continued my way by not going under her arm pits but choosing another way of holding her. We were also warned that people could and would often fall out of a lift and could be hurt. Thanks for alerting us to dropping patients accidentally falling out of slings or whatever.

The search for a lift begins. The broken arm accident happened the day we brought Jeri home from Rehab. The nursing service ordered a lift from Medicare. It was a little shocking to see what Medicare sent Jeri. It looked like it belonged, like the bed that was sent, in the Smithsonian also, not our bedroom. I was beginning to feel we lived in a museum! Well, it wasn't quite what we had in mind but it worked, for a while. It was a hand pumping lift. Funny, we didn't like it, neither did the nurses - hand pumping Jeri up and down? Jeri was bound over to floating in space.

Why can't we get an electric lift? Why can't we pay the difference if need be. Good questions. Now let us get the answers and get the lift she needs. Put our gloves, boxing that is, back on and do our job. Here goes:

We knew this was going to be another difficult request. Our nurses told us an electric lift is the only way to go. It really was helpful when the nurses supported us. The word was out about us and the word was you're not going to get an electric lift paid by Medicare etc. We had different case managers involved and they were for us but often didn't try hard enough or did not use their implied authority. They really were for Jeri 100% but their supposedly authority was more like begging than doing. This went on several months with no progress. It looked pretty hopeless when our last case manager working hard to get the lift came in to tell Jeri that, "No electric lifts were being approved, there's nothing more I can do." This came from Medicaid-Waiver! End of the line? I then decided to find someone higher up to talk to about this. I did find a name and planned to get in touch with them. Before I did that, somehow, an electric lift was delivered to Jeri within a month after being told, no way would we get one, we had one.

But wait, there's more. Something's fishy about this climax. Among questions were: Who approved it? Who paid for it? Will we receive a bill? It was back to the drawing board.

As far as we can tell:
Jeri's "Ohio Home Care Program All Services Plan" for the period 12/17/2007-12/16/2008 showed an approval on 3/25/2008 for an electric lift costing $7,064.88 to be paid by Medicaid. Later in this services plan, it showed "Lift to be billed to Ohio Home Care Waiver."

Apparently there were two case managers involved in this somehow, especially since one told us Waiver would not pay for a lift. I believe the other case manager had an already approved Medicaid (per a note from the selling company).

Jeri did receive a bill for $7,064.88 from the company selling the lift and saying she "would be responsible for any amounts not paid." I called the selling company telling them they had better get to Ohio Job & Family Services, who they had said they billed, and find out what the hold-up was? We never heard any more and did not receive another bill.

Now a little bit about using Jeri's new lift.

This was a really nice safe lift. The nurses liked it and to Jeri, it was a big improvement over the old one. It operated quietly and you could raise and lower Jeri smoothly. But lest we forget, it was still a lift Jeri had to face every day. She still hated this but could do nothing about it. Not a very pleasant feeling. We did have to be careful moving her from one or two rooms to her bed. We had a family rule that there always had to be two people moving her since we had heard of people sliding out of lifts and getting hurt. Jeri still disliked the floating involved. What made it more uncomfortable was that going through rooms that were carpeted, the lift's wheels would turn and the lift would stop and then get started, causing Jeri, in her "sling" to bounce a lot. Floating Jeri back to her room was no time to be funny. One night, innocently enough, putting Jeri in the lift to put her back to bed, a new nurse, cheerfully said to Jeri, "Are you ready to go for a ride?" I cautioned the new nurse to be careful of being too cheerful putting Jeri in the lift. Just talk to her like saying you would try to be gentle with her and move her as smoothly as you can – something like that. In other words distract Jeri. In her place, what would you want someone to say?

SUCTION MACHINES

Jeri did not have need of a suction machine for many years. Two or three times she was tested in a hospital for swallowing but each time she showed no problems. Her food showed going down the way it was suppose to go. When she did begin showing signs of choking, it seems we could handle it with little effort. It was no serious concern for many years. Her breathing energy because of MS (now don't blame everything on MS) became slightly weaker which affected her taking deep breaths – the doctors noticed this in listening to her heart and telling her to take a deep breath. They were able to get a good reading on her every breath. She seemed fine always well into later years.

In our early use of the suction machine, we had one at home but rarely used it. I remember the kids telling me every so often, "Dad, Mom sounds like she needs the suction machine" as she would cough a bit. Sometimes I listened to them and sometimes I just kept an eye on Jeri. This one seemed to be getting old, so I took it to our regular equipment company to get it fixed. I thought it was ours we had it for so long. They checked the serial number and said it was theirs. When we looked at the original invoice, down deep in the invoice mentioned it was a loaner. At least I hadn't thrown it away. They gave us a new one.

Because her choking increased slightly, we began taking it with us on trips, were able to get a newer one in 1994 which lasted through 2000 when we got our last one. We kept hoping they would get lighter but the last one, the lightest, weighed 10#.

Even though we rarely used it on trips, we still took it with us. Carried it in one of our luggage pieces and always kept it near us on trips including in our hotel rooms. When we did need it, we were really glad we had it.

One trip, we were using it in the hotel a lot when the battery became too low to use. We could plug the machine into an electric plug but would have to wait for it to recharge. When it recharged a little bit, we would use it a little and plug it in again. I was afraid the battery would not recharge then we would have another problem.

When we were on a train and would go across country, looking back: you mean we (I mean "I") carried that 10# suction machine all that way and didn't need it? "Rattlesnakes!" (just one of my dumb sayings, easier than counting ten) Actually, I was glad we didn't need it and I'm sure Jeri was to. It meant she was breathing and eating good, meeting people, having attendants sit with her and having a very enjoyable train trip. It doesn't get much better.

**Suction machine replaced by napkins..........
better sit down for this one. No, I'm not making these up as I go along.**

While Jeri was maintaining her health quite well over the years, her strength was being weakened somewhat in her breathing. Eventually she became choking a little more often. Well, with MS, what do you expect?

With a suction machine, first of all, you don't carry one along with you walking or otherwise. I kept hoping one would be invented but in the meantime, you don't carry one in your pocket either so you try to clear one's throat manually. Secondly, you don't carry a large battery or have a place to plug a machine in. So since nothing else was happening, we made a discovery very "unmedically" about her casual choking.

Even if you do have access to a suction machine, you have to be carefully how far you go down a person's throat to clear it. You can cause the person to choke more if you go too far.

To simplify, I found out by putting a napkin **slightly** down her throat, the mucus formed as a sticky web and would stick to the napkin. I simply would pull the napkin out and could hardly believe what I was seeing. All this mucus would be on one or more napkins and more hanging on just like a large spider web. Jeri's throat would be clear and she did not need a suction machine to do it. Sometimes she would go weeks with a clear throat, not needing a napkin or anything. When the mucus returned, I would use napkins for a few days until it would clear again for a period of time. Often I would have to use several napkins to clear her. Not very professional but this worked for I would say several years and several trips we made.

Jeri and I were always eating at our same favorite Bob Evans restaurant two or three times a week for two or three years. The staff and management who got to know Jeri would put us in "our" back table, if available, and Jeri became Queen for a day. They knew Jeri had MS and would see that she had plenty of napkins (soon to become ours) to use in eating and actually take with her. On a Sunday or whenever, sometimes our entire family would join in going with us.

We did keep the napkins and we would carry them on all of our train trips. Actually, I would stuff some in all my clothing pockets to be sure I always had napkins handy. It worked unbelievably well.

The moral of the story is perhaps this is not the right way of handling this but families and nurses etc have to try what they feel comfortable with, what with MS being such an "outlaw," that real medical treatment is not always available.

ALERT ALARMS

Now here's a problem that we could not fix. Did we try? Hear us out.

When Jeri stopped walking, compounded with being unable to talk, it took us a while to realize that putting these two symptoms together, we had two problems: Communication and Fire Escape. These gave us a lot to think about. We knew one reason for Jeri to be on a computer was learning a way to communicate. That was one of two goals in learning the computer. Her MS doctor asked us, "How do you communicate with Jeri?" We had answered this question early in the book on the page that read **"How do we communicate with each other?"**

We told him we had different signals we used and were careful of not asking Jeri questions but rather would make statements that she could smile or nod her head. Over the years, she became helpless in such situations. What would work? Oh, a button alarm? How would she press the button? Make a sound? How? I tried placing a tin can on her bed that would roll off and make noise in which case if we were in another room, we would hear it. In a way it worked but only in practice. How do we get the can to move off the bed? Another idea - I called 911 and briefed them on this and asked if they had any ideas? The person said, "No, but if you hear of a way, let us know."

The fire marshal visited us, looked around, talked with Jeri, and said, "If you have a fire, she's not getting out."

Talking with various companies about this, they all said what they had they could help Jeri. After finding out what Jeri could not do, they admitted they had nothing to help her with.

Finally a salesman with equipment he brought with him had a real possibility. He set it up, had us go to another room and somehow had Jeri making an alert sound. This really looked good. How much was it? How about thousands of dollars? He named how much. Doesn't matter It was out of our league and I don't think we would ever get Medicare etc to cover it. He had no answer for how it might be covered. There were no more suggestions. We went back doing things our way. We always had a trip, primarily train, lined up. Now this was the fun time. It was time to go. We will find a way to communicate.

CAR

An introduction of car and its relationship to MS – is one of being mandatory for any additional hope of medical and morale help. Perhaps a car should be listed like a wheelchair as "Medically Necessary."

We used a car which we liked better than a van that a wheelchair could be used for. No question to the van being better for wheelchairs. But were they better for the user? It depends on the user.

We found vans to be too expensive for us. Our comments were always:

Do not count on free vans.

Get in your car out of your wheelchair. A car seat is much more comfortable.

Obviously a van is better for a doctor visit etc where you can stay in your wheelchair. You can't have it both ways unless you can afford it.

Jeri even designed, for one car we were interested in, her colors she wanted. She picked tan on the outside and green on the inside. The dealer was shocked and wasn't too happy. Jeri using her "why not" approach stuck to her choices. I don't think they ever had a combination like that before. I think the dealer wanted Jeri to pick a car he had in stock. The dealer said ok but he would have to order this car from the maker. So order the car from the maker. Jeri liked it and was proud of getting to do it her way.

We were often asked why we didn't get a van for Jeri. Car dealers would sometimes advertise help for those needing a van or a car that they could help pay for. All we ever discovered that a dealer would give us free was a possible swivel seat for Jeri to sit on that would allow her to get in and out easier. What about the expense for the rest of the car or van?

We stayed with a car that would work the best for us. Jeri simply enjoyed looking out her front windows, sitting on the right seat and feeling like she was like everyone else. Take a drive in a seat you can see out of easily. Forget the MS.

Family living in a car..........in our case, most of our years were with one car at a time.

All three of our children managed to scare us with each taking their one turn at almost drowning at different motel pools as we traveled in our car. Jami was about four when she walked politely backwards to the deep end without missing a step, went feet first down under. We saw her from the other end of the pool and quickly got to her. By then she had come up head first without any sign of fear. We asked her if she was ok, she said she was fine, that she just said, under water, "Mother Mary, help me."

Now Jodi, sitting in her own little water float decided, apparently, to see what it looked like upside down. She leaned over and surprisingly, she did get to see the underside head first in the water upside down. However, she could not right herself back up. Jeri and I got to her pretty quick. She didn't choke or cough at all.

Both girls held their breath very good. I don't remember where and when Jeff took his turn. No one else does either. I remember him doing something like this because I remember telling myself, "Now, all three have given us this scare. Now we can relax."

Asking Jeff recently if he remembered needing help in the water, he said he did not remember. He then reminded me that he was younger than Jodi and Jami which would have made him under four years old.

A new family car rides that we enjoyed together over the years in spite of Jeri's MS.

Traveling in our car between 1969 and 1971, I found a large number of brief notes Jeri had hand written reference our traveling. Jeff's name was not mentioned, perhaps because he did not show until 1973. That was nice of Jeri to leave notes for us. I think some of her notes were cute enough to repeat. So briefly at random, here are some:

Jodi and Jami swim in Lake Michigan 1st time.

Jami's shoe fell out of Jack's pocket into Lake Michigan and floated away in the wake. We never found it.

Took ferry to Mackinaw Island. On our return on the last ferry, fog had set in. On a prayer, we barely missed hitting a light house.

Jeri, Jack, Jodi went swimming in St. Lawrence River.

Jeri: Playground with chain bridge. (When in Canada we would always look for playgrounds for our children to stop, use and see if there was anything different. This chain bridge was different. We took drawings of it and built one in our backyard connecting two play houses already built. It became a favorite in our neighborhood).

Auto to bus to Subway to Expo 67 Montreal including a mini rail ride over fair - Expo 67 ended in 67 but continued most of it under a different name from 1968 until 1981.

Sunday, June 29, 1969 Jeri wrote, "on to beaches-----Lake Ontario water: cold & windy but I braved it!"

Another story as we remember it was in July, 1975 when we were on our way to Pipestem, West Virginia. We stopped at Beckley, West Virginia where a film was being made for TV. With us was Jodi (age 10), Jami (age 5) and Jeff, (age 2). This film was being produced at a coal mine and the stars of the show were Claude Akins and Gary Merrill. As one knows, it is usually exciting watching a TV film being made. It is more exciting being real close to the stars. During a break in the action, Claude Akins was near us and Jodi and Jami. He saw we were trying to take pictures of him and the girls. He reached for Jami, held her in his arms and we took the picture. Now get this. Jodi received his autograph but Jami was in his picture! We received autographs from Claude Akins and Gary Merrill.

When we were in our car on our way home after staying at Pipestem State Park, somehow we ended in Nashville, Tennessee home of the Grand Ole Opry. The family decided they wanted to stay and watch the Grand Ole Opry show that night. Our stop was to be at Fort Knox, Kentucky the next day so I could show them where I played soldier. Now how can we do both? I realized I would lose this one since I was outnumbered 4 to 1, including me. We stayed. I had it all figured out. We watch the show and try to stay as long as we can in the theater and then head for Fort Knox in the morning. So we went to the ticket window and said we wanted five tickets. "Sorry, we are all sold out." Our jinx is working again. "What about standing room?" we asked. They didn't seem too happy with that because we had three young children. Jeri, where are you? Get your act going and say why not. We began a discussion with them that it would be ok, we could handle the children. Sold - we had five balcony standing room "tickets." I don't remember anyone else standing. Maybe that was what delayed them selling us standing room.

The theater was packed, seating that is. We had the balcony to ourselves. We bought pop corn and told the kids to sit on the floor against the back. Jeri and I sat there also. Anyway, the show started, the kids were having a great time. Suddenly a few people sitting in seats in front of us got up and offered their seats to us. We said thanks but our family seems like they are enjoying where we are. We would rather stay where we are and did so.

The show was great and people were leaving. It was around midnight. What do we do now? It turned out that another stage program was to be put on shortly. All people not staying for this show had left, so we moved downstairs to sit and rest. Not too many stayed so we were able to do this. We were ready to leave in just a few hours of rest. In the morning we were able to make our way to Fort Knox where we were to spend several hours. Now we were homeward bound.

By 1985, our children were growing up pretty fast but we managed to continue family car trips. We were in full force of five now. Jeri's first owned wheelchair in 1985 had been primarily because the children earlier, as mentioned, shopping at a mall recognized her difficulty in walking and wearing herself out and talked her into getting her own wheelchair in November 1985. This was a major change in our family but actually it was a good one. Jeri seemed more comfortable, relaxed and used "Let's do it" more. So we got Jeri back with us. Now we were all comfortable once again.

Our three children always stayed close to Jeri. They never understood MS but then no one in the whole world understood either. They were on board for the duration, sometimes a rough trip that Jeri made look easy. So what's the problem? If mom can do it, we will help. This they did in many ways and I'm sure they were glad they came. It was their decision. Jeri showed them the way. They learned very well that there was only one way, the hard way.

They made their own productive choice, not ahead of time or by someone else. Over time they just seemed to fit where needed and how they could best help Jeri. There was nothing magic about that.

Eventually our three children, while keeping abreast with Jeri and me, began their own families. Jodi, living her married life with three young children in Livonia, MI worked with case managers, kept lining up nurses, talking with doctors etc. Jami married with two children, was only one mile from us and was Jeri's prime nurse, always teaching nurses, watching Jeri closely for her needs etc. Jeff married with two children was always nearby helping lifting Jeri, making wheelchair parts etc. All three were backups for Jeri whenever needed, which was usually often. No complaints from them and they never talked bad about their mother. We were always proud of them no matter what they did and helping Jeri the way they did, we won.

But let's get back to our car traveling in 1986 where we were still able to have our fast growing children with us. We had a revitalize reaction – out of our way MS..........and 1986 was the time to hit the road. Two major car trips did it.

Trip one (June 1986) was in DC for a five day stay at the Radisson Hotel in Virginia. Staying at the Radisson was one of the first times we had the children with us at a luxurious hotel. Add our big white station wagon to this and we felt we were really traveling in style. Jeri was riding her first wheelchair which was easily put in the car as Jeri was resigned to her front seat near me. We did the normal trek around the many sites including Arlington, Washington Monument, the Capitol, the Basilica National Shrine, even to the Navy Yard to tour a Navy destroyer. We also had with us tickets for a tour of Kennedy Center. To top this we had been told by a Representative to Congress that special arrangements had been made for our family to tour the Pentagon. Further instructions were that Jeri would take the tour in a cart with Jodi and Jami while I would be taking the regular tour with Jeff (walking). They would be separate because of not being able to put wheelchairs in with a group.

Of course, we had to be different. The guides meeting visitors including us at the Pentagon were kind of surprise to see us. The tour, through several halls, caught the tour guides a little by surprise when our family having five including one in a wheelchair appeared. The regular tour took visitors walking around in a group. They were not prepared for a wheelchair. They huddled together to decide what to do. They did put Jeri, Jodi and Jami in a Cart and left Jeff and me to walk. Actually, I remember Jeff and me just walking along with the Cart. It was interesting and educational. There was, even back then, instructions that "Visitors must undergo airport-like security checks before the tour begins and stay with their group throughout the tour." I don't remember that one. We were on our own tour together as planned.

Trip two (December 1986) took us to Walt Disney World in Florida, by our station wagon, of course. It was Christmas Day when we spent the whole day there. We had driven a whole day and all night to get there. The kids were able to sleep in the car. We were disappointed when driving down from

Bowling Green we thought we would see a lot of Christmas decorations all the way. There were very few. It was like well we traveled on an interstate highway, so much for scenery. We had a great family time there. Jeri was able to stay in her wheelchair for just about everything. We had even brought a few wrapped Christmas presents for everyone and opened them in our hotel room where we stayed once more at a Radisson hotel. We went to Mass on New Years' Eve and then went out to find a good restaurant to eat and celebrate. Well that was our intention. We learned that on this date, if you did not have a reservation "years" ahead, forget it and go home. We searched everywhere for a restaurant that was available. We finally found one not too attractive and more on the hamburger side but it was our celebration. We would make it work.

I found three Disney World 15 years celebration tickets among our souvenirs we had brought home which read "If a prize name appears in the box above, you're a winner." Well, two read "sorry no prize today." One read you're a winner "Disney Visor." So we were

 winners, I guess. The tickets were dated December 25, 1986. From our souvenir newspaper,  there was a list of prizes being given away in the order of importance. In the eleven categories, our winning ticket was tenth. See we did win. We were not last.

Again we enjoyed our hotel, went swimming while we stayed a few days. Jeri enjoyed this and I found her out on a bench getting a suntan. It's funny but

wherever we went, Jeri was not a handicapped person she was the smiling star of our family.

While in Florida, we spent a day at the Kennedy Space Center. Once more for our children, they were getting a good education. From there we headed home.

We stopped and spent New Years' Eve in Nashville again at a Radisson. We were disappointed somewhat when there seemed to be no activity outside. It was a quiet evening in our room. The next morning told a different story. Downstairs in the lounge areas, the place was a first class mess. Someone had a good time. Good thing we didn't go down that night. I think the kids would have really liked it.

Again, we had a great vacation.

Jeri with her progressive MS did not change enough to be noticeable except for her walking and tiring. Nothing seemed to be happening to MS research either. Our children did not understand MS but it seemed to affect the kids to want to help Jeri as time went on. Their going with us on trips helped Jeri a lot. On the other hand, Jeri and I were picking out some pretty good trips to go on — free to the children.

Another major car trip that became interesting without our planning any surprises began Wednesday August 4, 1993. We would drive 2,062 miles, arriving home Friday August 13, 1993.

OUR FIRST ASA PICNIC AT VINT HILL WAS IN 1993

We had heard about ASA picnics being held at Vint Hill. It gave me an idea to drive there with Jeri to show her an Army camp where I had been stationed many years before. On August 4, 1993, Jeri and I alone on this trip, headed for Virginia.

A little background:

Vint Hill Farms Station near Warrenton, Virginia was an ASA post for many years. The Army had chosen  this area to establish an ASA secret camp for intercepting messages. A large barn was there for primary training and actual military operations. It was a perfect building to look like a working farm. Had it been that? Originally possibly yes but when the government bought Vint Hill in 1942, it became a military post eventually used by ASA. When Jeri and I did our original ASA Book, we found pictures of this barn being rebuilt in the early forties by the military. Vint Hill Farms was our nation's first large listening post.

Another discovery was a state county road that cut right through Vint Hill that was used by residents in the area. By then the Army had established a MP station right at the entrance which military personnel used, by ID, to get into the camp. So what about all the residents? The country road stayed and the residents were given their legal rights to use it!

After finishing training at Fort Knox, Kentucky in 1951, I was sent to Vint Hill Farms Station either to be assigned there or sent overseas. An interesting remembrance was when several of us checked into Vint Hill, after finding it, we were wondering what we were into. Another soldier already stationed there asked if we would like to know what all the telephone poles were for at the camp entrance. Of course, everyone wanted to know. He said, "I will tell you, It is an obstacle course for pigeons."

Jeri and I arrived in Warrenton on Friday and checked into a Hampton Inn. We met my brother, who had been in ASA, and his wife there. We explored the Manassas Civil War battlefield which was pretty good but nothing like Gettysburg. The next day It was on to the picnic plus it was a grand time for Jeri to take an active part in an ASA activity at an Army post for probably her first time. There were 350-400 ASAers and guests there – we didn't know anyone. We did what we had learn about ASA – introduce yourselves, you're among the best friends you may ever meet.

During the course of the day, a retired Army general, a former ASAer, gave a very good talk about ASA – **what it was and what its mission was**. This surprised me because I thought we were still covered by our ASA "life time oath" which apparently had ended, perhaps because ASA was officially ended **1 January 1977.** I was especially grateful that Jeri was present to listen to this talk. She finally learned what ASA was.

After all the music, a few drinks, and by now everyone (well, perhaps a few) knowing each other, we went to a dinner that was beyond explaining and was served in an original building built in 1860. It was a Mongolian barbeque feast starting with a salad then came all small pieces of beef, pork and turkey topped with sauces and red wine, all stir fried together and served with rolls and coffee. Price was 60 cents an ounce. Our bill was $6.40. Now that was a party.

This meal was interesting to me because 42 years earlier I was on KP at this very house which was then the officers living quarters. Their meal mess left for us to clean up was terrible. Here I am now eating like a celebrity in the same house.

The next day the four of us went to church in Warrenton and then we went swimming. When my brother Tom and his wife Betty left to go home, Jeri and I drove into DC. Of course, I did what I was best at, we got lost ending up at the waterfront. From there we found our way to Arlington Cemetery. I pushed Jeri up to the "Unknown Soldier" a long walk up, not bad coming down. Arriving back down, we were told we could have driven up! The next day we drove to Williamsburg, ate lunch there (not very good), saw a little of the "restored village" but left – did not think much of it.

From there, Jeri and I made our way to Norfolk where we took a three hour harbor tour in the evening and then went back to our hotel after dark. It took us about two hours to find it. The next morning we took the naval base tour (of course, a $2.50 tour).

Next, A PEACEFUL CAR RIDE for our first visit to Virginia Beach.....wheelchair acts like a horse and throws Jeri to the ground.....Now who or what would do something like that to Jeri?

After the naval tour, we finally headed for Virginia Beach where we could now take a break and enjoy the ocean and everything that went with it.

We arrived in the afternoon of August 10, 1993, parked our car several blocks away and walked to the beach. We then decided to get something to eat, shop around and then have a lovely evening on the beach. We never quite got that far or eating or shopping or a lovely evening on the beach.

Within a couple of minutes on the beach, we began walking towards the street to find a place to eat. As I looked up and down the street for a nice eating place, behold a hidden curb in the sand where I pushed Jeri down the curb right off forward from her wheelchair. She tumbled out and landed on her face on the cement. A nasty cut on her forehead just above her right eye was bleeding. Her sun glasses she had on were knocked off her head with the left glass well scratched but neither eye glass broke. She said, "I'm ok." A lifeguard was near, came over and called for an ambulance. When they came and put Jeri inside I told them not to leave until I get our car and follow you, otherwise, how would I know where you took her. As I got into our car and started back to them, I found out that they did not wait. I could see their light flashing and began speeding to catch them. I couldn't catch them but I kept them in view long enough to see which hospital they took her to. I pulled in, parked and went to the emergency room where the hospital staff was already working on her. Jeri ended with 11 stitches in her forehead (a bad cut over her right eye}, a cut under her nose, on her arm and cuts on her right shoulder and knee. To top it off, she had a broken bone in her right ankle. She was smiling as if nothing happened. She had the nurses and doctors smiling too. They looked at me and said, "You should have been arrested for reckless driving."

So to finish with Jeri, they put a splint on her ankle and leg and said she was to have her doctor put a cast on it at home. Jeri responded with, "At least now I look like I belong in a wheelchair." So after a six hour visit, they said she was ready to leave. I asked Jeri, "Do you want to go home or continue our vacation?" Silly question since I already knew the answer. "Finish our trip," she answered.

I said to Jeri, "What are we going to tell the kids when we get home. They won't let us go alone on any more trips." "She said we won't tell them." Good point.

We never did get back to the beach but we did continue our trip which took us to Beckley WV and then to a prime favorite of our family, Pipestem State Park in West Virginia. We checked in and the next day we had lunch by way of their freight elevator and a walk through the kitchen to get to their dining room.

It was now Friday August 13, 1993, definitely time to go home. But no, we didn't want to go home yet. It seemed over the years of our car traveling, on our last day we always had to make one more stop if we were going home. From the west, we would stop for a picnic and swim at Lake Erie's "East Harbor." If we were coming from the east, it would be Pennsylvania's Lake Erie's "Presque Isle." From where we were on this trip at Pipestem the stop was "Hartville Kitchen" near Kent. As usual at this stop, we took a lot of home cooking back to our children.

We finally arrived home. They at first did not notice anything until later when they asked Jeri, "What's that on your leg?"

OUR SECOND ASA PICNIC AT VINT HILL

 **WAS IN 1994** when Jodi and Jeff drove Jeri and me to it. We left Bowling Green August 4 at 2:30 am arriving in Manassas, VA Wednesday, August 4, checked into our Hampton Inn for four nights and went swimming at the hotel. On Friday we went into DC to the Capitol, Arlington Cemetery, Ford's Theatre and the Hard Rock Café. Saturday was the picnic.

The picnic was sponsored by the Vint Hill Farms Station Warrant Officers Association and again there was a large crowd at this beautiful perfect place to have a picnic. Since it was already owned by the government and had carried on a modern intelligence program, it seemed wrong to tear it apart. One retired officer who spoke about this made a good point when he said that, "yes we now have satellites to do all ofthis but the day may come that they can be shot down." Somewhere along the "way" we were asked to write letters to the governor of Virginia questioning the wisdom of getting rid of Vint Hills Station. We did this but had no reply.

Soon, it was time for another Mongolian barbeque feast which I had already reserved four dinners for 6 pm.

The next day, Sunday, we went to the post chapel for Mass. This was not quite an ordinary Mass. It was one I had always wanted Jeri to attend. This was a surprise for me when I found there was still an active chapel at this Army camp. To me and perhaps others in the service, there was no comparison to attending Mass at an Army chapel. It always seemed so different, yet it wasn't. The Mass is the same everywhere. An Army camp Mass is usually well attended, quiet, sermons quick and to the point with little preaching etc. It just seemed to always have more meaning and Army chaplains were at their best.

Still Sunday, we went back to DC to go to the Smithsonian, Navy Memorial, National Archives, Washington Monument and then all together to the Smithsonian Castle. It was then back to our hotel to get ready for our leaving the next day.

We weren't finished yet. Monday we went to Ft. Meade, MD to visit the Center for Cryptologic History. We were allowed to visit this Museum adjacent to Ft. Meade but not Ft. Meade itself, home of the National Security Agency, which became active in intelligence shortly after ASA was established.

After touring the museum, I had one question to ask the person directing us. I had noticed that the only reference to ASA was a small banner hanging on the wall. "Shouldn't more credit be given to ASA?" He didn't know how to answer this and directed me to the "comment" suggestion book at the entrance. He said, "Write your question in that book." I did and never received an answer!

While touring the museum we found the most interesting thing they had to show us was the well kept secret by Germany, the Enigma. This cipher machine was used by the German forces during World War II. It had many key settings and machine configurations. To find one here at the museum was a pleasant surprise. They briefly showed us how it was used and allowed us to try. Since Jeri could only watch, because of her MS, we decided to send our first and only message to Jeri and surprise her. With a little help from the museum staff, we "sent" a message to Jeri on the Enigma. This is the way we did it:

This was 8-8-94. The attached was "sent" on the Enigma:

(Rotaries were set at 09-02-14)

Message "Hi Jeri" was "typed" on the keyboard using:

H → Y   J → O
I → K   E → F
            R → A
            I → L

To decrypt: Set rotaries back to 09-02-14

"Type" YKOFAL → would light up
each letter of "HI JERI"

We then headed to Baltimore, Maryland. Jodi knew someone there that she worked with when both were at the Detroit Tigers. She found the person and we all took a little tour of their new Baltimore Baseball Stadium.

Now it was time to head home. This time we went by way of Interstate 80 stopping in Lancaster, PA for good eating that we had been to before. I think everyone but Jeri was worn out. No MS on this trip. Why stop?

OUR THIRD ASA PICNIC AT VINT HILL WAS IN 1995 when Jodi drove Jeri and me to it.

This was to be our last ASA picnic as we later found out why. We would miss it. Jeri would miss it. How could this have been the last? Well it seems the US Government had other plans for Vint Hill – to close and sell it.

As the saying went "Save the best for last." This picnic was a good one, even served the same menu and was sponsored by the Warrant Officers. Several activities included one giving away an Army history book. Jeri and I decided to sit down and watch. A Warrant Officer had a question for someone to identify and receive the book. The question was taken from way back before World War II and was about the US Army getting more involved in intelligence work by intercepting and listening to messages. The Secretary of the Army was against this and said, "Gentlemen do not listen in on other people talking." Who was this Secretary? I quickly answered this almost before he finished the question and yelled out who it was. We won the

history book. Well, it so happened, I remembered the name because I had read about this just recently. People there probably thought I was brilliant to remember an old story  like that and to answer so quickly. Jeri was sitting right with me and kind of knew I had the answer so she didn't give it much value. Well, I thought it was cute. I never did that before.

During the afternoon there were some displays of Army equipment including a newly developed "night helmet" that had a mask attached that you could wear and see in the darkness. They put one on Jeri. She did good and enjoyed doing this show and tell. With MS, Jeri was most excited when she was "involved" in something herself or with others doing something meaningful and/or fun. Putting that newly designed Army "night" helmet on her was a good example otherwise she would have been just a spectator. Better yet, if Jeri was helping them test this helmet, she had to feel proud. I wasn't even asked to test it.

Well, after that excitement, we decided to go to the dining room of my former KP hangout so I could dirty more dishes and let someone else clean up. As Jeri, Jodi and I sat down for another great meal a warrant officer came over to serve us or was it to come over to see Jodi? He sat with us for dinner but was talking to Jodi more than us.

Jeri and I made our own way around the picnic area. We happened to sit down with a retired General who had been an Army Inspector General. When he introduced himself, I introduced Jeri and myself. For something to say, I said, "I have a question for you. Would you have any idea of how I might have gotten into ASA? I never knew and was never told." He said well what was your MOS? (Military Occupation Specialties) I told him it was a tankers MOS. A surprise look and a quick answer – "Well I don't know how you got in but I do know we certainly did not need any tanks."

After leaving the picnic, Jodi drove Jeri and me to Atlantic City and DC. At the White House, we were fortunate to have three tickets for the "two-floor tour." Normally the tour was a one-story tour. We soon had a problem. Jeri did it again! When our tour group was finished on the first floor and moved up to floor two by stairs, we could not follow because Jeri was in a wheelchair. Read on:

We hesitated a second. Within that second, a Secret Service Agent was upon us dressed in a regular suit and said, "I will take Jeri and one of you up on the elevator." We left Jodi to walk up the stairs while the agent pushed Jeri in her wheelchair with me following through a couple of hallways where there were folded metal chairs lined up. It was a bit exciting. Here we are in the White House, having left the tour group, and taking our own tour. We entered, of all rooms, the kitchen. It was quite busy. Surprisingly, it was quite small. The pots and pans hanging from their overhang were very clean but also very used. We were taken to the kitchen elevator. The two of us and Jeri in the wheelchair barely fit into it. As we got on, I noticed someone had written in chalk on a chalkboard on the wall "Breakfast today – Pancakes." As our new found friend, the security agent, went to press the button, another man came quickly to get on. He was dressed in a tuxedo, obviously the one in charge, the chef perhaps? Now the elevator was a bit crowded. Before we started up, for something to say, I asked the man in the tux, "Is this really the White House kitchen?" He was very serious looking when he got aboard, but my question surprised him. "Of course," he said, "It's the only one we have." He was really smiling by now. We arrived on the second floor and our security guide was able to catch up to our regular tour. I think Jodi wondered where we were all this time. I wished she had gone instead of me. She would have enjoyed it and have something to remember. I know Jeri enjoyed it – having her own Secret Service Agent pushing her through the halls of history. Wow!

Before being home bound, we had one more stop to make. We had Jodi drive us to Ft. Meade, MD to visit the Center for Cryptologic History. This was our second visit to the museum but since we were close by we wanted to see if it had expanded which it had. Now we can head home.

My skillful car driving taking Jeri and me on our trips around the country ended suddenly in none other than Bowling Green, itself……….

By car, Jeri and I did a lot by ourselves, with me doing the driving. It came a time when I decided I was not going to drive any more. What helped me to decide was that it was time to renew my driver's license. The license bureau refused to renew it (year 2000). I was surprised and a bit upset. I thought Jeri would be upset also. When I got home, I told Jeri,

"They would not renew my driver's license." She said, "Good."

Not able to drive caused a new problem. It didn't take us long to adjust. By analyzing our situation and intending to remain independent, we found we could walk to a nearby coffee shop, the hospital was only a mile away and even walking downtown was enjoyable. Free rides, often with "donation appreciated" signs helped but all agencies offering this transportation had "gimmicks" included which made you learn them or do without. Jeri qualified for Medicaid car rides but their rule was that the Senior Center had to do it before they would. And then there were restrictions like only available within certain miles, limited trips reserved in advance etc. We used these services by accepting our situation and while accepting it worked, it was not easy.

People, when finding out I could not drive, would offer to take us shopping or even to church. This was nice and appreciated but we felt this could lead to more problems. We did not want people to feel they were always "on call". It could become unfair advantage. For example asking someone to take you to church every week would be unfair to them. On occasion, it could work but this could work into a regular ride. Eventually our three children began driving us.

Our Station Wagon Jeri got for $7,000 ends its faithful service by running out of oil on its last one block trip!

As mentioned earlier, It was in 1980 when Jeri entered a bidding contest between the car dealer and me. Jeri let go her $7,000 offer and it was all over. The station wagon was ours.

In an early trip in our new wagon we no sooner left BG when the transmission went out. Stopping at a garage it took a while to get it replaced and there was a problem as to who would pay.

We continued our trip and many trips after that including our two and half years back and forth to Kent. The car was excellent and served us well, even when we pulled into a trailer park to spend a night and when we asked them if a station wagon could also stay there, they answered, "Of course."

When Jodi was using the wagon in BG, she was hit by another car which smashed our left side back door completely. It could not be opened. It looked terrible all bent and damaged. The car itself took a pretty good hit on that side but this wagon was one tough car. When the car was hauled to some distant lot probably to be destroyed, we found out it could still be driven. So we kept the car and continued using it. The one door could never be opened and the car itself drove down the road a little sideways. I understood it soon was recognized anywhere in BG. One suggestion to us was we should enter it in a car demolition derby.

The ending was near in a rather undistinguished manner. One day I took it to a gas station to have the oil changed. When I went to see if it was ready to pick up, I paid the station and drove off. Our station wagon went one block and conked out. I walked back to the gas station. They were surprised, did a little checking and found out the employee changing the oil, drained the oil but then forgot to put oil back in. The motor apparently was destroyed. When we asked what it could cost to repair it, the owner said it would probably take a new engine but wouldn't be worth it. He was nice enough to say it was their fault and he offered us cash to buy it.

So after over ten years and over 100,000 miles service, our best car ever was out of oil.

BUSSES, TAXIS, SUBWAYS, RENTAL CARS, AIRPLANES, ONE NYC POLICE CAR AND ELEVATORS - (elevators – travel?)

BUSSES

On a trip to Cincinnati......to go to our Army reunion at Ft. Mitchell, Kentucky, there was no direct train ride to get to Cincinnati. We would have to go to Chicago first. We then decided to ride the bus from Bowling Green and then take a taxi to the reunion. We had prearranged to have a bus with a lift on board to pick us up in BG. The driver stopped for us but found out the lift would not work. The driver said, "I will not leave Jeri behind, I'll get her on." He carried her on the bus and placed Jeri in her wheelchair back in the bus where wheelchairs would be near a door tied down. He apologized and said, "In Cincinnati, we won't have this problem. They will fix the lift right there at the bus station and we will be able to use the lift door back there to get Jeri out." Arriving at the Cincinnati station, the worker there could not get the lift to work either and could not open the lift door in the back where Jeri was. The driver said, "We will carry her out." The bus was filled with passengers heading south. One passenger came forward and told the driver, "I'll help you carry her." All the other passengers stayed in their seats. The two men lifted Jeri and the wheelchair up above the passengers as far as they could go to the ceiling, over the heads of the passengers. They carried her through the narrow aisle to the front and out the door steps of the bus and onto the pavement. Unbelievable! I could only watch. I not only wanted to thank them, which I did, but I wanted to give the man that helped something. When he got back on the bus to go to his seat, I handed him a five dollar bill and said I really appreciated what he had done. He refused the tip and "yelled" at me and said, "Don't you ever do that!" Wow. I was a little stunned. I asked, "Do what?" He said, "offer someone money when they offer to help you." We never forgot that message and I certainly learned from it.

From Cincinnati, we were able to take a taxi to our reunion in Kentucky. We further decided to not take the bus back to BG but would take the train to DC from Cincinnati. This part of the story is continued within **"Train Destinations, Reunions."**

Bus to Disneyland.....even going to one of the best entertainments in the world, one sometimes has to accept people as they are.

We were staying at a hotel outside Los Angeles but close to Disneyland. Our daughter Jami and her husband and son were with us. We had come by train and decided the first morning there we would catch the hotel courtesy handicapped bus service to Disneyland. The bus was crowded but we were able to get Jeri and her wheelchair on ok. As the bus pulled out, we found ourselves standing in the aisle, all seats were taken. The bus driver was in a hurry and you had to hold on pretty good. As I was holding Jeri the best I could in her wheelchair and maintain my balance at the same time, I noticed a sign over the large side seat which read "seat for handicap passengers." There were four people sitting in it. None got up to offer Jeri their seat. At the next stop, I asked the driver about the people sitting in the handicap section. He quickly responded abruptly saying, "I'm not going to ask or tell those people to move." We hung on to a very wild trip to Disneyland. This happened on four trips on the hotel's courtesy bus service to Disneyland in which they failed to tie down Jeri's wheelchair. I understand in our case, if people are sitting in these seats, the tie downs are under the seats. I had mentioned this to the hotel but they said since they contract this out, they were not responsible. Later Jeri told me she was very scared going through Los Angeles in a fast moving bus being held just by me. I learned that there is an amount of fear riding in a wheelchair when you can't control yourself. Jeri proved this.

Out of curiosity, I called an 800 number which turned out to be the Justice Department to question them on this tie down business. They thought the hotel could be held responsible if only for negligence. They wanted me to file a complaint and suggested two different phone numbers they gave me to call. I didn't feel this was up to us to call because I was only after information and we were traveling. Well, we let it go at that. No one got hurt. This was to be a happy time, let it be. Looking back to my call to the Justice Department, I question why they didn't handle my call as a complaint and do their own testing as to what I said. With us traveling left us out of that picture, I think they should have thanked us and say they would check it out.

As far as Disneyland, we obviously had a great time. Jami and family went there three days while Jeri and I went two days.

TAXIS

As a general rule, if you are in a wheelchair, taxis play an important part in your getting around. Taxis can answer your needs when nothing else is available. From our experiences, taxi trips are never the same. While they all serve the same purpose, the drivers are all different.

Reference wheelchairs, taxi problems are tough to handle. You, yourself, have to know what you are doing, where you want to go and even where you want to SIT in the taxi. We rarely found a taxi that knew how to handle someone in a wheelchair. I or a daughter or whoever was with us had to take charge and tell, not ask, the driver what to do. As a rule, they were fairly polite but rarely would help you in and out of their car. In Jeri's case where she could not help herself, I would tell drivers she had to ride in the front seat. This was because the back doors never opened wide enough to transfer a person into without difficulty. Not only would the drivers not like the idea, it usually meant they had to "clean" up their front seat where they kept all their needed papers etc. As far as fares went, you better do some homework, don't even try to argue with the driver and being handicapped usually meant nothing to the driver. We found out being nice to them helped somewhat and sometimes a lot. You'll rarely know what it will cost you and with those that use a meter box counting machine that you can see, your tab shoots up pretty fast, even at red lights.

A couple of taxi trips follow:

A stranger appears out of nowhere to help Jeri.........on one trip coming out of the main entrance to Union Station in DC from our train, we were aware of taxis being waiting for passengers. We decided to take one to our hotel. When we saw all the taxis waiting in a single line along the curb and then saw this long almost complete large circle of people waiting their turn for one, we were stunned. We have no choice. It took a long walk to find the last person in line. One taxi at a time one or more passengers at a time getting in, we will be here forever. This large circle of people with patience for a taxi, and waiting peacefully, was almost unreal. So, as usual, Jeri waits. This time we had a lot of company. We could see the taxi loading area in the distance. Someone was controlling the loading and making them move fast. This person had no uniform, even just looked like someone helping.

Everyone being patient, we shall do the same. We had not moved more than one or two steps forward when a lady stood about thirty yards from us waving to come to her quickly. Not knowing what she wanted, we did what she waved us to do. We stepped out in "nobody's land" and began following her. She was taking us to the head of the line! I thought wow this crowd is really going to boo us. Nothing happened. We followed, sure enough to the head taxi waiting for us to get in. This lady was next in line but she had given her place to us. How did she see us? How quickly she acted. We never even got to thank her. Amen to all the good people we met on our trips.

This next example is easy to explain even though we got caught off guard. In DC, Jeri and I were planning to call for a taxi to take us somewhere. We also had a delivery for a secretary we knew in our Congressman's office. When I told her we were planning to go somewhere in a taxi which would take us right pass her office building, she said don't bother stopping, I'll wait for you in front on the sidewalk and you can give this to me right from the taxi. That was a good idea. The taxi picked us up and as we proceeding to head to our destination, I told him to just make a brief stop at the House office building. An office secretary was waiting on the sidewalk for a delivery we would give her without our getting out. He did this. It took about five seconds. Surprise, he charged us for two trips.

SUBWAYS

We knew a little bit about subways and their poorly kept conditions and the rush on and off of them. But now we are talking wheelchairs getting on and off. We had never ridden a subway by ourselves before.

On our Amtrak DC trip in September 2000 to attend our 8th ASA reunion in Arlington, Virginia, we stayed three days at the hotel there and when it was over, it was then time for us to move on to College Park, Maryland to continue our book research at the archives. How to get to College Park? On the map it looked like about a thirty minute ride on the interstate circling DC. Our ASA friends Elmer & Alice Yeakel offered to drive us to our hotel there. It took about an hour and a half to get there. We couldn't check in yet so we decided to store our luggage and "practice" becoming subwayers. We had intended to go by bus to downtown DC but after checking all the different busses and ways to get there – forget it. We will try the subway. We liked it. It was a fantastic subway system. If only we knew how to at least get on and off. I envisioned pushing Jeri on first and the door closing between us. I told her if that happens, I'll catch up to you? How? I don't know. By the end of our stay in DC, I was able to get our subway tickets out of the many machines all by myself and I didn't lose Jeri even once. To go through the turn stills which could not, in those years, handle wheelchairs, we had to get the one and only station employee to get us through.

To go to downtown DC was easy with several stations to get off at. Returning to our hotel station was "better know which station you want off at." I solved that problem by counting the number of stops before the one we needed. In this case it was ten. Now on one return trip, we got on easy, sat down and holding the wheelchair tightly, I started counting the stops. Stop one was easy. Stop two not only stopped, it never started again. Now what's wrong? The inside car lights started flickering. So we just waited. But by then we had notice not only regular riders were getting off at their stop but everyone in our car was off. The blinking lights must have been telling us to get off. We looked outside. People were waving us to get off. So we got off. What it was, that train was being taken out of service. We would have to reboard on the next train through. Ah. Now we know, watch for a blinking the next trip. We often wandered what would have happened if we had ignored it and stayed on. Probably it would have been a free ride to their barn. We should have stayed on.

While in College Park, we depended on the subway and used it for six round trips. By then I was pretty good using them! Well, not really. We spent about 30 hours total at the archives but found very little. Some days, Jeri was in her wheelchair nine hours in a row. To do what we wanted to do besides research we also went sightseeing. Jeri did it without a single "grumpy." Remember, in a wheelchair, there aren't many accessible places to visit and probably worse in those days. If I questioned her if it was time to get back to our hotel, she would say no. This is what we came for. I knew she hated the sidewalks around the main attractions but never once complained. Now these were the ones recently built with "soft" cinders and with no breaks – all continuous large sidewalks. They were and are bumpy for wheelchairs.

We did do a lot of Christmas shopping – at the museums and gift shops in federal buildings - we had fun. Of course, we had to carry what we bought with us, even on the train returning home.

RENTAL CARS

Our first car rental was in 1990 and is included in our "round the country trip" in 1990.

Our second car rental was in 1993 when Jeri and I rented a car to go to Two Rock Ranch in California. This was our last rental car – twice was enough! You're read this horrendous day in the 1993 train story.

AIRPLANES

Flying for Jeri seemed normal enough for us to get around the country and we had intended to make use of this means along with trains.

The first time for Jeri and our daughter Jodi to fly was in 1970 when we scheduled a trip to Disneyland in California and started the trip by airplane from Akron, Ohio to Chicago. Later we would finish our return trip by flying from Chicago to Akron. In between, we used the train. Jeri did not have MS at this time nor was she aware of such a "medical" term.

Jeri, as usual, made her first trip just a bit more interesting. She asked to sit on the aisle side rather than by the window. Once we were high in the air, I told her to look out the window and see just where she was. She stood up, leaned as far over towards the window that she could without moving her feet and remained motionless. I asked her, "What are you doing?" She said, "I don't want to tilt the airplane."

This completed her first two trips by air and covered 600 miles. Jeri and Jodi (who was four years old) looked so very nice traveling in exact mother and daughter green outfits made by Jeri.

Plane ride number three and final ride occurred in 1999 and was from Churchill, Canada to Winnipeg, Canada, covering a one way non-stop of 1,060 miles. For this trip, she was in a wheelchair. This story is told in more detail later under "Churchill."

One year we decided to fly to Las Vegas for our Army reunion. Then she did have the MS. Jeri agreed and we thought this would be rather easy since we knew they took passengers in wheelchairs. We called one of the major airlines and told them who we were and would like to get two round trip tickets to Las Vegas from Detroit. It went fine until I mentioned Jeri was in a wheelchair. The person quickly changed her tone and began saying that there would be some long layovers in some cities that Jeri would have to contend with, obviously becoming nervous and negative. She made no attempt to try to help us. We finally said never mind, thank you and hung up. We tried another major airline, same reaction. So after about an hour of listening to excuses (they avoided saying NO), we gave up. I told Jeri, let's call Amtrak and see if we can still ride with them? No problem. It was on to Las Vegas via Amtrak.

ONE NYC POLICE CAR

You might say this little story started in California. During a 1996 trip, we stayed at a hotel for a week to visit Disneyland. There were several disappointments about this hotel. We eventually received some refunds including a gift certificate from their home office to be used at any of their hotels. A year later, we were in DC and decided to use our gift certificate. So, by train we went to New York City. We checked in with a really nice hotel not too far from the theater district. Normally we would not stay that far downtown in NYC because it is more expensive. This time we were treated to two free nights in a fashionable hotel which we were not able to do too often.

Jeri loved New York City's Broadway plays. We decided to see if we could get tickets to see "The Phantom of the Opera." at the "Majestic Theatre?" Being in NYC for two days and seeking play tickets for the next day was wishful thinking. As usual, I listened to Jeri and we called the theater. Tickets ranged from $45 to $90. We were told that they were sold out for the time we wanted tickets. I then asked what plays might be available, that Jeri was in a wheelchair. They said in that case we do have two wheelchairs tickets for the "Opera" but tickets are not refundable. I asked how much were they? They said $7.50 each. They sold us two handicap tickets for $7.50 each for the next evening. Each ticket was printed **SPECIAL WHEELCHAIR TICKET**. While on the side but in reserved seating, we were 6 rows from the stage. This Jeri I knew was becoming impossible to live with! How exciting. Now we get to see a live Broadway show for almost free. (I still have the two stubs from the tickets. I wonder if they have any value).

The next day, getting ready to "step out" to go to the theater, Jeri as usual, looked perfect. Our hotel doorman hailed a taxi for us and we were off for a "night on the town." After the play, which was excellent, was over we made our way outside. Leaving the theater, the marquee was still brilliantly lit. The doorman hailed a cab for us. It pulled up right at the curb but with the driver side next to the curb facing straight ahead. This was at 11 PM and we were affecting traffic. I then realized that we were on a one way street with three lanes, one of which was the no parking lane in front of the theater. I would have to transfer Jeri quickly while out in the street, near the second lane with oncoming traffic, not a very safe maneuver. We almost always had to put Jeri in the front seat because the back seat, especially if I were alone, was most difficult to get her into   because doors would never open wide enough to do so easily. Meanwhile, the cab driver did not offer to help (this was normal) and was busy cleaning off the passenger side of the front seat where I would seat Jeri.

So, on a semi-darkened street, I wheeled, as carefully and as fast as I could, Jeri from the sidewalk, around the car to the front seat door on the street side and opened it wide. As I started to lift Jeri to transfer her, I heard this screeching of a car behind us that speedily pulled up behind us and, sideways, turned to block traffic behind us and also part of the next lane. I looked up. It was a police car. I thought this isn't good. Now I am in trouble.

There were two policemen who quickly jumped out. One began stopping traffic while the other headed straight to Jeri and me. When he reached us he said, "Can we be of service to you?" Wow! What a surprise. He helped getting Jeri in, being very pleasant and really great about it. He then took the wheelchair, folded it and put it in the trunk of the taxi. We thanked them and they said "no problem" and we went on our way, not even a ticket for any number of violations I committed. I was always sorry I never took their badge numbers. I would have sent a letter to their police department. As for Jeri, was she scared? I never thought to ask her. In any case, Jeri and I had a nice quiet evening in New York City at only a cost of $15.00, a couple of taxi charges and help from a couple of nice officers. More of this story is included in our June 2 1997 train trip.

ELEVATORS

New York City

Macy's Department Store at 34th & 35th Streets......Shopping and eating in Famous Macy's on Fifth Avenue was a sudden decision we made on our last trip to New York City. This was in 1997 and we were already staying downtown. Actually we were just walking around seeing the sights when we came upon Macy's. Using Jeri's worn out "Let's," we walked right in. My big "suggestion" – let's eat here too. In department stores like this you could always find pleasant dining rooms, usually on an upper floor. There were ten floors here and I think I found where there was one on the 6th floor. So we will get off on 6. The store was packed. I added let's stop to shop on one of the floors first and then go up to eat. There were plenty of elevators (I would say 10-12) to choose from. We had no problem getting one since we were on the ground floor where most people were getting off and on. With the wheelchair, people would step aside to let us on. I think it was then the third floor when we got off to shop. We didn't buy anything yet when we decided to go eat first. We went back to elevator row and waited only a few seconds when one opened its doors. It was packed going up. We waited for another one and then another and then another. All packed or others beating us to one. The elevators did not wait long – either you were in front of it to get on or wait for the next one. We tried to guess which one we should stay near. That didn't work. We tried running to get to one. That didn't work to well either. By now, I don't know about Jeri but I told her to "forget the shopping and eating, if we ever get on one to get down, we're on it and we're out of here." We made our escape by making a timely "run for it" by choosing the one closest to us as it opened its doors.

Washington, D.C.

Washington Monument......I'm not sure what attracts tourists to not only seeing this monument, but also wanting to go up it, by elevator or walking. Walking up and down use to be allowed but they began finding the cement steps getting worn and needing repair. They now allowed only on occasion one to walk it. It then became primarily required to use the elevator. If you've done this once, you have seen everything. Nevertheless, it was popular. I suspect that Jeri and I have been on it about seven times together. Early on, with Jeri in a wheelchair and with a long line waiting, we were always escorted to the head of the class. No charge. Not much room at the top but you could stay as long as you wanted. People were always patient up there to allow everyone to enjoy the four small windows with different views. You had to stand to see out although they did have small platforms for children to stand on. So how was Jeri to see out? An attendant had a drab olive brown military periscope (looked like from WW1 or 2) that she handed to Jeri. Because it had a short bar to see over with, it was pretty well useless. We tried holding it over Jeri's eyes and judge where to point it. It was better than nothing. She got the idea and was able to see enough scenes to enjoy it.

As we returned to DC, we were ready to work the monument into our schedule. This happened several times. Each time the head of the line with no charge was allowed for Jeri. She also received her "own" periscope, the same periscope she had used each time. It was beginning to look like it was from World War One. These times, they would lay the periscope on her lap at the entrance to the elevator. I think she appreciated this concern for her and valued the periscope even though it was becoming very old as many other sightseers were making use of this same periscope.

To continue our own entertainment on one of the early trips up the monument, I asked Jeri if she remembered seeing red lights shining from the monument. On TV, if you looked closely when they showed the monument, you could see these lights on. I told her the next time we go up the monument, I'm going to find one of those lights and take a picture. So Jeri and I looked for one of the red lights. We found one way up above us built into the outside wall. Jeri watched me move into position to see if I could get to it. Jeri and I now have a picture of a red light shining outside the top of the Washington Monument. The story is, if Jeri can't see everything going on outside, she will join me in doing something inside.

On a later trip there, they had a surprise for us. No head of the line. Jeri waits in line like everyone else. They had discontinued moving handicapped to the head of the line. We had seen enough and bypassed the monument thereafter. The lines seemed always to be very long with a long wait because the one elevator they used only held perhaps ten people.

Lincoln Memorial......visiting this memorial several times with Jeri, it was a case of not knowing there was an elevator at the "building." Jeri would see "Lincoln" inside from outside but from beyond the many steps into the memorial. One later visit we saw a small sign, well "hidden," on the side of the building with an arrow reading and pointing to where there was an elevator. I think it was meant for handicapped. The elevator was old and quite small but everyone was using it. Once again we found ourselves waiting for an elevator. We moved Jeri into it and for the first time, she was able to see this monument up close. Again it had to be exciting for her. She enjoyed normal living like this with everyone else.

Smithsonian National Air and Space Museum...... This was one elevator we did not have to wait for. In this museum we found the best gift shop in town. It was in a large several areas of different gifts for everyone. I suspect we eventually shopped there ten different times but only after we found a way to get to the basement where it was located. We saw the stairs on our first trip there but no elevator until we were directed to the one and only express elevator "reserved" for handicapped and wheelchairs. It was closer to a "dumbwaiter." There was only room for one in a wheelchair and one other person, me, the driver to be. A clerk opened its door and showed us how to operate it. She disappeared and I pressed a button. It was a slow and noisy ride down to the basement floor. I then could not figure out how to open our cage door to get out. I waved to a clerk for help. She had to figure it out also. I then asked, "How do we get back up?" She answered "the same way you came down. You may need help." We went shopping. When we were done shopping, we had a hard time finding where we had left our ride. We knew it was in some out of the way corner. We had to ask someone.

At first Jeri and I didn't like our new friend but since it was our only way up and down, we went for it. Would you believe we began to like our new found ancient wheelchair elevator? Every time we were back to DC and went shopping there, it was always there waiting. All the times we used it, I don't remember seeing anyone else using it. We did notice that it was getting worn and older.

On the lighter side, it seemed to us that this relic was in the right place at the right time. It certainly looked like it belonged in a museum. Perhaps others looking at it didn't realize it was there to be used. Finally on our last visit, a regular passenger elevator had been installed. Now no one had to walk down steps to get there. I wonder what happened to our elevator.

Bowling Green, Ohio

An Avon Dinner Invite ...... Jeri and I were invited to a local area Avon dinner, a place I can't recall where except it was about ten miles away where we would drive to. I usually expect the worse on an invitation so I called the person handling it and asked where this dinner was being held, in a restaurant, hotel or where? She told me where and said it was being held upstairs. I answered, "I assume then that they have an elevator. You know, Jeri is in a wheelchair." She said she wasn't sure but she would call and ask them. She did call and called me back and said, "No problem, they said they do have an elevator." Fine, thank you, we will be there. Our dinner time was approaching when I got Jeri dressed looking really nice and put her in our car for one of our few nights out. We arrived in about thirty minutes and found our dinner was upstairs. We looked for the elevator but could not find it. An employee asked us if we needed help. We told them we came for the Avon dinner being held upstairs and were looking for your elevator we understood you have. "Oh, we have an elevator, but it's a "dumbwaiter."

We never made it to the dinner.

San Francisco

Our 1996 train trip included a stop in San Francisco. With Jeri and I were our daughter Jami, her husband Craig and their son Dylan. We were staying at a downtown hotel. In the lobby getting ready to go SF sightseeing for the day when the President of our ASA reunion group, Jack LaDove heard we were in town and surprised us. He said he would show us around and we began with a trip down to the waterfront. To get there, we entered a building and found an elevator to take us down to sea ground level (as you probably know, SF is very hilly). We saw no one in the building. Jack, our new guide directed everyone to get in the elevator. He started to see which button to hit to go down. As he continued hitting each one, he must have hit down and at the same time an alarm. It was a really loud one. He could not find a way to stop it nor the elevator. We had to wait until the elevator stopped itself. The alarm was at full blast. We had no way of knowing who the alarm was for and expected one or more to come out of nowhere to find out what was going on. Jack yelled above the noise, "As soon as we get down and the door opens, run for it, let's get out of here as quickly as we can." We never did see anyone and the alarm kept going off as we left the building.

Jack did stay with us the entire day. He lived there. He even showed us how to help "turn" the trolley cars around. These were the ones operated by underground cable, the pride of San Francisco. We had a good time. I think Jack did it because of Jeri whom he always made a fuss over at our reunions. She would always laugh with him. He always liked Jeri this way. I don't remember him ever cutting up with others or making them laugh.

More of this story is told in the **"April 1996 train section."**

Canada – Winnipeg Train Station

The large freight elevator at Winnipeg's train station became our only means of entering their station or boarding trains to leave. Regular passengers had a long row of steps to climb both ways. You were not allowed to wait on the platform for trains plus we were usually in for a long wait there anyway. We were introduced to our new elevator, probably the largest one yet, on this our first visit and began to feel like celebrities because of the service we received using this method. Because we used this station many times, we began to recognize employees and they, us especially Jeri (the wheelchair helped people to recognize us). They suggested we leave our luggage in their work area right off the elevator rather than check it in and then have to check it out. They would watch it for us. We never lost any luggage and it was a convenience for us. One attendant who worked in this area and who we got to know quite well (never knew his name at first) recognized us every trip and would always wave or come talk with us. He seemed excited every time to see us. He looked like a twin of our nephew. We always liked and felt comfortable in this station.

Restaurant and hotel elevators – US and Canada

Restaurants - When they were located upstairs, restaurants would have an employee take us to their freight elevator for our tour which usually included by way of their kitchen. We undoubtedly saw more kitchens than anyone traveling.

Hotels - Obviously it was normal for hotels to have elevators. The one concern to us was always where we would have our room in the hotel in case we had to get out in a hurry. Rarely did a hotel have rooms on the ground floor. They would respond with, "we will reserve your room that is nearest to the ground floor," which would mean second or higher floors available. We dared not argue this – take it or leave it - they could only rent what they had. Now the real problem was when they would say, "We will give you a room close to the elevator." But as everyone knows, "when there is a fire, do not use the elevator." I walked (like Jeri always said) myself through how I would get her down the stairs in her wheelchair without help. One floor, going forward or backwards, I could probably handle. More than one floor would be difficult. If one person would help us, we could handle several floors easily but it would be a bumpy ride for Jeri. Fortunately, we never had to use our escape route.

TRAINS

An introduction: Ah! To trains? To distract MS? To take an adventure? How sweet it was for Jeri and family! As you will see by reading, we stumbled into an excellent way to live with MS. Try taking a train ride. We lived the easy way to find out by traveling our way of where to go and what to do – with unexpected excellent help from train personnel. A 19 day train ride for Jeri and me alone? Impossible! Excluding Jeri, of course, I don't recall ever hearing a MS patient saying, I need a distraction from MS, "let's" take a train ride.

Outside of our wheelchair accident at Virginia Beach, Jeri never had to go to an emergency room or see a doctor in any of the trips, trains, cars etc, we took. I don't remember her ever getting sick traveling!

One more thought to our following train suggestions. While seemingly applying to one in a wheelchair, most of our explanations can very easily apply to anyone traveling.

What to take with you on the train or any traveling – this is where those not handicapped get to take their time in selecting on their own time and enjoying what they will take – always too much. Jeri, now with MS, and I always planned at least a month ahead. We planned together and found enjoyment in doing so. Too far ahead wears one out and being selective is important because of not only limited space but because of more medical and other needs – medicine, clothing changes etc. Add a wheelchair with a small tool and you have more to take care of. For a long time, we did not take a suction machine with us. As Jeri began choking more, we thought we better get a lightweight machine. We found the lightest one we could, only ten pounds! We always carried it in one of our luggage bags. Ten more pounds for our luggage. Funny, on the train, we never needed it. In hotels, a few times we did.

A last thought for checking what we needed, then it's "all aboard." We needed a little relaxing energy and all thoughts of our trip to be once we were underway. It is strange that Jeri, without trying or intending to draw attention did just that. Our intention of traveling was because we wanted to – just blending in with the scenery and meeting strangers on our way even if in a wheelchair. We never expected Jeri to have an effect on people. Actually traveling by car, going to church or selling Avon for 25 years would be a poor way of affecting people if that were our intent. Attending our Army reunions did affect people – Jeri was seen. Only on the train and the destinations involved did it appear that Jeri did have an effect on people. It was only when we started getting many compliments about traveling and the fun we had. As I said earlier, one letter told it all: "How can this be?"

Note: If you never take a real train ride, you are missing something but enjoy it with us in this book. In case you do take a ride, let me explain something you may experience and never know why. Should you be on a long train trip that may take one, two, three days, whatever, a day away from your train and sleeping will probably feel good. But wait, that first night "away" from your train may feel you are walking and balancing yourself on the train, even if you are not on it. You may be surprised that a long train ride can do this to you after you get off. Your attendants will understand this one. It happens to them also. Another important "last thought" — when you have your first "real" train ride and you can walk throughout the train, you will have to learn to walk on a fast speeding train -- children love this part, you will have to learn that it is not so bad after all even falling into passengers sitting in their chairs, catching you and smiling at you. They will have already experienced this and are glad to be of help.

Most trains are called "working trains" which means there are no special tourist guides aboard for explaining sightseeing. Most attendants, however, can or will help identifying things to watch for. Other than all of this, you can be your own guide as you begin to learn from others aboard, just get to know them. I met someone from Germany once and in making friends with him, I asked him how he would pronounce our German name, Schroeder. He explained it to me and for the first time in my using our name, I could actually explain how and why we pronounce it the way we do.

As for fun with attendants and conductors they like to exchange greetings etc. We tried to get one conductor confused once when he was taking our tickets. Being on a long trip, we had a stack of tickets for him to go through and pull out the ones he needed. It was taking him so long going through our tickets I looked up at him and said, "Jeri and I are running away from home." He was not distracted as he kept pulling out tickets and soon said, "Sometimes you just feel like doing that!" We were the ones fooled. I think he must have believed us.

To introduce you to our train travel adventures and to show you which train we "liked" the best, following is the train mileage we rang up between 1990 and 2006. TOTAL mileage was 84,201 miles: VIA Rail 42,136 miles, AMTRAK 42,065 miles. Looks like a tie. Actually both trains were very good.

Amtrak (US) and VIA Rail (Canada) were just right for Jeri and me - service, food, helping Jeri, often just talking to her.

The following suggestions, stories etc are intermixed with Amtrak and Via Rail since both have similar suggestions, stories etc. Separate stories in more detail of both trains are completed later in the book.

Traveling on trains, our destination was always the train. To get our traveling under way and with all the arrangements needed to do so, we always were relaxed when "our" train started moving. We knew we would have a good time even if our secondary destination turned out not so good.

We have often explained that travel, especially trains, can be restful and exciting. Tell yourself that small upsetting things against you in a wheelchair are going to happen, so what. "I'm not going to let it spoil my trip." Other passengers, especially the attendants, will be there to help us. So true! Obviously it is more comforting to have someone with you. When two people somehow do things like this together, each one is proud of the both of you. We did it!

As we know, people confined to a wheelchair want to be independent but traveling on a train alone can become a burden to attendants and upsetting to the person themselves. If you're alone, it can work but can be a bit more difficult. You're there to enjoy yourself. Better to do it the "right" way. Have someone with you.

"Red Caps" – For any major traveling or if in a wheelchair, Red Caps are almost a must. While not directly related to trains, this Red Cap service is generally free, but one should tip. They will help you board early and help with your luggage, all the way to your assigned car and seat. In a crowded station, they will probably be your best friend. How do you identify them? Amtrak and Via Rail both use them at large stations. They wear a Red Cap! At stations they serve, we found that they usually have a marked section to identify where you can find them. It works well. Our most recent traveling taught us to trust them but still took their name or whatever if they were to take our luggage from us for boarding or to hold. You usually traveled with your luggage nearby at all times unless you check it in at the station luggage office to send it ahead to another station, which is often an excellent idea. Check only what you don't need. Actually you can check it broken down to one or more stations you expect to be at and pick it up as you go along. Our family never lost a piece of luggage traveling by Amtrak and Via Rail.

We use to do some of our traveling by going through a travel agency. Without a wheelchair, this worked well. With a wheelchair, it was not too good. After we learned more, we still did do some of our traveling through a travel agency.

We learned that travel agencies would direct a person as to what to ask in making reservations or, in some cases, did it themselves. They would advise you to be specific in what you need. This is very important for handicap travelers. For example, you might be told to get the exact measurements of the bathroom door. This can hardly be known by a person taking a reservation. About all they can tell you is if the room is handicapped accessible, whatever that meant. This is why we did a lot of the reserving - to get general information without being too demanding. Face a bathroom door too small to get your wheelchair through when, or if, you get to that problem. We had it happen several times.

Understanding the difficulties trains have to contend with behind "doors of passengers" to serve them well.......... The trains were always under pressure to maintain their schedules. If the train was starting from an originating station, there was an exact preset time to leave. This did not always work for them. Jeri proved them a little wrong.

Sometimes the train waiting to pull out had to wait for another train having passengers to transfer. Actually, it had to be near impossible to maintain a perfect schedule, pulling over for freight trains, weather etc. Anyone who has by train knows, getting behind schedule meant shorter stops at stations or going faster to make up time, usually both. We would rather the train keep a safe speed.

At most train stops passengers are allowed to get off the train to walk a bit, look around or even buy something (newspaper?) on the platform. You get off to wander when a car door is opened and a stool is placed to step down on to get off. The attendant of that car would stay by the door and was always nice just to talk to and ask questions. Beware! Do not wander too far. Just be sure how long the train is stopping if you go inside the station. The attendant will not leave their area to find you. The train will not wait. If you are not back aboard, you're on your own. Your attendant will collect your belongings and the train will leave them somewhere for you. You can pick them up later by calling the railroad and asking where you can find them. This never happened to us but we have seen it happen. When Amtrak serviced Las Vegas by train, we were told it happened all the time as passengers would go inside to gamble and forget to get back on in time. One idea we had if we missed the train, we would try to find a taxi to take us to the next train stop to get back on board.

Probably the biggest complaint from passengers is the train being late. Relax. The train will get there. Besides, railroads go to a rewarding program to satisfy lateness. If the train we were on was running late – who cares, we usually weren't going anywhere special. At times we were glad because if it were very late, we stood getting a refund or something.

Help the station staffs and train crews do their job. You will win. With wheelchairs, it is difficult. You must plan ahead. You will also learn more with each trip you take. Train language can be difficult to learn but you will learn. The first best way is to order your ticket requirements through a "live" ticket seller. Identify yourself in a wheelchair. If necessary ask for one who is experienced with wheelchairs aboard the train. There, half of your problems are already solved.

After a few trips, we learned to be specific as to what we needed aboard. In coaches we learned that certain seats were meant for wheelchairs, even if not marked that way, for example to seat handicapped people near the restrooms and also help them to debark the train. Now where the train car was a "handicapped" car, certain seats were reserved and your ticket should read that. We found out that because I needed to be sitting next to Jeri, our two tickets had to show that and that we did not need a wheelchair tie down. On one trip our tickets indicated one tie down and one regular seat. This meant Jeri's wheelchair would be tied down with her in it, in other words, this tie down replaced one seat, in which case the person stayed in their chair for their trip. I quickly realized our tickets were not done right. I explained to the attendant that we did not need nor want a tie down, that we needed two seats side by side together, otherwise Jeri would be slipping up and down etc. They understood and, while it affected the tickets and seats, they were able to make the change with little problem. We thanked them. It was partially our fault and we learned on this one. The next time we would have to explain to our ticket seller a little better. Of course, when you solve one problem, another will take its place. In this case of us transferring to two regular seats, what happens to the wheelchair? This is tricky. Don't panic. You always want your wheelchair nearby and available to YOU. The crew may simply take it to a closet or somewhere on the train. You have to know what they have done with it, so have them show you. They will be glad to do so but you had better ask. If attendants change shifts and your wheelchair attendant is no longer aboard and you and a new attendant have no idea where your wheelchair is, now you can panic. Since we always used a lightweight travel wheelchair, we usually could put it behind our seats if space was available. If traveling with someone, the lightweight chair is the best to use.

You always made sure the trains had their little "Washington" wheelchair aboard to allow you to be moved from car to car. You would always alert the person taking your reservation that you would probably need the use of this little "miniature" wheelchair and the manual outside lift kept at stations to get you on and off.

The information you give in making a reservation would usually be put on the train's (Amtrak) Conductor's or VIA Rail's Service Manager's manifest. They valued this information before and after you boarded because it helped them give you the service you needed. Along with making train reservations, you would also line up hotels convenient to the trains. Nice, but old, hotels in Canada which were right across the street from the train station, had been established years ago when the railroads themselves owned the hotels. They found train travelers often had no place to stay and eat. We used these hotels often, especially if we were catching a train the next day or so. They were great for us because we would not have to use a taxi. In Toronto, we often stayed at the beautiful Royal York. They had a prearranged procedure that, if you were staying with them, a Red Cap from the train station would bring you and your luggage across a very busy avenue and get you checked into the hotel. When you were to return to the station to catch your train, a uniformed hotel bellboy would take you and your luggage back across the avenue and check you into the train station.

So now you are on the train in a wheelchair or handicapped for some other reason. Amtrak had one way of handling this situation by having sections for those handicapped. This was available in two level Amtrak trains. Via Rail used their regular seating cars including some handicapped cars but had no special sections. Both ways worked but Amtrak's service was a little better for those needing help by being more all together in one section. This would be the lower half available car designated handicapped and/or seniors because they were unable to get upstairs very well. We, of course, experienced both methods. Both had advantages.

Using Amtrak as an example, I would be with Jeri in the lower car where there were 13 seats available. Now each trip was different meeting others. Some passengers needed more help and some were probably not often real happy with their handicap. But wait. On this trip we were in our "private" handicapped section and soon got to know everyone. We began having more fun than those people upstairs where there were almost too many passengers meeting others. This trip when Jeri needed changed, our whole compartment became excited and wanted to help. Now follow this awakening to want to help. One came quickly saying I want to help. Another said I'll get my blanket hung up for privacy. Our entrance door (the only one we had) which we could control ourselves by hitting a few buttons was used by another person for our privacy by putting a blanket on the window of the door and a sign on the outside of this door which read: "Room closed to men including attendants." WOW! No outside problems developed. Our Room Rules had spoken.

All passengers in this handicapped, seniors only half car (the rest of this layer car was for all restrooms in this car) usually were quick to volunteer, some would wait to be asked. There were two more reasons that they volunteered (whether they realized it or not) and it was because they were tired of talking or sightseeing. They found what they needed most – helping others with meaningful help to them and feeling good themselves.

One strange part of having someone to help us, either on one level or two level trains, I usually would not ask for help quickly. If it applied to an attendant, they would be the ones to ask first. Depending on the problem I would ask a man to help me (moving Jeri, for example) or a woman for personal problems (changing her). To do this I would observe passengers for a while. It seemed amazing but after about thirty minutes, I knew who to ask. It worked every time. I only remember one lady saying she didn't feel capable. I thanked her and found another.

All of this planning and going places helped distract us from the MS. It was not unusual for us to have posted on a room wall at home the schedules of our next three trips. Planning a trip yourself or with someone ahead of time can be exciting. Doing most together with help as needed from a train reservationist will give you experience and fun right up to the day of your actual trip. When you get seated in your seat, you will say, "We did it." To expand more, when you get on your train and can answer other passengers' questions such as how do you open the automatic door, you will be proud of yourself, that you now belong.

One puzzle traveling in a wheelchair by train or just walking and being on the streets in one's own wheelchair was when strangers would approach Jeri and ask for a handout. As all people know walking streets and having strangers ask for this kind of help is not usually welcomed and each person has their own way of either helping or not helping. However, asking someone in a wheelchair was news to us. Why someone confined to a wheelchair? I always thought we were immune to any type of solicitation believing that the person asking for a handout would always feel sorry for someone in a wheelchair and leave them alone. Just the opposite, we were prime targets. It always appeared to me that they had no respect or cared that a person was in a wheelchair. Or did they feel the one in a wheelchair was more understanding? I was usually very careful on giving money out this way based on not knowing if it would help a person. In asking Jeri to give something, I would say no and let it go at that. There's always an exception. One time in DC we found ourselves trying to walk to the capital building but soon realized we were going the wrong way. It was hot enough that day to walk let alone the wrong way. A stranger approached us and looked for sure that he was going to ask us for a handout based on his appearance. I beat him to the punch and asked if he could direct us to the capital. He walked with us to the corner and pointed to which direction to go. He was right. I gave him probably a dollar and he seemed to appreciate this and thanked us. Now normally I would not have given him any money but it was obvious he needed a little help. Obviously, we did too!

After a train trip, letters would be sent to train "customer relations" or whoever

To give you an idea of what might be in such letters, we selected one of our letters, left excerpts not needed out and showed the principle comments. The one chosen with interesting comments to print was the one on our Amtrak trip of September 1994 which reads like this:

October 31, 1994

Office of Customer Relations, Amtrak
60 Massachusetts Ave., N.E.
Washington, D.C. 20002

We have just returned from another major train trip and hope you don't mind our comments again since we have written before. Actually our main purpose is to pass on to you a few names who were extremely courteous and helpful and make one want to travel Amtrak.

Since my wife Jeri (Geraldine) has multiple sclerosis and is in a wheelchair, our trips are always different, challenging and interesting. We have the feeling at the end of each trip "we did it." You haven't traveled until you do it in a wheelchair – try it.

We still don't feel Amtrak sells itself enough – meeting and making new friends (we've never met an "enemy" on board), the friendly crews (and at stations too), delicious reasonable meals, careful luggage control, etc. The one question we get at home is does anyone ride Amtrak? They are amazed at our answers. I sometimes get carried away and have to tell people, no we do not work for Amtrak.

Anyway, to pass on names of people who were really nice to meet:

(Five Amtrak employees were named with what they did for us plus Toledo Station.)

Obviously with a wheelchair, we are concerned with not having problems or causing problems. We understand and fully agree that when we travel, we are on our own and this is fine. I transfer Jeri, feed her etc. We don't expect Amtrak to treat us differently. However, we do admit a little extra help means a lot to us (like some attendants will give Jeri an extra pillow or two, or they will help us get seats side by side, etc – attendants have been great).

Note: A few, hopefully, constructive suggestions followed.

Thanks so much for your interest. Hope we are able to contribute towards Amtrak's success.

Jack and Jeri Schroeder
38 Dogwood Ct.
Bowling Green, Ohio 43402

X-Copy: Mr. Thomas M. Downs, President, Amtrak

The response from Mr. Downs:

December 2, 1994

Mr. and Mrs. Jack Schroeder
38 Dogwood Court
Bowling Green, OH 43402

Dear Mr. and Mrs. Schroeder:

Thank you for your correspondence of October 31, 1994, which was also sent to our Office of

Customer Relations. As President, I will respond for the Corporation.

Passenger satisfaction is of utmost importance to Amtrak. Therefore, I am glad that you enjoyed your most recent trip with us.

I am pleased that you found several employees especially helpful and considerate. Our people of all levels in Amtrak strive to provide comfortable and convenient service for all our customers, and they appreciate knowing when their efforts are being noticed. The employees you mentioned by name will be commended for their outstanding service.

In addition, I appreciate your comments concerning ways in which to better our service for those persons who have disabilities. Comments from our customers play an important role in our assessment of Amtrak's services. While we are unable to implement many of the suggestions received, we remain receptive to constructive feedback. I am forwarding a copy of your letter to the appropriate management, for review.

Once again, thank you for taking the time to write. I am pleased with your continued interest in Amtrak, and have enclosed small tokens of our appreciation. We look forward to having the opportunity to serve you in the future aboard Amtrak.

Sincerely,
(signed Tom Downs)

Thomas M. Downs
President

JERI HOLDING UP TRAINS

On a side trip to Atlantic City (on our way to our ASA reunion in Florida September 1994), we were on a train from Toledo to DC where we were to transfer to the "Atlantic City Express." Amtrak had assured us when we made reservations that we were in everyone's manifest. Our conductor had nothing in his manifest expecting us. Our train was over 3 hours late when we arrived in DC and had only 30 minutes to change over to the Atlantic City Express. With getting luggage, having a wheelchair and finding and getting directions to which track the Express was on, we arrived minutes before its scheduled leaving. Sure enough, it was waiting for us. The crew was sitting out in the sun. They looked at Jeri and said, "So you're the one holding us up" laughing. It wasn't over yet.

After getting a lift, they had problems with it and with four Amtrak personnel (including the conductor) working on it, they finally got Jeri aboard, causing the train about a 15 minute late start. The conductor reacted to this very professionally and apologized to us for the inconvenience. He asked us to write up a report for him since he didn't like not being ready for us. It did not bother us – we were more concerned with causing the train to be late. Throughout our trip to Atlantic City, the conductor was very considerate. We thanked him. We also included his name on our "list of names who were nice to meet" letter to Amtrak Office of Customer Relations.

Jeri not only holds up the VIA Rail "Canadian" but they had to also move it for her..........this story happened several times in only Winnipeg and with Jeri aboard or waiting to board.

This train would always have about 25 cars and probably about 400 passengers. The train's schedule, traveling east or west, required it to stop in Winnipeg and all passengers would have to get off the train and platform for one hour to allow maintenance or whatever on the train. The tracks were on ground level while the waiting room was down a floor. The passengers had to walk the stairs down. Gates would be closed and then be reopened to allow them back on the train. The first time Jeri and I were on this train, we were in our own sleeper. The train came into Winnipeg but switched tracks as it approached the station. The train stopped at the station but short of the long platform which wasn't long enough for the whole train. We knew we also had to get off the train for the hour but our car was about two cars from the end of the train and part of our car was on the tracks that we had just got off. Now we started watching if another train were to come by. What then? We were getting a little concerned to better either move or we better get off. Other passengers in our car had already moved forward to other cars to get off. The problem was that they were unable to move Jeri, because of her wheelchair, forward to other cars.

Our attendant called on his phone to the train engineer and told him the train was not all the way on the tracks, part was still on the other tracks. It was decided that we were to wait until everyone was off and then they would move the train forward to reach the platform to get Jeri off. Well it did work. The attendant would continue guiding the engineer to where to stop on the platform. We were then taken off the train and moved downstairs by way of the freight elevator to the waiting room to wait like everyone else.

As stated, this happened several times with us. The same procedure was used with our attendant calling the engineer and saying we are not all the way on the right tracks back here to get Jeri off.

Could there be a second side to this story? Why not? This first part covered Jeri's being on the train entering Winnipeg. There were other times we were already there. Fine but why would there be a problem such as this first one? Let us find out.

When coming from Churchill on the train, our train's end of the line was Winnipeg. We would arrive in the morning and wait for the "Canadian" in the afternoon in the waiting room. We would often be the only ones waiting. This was where we got to know the Winnipeg staff better including riding the freight elevator and their taking care of our luggage. We felt almost at home in Winnipeg.

An example of one of these trips from Churchill, the following took place:

The "Canadian" arrived heading to Toronto. As we expected, all passengers had to leave the train. "Our" waiting room became packed with hundreds. When the "all aboard" sounded the waiting room quickly became in complete desertion except for you know who. We had been told to wait for an attendant to take us up to the train. The attendant returned and had "new" news for us. The train had to be moved to get Jeri on! He would come back and get us. It sounded like thunder but we could hear the train moving up above us. Apparently everyone was aboard. Jeri and I kept listening to the train moving. We were hoping it would stop within a minute or so. If it didn't, the next train would be two days later. The train stopped. Actually other than being a little anxious, we were never concerned. So being relieved, we started making humor about all this. Our attendant came, took us up on our elevator and we were then on the platform heading towards our sleeper.

As we knew so well by now, every time your train would stop, passengers would congregate looking out the windows to see why. In this case, we were still on the station platform. The train had only moved a few yards. Why did it stop? Passengers often said "there must be a celebrity getting on the train this way to avoid crowds." Well there wasn't any celebrity and when they saw Jeri in a wheelchair, they knew the reason for the delay. As they kept looking, I couldn't resist this: The attendant was rushing Jeri to our sleeper. I was next to the wheelchair and only a few feet from the passengers who were watching us. I decided to make them either laugh or get mad at me but I started holding and pointing my finger over Jeri's head and at the same time looking at the passengers. You could not hear through the windows so I would yell that "it was her fault" for being late in which they could read my lips. The surprise was on me. When I said it was her fault, the attendant pushing Jeri yelled out "Oh, it's nobody's fault!" He was very serious. I quickly told him I was only kidding. I think we all had a laugh.

JERI HOLDS UP MORE THAN JUST TRAINS

At Disneyland, Los Angeles, 1996 Amtrak train trip..... Jami and her son Dylan took Jeri on the ride "Star Wars." The theater where it was held had individual seats in which you had to be firmly tied in since there was a lot of shaking to the seat and the person in it. Jeri was transferred from her wheelchair to the theater seat and tied in. The room was darkened so it was hard to see others. The movie started and soon the seats began to shake and Jeri began sliding out. Jami, being tied in also, could see Jeri sliding but could not reach her. A monitor evidently caught what was happening. The movie stopped and the lights came on. Jami said she could see mom who was sitting there laughing. The staff reached Jeri before she hit "floor level." They asked if she wanted to get off. She said no, that she wanted to stay and see the rest of the movie. They tied her back in and restarted the movie. (Dylan)

From our family "five bears' stories" (see section Christmas time, MS style) is a story which seems related to the above true story, written here as originally written:

Grandma Lost In Space

One day Papa Bear took the five bears to an amusement park. Grandma was with them.
Papa Bear said, "I want you to see It's a Bear's World. It's the greatest show ever."
"What is it?" asked Peanut Butter Bear. "Never mind, you will know when you see it,
I want it to be a surprise to you. There's nothing like it. Bear, you will be surprised. I can hardly wait."
Peanut Butter Bear. "I don't want to see it."
Papa Bear. "What!?"
"I don't want to see it. It sounds gross. I want to see the space show."

Papa Bear. "What space show?" Never mind, you and we are all going to see It's a Bear's World. I've waited a long time to show this to you and we are going, that's final!
Nothing's stopping me from showing it to you! Understand!?"
Peanut Butter Bear. "Understand what!?"
Papa Bear. Looks like another one of those days with Peanut Butter. I'm not going to let him win. He is going to It's a Bear's World or else.
When they got inside the park, Peanut Butter Bear said, "I want to go to the space show *NOW!*"
Papa Bear. "Peanut Butter, **NO,** we are all going to...."
Grandma spoke up and said, "I'll take Peanut Butter Bear to the space show."
Papa Bear, laughing. "You? Alone? You got to be kidding!"
Peanut Butter. "OK, then, I'll take Grandma."
Papa Bear. "No way will you take Grandma." OK Grandma, you're asking for it. Tell you what. I'll let you take Peanut Butter now and we will wait for you here if you promise to go to It's a Bear's World afterwards."
Peanut Butter. "It's a deal."
Papa Bear. "I'm not asking you Peanut Butter, I can trust you about as far as I can throw you. I'm asking Grandma."
Grandma. "It's a deal." Off they went. (Kelly)

A short while later, Peanut Butter came strolling along, touching everything he could and humming, probably, some bear song.
Papa Bear. "Oh there you are Peanut Butter, it's about time. Let's go. We keep it up and It's a Bears World will close before we get there. Where's grandma?"
Peanut Butter. "Uh Uh Oh Uh."
Papa Bear. "Well?"

Papa Bear. "Peanut Butter."

Peanut Butter. "Well, she was with me."

Papa Bear. "What do you mean was? I know she was with you. I want to know where she is now? Anyway, you were supposed to be with her, not her with you. Where is she?"

Peanut Butter. "Well we were in the space show. It was very very dark. The show was really super and...."

Papa Bear. "Forget the show, tell me where is grandma? Where is grandma?"

Peanut Butter. "I'm trying to tell you. It's kind of hard and I'm still not sure what happened. In fact, I'm not sure they found her yet."

Papa Bear. "Found her? What do you mean, found her? Is she lost?"

Peanut Butter. "It's a little strange."

Papa Bear. "Peanut Butter, if anything strange, it's you. Now tell me where is grandma?"

Peanut Butter. "She's lost in space."

Papa Bear. "Peanut Butter. Now listen carefully. Tell me nice and slow, what happened?"

Peanut Butter. "Ok. We were sitting in our seats when the seats started moving backwards and forward, backwards and forward and all of a sudden this big huge large space ship came flying right up to us. It scared me so bad, I closed my eyes."

Papa Bear. "Peanut Butter, that's part of the show. It's meant to scare you. What happened?"

Peanut Butter. "I opened my eyes and felt myself moving awful. I felt like I fell right off into space."

Papa Bear, "Then what?"

Peanut Butter. "That's it, it was over. The lights came on and people started leaving."

Papa Bear. "Then?"

Peanut Butter. "She was gone."

Papa Bear. "Gone?"

Peanut Bear. "Grandma was gone."

Papa Bear. "What do you mean grandma was gone. She couldn't just disappear."

Peanut Bear. "Grandma did."

Papa Bear. "Did you look for her?"

Peanut Bear. "I looked everywhere. I looked up. I looked down. I looked over. I looked across. She was gone. So was the space ship."

Papa Bear. "Did you look under the seat?"

Just then two attendants came helping someone that looked like grandma. "Look what we found under the seat." It was grandma.

Papa Bear. "Now Peanut Butter, are you satisfied? What if we had left? And without grandma. What would we have told everyone?"

Now that that is over with it's on to It's a Bear's World. "You're going to love this after what you just put us through Peanut Butter."

As they neared a very quiet it's a Bears World, a very large sign read CLOSED FOR REPAIRS.

Papa Bear. "Let's go home." (Chloe)

The first story above at Disneyland was a true story in 1996 at Disneyland about Jeri, aka Grandma and aka as Gram. It seemed to fit a fiction children's story (above) our family wrote around 1975 as one of our five bears' story which is explained more in **A LITTLE BIT ABOUT US** .... in the section **Creating our own home entertainment for our children as they grew.**

DESTINATIONS

Amtrak US and VIA Rail Canada.......... similar yet different...the engines, coaches, dining, sleepers, stations etc, were not much different. Both trains traveled north, south, east and west on same gauge tracks. Both pulled over for freight trains. Attendants - One couldn't tell the difference. Prices – about same except one used Canadian and one used US monies. We liked the Canadian dollar and two dollar coins – no paper money for these. They both used identical lifts for Jeri and handicapped. Scenery going through the western mountains – we found one little difference. Amtrak used valleys and mountains. VIA Rail seemed to like the valleys following rivers. The difference to us: One minute Amtrak was roaming in and out of the valleys, the next moment, their double header engines were puffing snake routes up to the tops of mountains and down again. It was beautiful seeing both valleys and mountain tops. VIA Rail scenery along the rivers thrilled the passengers looking and stretching to see how high and pretty the mountains looked.

Probably the most interesting happenings on trains for passengers, to awake them or to get them involved and away from boredom would be "Why are we stopping?" A freight train flying by, you would see but if it stopped, everyone wanted to know why. Furthermore, their attendant was expected to know when and why, which they often did not know.

Since VIA Rail did not come to the US, Amtrak traveled to Canada. Amtrak had several routes into Canada. Why one day when Jeri and I were on a VIA Rail train our way back to Windsor, Canada, I looked back through our car window and there was an Amtrak train. At one stop it pulled up right behind us. We were the last car and could see out the back. Now I knew

Amtrak did not use this route, or did they? It's fun being on a train like Amtrak and VIA Rail.

US AMTRAK – A preliminary train trip before Amtrak makes an appearance.

Our first family trip by air and train (Amtrak wasn't created yet. They took over May 1, 1971) was in 1970 when Jodi was four years old and Jeri and I were along for the ride. This was to be Jeri's first and last ride on a train or fly in an airplane without knowingly having "MS." She proved this by running all over Disneyland and all the other places we visited while carrying Jodi with no such signs of MS on trains or airplanes. In fact there were no MS signs period.

Jeri and Jodi had never been on an airplane. It was time for them to learn but which one would be afraid? We didn't ask them. We were planning going all the way to California for our family's first train ride. We also planned on meeting some of Jeri's family in Los Angeles and definitely to visit Disneyland. We decided to fly from Akron to Chicago to catch our train. There is more on Jeri's flying under section **"Airplanes."** Our first "real" family adventure together looked like the following was going to be "who's in charge" and "will we get to where we are going."

Akron/Chicago United Air Lines 5/25/70
 Dep 11:10am Arr 11:22am

Chicago/Los Angeles Santa Fe El Capitan 5/25/70
 Dep 6:30pm Arr 9am (5/27)

Los Angeles/San Francisco Southern Pacific 6/1/70
 Dep 8:30am Arr 6:15pm (6/2)

San Francisco/Chicago Union Pacific 6/4/70
 Dep 12:30pm Arr 11:59am (6/6)

Chicago/Akron United Air Lines 6/6/70
 Dep 3:50pm Arr 5:58pm

We covered the above trips with a lot of exciting joys. When we got off the airplane in Chicago to start our first family trip, Jeri did what she was best at — having a picnic at Lake Superior topped with shopping at the stores in Chicago. Since our Santa Fe train was not leaving until 6:30 pm, this was what Jeri had us do. No voting in our family. In spite of her throwing in "shopping," we had a good time. We were on vacation at my expense.

Our travel was courtesy of United Air Lines, Santa Fee and Union Pacific Railroads. This blend of trains added to the scenery and the many different ways of traveling by train.

Jodi would sit on my lap on the train as I would point out different sights. I would tell her, "Look at that animal." She would always answer, "Oh, yea!"

We never even talked about getting a sleeper probably because of the expense. We quickly enjoyed being in a coach car sitting during the day, putting the back down for a nap or sleeping at night. We learned how nice it was to meet others. They were doing what we were doing - roughing it. Jodi, as a four year old, found a home including new friends. It was great.

One unexpected popular news story making the news had been our Kent State University student uprising May 4, 1970. When passengers learned we were from Kent, they would want to know all about what happened, who was at fault and who won? This was not exactly what we had in mind to talk about.

Now the following "had to happen" to set the tone of all of our future train rides we were "destined" to take. Our train caught on fire.

Jeri, Jodi and I were in the dining car when thick smoke started coming into our area where we were sitting. It happened fast enough that the crew told everyone to quickly go back to your seats. We took Jodi in our arms and without being able to see through the smoke, we covered Jodi and went through blindly to the next car. The kitchen had caught on fire. The crew handled the fire without even stopping the train.

Arriving in Los Angeles, we were met at the train by Jeri's relatives and spent several days with them entertaining us and getting to know each other. They had not seen Jeri for a long time.

Taking Jodi to Disneyland in California in those days was the cream of children adventures. We always remembered Jodi (and us) always riding a "boat" through "It's a Small World After All." We took Jodi through several times. She didn't want to leave. By near the end of the day when the park was soon to close, we found ourselves on the other side of the park away from "Small World." Jeri did seem to get tired but then so was I. We did do a lot of walking. Jeri said, "Let's take Jodi back on one more ride on Small World." Could we make it across the park in time? We started running, Jeri carrying Jodi, and ran all the way across. It was to close at five o'clock. We made it to the ride five minutes ahead of closing. We did it! Reaching out to buy our tickets from the person running it, he said you're too late, we're closed. Now wait a minute, we're five minutes before closing and it's still running. He said, "We go by the time the last ride ends, which is five o'clock. The last ride has already left." He would not yield.

After a week of seeing all (well most) of the sights of LA and Hollywood plus wasting an evening at a laundry, It was now time to head for San Francisco for a quick stop on our way home.

Our train trip to San Francisco along the ocean was relaxing and a beautiful ride. A 423 mile trip took us to our "favorite" stop, Oakland. San Francisco was built on a peninsula at the northern end and is separated by the Pacific Ocean and San Francisco Bay. Apparently some look at San Francisco as a "city" not as a peninsula. Trains were not able to go directly to San Francisco but could only go to Oakland. Ferries were used to move passengers to SF. When the Bay Bridge was built, it apparently was when passengers were transferred by bus to SF.
That was the way we were transferred – Jeri was not in a wheelchair.

We arrived in SF June 2 and checked into the Manx Hotel near Union Square for a two night stay. Our train to Chicago would leave SF at 12:30 pm. So what to do in SF? Well we discussed that. The Manx had just installed new automatic elevators. We could ride those for a while (sounds like my suggestion). The famous cable cars passed our hotel doors – but we can do that anytime on another trip. Jeri's smile comes on. "Let's" go to Sausalito. I've heard about it being a nice place to visit – sounded like a good idea - map reading time. It was just across the Golden Gate Bridge. We shall find a bus that goes that way. The next day we made our way to the bus station and found out which bus we should take to get there. I think this was Jeri's and Jodi's first ride across that bridge.

We got off at Sausalito and began walking to see why this area was so popular. It was a very hot day and Jodi walked with us. We decided to look for a nice place to eat. There seemed to be a lot of restaurants on different streets. We were near the bay water which meant we should find a good fish restaurant. Well this was easy. They were all fish restaurants. Jeri chose one we should go to. It was on none of these streets. It was a sign that advertised a hotel and restaurant and how to get to it up a hill. Let's go.

It was a steep and long walk up. As we approached the hotel and restaurant, it was a beautiful but obviously elite place to have dinner. By now we were looking pretty worn out and getting hungry. We entered the restaurant lobby which was beautiful. A well dressed (tuxedo?) receptionist greeted us and took one look at a family that looked like they just walked all the way up a steep hill just to eat. "May I help you," he asked. Yes, we would like to eat here. The answer came quickly. "I'm sorry but you have to be dressed properly and men have to wear a suit coat." Jeri began talking to him. After a few minutes the person said wait here, I'll be right back. He came back carrying a coat for me to wear. We were invited in. We were excited. This was unexpected, also surprised that they were letting us in. Our meals, I'm not fond of fish but I sure wasn't going to order a hamburger. I ordered swordfish. It was delicious. Jeri ordered lobster and was at her glory. They even showed her how to cut and eat it. Jodi, I can't remember what we got her. Maybe it was the hamburger. We took our time. The view from our table was a broad look overlooking San Francisco Bay.

As we finished and made our way back down to "civilization," we were glad we came. It was something to remember.

We caught a bus back to our hotel – of course going across the Golden Gate Bridge.

We found out years later that this hotel had been converted to a very expensive Rehab for people having drug problems.

On to Chicago was our call for the next day. This time it was riding the Union Pacific, a two nighter through the west in a coach car. This was fine because Jodi would again meet friends and not be "confined" to a room. Meeting friends was more important to her than watching mountains. Break time for her was again sitting on my lap saying, "Oh yea" as we watched various animals, scenery and everything else that belonged to the west. With Jeri along side of us watching with us – it doesn't get any better. Going through the west, the towns, cities, cowboys, stepping outside for a breather at stops, eating great meals in the dining car topped off with the people we met – I don't remember any train problems – it most certainly does not get any better. The two days went too fast. We don't want off. But we had to get off. A plane was waiting for us.

After waiting about four hours in Chicago and making our way to the airport, we boarded our United Airlines airplane for about a two hour ride in the skies to Akron. Jeri had made two green suits for Jodi and herself for this trip. Before we got on the plane, she dressed Jodi and herself with these suits. Getting off the plane at Akron, they really looked pretty. I had someone take our picture as we walked away from the plane. What a nice ending.

In between this trip (1970) and the one following (1990), our time was spent with MS, wheelchairs, computers, etc and everything that went with these problems plus many many good happenings topped with two additional precious children called Jami and Jeff. We still traveled by car but now we had our total family with us. We did not get back to the trains until 1990 thanks mostly to our remarkable Jeri.

Many years later, like 1990, we put together our "trip around the country." I'm not sure whose idea it was but Jeri would agree to any Amtrak or Via Rail train trip. Either her or I, it didn't matter. Our children had no vote in this trip or any train trip for that matter. This one we kept secret for a while. They, not us, were getting older and, like many children, it was time not to be seen too much with your parents, even though you loved them. Jodi was 25, Jami 20 and Jeff 17. We wanted them to come with us but we did not invite them. We let them decide. They knew we were planning a train trip. One day, one of them asked where we were going. We told them to Chicago, Seattle, Los Angeles, New Orleans, Chicago and home. They said, "I want to go." The other two followed. Later a friend of ours, Rhonda, heard about us going and asked if she and her daughter, Rashelle, could come with us. I reminded her that we were jinxed especially on trains. She answered, "Oh, I don't believe that." We said ok if you are sure you and your daughter want to come. Welcome aboard. Now this was to be a fifteen day train trip. Funny but strange things will happen.

After we arrived home, Rhonda came to me and said, "You made a believer out of me."

Being quite new at railroading and mixing wheelchairs in, we had gone to our AAA and worked with one of their girls to set our "round the country" trip in order. When our trip was finalized, I told her about our jinx. She wished us luck and that nothing would go wrong. I guaranteed her that things would go wrong. We had already lost our sleeper from Los Angeles to New Orleans and would have to go coach on that one.

Let the adventure begin.

Boarding our train at Toledo, the work crew did not seem to know how to put Jeri aboard. They had the standard lift but did not seem to know how to use it. Jeff carried Jeri aboard.

Seven of us arrived in Chicago with 27 pieces of luggage. There was a two hour wait here for our next train. Unloading here became a problem so we hired a Red Cap to take our luggage. He said to meet him at a certain gate in about an hour. This was to be our first experience with a Red Cap. Free assistance with baggage was available from Red Cap attendants. We learned to use them wisely which meant they usually deserved a tip especially because in most cases you really did need them. We soon learned not to trust them to show up to get us aboard, so for several train rides we were very careful to keep our luggage in sight and remember which Red Cap was helping us. Even Amtrak personnel warned us to watch them carefully. A few years later, they actually became very trustworthy and dependable. Meanwhile in our present case, we became concerned because our train was about to leave without us. The Red Cap showed up just in time with our luggage. We lucked out just in time. But wait, Rhonda thought one of her suitcases was missing containing $100 worth of cosmetics. I told her it was a good thing it wasn't anything important.

I think Jeri and I had our first ever "sleeper." It was not the kind we would ride in future rides but it was our first private room. We enjoyed it, as did our other adventure members. We found our room was for handicapped but it seemed to be more of a "cell." It had one small window. It was in the downstairs level and at the end of that car. To go to the next car, one had to go upstairs and over. As a result, we met few people and we seemed too alone. This is one reason we liked coach seats better. We also liked one level trains better. Two level trains were new and well liked. One level trains were used where there were tunnels etc to go under in which the two level trains could not use. Our train being two levels we were not able to get Jeri up steep narrow winding stairs to the upstairs. Jeri was stranded to the lower level.

Back to our story, all our own family came to the rescue. We had a complimentary wine party in our room. Our sleeper included wine, juice, coffee and snacks plus meals for two, Jeri and me. Later we had another get together in our sleeper. We only had one chair but we did have the commode. I sat on it to eat. I believe it was Rhonda who came up with "Jack eating Jeri's desert of pie alamode on the commode." This was ok until someone (Rashelle?) "accidentally" hit the flush button. I thought I was going to lose everything!

As our train headed for Seattle, It wasn't too long when we came upon a freight train that had a "derailment," which meant no overturned cars. We were learning the language. We watched them putting a freight car back on the tracks. Our train was then warned to slow down when a train in front of us carrying something from the derailment said they were afraid the tracks were damaged so they had to have an inspector go ahead of us. I don't know if he was walking or running but after a while, we were back moving fast to make up time.

Later in the evening, our train was stalled on top of a mountain at night with our lights all out. I peeked out our door and saw two crew members working on our car with an apparent electrical problem. One held a tiny flashlight while the other was looking for what was wrong. I took my tiny flashlight out to see if they could use it. They "surprised" me and said "No." Back to our coach seat and tell Jeri, "I tried." She laughed. Why was she always laughing at me?

Besides watching animals along the way, on top of another mountain, we watched a forest fire in the distance and airplanes dropping liquid or whatever it was on the flames.

The first night aboard, we took it upon ourselves to make a few changes. Jeri was in the lower bed, Rhonda was in the upper and I was 30% in the lower, 40% hanging out, 20% on a suitcase and 10% missing. Jeri seemed to sleep well in a lower bed when we would get one for her. She could stretch out good and I was nearby to turn her periodically, which was critical for her. Meanwhile the train was really moving going probably at their top speed of 79 MPH. In the lower floor of the train, you were real close to the tracks and could hear and feel the speed. It seemed our speed was indeed fast. I resigned myself we were going to go off the tracks and went to sleep.

Then the toilets went out. This was not good. It seemed like a problem that had to be solved. The toilets also warned you not to flush them in a station. By now I learned that Rhonda was writing that she feels like "I'm a hostage on the Schroeder's All American Nightmare. I had better be rested for the next catastrophe."

The next morning the "no flushing" warning sign was still on. The sightseeing and lounge cars had been removed so we were now roughing it.

Arriving in Seattle three and a half hours late, it took two taxis to get us to our hotel for a one night stay. Our train crew stayed at the same hotel and Jeri and I got to meet some of them. Talking to the Steward, he thanked us for complimenting him on the food and called the Chef over to meet us. Our attendant was there also. Everyone liked him and he had helped us detrain and get the taxis.

The rest of that day we spent sightseeing. Jami, Rhonda and Rashelle went up the Space Needle. Jeff went looking for a shop that could fix his radio. Gee, we let Jeff at age 17 wander around a large city by himself? Times were different, maybe safer then. We stopped a bus to take us to the

 waterfront but the driver did not know how to get there. We left him talking to himself and walked. Not much to see there, we did not like the area. This was the time when it seemed many cities were making Spaghetti Restaurants out

of abandoned factories. Very steep hills made it hard to take Jeri up and down plus sidewalks were pretty bad. Up we went and we found our Spaghetti Factory where we had a nice family dinner. We probably walked 25 blocks that day.

Next morning at 10:30 sharp it was time for lift off. Our second taxi was late picking Jeri and me up. When we got to the station, it was lined way up. Our family was strung out throughout the line. A Red Cap spotted us with the wheelchair, grabbed the chair and began running through the station, to the train. As we passed the line, we told everyone (belonging to us) to get out of line and follow us. We kept our eyes on the runaway wheelchair with the Red Cap pushing it and someone in the chair hanging on (Jeri? I hoped so). Surprise, at the train there was no lift and they did not know how to get Jeri on. I butted in and said I could get her on. The attendant was not too happy with me and said it was their responsibility.

They then tried lifting her and bent the side panel of the wheelchair. Now it was all aboard for Los Angeles. Incidentally, later we did file our first and only claim with Amtrak (none ever for Via Rail) about the wheelchair damage. They sent us $50.00.

It was a beautiful ride down to LA, a one overnight trip. The conductor was announcing instructions and stops over the speaker system right next to our sleeper. He was very entertaining in making announcements good and not so good. He would always begin his announcements with "Ladies and gentlemen and boys and girls..........in one case continuing with "you get off the train, you pay the taxi to the next stop. The train doesn't wait." We saw it happen several times. The attendants would collect the left behind luggage etc from the seat and have it available at a station for them.

While on our way to LA, at one stop you were allowed to get off and walk around, I was looking through our window to the outside when I saw Jeff taking his time walking around. I pounded on our window and motioned him to get aboard. Fortunately he did, in time. Jeri and I talked about this one. What if he had missed getting back on? He had no money with him. We decided to give him a credit card. He sat down with us and we handed him a credit card, to be used only if need be and don't lose it. He took it and said I won't lose it. I reminded him again. He said, "Dad, I won't lose it." Within an hour on the train, an announcement came over the speaker for Jeff Schroeder to come to the dining car. I said to Jeri, now what. I better go up there to see what's going on. I met Jeff part way. What happened? "I lost my credit card. It was in my wallet."

A little more to this was that the dining car crew knew Jeff, if only from his wallet and could have easily given it to him. But they had their way to entertain passengers by announcing this over their speaker.

We were five hours late arriving in LA after midnight. We took our luggage (26 less one if still missing a piece) into the station, sat down and waited to decide how we would get to our hotel. We knew the name but did not know where it was. We would need two taxis. The taxis were outside waiting with their drivers sitting around in a group waiting for passengers to come out.

I told our group I was going to find someone to maybe tell me which taxi service was the best to go with. They waited while I went up to the nearest window which had someone behind it. I started to ask the girl my question but she interrupted me and asked me if we were on the train that just came in. I said yes. She began writing a note and gave it to me to take to the window she had written this note to. Fine whatever that meant. I found the window ok, gave the person the note and she handed me $50.00 cash for our train being late. Wow. Forget my question. She gave me the answer in money. I went back to our group holding up $50.00. They had wondered what happened to me. I told them to sit still that I was going outside to the taxi drivers, hold up $50.00 and asked them who would take us to our hotel for this. That was easy. We were taken to our hotel which took about thirty minutes. It was a Hampton Inn at the LA airport.

The next morning it was breakfast at the Hampton. We were right at the airport – every 30 seconds, an airplane went by. We rented a Taurus station wagon and that first afternoon went to a nearby beach and carried Jeri to the water but didn't put her in because of deep and hot sand. We went back to our hotel to clean up. Jodi and I went out to get pizza to bring back. I took a wrong turn and we were on a LA freeway going out of town. One and a half hours later we returned with pizza. Friday we spent at the Universal Studios. Jami, Jeff and Rashelle were invited to see filming of "American Gladiators" which was shown on TV the following September. Saturday we took Jeri to Monica Beach. We pulled her backwards in the sand and got her into the water. The waves were high, water salty and pleasant after getting in.

The next day being Sunday, we were able to go to Mass in the morning and then drove to Hollywood and around Beverly Hills and ate at the Spaghetti Factory. It was then time for us to check out to catch our train to New Orleans. We drove to downtown LA and checked our car in and waited for the train.

We liked LA. This was our second visit there. Years later, after two additional visits, it seemed different. It was much larger with many buildings added. We didn't like it anymore and did not return.

Our four great days were up and we boarded our train for New Orleans. In the train station, we had to go through a "fruit inspection" to see if we were carrying any fruit. For whatever reason, we lost our sleeper and Jeri and I were assigned to stay in the lower level in the handicapped section. This was fine with us since the sleeper really didn't work well and besides, sleepers are expensive. This handicapped section had the regular 13 seats and was needed because the train we were getting on was two levels with narrow stairs. This section eventually became known as for seniors also. So Amtrak was improving.

Being assigned to a handicapped section can cause unnecessary problems. Early on we felt that the crews did not know very much about helping handicapped passengers. On our train to NO, we witnessed a situation in this section when the conductor appeared and said he needed one person to go upstairs because the seat they were using was needed for someone else. The person he chose was the personal attendant for a person in a wheelchair. He refused. The conductor should have thought this one out before saying to this person that they had to move upstairs or they would make him get off the train. The patient in the wheelchair returned that statement by saying, "If you put him off, you will have to put me off also. I need him." My needing to take care of Jeri made Jeri and me think I might be next told to go upstairs. I prepared myself for that one. I was not about to give in especially if threatened. Anyway, the conductor backed off and left. This was because of their not knowing how to handle these situations ahead of time. There were other methods the conductor could have used. Offer to help another person less handicapped to move them upstairs and offer them free passage for the future. Once a passenger is aboard, I believe the railroad is responsible. We ran into this later in another train when I had to tell them that they were responsible, not the passenger.

Going across the hot areas with little air conditioning and not much to see made this first trip across our last trip this way. It was a little interesting — riding along the Rio Grande and seeing poverty in Mexico, viewing them wading in muddy water and later viewing the Air Force junk yard of airplanes.

Arriving at New Orleans for a three day stay, it was different. Jeri liked it and we made it a point to see Pat O'Brien's music entertainment bar. Jeri liked this also. They would not let Jeff and Rashelle in so we had to send them back to our hotel by taxi. We stayed for an enjoyable evening. When our three days were up, Jeri and I decided we would be back. We did come back, once more and Pat O'Brien's was still there.

Our trip to Chicago was on a one level train which allowed us to be all together again in the same coach car for one overnight. With just one overnight, it was much easier than having a sleeper. Two overnights for Jeri was too much. Our train did have an original 1948 dome car to sightsee from "upstairs." This car showed its age with broken glass in some windows. That night in the lounge car two fellows were playing guitars and Jeff was playing the "drums" on anything he could find. They had everyone singing. Now that was a real train for real people!

Arriving in Chicago completed our circle around the country. Having a six hours wait for the Toledo train, some of us headed for a festival at a lakeside park. Others headed for shopping at Marshall Fields. Back at Union Station with one and a half hours to spare, we went to check if we could get an early boarding. A Red Cap came up to us and said he had the best Red Cap and directed us to him. This Red Cap said to wait where we were, he would come and take us aboard early. I made sure I could recognize him if we had a problem. As time grew short, we saw him hauling someone else's luggage towards the train. We may have a problem here. When we saw the computer screen flashing "loading" on our train, we knew we had a problem. We rushed down to the tracks where we found everyone else already on the train. I was wondering how I could stop the train if it started moving. I had learned the train would not move until all the loading "stools" were back on the train. We had a reprieve. One outside attendant told us to go on up several cars to board. The attendant there said he was filled, go back. Back we went. By now there were no seats together. The conductor got off to see if he could help with the wheelchair. There was no lift. Each car was supposed to have a handicapped seat. Jeff was going through the cars trying to find seats. He found a seat in the next car and carried Jeri onto the train and to the next car. We were now scattered throughout the train.

I explained to the conductor why we were late because of the Red Cap. He said they do that all the time. The attendant apologized for Jeff having to carry Jeri on and through to the end of the next car. He later said we had a very nice family. He also as we neared Toledo asked if Jeff could carry Jeri off. He seemed to appreciate this and said this was his first time as an

attendant, that he was not told anything other than go to his car.

On to Toledo – we didn't know where everyone was. I believe Jami was sitting with a fellow her age and I think became friends. We had sent our luggage from Chicago to Toledo.

Arriving late at night, we went to pick up our luggage. The people in front of us were told their luggage would arrive the next day. Our luggage – There it was.

End of a perfect trip!

And it was perfect. We were all together for a family vacation.

A boost for Jeri – whatever we did or wherever we traveled, she was alert and enjoying life. We were always so proud of her. She was a real trooper and affected a lot of people without even trying. This first major train trip taught us why Jeri and I did not like sleepers. From this point on, while we did use sleepers a few times primarily so she could rest more, she and I both preferred a coach. Jeri became part of the passengers – they could see her smile, watch her, help her and understand what she was doing on a train – enjoying life in spite of. Passengers on and off the train continuously would approach her and congratulate her for what she was doing even telling Jeri that she was their role model. They felt good and Jeri felt good. I was always stunned when people would do this, it was so great. Never had we intended to get such comments. We were traveling because Jeri and I were together and wanted to do things.

This first major train trip shows a lot of "ups" for Jeri. What no "downs?" Not on our trains. It does show like we were ahead of our time. This is similar with what we say about Jeri and her computers, where Jeri seemed ahead of the handicapped computers and that she was the explorer based on that so many new handicapped items came along after Jeri. We seemed to have similarities between the computers and the trains. After our early major train trip with Jeri in her wheelchair and the fact that crews were not very well trained for handicapped passengers, we did feel like we were learning along with the crews. Since we did not see very many people in wheelchairs riding the train, Jeri did seem like the explorer for handicapped future riders without knowing it. The trains and especially the crews eventually became very good.

1992 MAY -- Jeri and I take a strange ride by Amtrak – to Montreal!

Not quite sure how we did it but we did. We were not too sure of ourselves alone yet in traveling by train but let's try this one to Canada on a US train.

It was all by coach and we left Toledo at 03 May 92, a Sunday, arriving in DC the next day. We stayed overnight there and boarded Amtrak Tuesday heading for Montreal. The train had no handicapped cars so we were put in an empty "recreation" car seating us at a table with our luggage. Not too comfortable because it left Jeri in her wheelchair all the way to Montreal. But our train was moving, that's all we needed. We did have nice views of scenery, no extra charge. Then our first problem came aboard. We laughed at this one, but we had visitors who did not laugh. We reached the Canadian border where the US Border Patrol, four or five strong came aboard where we were. They told us we had to go back to our car. "This is our car" we said. The train had no place to put Jeri. They did not appreciate this and dwelled on it for a while as to what to do. So Jeri holds up a train for Border Police. They finally told us what they were doing and that we were not to get in their way. They were checking everyone on the train and anyone that seemed suspicious, they and their luggage were to be brought back to this car for the officers to check it out. Several passengers were brought back and we had a front row seat to watch what happens at a train border crossing. Hey, this was interesting. They went through luggage, then would tell passengers they could repack their belongings and go back to their seats. One passenger, however, was told he had to leave the train at the next stop. Meanwhile the train was waiting for them to finish. After one hour they released the train. Would you believe – we were never searched.

About this trip itself, I'm not sure why we went to DC first for just one overnight stay to catch the train to Montreal. I would guess it was because we wanted it to be a round trip on different ways to go and return and thus see sights we had never seen before.

We never cared much for Montreal not only because you really had to know French to enjoy it but also because the sidewalks etc for wheelchairs to get around seemed difficult and also there seemed to be nothing that would be attractive to us especially with Jeri in a wheelchair.

Getting on the Amtrak train from DC to Montreal, the distance was about 550 miles. Leaving DC at 4:10 pm, we were scheduled to be in Montreal at 10:45 am the next day, May 6.

For about four days we roamed around Montreal taking it easy and finding out Montreal was not too bad after all. But, here went another sudden, and without good reason, a real "wreck." We had a flat tire! Actually it was a broken wheelchair wheel. I had mentioned earlier about their sidewalks and how bad they were for wheelchairs. Pushing Jeri uphill in the busy business district, I was going over and hitting the large stones which were in fact their sidewalk. The front plastic wheel crumbled to little pieces. By now I am holding Jeri in her wheelchair pointing the front up in the air off of the sidewalk. Interesting, the sidewalk was very crowded – it was closing time for all the stores – not a single person stopped to see if we needed help, perhaps because they spoke French. My first reaction was to see if there was a nearby wheelchair company. Now I knew that was not going to work, even if there were one. Where would it be? To the few people who slowed up to pass us, I tried to use signals by pointing to the broken wheel thinking they might know where we could get repairs. Well this was a waste. Should I call Triple A? Naw! That also would probably be a waste, more funny than realistic. One more idea, we were right outside a business building. I'll go in there to see if they could help or if I could call someone. Call someone, who would I call? I think I was beginning to panic. I went inside this building. There were workers still there and one was seated at the entrance desk. I tried to tell the man sitting there about our little accident but before I could finish in English, I scared him so much I think he thought I was going to mug him. I left in a hurry and just remembered I left Jeri almost face down in her off balance wheelchair. In situations like this, one of us should panic. Isn't it usually the wife? Finally I managed to stop a taxi. He asked no French questions. No English either. He looked at Jeri like she was badly handicapped, the way she was hanging onto the wheelchair without sliding forward. I put Jeri and the wheelchair into the taxi and mentioned and pointed to our hotel. At last, someone understood, a little at least and money helps. I was able to get Jeri and the wheelchair into our hotel, again facing funny looks from people there. Fortunately the next day we were scheduled to get a taxi to take us to the train station to head home. I got Jeri out of the taxi and with her riding on the back wheels with feet up in the air, we headed for the train. One plus was with her riding this way, she was unlikely to fall out. When the train attendant saw Jeri, "he asked why did we keep her feet and wheelchair up in the air?" I told him to look at the front wheel. "Oh, there is none."

Leaving Monday, May 11 at 10 am (hey, we even enjoyed the stay – it just wasn't our favorite), we deliberately had our return schedule set up so we could stay on the train longer along the Hudson River Valley. Our tickets were shown as getting off at Poughkeepsie, NY. We then could catch the Lake Shore Limited back to Toledo via the northern route through New York State. Our conductor met with us and thought it would be better for us to get off at Albany to catch the Lake Shore Limited back to Toledo. He explained that the station in Poughkeepsie was small and, that there would be about a three hour wait in late evening to catch the Lake Shore train there with little to do. He said Albany-Rensselaer was a much larger station and busier to help you. We agreed and thanked him.

At the Albany-Rensselaer station the conductor was right. It was an active station and a safe place to wait. One more normal slight problem we were use to and could handle pretty good was getting Jeri changed for a long ride home. I timed our wait there close to all aboard time to change Jeri. They had a nice roomy women's restroom for me to change her. We asked the station if there was someone available that could guard the restroom door while I changed Jeri. They found someone. This would be easy for me. Half way through this change with new clean clothes on, the restroom door opened. We had company. Our guard was gone. I'm on my own. The lady walked in, I apologized to her but that we were almost done. She smiled and said, "That's ok. No problem." I think she asked if she could help, as they always would. Well, the door kept opening and I kept apologizing. I finished as quickly as I could so we could leave. No problem. Goodbye Albany, hello Toledo as we arrived back May 12, a nice 10 day trip. The trip back to Toledo was delightful. We came to believe that this Lake Shore Limited was one of Amtrak's best scenic routes. A climax to this story was that the next day in Toledo, a company gave us a new wheel.

1992 October – the Amtrak routes that took several puzzles plus six trains to follow our designed trip between two countries.

On this trip was Jeri and Jack, our daughter Jodi and our family friend Rhonda, who has been pretty much part of our family since we arrived in Bowling Green. She was one of the first regular nurses to care for Jeri. We mentioned Rhonda being with us in our "round the country" in 1990.

Reference this current mystery trip, Jeri and I kind of passed the others as we traveled along two different schedules planned by, "I don't know who." Using all aboard passes was a nice way to travel – you could choose where you wanted to go.

We four left Toledo Friday October 9 on Amtrak's "Capital Limited" train arriving in DC the next day. In DC, we all watched live the filming of "In the Line of Fire" starring Clint Eastwood.

After two days, we left DC Oct 12 for New Orleans by Amtrak's "Crescent" train arriving the next day, Tue, the 13th for a four night stay.

At New Orleans, Jeri and I had been introduced by Jodi and Rhonda to Pat O'Brien's, in the French Quarter in 1990 when we did our round the country trip. We knew we would be back some day but did not expect the return to be two years later. So here we are again. Probably about the only bar that Jeri and I ever enjoyed. We spent a couple of evenings this time that lasted several hours each. She enjoyed being there.

Actually, I enjoyed it to. We thought we would return again soon and even went into several hotels in the French Quarter to see their prices and facilities. We took brochures home with us but we never quite made it back. At home we were amazed at how many people, when they found out we were in NO, would ask, "Did you go to Pat O'Brien's?"

One of the most interesting comments we had ever received from all of our train rides occurred on this trip from DC to New Orleans. Pushing Jeri in her wheelchair on this long platform in DC to our train car, we didn't know which coach car we had but as we came to one with an attendant waiting outside, this was our car. He helped get Jeri aboard and to our seat. Jodi and Rhonda were in the same car with us. This was an overnighter that we got on early in the evening and arrived in New Orleans at seven in the morning. A trip like this, especially going to New Orleans, would usually be a fun trip. Ours was no exception. I don't think Jeri slept at all that night. She apparently thought she was part of the fun. Our car was "jumping" pretty good and included our attendant who helped Jeri on. The next morning we were up and ready to go. Jodi told us later about an incident that happened, behind our backs. Now what? She said our attendant who had helped Jeri aboard said, "I owe your mother and dad an apology. When I saw them coming down the platform with your mom in a wheelchair, I said to myself, oh no not another wheelchair. I watched her on the train, she was just great. I then told myself that I was going to have to change my thinking about wheelchairs."

Now we split. Jeri and I left NO (by Crescent) Saturday the 17th heading to Wilmington by way of DC. We changed trains there, to see my brother and family for a few hours, and then boarded the Montrealer train heading to Montreal arriving Monday October 19. Jodi had told us she would meet us in Montreal to go back with us to Toledo.

Jodi and Rhonda left NO (by City of New Orleans) Saturday the 17th heading to Chicago. In Chicago they changed to the Capitol Limited and headed for Toledo arriving Sunday the 18th. In Toledo, Rhonda got off while Jodi changed trains and caught the Lake Shore Limited to New York City arriving Monday the 19th. Jodi wasn't done yet. After spending the day in NYC, she caught the Montrealer heading to Montreal, arriving there the next day, Tuesday October 20. Finally, Jodi knocks on our hotel door at 3 am carrying one piece of luggage as if she was on a trip. "Where have you been?" we asked.

We weren't through yet. With Jeri, one never gets "through" – we loved her for it. Well the next morning, Wednesday October 21, we still had another trip to make – go home. We decided to go by train. Why not, we still had tickets. It was still Amtrak (the Adirondack) in which we boarded in Montreal and headed south through New York state to Hudson, NY where we changed trains to get on the Lake Shore Limited to continue our scenic trip through New York all the way to Toledo arriving Friday October 23, 1992. Now this was a train ride or rather several train rides. It was different to Jeri who showed no signs of tiring. It doesn't get much better. What MS? When's our next trip?

1993 April TRAIN RIDE – Jack & Jeri – I can't believe we did this one ourselves.

Our train trip of April 1993 was for Jeri and me only. We were on a 15 day trip that covered Oakland (San Francisco) by way of Las Vegas and Los Angeles and back through Chicago to Toledo. Throw in Petaluma and we have a wild one.

Our Jami and her husband Craig and their son Dylan drove Jeri and me to Toledo to catch the train. While waiting for our late train to come, another Amtrak train, the Toledo-Detroit train was there and empty. It was waiting for a later departure. Their conductor took us, except Jeri was left to watch, on a tour through this train including letting Jami and Dylan sit in the driver seat of the last car that could actually control and pull the train. They were thrilled.

Getting on our 19 car train in Toledo heading for Chicago, the attendant on board, when he saw Jeri in a wheelchair, yelled out that they had no handicapped cars. The Toledo attendant found a car with two seats and, with their lift, got us aboard. I then had to carry Jeri around an enclosed room through a narrow hallway to our seats. Our Toledo attendant refused our tip to him as did another fellow, a passenger from Denver, who helped us on and eventually off. Once on the train and seated, a lady attendant came and said there were two handicapped cars on this train. We decided by now to stay put. She later asked our name because Amtrak would be upset over my having to carry Jeri and the fact Jeri was not in a handicapped car (nothing came of this). Different ladies came by wishing Jeri well. This was not unusual. Friendships always started early on long distance trains. I think also that the fact Jeri was in a wheelchair was actually becoming something new in train traveling. I was always surprised how few wheelchairs we would find aboard trains. Again, Jeri seemed to be the explorer to lead the way. As trips went on we did seem to see a few more wheelchairs. The trains were becoming very good for and with them.

Leaving Toledo April 20 three hours late at 1:30 pm we arrived in Chicago at 6:30 pm four hours late and missed our connection to Las Vegas. So were we off to a bad start? No, we just earned a free overnight stay in a nice hotel. We would have to wait until the next day to catch the train. The crew (no lift) carried Jeri and wheelchair off the train. This was the first time we used our new green lightweight wheelchair, which we had to buy ourselves for much easier traveling by train. We were then taken to a private entrance and Amtrak gave us vouchers to use for a taxi and food both ways plus a voucher to a Ramada Inn on Lake Shore Drive. When we got to the hotel, I took Jeri out of the taxi and onto her wheelchair. The wind was terrific. I asked the driver to hold the wheelchair and also the pads Jeri sat on. The pads took off in the wind down the Lake Shore Drive with the driver running after them. Meanwhile, I'm lifting Jeri and found no one holding the wheelchair. The driver returned with two well soaked pink pads. Grabbing our new Avon travel bag, he broke one handle off of it. The second was broken off later by another taxi driver.   We took our time getting up in the morning. Our third floor view faced Lake Michigan which was a beautiful scenic morning. We began Day 2 of J&J Odyssey. Breakfast was courtesy of Amtrak, plus everything else including our taxi back to our next train.

When we arrived at the station, we found a new lounge for handicapped passengers. This was great. From here on, every time we passed through this station, we used this lounge. Now Amtrak is learning. This lounge was used for waiting for trains, changing clothes, watching TV etc. One would check in at the desk where there would always be a desk clerk and attendants to take you to your train. They would keep your time for boarding and alert you to get ready.

Next day we boarded our "new" train and got back on a delayed schedule. It worked fine. Had to adjust some overnight stops ahead of us by one day but this was to be expected. We left Chicago April 21 instead of April 20.

Trying to get Jeri in the restroom on the train, the wheelchair would only fit sideways with me in the restroom. We tried it once but resorted to changing Jeri in our seat, which always worked. We had no problems getting other passengers to help.

The train made a long stop in Denver. I decided to get off and write a post card back to Jeff. It read, "Now in Denver-lots of snow in the mountains-warmer here-am in the station-mom's still on the train-she said if I miss the train-see me in Vegas."

After leaving Denver we entered the Colorado Mountains and found (it was April) snow all around us. One might be surprised at the next remark. Jeri and I learned to love riding the train through snow. It is always beautiful.

On the train a couple across from us was from Florida going to Vegas. It turned out she worked at a nursing home and would help me changing Jeri. The night before, after we asked them, two lady attendants offered to help but were not overly eager to do so. I told them I would call if I needed them. In such a hesitation I would not call. I was always conscious about someone being concerned in changing a stranger. I would explain that I would do the lifting and changing. I only needed someone to balance (not lift) Jeri while I changed her clothes or removed or inserted a brief and then help me raise her slacks up.

People who knew how to do this would sometimes say I can help you whatever you want done. This is also covered in another section of the book.

Arriving in Las Vegas, we stayed at the Union Plaza Hotel in the area known as Downtown Vegas. It was Jeri's and my first trip to Los Vegas. We did it alone. Inside the hotel was where the Amtrak station was located. After checking in at Amtrak, we found the entrance to the hotel leading to the lobby. We had a strange thing happen. I took all our luggage piled it on our wheelchair (Jeri was underneath somewhere), grabbed both handles of the wheelchair and began moving this through the hotel door and onto a rather steep wide ramp to get down to the check in area. As I walked slowly down the ramp, the two chair arms I was holding tightly were slowly being let down onto the ramp and Jeri's legs and feet were slowly going up in the air. I could not hold the wheelchair arms up because of the weight and I let the arms go down until they hit the ramp. The wheelchair and Jeri were still in the up position. So were Jeri's legs. When the wheelchair arms hit the ramp, everything stopped. Jeri's legs were still up. We were stranded half way down this ramp. The weight of the luggage placed mostly behind Jeri had caused a shift in balance. I could not lift the load of luggage back up until others saw this funny happening and, laughing, came over to help. We do have fun in funny ways!

In checking in at the desk where we had reservations, we asked for a handicapped room. My mistake, I never included it in our reservation. They nicely said they would have one for us later that day. We waited because checking the room we were to get we were not able to get the wheelchair in. We rested this day and "hit" the machines the next — slot machines everywhere!

The next day, breakfast, swimming in the afternoon, had a prime rib dinner and Jeri hit the machines! The following day, it was going to church, riding a very good handicapped bus down and back to where the city had added more hotels. Later, it was to a buffet at Circus Circus Hotel for $3.00. It was packed and hectic. They took Jeri in her wheelchair and me out of the line and moved us up front. Food, swimming and "donating" money the next day kept Jeri happy and me looking for the "penny" machines which were almost non-existing. Actually we were big spenders, at least to us. Play the nickel slots, loose a few quarters and let Jeri choose which machines to play. While we were at the casinos having fun, I don't think we impressed the casinos using nickels – no casino ever served us a free drink as we fed the machines. While I was always losing what Jeri had allowed me - $20 once only then back to her standard $5.00 and out – she was always winning. You see. It was not only Jeri having her "ups" and "downs," I wasn't doing very well either.

Another day, we had lunch with the couple from Florida we met on the train. We then took the bus down to what was called "The Strip." Our Jeffrey had asked us to bring him something back from the Hard Rock Café. We heard they had one here but where was it. We asked someone who told us what street it was on. We followed their directions and walked about two miles to the street it was suppose to be on. When we got to the corner of the street I looked up and down that street on both sides and could not find a Hard Rock Café sign. I finally asked someone if they knew where it was. They said, "You are standing right under it. I looked up, they were right."

After shopping for Jeff and since there were no sidewalks there, we found another way back to the casinos. I was pushing Jeri pretty fast to get back when we came across a couple who turned to say hello to us. I looked around quickly to speak to them and ran smack into a telephone pole or rather, Jeri did. I said who put that there. The pole was ok so we continued heading for a place to eat which was the Flamingo Hilton. By then it was dark so we were able to see the strip at night. We thought the downtown area was nicer. Boarding the bus to take us to our hotel, it was packed and their lift was at the back door so it took a little longer to get us aboard. The lady driver was nice and patient even though she had a packed bus.

The next day we celebrated Jeri's birthday. It was breakfast then taking her shopping, then swimming in our beautiful large outside 5th floor swimming pool topped off with Jeri winning 100 nickels from the machines. Now to us this was fun. Jeri had her hair (trim and shampoo) done at our hotel. It took ten minutes and cost $35.00. She looked great.

Leaving in the morning to catch our train right outside our hotel, we did the normal thing everyone else would do. I had two quarters and lost. Jeri on her second quarter hit 10 quarters and then 4 more – time to leave. Bye Vegas. We'll be back. We did return.

It was on to Los Angeles. When we arrived, we asked a clerk at the station where a certain hotel was that we had reservations for. They told us it was two and a half blocks away, to take a taxi. We went outside the station and asked a taxi to take us to this hotel. He said he never heard of it. Another taxi we asked pointed us to a limo that would take us there. We asked them and they said "No." However they also said that the hotel we wanted was right across the street from us here at the train station. We walked over to it. Who said traveling is fun. It couldn't have been me, Jack.

The hotel was Oriental in a questionable neighborhood. "Ah so desu ka" if it was Japanese. I may like it here. It turned out to be real nice. We did not want to go out at night so we ordered Pizza. It wasn't very good. So as we stayed in the hotel and discovered something we didn't know what to call it. I think Jeri knew that it was a tub by the name of Jacuzzi. Well even I could tell it was a tub. This one though apparently was used for massages. It looked inviting to Jeri. It looked interesting to me. So, let's get in and turn the water on and see what happens. It was easier said than done. So how do we get in? This was easy. I lifted Jeri put her legs in first and slowly dropped her into the water. I got in. Now what do we do? I got the water on and saw a button which I pressed. Ah the hot water turned to bubbles etc. Now this felt good. Jeri loved it. After a while, we decided to get out. Now that was what I was afraid of. How can I get Jeri out? Somehow I did it without yelling for help.

Now the next morning when we went across the street to the train station, it was beginning to look like our jinx was not in Disneyland, it was right here in LA. To get to our train all we saw were large ramps to lead you up and to the trains. We were told there were no elevators. We did not see any Red Caps but we did see an Amtrak employee about getting to the train. He told us to go to a place and wait and he would see that we get aboard ok. Since we learned long ago not to be too trusting we waited for a good while and finally seeing a Red Cap we asked him to get us to our train. He pushed Jeri up the ramps and to our train. Score one point for Red Caps. However it wasn't exactly over yet. On board this double-decker car an attendant "too" firmly ordered everyone not handicapped to get upstairs out of the handicapped area. He said the train was going to be very crowded and he needed the room. He left and we never saw him again even though he scared a couple of people into leaving and almost scared me in going upstairs which I would not do. As it turned out the train was not crowded and the handicapped lower level was never full.

As we headed for Oakland we found we had nice people in our lower car. One little three year old girl was with us with her mother. The 3 year old could not walk (yet). Her mother had been in an earthquake when she was expecting and was thrown down.

Comment: while Jeri and I liked the single level cars better so everyone is together, we learned to like the handicapped lower car where we would always meet children etc and who really enjoyed riding on a train. What handicapped travelers? In many cases Jeri helped a lot when children would talk with her and she listened. They had no idea Jeri was handicapped until she got off the train in a wheelchair. A lot of adults didn't know either that Jeri was handicapped. One passenger saw our wheelchair behind our seat folded and laughed. He said, "I see you brought your golf cart with you." He couldn't believe it was a wheelchair.

Arriving on time in Oakland to meet an expected Hampton limo, there was none. They said they had a message that we changed schedules. They said they had no limo available, that we would have to take a taxi.

This Amtrak Oakland station was small and old. We had to claim our luggage which had been put out in the yard. It was dark and we had a little trouble

371

finding the taxi area. We found a taxi and a real nice driver, who said it would be about $17-$18 to the Hampton Inn. When we got there, his meter read over $20. He only charged us $18. Helping us out of his cab, he broke the other strap on our big new Avon bag. He was honest enough to show us what happened but was probably afraid I was going to ask him to pay for it. I told him it was ok – it was partially broken anyway. Inside the Hampton, the limo driver that was to pick us up was very apologetic in the mix up.

A PEACEFUL SUNDAY CAR DRIVE TO THE PACIFIC OCEAN AND BACK ALL IN ONE DAY – IT DOESN'T GET ANY BETTER OR WORSE.

Since we had decided to stay in Oakland where we would get our train for our trip home, we were on our own. There will be no San Francisco visit this trip. So what do we do today? It was a Sunday when I had an idea. This was my first mistake. Since I was stationed in Petaluma (about 30 miles north of San Francisco) at "Two Rock Ranch," I thought it would be nice to take Jeri to see it. Jeri was all for it.

We would take a shuttle bus to Oakland's airport and rent a car. I began our routine map reading which never worked in the past, why should it work now? To get to our highway north, we would have to drive all the way from Oakland across the Bay Bridge through downtown San Francisco to the Golden Gate Bridge. Driving through San Francisco, me? We did not want to see San Francisco this way but how do we get to Petaluma. Being Sunday, I told Jeri downtown San Francisco should be easy with little traffic. It was busy just follow the route we were on, cross the bridge and then an easy summer ride up north. We did arrive in Petaluma in which I showed her around and we went to church there. I remember the church. Mass was in Spanish. I don't remember that. There were lots of pretty noisy kids there. I knelt down on chewing gum. When I asked the lady distributing communion that I needed another one, she hesitated and gave a host to me with a funny look. Maybe the look came from my asking in English. I did not know Spanish.

I did not remember which road to take to "Two Rock." When I saw an older man, I asked him how to get there. He said he remembered where it was and would tell us. He also said, "By the way, what did they do there? No one in Petaluma ever seemed to know."

We found our way there but found out it was now a Coast Guard Station. At the entrance they said the Army had let it run down and the Coast Guard took over. They welcomed us to drive around. I recognized a couple of buildings still standing. Bunkers with communication equipment were still there. Anyway, Jeri saw what a "Two Rock Ranch" looked like.

We started our way back. Looking at our map I said to Jeri, "Let's take the shore road back to San Francisco it should be a beautiful ride back." Jeri was all for it. This was my second mistake. At first the road was nice and the ocean great to watch. We slowly stayed along the ocean, not many cars were seen. The road turned into a curving winding up and down zigzag road that we had to go slow on and I had to watch the driving. I don't even remember seeing another car going either way. Of course, I wasn't looking for cars I was looking for a cut off to the main highway. I had enough trouble staying between highway lines, if any were there. No road signs that I remember. It seemed never to end and it was going to get dark soon and we had to return the car before dark. At last, a cut off. We got back on the main highway going into San Francisco – it was as packed as could be. We reached the Golden Gate Bridge and paid the toll of $3.00 – you were only charged this going into San Francisco. After crossing the bridge, we made our way, a second trip through San Francisco and through a very busy downtown back to the Bay Bridge and across to Oakland. Good. Oh Oh! About when I was thinking we were back in Oakland on the right road to the airport, I found us two or three lanes on a busy road from the lane I was supposed to be in. It turned out I could not cross over. I turned off at the next exit. This was my third mistake. There was no turnaround road to get back on. Now we (I mean, I) was totally lost and going the wrong way. We then were driving around looking everywhere for signs to get us off the road we were on and back on the right road. By now, our jinx had to be at work and I'm sure Jeri was praying. The road we were on "sightseeing" Oakland came to an end. There were no signs which way to turn. I thought I would turn left and hope. At the last second I turned right. There was our interstate sign we were looking for. We made it to the airport, turned our car in phoned our hotel to pick us up and found Jeri exhausted. Was it a good jinx or did Jeri save us once more?

Actually we did what we wanted to do. If not one of our better fun days, it was certainly a new experience. Forget renting cars, next time we will take a train.

Next day we were up at 6 am, had our Hampton breakfast including a couple of donuts for our train ride and got in our limo to the train station. The driver was the owner, very nice and helpful and careful. He locked all the doors as we approached the station, area too dangerous he said. He helped us out, got a cart for us and refused any pay at all. An Amtrak girl said she would help us on early. She never came back. So what else is new? We boarded with everyone else including those passengers brought from the downtown office by Amtrak bus. We had scheduled a coach car for two overnights back to Chicago on this train, the California Zephyr, the best passenger train in the US.

Our Amtrak attendant was super, one of the best we ever had. Paulette, her name, from New Orleans (she gave us her full name and full address), helped Jeri so well, it was like we knew her a long time. She helped me several times to change Jeri in her seat rather than a difficult change in the restroom. She would bring Jeri's meals to her including extra for me.

The beautiful California Mountains with plenty of snow and us going through a free 2" snow storm was a wonderland in itself. This was soon to change from liking watching the outdoors to watching something else called termites at Glenwood Springs, Colorado. Apparently, at that time anyway, this area had them. One person said swarms are attacked by birds for food. After we left Glenwood Springs and talking to others, I said they look like flying ants crawling. Later back in my seat trying to sleep, Jeri punched me, said something and pointed to her window. I didn't understand her and asked if it was important. She nodded yes. It was a termite crawling up her window on the inside. Give me one termite star for one kill.

On long distance trains you are always told that what is nice about trains, you can take a nap anytime you want. We do it all the time and it is really nice except you find out that your nap has a wake-up call about every 30 minutes, if you are lucky. The call comes through the announcement loud speaker. It may be for dinner, it may be for approaching your station to get off. Some are funny calls. Some conductors are good at this to entertain passengers. Some calls sound funny but mean business. We had one call like this that said, "The person smoking an illegal substance in the restroom of this car had better quit or appropriate measures would be taken."

Coming out of the mountains from way up on the mountains, especially at sunset, and seeing way in the distance valley and seeing Denver is something worth seeing. Going the other way from Denver going to the top of the mountain, and seeing two or three engines in front of your train zigzagging up the mountain pulling all the cars is another worth watching train sight. Jeri and I have been able to do this several times. No wonder the train is the way to go with MS.

On our current trip now, coming out of the mountains, we could see a large pretty lake below. The conductor got on the loud address system and with full knowledge and excitement in his voice to tell us about the lake said, "That lake you saw from above is the................long pause..............I can't recall its name, oh well you all know it anyway!"

From Denver to Chicago was about a five hour ride. We arrived about one hour late in Chicago and made our way to the handicapped lounge for another wait to board either the Capital Limited or the Lake Shore Limited (both stop in Toledo), a four hour trip. Now the train to Toledo from Chicago always seems crowded. Most passengers are going to DC or New York City. One nice thing in Toledo, the trains either way have a scheduled stop there for 10 or 15 minutes which allows time to get off and, in our case, get Jeri off because she is in a wheelchair. When we arrived,

Toledo attendants met us and took us up on the elevator to the waiting room where we found Craig and Jeff waiting for us. We claimed our luggage and the trip was history.

I think about now Jeri and I were exhausted from two nights on the train and all that went on. Was Jeri ready for another trip? Well we still had two car trips scheduled this year and another train trip scheduled for next year. If Jeri wants to do it, I can do it. We kept our schedule.

APRIL 13, 1996 - DYLAN'S DESTINATION: DISNEYLAND BY AMTRAK, OF COURSE.

Dylan (Jami and Craig's son) was Jeri's and mine first and only grandson out of seven. We shall find out if he is our jinx. If he is, he walks home.

This trip had all the signs of a pleasant adventure. We had a pretty good agenda with destination stays in Las Vegas, Los Angeles and San Francisco. By now Craig knew me well enough not to trust me. I asked him if he would be in charge of our 15+ luggage cart.

In Toledo, we checked our luggage in for Las Vegas and Los Angeles. Leaving Toledo at 9:04 am on the Lake Shore train, we had electrical problems and arrived in Chicago six hours later (normal time was four hours). To add to the problem, our train had to turn around, stop and check its brakes and then back into the station. Sometime before this, another train could not stop and ran into the station. So they changed the train methods of entering Chicago station. Fortunately we had not checked any luggage to Chicago – we barely had time to change trains and to load what luggage we had with us on this new train. The Red Caps had taken all passengers luggage on their cart to the cars while passengers were still in the station except for ours because we had not arrived yet and our luggage was still on our train. As we arrived to change trains and luggage, Jami's family had a Red Cap take their luggage to their coach car. Jeri and I had a handicapped sleeper reserved and we had a Red Cap put our luggage on a cart that he would take to our car. Meanwhile Craig still had one large piece of his luggage he was carrying. I told him rather than carrying his piece of luggage, just throw it on our cart being delivered to our car and he could pick it up later. Jeri and I were at our car waiting for the Red Cap to bring our luggage. We were last on his list and as he began unloading the cart, we watched to identify ours. He had one piece left over. I told him it was not ours. He left. When Craig came to pick up his one piece of luggage, I told him we didn't have it. Then I remembered, it was his luggage left on the cart. I found Craig and we got off the train, about 20 minutes before the train was to leave to see if we could find his luggage. We half ran all the way back to inside the station to the waiting room. No luggage. We started back to our train and half way there we saw a large cart sitting by the side with one piece of luggage on it. There it is. Craig grabbed it. Now we ran back to the train with barely any time remaining. With Jeri alone in our car and Jami and Dylan alone in their car, who knows what if we had missed the train – but we did not miss the train.

Now that we were tucked into the Desert Wind at 3 pm still Saturday, April 13, it was time to sort our clothes etc and get ready for Jeri and me to have dinner served in our sleeper, this one being in the lower level. Now a new problem to solve showed up. I don't mind new problems. It is repeated problems that are hard to solve. It looked like we would have a problem with allowing Jami, Craig and Dylan to come to our sleeper room because they were in a coach car. Trains sometimes kept the coach passengers on their side and sleeping car passengers on their side, the dining car being the dividing car. Getting to the right person, this time our attendants, they worked it out for us even to allow what foods Jeri and I did not want that our family could use ours in the dining car. How sweet it is. If all people would only learn how to be a train attendant, wow!

Next stop - Las Vegas - as we finally got out of Saturday to welcome snow all around us, we stopped for an hour at Denver. Jami, Craig and Dylan had been eating in the dining car while we had been getting just one meal each time. I asked for an extra piece of apple pie and said I would pay for it. They said they could not do it that way. They gave me the extra piece. By now I was confused as to who was paying what. When that happens just let it stay its course and don't ask questions. When it was time for lunch we found out there would be no lunch today and possibly no dinner tonight. Now what happened? We learned that the dining car had a water problem and could not get the temperature high enough for cooking. Jeri and I were given two coupons to use in the snack bar. We weren't seeing much of Jami just now so we didn't know what was happening with them. Later in the afternoon, I took a walk over to the coach car to see Jami and family. The train had stopped. I looked out the car window and saw a KFC truck backed up against the dining car unloading chicken. This was good news. I mentioned to the other people in Jami's car that we were going to have chicken for supper. I further learned that everyone in the coach cars would get free boxes of chicken for dinner without any charge but could not eat in the dining car. The passengers in the sleepers would also receive "free" chicken served on plates with desert. Being in a lower level handicapped sleeper, we wondered what we would get. We got chicken but no desert.

Where we were in our lower level car with the only entrance being our front door, we were often forgotten by attendants and passengers except for the fact restrooms were right outside our door. Keeping our hallway door opened most of the time, we would meet people who could see and speak to us, sometimes asking us which restroom was open. I suppose this was one way of helping people. The dining car was closed for the rest of the trip. Restrooms remained opened.

The chicken mystery ended but the train was now crawling in which case I could now write without all the bumping and shaking. I didn't have anything to say. Now we were stopped in the middle of the mountains. I saw deer outside but there was no story there and I never did know why we stopped but remember we were in an isolated room with only one entrance. Comparing our elite car with other trains we have ridden, I think our room was converted from a large restroom that passengers could dress in.

We arrived at Vegas one and a half hours late at 9 am at our hotel Circus Circus. Even though checkout time was 11 am, we had to wait until 2 pm. They said they didn't kick people out. While waiting we ate at the buffet, lost a few coins and had Dylan with us at the Midway, for the children's free circus. While the hotel is geared for kids, an employee told us that Dylan was not allowed to watch us at the slots.

Walking the strip in the evening we watched the pirate show twice at Treasure Island, an outside show of two sailing warships shooting at each other with one getting sunk – excellent. The next day after another buffet breakfast, we began playing the one arm bandits. While losing my nickels Jami came along and I turned my machine over to her. She promptly hit for 80 nickels. In the evening we went to Caesar's Palace – an excellent show inside where the "statues came alive."

Next Stop – Santa Ana (Los Angeles) – after two nice days in Vegas without losing much but enjoying walking around seeing all the expensive facilities built with losers' monies as I heard it once said, we sat back in our train relaxing and preparing ourselves for a beautiful hotel we found to our liking in a catalogue. I was excited to tell Jami about this hotel and showed her a picture of it. Before we left home I told her she was going to be surprised with this hotel. Well we were surprised but first we had to get there.

We went through a travel agency on this one who was sure we had a winner when we picked which hotel we wanted. Our trip was set up to let us get off at a station nearest the hotel. It turned out to be one station too soon. Oh the train left us off all right, on a platform with 15 pieces of luggage and no one in sight. We tried the little station. It was locked. Could it be no one knew we were coming? Our train had left. We learned later that the hotel we were staying at would have picked us up free at the next station. We were now still alone with no one anywhere in sight. We had to find someone (no cell phones in those days) to call a taxi for us. Finally someone walked by and said they would call a taxi for us. Three taxis came. We were hoping one taxi would work. We had to use two taxis. I knew this was going to take a little bargaining with the taxis on this one. We asked the driver of one who seemed to be in charge, why so many taxis all we needed was one van. We were told that with our luggage it would take two taxis. We made an offer for what we would pay for two taxis. Actually if they did not accept our offer what could we do with no one in sight and our luggage stacked next to a closed station. The one in charge accepted our offer. He drove some of us to the hotel and was very pleasant about it. Our second crew told us the driver they were with complained all the way to the hotel that he should have been paid more.

As we entered our hotel to spend the next week relaxing, swimming and getting to Disneyland, our surprise was spelt shocked. Our travel agency had made reservations for a 3-night package plus 4 extra nights. When we checked into the hotel, they said we only had the 3-night package, that the other 4 nights had been canceled. Not so. There was no cancelation. They put us down for the 4 extra nights. We then showed the desk our confirmed price of $844.44 with all taxes. I checked the next day to confirm the price. They said the total price would be $884.44. I asked why the increase? They said the Disney price went up. I asked how much did the Disney price go up? They did not know. The acting manager said let me see your copy of the confirmation which showed $844.44. She said she would see that our final bill would be $844.44. Our bill was $866.05 including $3.50 of phone bills.

We finished checking in and found our rooms, I mean "suite." I had a cold and asked if the desk had any over the counter cough medicine. No, they did not. I asked, "How far was the nearest drugstore?" They said, "a few blocks, but you can't walk to it because of its location and there are no others close by. Last night in our parking lot, one of our employees was mugged. You had better stay here." We stayed.

To sum it, this was an old hotel in a bad location, no restaurant, an outdoor unheated swimming pool (we got Jeri in it twice but it was too cold and never used it again), poorly furnished rooms etc. Since I and especially Jeri never gave up easily, we had an idea. We asked the desk clerk if their shuttle would take Jeri and me to a mall. After a while a driver brought their shuttle van to us. Being a high van, I tried twice to lift Jeri up to the front seat. It was too high and the driver made no attempt to help us. Jami's family had gone to Disneyland. We abandoned that idea. We asked if there were any eating places in the area. The clerk pointed one direction and said there might be something that way. We walked four blocks, found a couple closed (it was afternoon). We had a pizza delivered which was terrible. I said to Jeri, they have a "Happy Hour" here, let's see what they have. They had a bowlful of pretzels. I said forget it. We went back to our room and found a few peanut butter crackers. So our stay for a week was in jeopardy. We have been through worse conditions than this. We stayed.

They did serve a free morning breakfast. We entered the room to eat there the next morning. When we saw them emptying a big sack of frozen potatoes on the stove and the tables of their "dining room" looked a little used - we were turned off very quietly and quick. We had to eat there, we had no choice, and we did so each morning. It never got better. It only got worse.

Note: We did recover some of our payments to this hotel when we got home but it took a few phone calls for a couple of small refunds. It wasn't good enough.

Locating the main offices of this chain hotel system to talk to someone high up, we reached a girl who answered the phone. I said we had a problem. Before I could explain all the details, she asked, "What can we do to satisfy you?" This stopped me "in my tracks" and I hesitated to think of an answer. She said, "If we give you some coupons and free room tickets for another stay in one of our hotels, would this help?" Problem solved that quick. A year later we stayed at one of their hotels in downtown New York City.

Note: The section of this story about our courtesy bus rides to Disneyland is written in **"Busses"** section and titled **"Bus to Disneyland."**

We survived the week at this hotel and actually, making the best of it, we enjoyed our make shift adjustment to crowded rooms, poor food and no one getting mugged. Did Jeri enjoy her stay? She made no bad remarks about it. Anything away from MS was good. The only thing I remembered she didn't like was that she was scared on their busses taking us to Disneyland speeding through the streets and her in her wheelchair not tied down. I guess anyone would be scared that way. So remember anyone you see in a wheelchair flying somewhere being pushed, they just might be a little scared. It was on to our next adventure.

When our "hotel" stay came to an end, we asked the service girl if she could take us in the morning to the Fullerton train station. She said "she could put us down but airport requests had priority." I told her we can't miss that train because it gets us to LA to make a connection to San Francisco. She said I could keep checking to see if we were still on or not. I kept checking all night right up to 6:30 in the morning. With the five of us in the van, we headed for Amtrak.

Everything was ok now that we were in the train station ahead of the train. Well not quite. When we checked into the station and showed them our tickets we were told that our tickets were to get us on the station we got off from. We would have to pay extra to get on here. My very tired mind said to ask to see someone higher up. The station master girl came to the window, listened to us and said, no problem. I will give you a note to the train conductor. The note read, "TO CONDUCTOR: You are authorized to carry this passenger between the stations specified without additional collection." The girl signed the note. The five of us boarded the train to head for downtown Los Angeles. We still have the note. We also sent this station girl's name to Amtrak Customer Relations in DC telling them how helpful she was.

We made our train connections from Fullerton to the LA station to catch our fifth train (out of seven for this trip) the Coast Starlight. Now we were heading along the ocean to Oakland (469 miles) where we would attempt once more to cross the bay and visit San Francisco. If we conquer that one, we should receive a "chumpion" award at least. We shall see.

We were instructed by Amtrak, that since their busses could not take us to SF, we should request a "pari-transit" to take us. This we did ahead of time and several calls to Amtrak assured us that the computer had us all set. Our train was two hours late at Oakland. We got off the train at 10 pm. An Amtrak bus was waiting for our train to take the passengers across to SF. The bus driver said he had no lift to get us on. He headed for SF. Anyway, we were expecting a pari-transit (whatever that was) to meet us and take us across the bay. Checking in the train station, we were told the van was there at 8:00 pm but had left. They didn't know either why he left. The attendant got on the phone and was told the van was in Emeryville, a station a few miles ahead, our train's next stop. Our train's conductor had not left yet to stay with us. He told us we could wait for the van or we could get back on the train and they would take us to Emeryville. Being pretty deserted by now where we were, we didn't want to be left alone. We decided to stay with the conductor and get on the train. When we got to Emeryville, the conductor pointed to where the van would be and felt everything was under control. He was even nice to explain everything we should see in SF. He then got back on his train and left. By now this conductor had spent a lot of time with Jeri which meant this train going to Seattle was delayed further. I like to think Jeri once again held up a train, shame on her!

HOWEVER, there was no van! We went inside the Fullerton station and the attendant did not know what happened. He thought it was in Oakland. He got on the phone to call the company supplying this van. They didn't know where it was either. Our attendant said we would have to wait while the van company searched. It was now 10:30 pm. There was a regular taxi driver standing there with his cab. We asked our attendant if we could let this taxi take us downtown at Amtrak's expense rather than waiting. I said we could transfer Jeri to this cab. The attendant said ok and gave the taxi money.

If anyone is still reading this "epic" there's more because we "ain't" done yet.

Amtrak's downtown station was at the Ferry Building where the busses would take and pick up passengers from and to Emeryville across San

Francisco Bay. We arrived at the Ferry Building at 11:10 pm. Two Amtrak ladies inside were very concerned about what happened to us. One of the ladies said, and showed me, the efforts they went to in trying to make sure nothing would go wrong. We appreciated their interest and while tired, never got upset over this because a lot of people were involved in trying to help us. The ladies called our hotel which was 1 and ½ miles from the train station and was to pick us up but they said their shuttle stops at 11:00 pm but that they would pay up to $7.00 for a taxi. The Amtrak ladies were nice enough to call a cab for us. We waited. They called again and were told one was on its way. It was now about midnight. The one attendant still there said we would have to wait outside, luggage and all, since she was told to close at midnight and was not allowed to stay with passengers past midnight. These two lady attendants told us they would see that we would not have a problem going back to catch our train.

Our family of five, including Dylan, was momentarily disturbed going outside at midnight in downtown San Francisco with a small child and our luggage. As we were setting ourselves up outside the cab came within about fifteen minutes.

End of story and trip? No sir. We still have a two night stay at our new hotel the Americania April 24 and 25 and then the California Zephyr and lastly the Capital Limited to Toledo.

The next morning when we came downstairs to the lobby, we found our friend Jack LaDove waiting for us. Now Jack was mentioned in the ASA section of this book in which he was our founder of our ASAPAC alumni association and had met Jeri at our first reunion. After one reunion, he invited us to a a semi formal dinner with him. Did Jeri get her wine – I would bet on it. There is also more about Jack LaDove and our family in the **"Elevators" San Francisco section.** As mentioned earlier, Jack spent the day with us, had lunch with us, took Dylan to the amusement park there as we walked by it etc. I think Jack was a good example of why Jeri loved going on trips, especially trains. She attracted many people to meet and talk with her, even becoming good friends.

Spending two days in SF gave us a little more time to explore. We took a great ride in a beautiful "ferry" boat all around San Francisco Bay. The pictures we took aboard this perfect size boat (for us) looks like we were the only ones aboard. It covered a large section of the bay including going under the Golden Gate Bridge twice – after going under it one way it eventually came back under it. Add this to Jeri's experience because now we could say we drove on the bridge and now we rode under the bridge. This would have little interest to most people traveling but when you have MS and you do little unimportant side tricks, it has a whole difference bearing of enjoying your life your way.

It was now time to repack and begin a nice comfortable California Zephyr trip back to Chicago in our own "state room" and having part of our family with us. Jeri wanted these trips to be endless and proved it by asking when our next trip was after arriving home. The amazing part was when we did get home, she never seemed tired. In fact even on a trip, she never seemed tired.

We read a lot about being tired with MS. Perhaps it is more boredom than needing rest. Early on Jeri switched from taking rests, as recommended, by being active doing things, dreaming, etc. She did little reading (because of eye problems) and little watching TV (too boring). Interesting, I once asked her why she was always asking a nurse to put her in bed to rest. She told me, "It was the only way to get away from them."

On the train Jeri would doze off often if nothing was happening but only for short periods. Now at night she slept pretty well even when the train hit 69 miles an hour bouncing better than at an amusement park. At that speed I would be wide awake waiting for us to jump the track. When you live on the lower level, you are not very far from the tracks and can hear every click of the train on those tracks. It put Jeri to sleep.

Back to heading to our hotel to get ready to check out, we stopped at the Ferry Building to check our schedule for the next morning. One of our two attendants was there and said everything was set for the next day. Be here at 8:00 am. A handicapped van would pick us up at 8:30 am. Now I would begin to get a little nervous as the time drew near to get back to the train. Jeri? This waiting never bothered her. I was always relaxed on each train when I was aboard with Jeri, her wheelchair, our luggage taken care of and the train slowly starting to move - This reminded me often how at home waiting for a no show nurse to come. It just didn't seem to bother Jeri.

We were at the Ferry Building the next morning at 8:00 am. At 8:30 am no van. At 8:45 am no van. The bus for the passengers catching this train was already there and left to take them to Emeryville to get to the Zephyr as it was scheduled to leave at 9:30 am. Our attendant called to see where our van was. They were told the van was somewhere at the Ferry Building, where they didn't know. When they found out they would tell the van to get to the Amtrak office in that building. The van arrived. It is now 9:00 am. The driver looked at us and said there were no seats in the van for passengers except for two in the front, one for the driver. He said he was told that he was to pick up a wheelchair. Nothing surprises us in our adventures. By choice we go with whatever will take us and enjoy it. The driver tied Jeri down in the back. Jami, Craig and Dylan sat on the floor. I was elected to ride in the only seat available. Now can we get to the train? I would estimate that we had 20 minutes left. I asked our station attendant if she would call the train in Emeryville and tell them we are on our way. I knew we were on their passenger list – how could they not know by now. The attendant said they would call the train. Now 20 minutes should get us there easily because we were very near the Bay Bridge and I figured we would be near the Emeryville station when we got off the bridge. Did this work? Not really. When the van driver asked the attendant standing there when we were ready to pull out how to get to the Bay Bridge to get to Amtrak – well you can't win every time. The driver started driving. Did he find directions? We will soon find out. We started to head for Oakland, I thought. But wait, I saw the sign Golden Gate Bridge - we are going the wrong direction. I said to the driver, "You're lost, aren't you?" He, panicking, said, "Yes. I told them not to send me, my route is somewhere else, I do not know San Francisco." I told him to turn around. He immediately made a U turn right into traffic coming the other way. I meant at the next corner. I told him to go straight until he sees a Bay Bridge sign, follow the sign and get on that bridge. Then when we get off, look for an Amtrak sign and follow it. This worked. We were on the road nearing the trains. It was

9:30 am. I saw the train about 200 yards away still there. I could still see one yellow step stool was still outside. There was an attendant standing by it. Our van could not drive to it. I quickly jumped out of the van, told the others to follow me and ran towards the train (they said they never knew I could run so fast). I was too far away to yell.

Waving my arms, I kept telling myself, "Look my way one more time." Finally, success as they looked, we saw two others jump from the train and come running towards us reaching Jeri and then running with her in her wheelchair and with our luggage back to the train. The attendants were thrilled to see Jeri and get her and us aboard, just in time. I would guess the train was now definitely late starting but made no issue of it. I later asked our attendant if they had received a call that we were on our way. He said he knew of no call. He also said when we arrived the train had already passed its departure time. So we did get treated well. I don't know what happened to our taxi driver.

As Jami, Craig and Dylan settled in their coach seat, Jeri and I crawled back to settle once more in a two day stay in our private car with the train track noise for entertainment. Actually, it was better than that. Jami's family spent a lot of time with us in our room. We had a lot to talk about. We had done a lot. We should have been tired but we were not. It was again an amazing trip with Jeri. No need to say more. Hello Chicago, hello Toledo. We'll be back.

Monday, June 2, 1997 at 1:09 am Jeri and I were back doing what we liked to do – getting on a train. It was another trip to DC, Atlantic City and NYC, a nice adventure of 10 days for us.

Getting on at one o'clock in the morning at Toledo is not a "piece of cake." It's more of an apology when you think you found not one but two seats we needed and you almost sit on someone sleeping. It is very dark at that time outside and inside a train car. A small floor light is kept on all night but no seat lights. If you do sit on someone, apologize nicely. They probably had to do the same thing when they boarded. We've never have seen anyone getting upset.

In DC we arrived June 2 and stayed four nights at Holiday Inn Central. Our Congressman had reserved shuttle busses for June 3, 4 and 5 to take us to College Park National Archives. He also had While House tickets for Jeri and me to take a guided tour. The tickets were dated June 4, 1997 while on the schedule we received the tickets were dated June 3, 1997. No matter, we took the tour. We also toured the new World War II Roosevelt Memorial.

Getting in and out of taxis was a job with a wheelchair so when we could walk, we walked.

Next stop was Atlantic City by way of a train change in Philadelphia and then two nights at Howard Johnson International Hotel near the boardwalk. We met my brother and his wife there where we walked the boardwalk, ate there and strangely found where the slot machines were. Did we win, I don't remember. I think I had less nickels after we left.

We then left Atlantic City, changed trains in Philadelphia and proceeded to NYC.

For Friday and Saturday nights, we did get to New York City and checked into the beautiful Radisson Empire Hotel. **This is the hotel referred to in our section "Busses, Taxis etc including "One NYC Police Car" and where we went to a Broadway show.** To add a little to this show and our "night out on the town," I think we were in a state of mind that rarely happened to us – dressing with our best clothes to go to a real Broadway show and mingle with the well dressed theatre-goers topped with meeting NYC policemen. The only part we did not do, was to have dinner after the show and join the night time society. Our reason: not hungry and tired. We went back to our hotel. I was so glad for Jeri that we could do this together and alone. She looked so beautiful dressed up so nicely as we got out of our cab at the theater with the dressed up doorman opening the cab and entrance doors for us. It doesn't get any better. So even in a wheelchair, you can have special nights out dressed in your finest with or without MS.

We also went to Radio City to see (I should say try to see) a movie and stage show. I had remembered a while back (actually before knowing Jeri) the times I had seen a movie and stage show at Radio City with their famous Rockettes. I told Jeri that I wanted to take her there. As we waited in a line with no one in it, I asked the ticket window cashier for tickets to get in for the show. She gave me a strange look and asked when the last time I was there, that the movie, stage show etc ended 20 years ago! We did walk to Times Square, took a tour of NBC and had dinner at a sidewalk café.

Leaving NYC at 6:30 pm, we headed back to Toledo by way of the Lake Shore Limited which, as mentioned before, we thought was one of the best scenic Amtrak trains to ride. Boarding at Pennsylvania Station the train took us up the Hudson River Valley then east through New York State arriving in Toledo at 8:06 in the morning on June 11.

When we arrived home we found our house cleaned, waxed, parts painted and grass cut by our family we left behind. Now that was the biggest surprise of all. We took them to Bob Evans and made them listen to our trip.

RETURN TO DC, OCT 2005 - JERI AND I.

By now one might think "again – DC?" Actually we were running out of train destinations, some even more than once. But tired of DC? Well, a little bit.

We still had research to do at College Park Archives, MD as we were just about ready to get our ASA book published. Arriving in DC by Amtrak on Sunday October 9, we took the subway to College Park and checked in at a Hampton Inn for five nights.

I remember the time when you told a taxi where you were going and they always knew where the location was. They were known for knowing their territory. Now it is not quite the same. One day Jeri and I took a taxi to the subway station, about two miles away. On our return trip to the same station, we went outside to catch a taxi back to our hotel. The taxis would wait for passengers on a street about a block from the station. No taxis in sight so we waited for one to come. While looking towards the direction a taxi would park, I briefly let go of the wheelchair. The sidewalk was not level and I had to race the wheelchair to the curb just as she was ready to go over. I sometimes think Jeri liked me to panic.

Anyway, that wasn't too bad. The taxi did show up so we now could rest easy back to our hotel. I told the driver to take us to the Hampton Inn. About two miles later, I didn't recognize anything on the street. Politely I told the driver that I thought he was going the wrong way. He knew the hotel name but in this case did not know where it was. With his meter turned on I told him to turn around and that I thought I might remember the street we came off from. We arrived back at our subway station ok – so far so good. I was hoping I could find our street to turn on. The only thing on was the meter. Another mile, I recognized our corner and yelled turn right and go about a mile, the Hampton is on the right.

When I told the desk clerks that a taxi didn't even know where you were, they were surprised. They gave me their address card and said next time show a taxi where we are. Actually this was a good idea for the future since we knew now, taxis didn't always know locations. I think they usually know "shortcuts" and I like to think many of them are honest. I can usually tell how honest when one actually talks to and helps Jeri. I know one fact. No one ever discouraged Jeri and I from doing things our way.

To continue with our shortest trip ever, just 8 days, we had free tickets for the Washington Monument, toured the WW2 Memorial, learned how to use the subway better and I didn't lose Jeri once getting on. This was our last Amtrak train trip but they did manage to extend our trip back to Toledo by five hours where we were met by Jodi and her "famous" three.

AMTRAK US and VIA RAIL CANADA SCHEDULES – date sequence - we used this just for reference, where we had been and added to it after every trip.

1990 (Oct) Amtrak
Toledo-Chicago-Seattle-Los Angeles-New Orleans-Chicago-Toledo (Around the country)

Jeri-Jack-Jodi-Jami-Jeff-and-guests-Rhonda & Rashelle

1992 (May) Amtrak
Toledo-DC-Montreal-Poughkeepsie-Albany-Toledo
(In and out of Canada by Amtrak)

Jeri-Jack

1992 (Oct) Amtrak
Toledo-DC-New Orleans-Wilmington-Montreal-
Hudson-Toledo (Jodi caught up to us in Montreal
to return by train with us)

Jeri-Jack

1993 (Apr) Amtrak
Toledo-Chicago-Las Vegas-Los Angeles-Oakland
(San Francisco)-Chicago-Toledo (Rented car to
Petaluma-drove thru 'Frisco twice)

Jeri-Jack

1994 (Sep) Amtrak
Toledo-DC-Atlantic City-Wilmington-Orlando-DC-
Toledo (ASAPAC reunion in Orlando)

Jeri-Jack

1995 (May) VIA Rail
Windsor-Toronto-Montreal-Halifax-Montreal-
Toronto-Winnipeg-Edmonton-Jasper-Vancouver-
Toronto- Windsor (Jeri threw a nickel into the
Atlantic Ocean, then one into the Pacific Ocean,
one week apart – from wheelchair)

Jeri-Jack

1995 (Sep) Amtrak
Toledo-Chicago-St Paul-Chicago-Toledo (ASAPAC
reunion in Minnesota)

Jeri-Jack

1996 (Apr) Amtrak
Toledo-Chicago-Las Vegas-Fullerton-Los Angeles-
Oakland (San Francisco)-Chicago-Toledo
(Disneyland)
> Jeri-Jack-Jami-Craig-Dylan

1996 (Sep) Amtrak
Toledo-Chicago-Las Vegas-Chicago-Toledo
(ASAPAC reunion in Las Vegas)
> Jeri-Jack

1997 (Jun) Amtrak
Toledo-DC-Philadelphia-Atlantic City-Philadelphia-
New York City-Toledo (Met brother/family at
Atlantic City)
> Jeri-Jack

1998 (Apr) VIA Rail
Windsor-Toronto-Jasper-Prince George-
Prince Rupert-Prince George-Jasper-Toronto-Windsor
(Northwest Canada - 30 miles from Alaska)
> Jeri-Jack

1998 (Sep) Amtrak
Toledo-Chicago-Albuquerque-Chicago-Toledo
(ASAPAC reunion in Albuquerque)
> Jeri-Jack

1999 (Aug) VIA Rail
Windsor-Toronto-Winnipeg-Churchill-Winnipeg-
Toronto-Windsor (1st trip to Churchill)
> Jeri-Jack

2000 (Sep) Amtrak
Toledo-Arlington-DC-Toledo (Research ASAPAC
history book and reunion)
> Jeri-Jack

2001 (Sep) VIA Rail
Windsor-Toronto-Winnipeg-Churchill-Winnipeg-
Toronto-Windsor (2nd trip to Churchill)
   Jeri-Jack

2002 (Jul) VIA Rail
Windsor-Toronto-Montreal-Halifax-Montreal-Toronto-
Windsor (Jodi-Katie-Jenny-Jami-Craig-Dylan-Chloe
met us in Toronto-all stayed overnight and we all
rode the train back to Windsor)
   Jeri-Jack

2002 (Sep) Amtrak
Cincinnati-DC-Toledo (ASAPAC reunion in Kentucky)
   Jeri-Jack

2003 (Jul) VIA Rail
Trip to Halifax **cancelled**-SARS outbreak in Canada
(Train tickets were refunded in full)
   Jeri-Jack

2003 (Sep) VIA Rail
Windsor-Toronto-Winnipeg-Churchill-Winnipeg-
Toronto-Windsor (3rd trip to Churchill, took a dog sled
ride)
   Jeri-Jack

2004 (Jul) VIA Rail
Windsor-Toronto-Montreal-Halifax-Montreal-Toronto-
Windsor (Rode on new train in handicap suite-Jodi-
Katie-Jenny-Kelly met us in Toronto-all stayed
overnight at Delta Chelsea and we all rode the train
back to Windsor)
   Jeri-Jack

2005 (Aug) VIA Rail

Windsor-Toronto-Winnipeg-Churchill-Winnipeg-Toronto-Windsor (4th trip to Churchill-met Jodi and her three girls for a 2-night stay in Toronto at Delta Chelsea, then all rode the train back to Windsor)
Jeri-Jack

2005 (Oct) Amtrak

Toledo-DC-Toledo (Stayed in College Park for research at Archives then back to Toledo and met by Jodi and her famous three)
Jeri-Jack

2006 (Jun-Jul) VIA Rail

Windsor-Toronto-Montreal-Halifax-Montreal-Toronto-Windsor (Last train ride)
Jeri-Jack

FINAL TOTAL FOR ABOVE TRAIN TRIPS:

Amtrak   13 (plus 1 LA train trip)   14 trips
(including two trips that included Canada)
Via Rail   9   9 trips

Total   23 Train trips

OTHER DESTINATIONS: JACK AND JERI AMTRAK TRAIN AND CAR TRIPS TO ASAPAC REUNIONS.

AN INTRODUCTION – When Jeri and I were invited to the first ASAPAC reunion in October 1993, I wasn't sure I wanted to go. It had been many years since those invited had served in Tokyo sometime during 1946-1952. Jodi drove Jeri and me to this first one which was in Kentucky. I don't even remember inviting Jeri to go. Why would she want to attend a boring Army reunion of has-beens? My error - this was one of the best things we ever did for Jeri. She loved going and the men and women then and thereafter took to her quickly and welcomed her as one of them.

Being in a wheelchair with MS? So what? This was ASA.

Listing the ASAPAC reunions Jeri and I were able to get to:

Reunion 1 1993 October Car Ft. Mitchell, Kentucky

This was covered under section **ASAPAC, REUNIONS.**

Reunion 2 1994 September Amtrak Orlando, Florida
This trip was by way of DC, Atlantic City and Wilmington. The train to Atlantic City was described under section **Jeri holding up trains.**

While we were settled in Atlantic City at a hotel just off the boardwalk, what was there to do here? I wish I  could say Jeri said to play the slots. We played them anyway. It was the 25 cent ones first but that was too expensive, the quarters went too fast. We found some 5 cent ones. Result for the day: Jeri was 3 dollars ahead, I was 5 dollars behind. Jeri made me put her 3 dollars in her purse. We usually were big spenders. Well, not really. We were through for the day, probably for the trip.

One more idea came upon us. Jeri liked to watch the Miss America contest on TV always being held in Atlantic City. Well, there was no Miss America contest being held while we were here but here we were, standing right in front of the building where it was held. Jeri wanted to see if we could at least go inside where the contest is held. There was something going on so we went up to a door entrance and went in. Inside we were told that there was a trade show going on but we were not allowed to go in. We simply  went back outside and went to another entrance and walked in where the person there said go on in and you can see where the Miss American contest is held.

After we were done in Atlantic City, my brother Tom (Butch) picked Jeri and me up to visit his family (Betty Anne and children Kim and Denny) for a few days in Wilmington. From there we headed for Florida by train.

We finally made it to Florida. The station's platform was not train level so we needed a lift to get Jeri off. The train was late so I walked Jeri down the steps with the attendant in front. They did not like my doing this but where was the lift?

Our ASA reunion attracted about 100. Jeri and I had a good time, getting to know more new people whom we had never met plus the ones Jeri previously met at the first reunion. We both felt more comfortable and were enjoying all of this. This was really all new for Jeri. She seemed right at home. To top off our stay there, Jodi and Bob (boyfriend eventually to become husband) had flown to meet us. We ended up touring the Cape Kennedy and space center. Since Jeri was in a wheelchair, the tour had its own bus to take us around. Being us alone, the driver was able to stop, explain and show us more. This was an "advantage" of living in a wheelchair. So if confined to a wheelchair, go for it.

Arriving back in DC, we found in those years that there were three levels of tracks entering Union Station. Some tracks were at platform level and some were at underground level. Our track was one level below platform level and underground where a lift was needed. No problem to us. By those years we knew the system. If in a wheelchair they would ask you to wait to get off, let the other passengers get off first. This we actually liked. At busy stations, passengers getting off would begin waiting near the exit early to be first off and sometimes it was like "everyone for themselves." There were also those who were saying Goodbye to their fellow passengers, some even exchanging addresses. We were the in-between where some offered us to go in front of them which we would usually thank them but that we would rather wait because it would take time outside to put the lift next to the exit door. Since the DC Union Station was an "end of the line" stop we had more time to get off.

Now in our case, our attendant, before the train stopped, came and told us to wait until all were off the train and the lift was put in place. They would then come to get us off. As usual, I would transfer Jeri from her train seat to her wheelchair. We were ready for the "all clear" signal. Now remember, all passengers had to debark here and would take the elevator up to the main floor. No new passengers would be waiting on our level.

We waited. We looked. No attendant, no passengers on our car, no lift. The large train area was abandoned. Panic time? No, it was just another routine inconvenience for us. Jeri knew that this meant going down the train steps with me with no one to help. Did it bother her? Actually not much ever seemed to bother Jeri. I had taken her down the steps many times alone. If I slip, we both go down. I never slipped. We were now on the lower paved floor. There was still no one in sight. No problem. The elevator was a short walk to it. No elevator was there. I looked up to see where it was. It was above us. I pressed the button to get it down. Nothing happened. Again, nothing happened. Just then a man was walking by and saw us. He did not look like he worked there but he stopped to tell us that elevator did not work. I think we knew that. He did say he thought the one across the tracks worked, try it. He disappeared. Somehow I got Jeri over the tracks even though there was no smooth crossing to do so. Still no people and I saw no train pulling in. On to our elevator – IT WORKED. It took us up to the main floor, the door opened and a lot of people were walking getting to and from their train. We walked off unnoticed and made our way right into the crowd. We thought it was not necessary to report what happened and get someone in trouble. We simply continued where we were going. A receptionist saw us and took us to the VIP lounge and stood guard at the men's room where I could change Jeri. Then back to Toledo at 6 am where Craig (Jami's husband) met us for homeward bound.

Did someone say that Jeri had MS? When did this happen?

Reunion 3   1995 September Amtrak St. Paul, Minnesota

Our train left us at St. Paul, Minnesota and then we went to our reunion at the Thunderbird Hotel in Bloomington, Minnesota. This was a nice quiet train trip in which we saw a little more of Minnesota and meeting new members and rejoining our previous members. One new member we met surprised Jeri with a beautiful small wooden table chest he had made just for Jeri. Our other surprise, especially for Jeri, was that being .9 of a mile from the "Mall of America" we were able to walk there and spend the day. This Mall, at that time, was considered the largest enclosed mall in the US. We still went to our reunion which included a banquet, which is always done especially since an auction is always held after our feast. Our own auctioneer Sam always put on a great show, usually better than the banquet. This would end our reunion until next year. The "Goodbyes" were so unbelievable that you almost had to come back. What a group for Jeri to belong to. Then it was back to Toledo.

Reunion 4 1996 September Amtrak Las Vegas, Nevada

This was our third trip to Las Vegas. At first we worked on going there by flying. We had decided this shortly before going and only had a few days to plan. The planning did not work. The airlines did not seem too interested in having passengers confined to wheelchairs. I think what did it was when I said besides the wheelchair we have to take a suction machine with us. When they indirectly discouraged us, I said forget it. I said to Jeri that I would call Amtrak quickly to see if we can still get a ride there by train. This we did. No problem. This is explained more under section **AIRPLANES.**

There were not too many of our group that went, probably because we teamed with another group to share expenses. We had a good time but Jeri and I both arrived at the same conclusion. We had enough of Vegas. We never returned.

404

Reunion 5 1997 October Car Louisville, Kentucky

Jeri and I have little information on this reunion. We drove to it alone. My leftover notes tell us that we stayed at the reunion five days, left and stayed overnight in Dayton. From there we detoured our way back to BG by way of "our" best restaurant ever, the Hartville Kitchen near Kent. When we were in that area, we always found time to go there. It still exists. If alone, Jeri and I would always bring back about $200 worth of cooked meals, pies etc for our family left behind.

We still had a great time at the reunion. Jeri knew everyone there and they, as usual, would have her at their table a lot. We were still working on our unit's history book and I mentioned that I had learned that there was a classified "Secret" report on ASA as to ASA's closing whether we should seek a copy of it. Shortly after, I sent the Freedom of Information office and requested a copy. Years later, I received a notice from the Freedom of Information that they had it ready to send me but was stopped by the Pentagon who wanted to know why we wanted it. We are still waiting.

Reunion 6 1998 September Amtrak Albuquerque, New Mexico

A bus tour with Jeri and I aboard to Santa Fe is described under section **ASAPAC, REUNIONS** and beginning with paragraph **Our reunion in 1998 in Albuquerque...**

On the train from Chicago to Albuquerque - with Jeri in a wheelchair, this two level train required us to be in the lower handicapped section of our now known 13 coach seats. We noticed a girl sitting by herself in the back seat. During the night with only a small floor light on, I was on an end seat with Jeri sitting next to the window. In this darkness, I saw someone crawling on their hands and knees. It was our passenger from the last seat. She was heading for her wheelchair to climb on to go to the ladies restroom. She was probably around 30 and fairly heavy with strong arms. She reached her chair. Jeri was watching and indicated for me to help her. I went to her as she was pulling herself up with her arms to get in her chair. I quickly offered to help and was able to do so to help her get into her chair. She then said she could get to the restroom just a few feet away. When she came out, she let me help her to get back onto the floor. Why the floor? The wheelchair was too large to move through the aisle. We were so pleased that she let us help her. Now this continued several times during the night. Each time we were able to help her. Now, a couple of strange things took place.

The next morning, this "trip" by the girl continued to and back from the restroom with us helping the best we could. The other coach seats were filled with other passengers. No one stood up to help. Jeri and I never expected that at all and Jeri being in a wheelchair herself must have felt really bad. When an attendant finally appeared in our "little corner of the train," I caught him quickly before he would leave. I told him that he had a problem here and explained what was happening. Being defensive, he said, "She should not even be on this train without personal assistance." I said I agree with you but the fact is she is on and you're responsible. You should tell your conductor this. I said furthermore, Jeri and I are getting off at Albuquerque while this girl is going on to LA and will need help. Just then one of our other passengers stood up and said, "We will take care of her."

There was one more "incident" in Albuquerque that bothered us to almost no end. Don't try this one. You won't like it. It was the train coming to pick us up to take us back to Chicago. As Jeri and I arrived at the platform to get on the train, I don't remember any station being there. We were told to go to the far end of the platform and wait for the train there. I think we were the only ones getting on, though that's no big deal. We were to be there early because we were scheduled to board the train at 1:26 pm. Easy so far, we could do that. Little did we know about the weather in this rather deserted "desert." With a lot of luggage packed on the wheelchair with Jeri underneath as usual, we walked to the end of the platform. No Red Caps at this one. We waited and waited. Heat became, to us, almost unbearable, especially with our traveling clothes on with no shelter, trees or indoor facilities in sight plus the elevation was 7,000 feet having thinner air. We waited well over an hour in that bright sun before the train puffed its way to us. To make matters a little worse, in those areas in the summer those days air conditioned trains were well thought of but it was hard to keep passengers comfortable trying to maintain a cool temperature. It was a case of being hot for a few minutes and then the air conditioning seemed to fade away. Did we complain to the crew when we got on? Nah! They were facing the same problem. We still enjoyed our trip.

Reunion 7   1999 October Car Buffalo, New York

Buffalo here we came, Jack and Jeri and 100 other ASAers and spouses. We drove to this one and stayed four nights. Almost everyone there took the bus tour to Niagara Falls. We didn't think they would allow us on the bus so we never tried. Anyway the "Falls" required a lot of moving around in a wheelchair to see them. After the reunion was over, since we were so close to the falls (about 20 miles), we decided to drive there ourselves. Never again - the traffic was so heavy that it took us nearly two hours  to get there. We did go to the Canadian side to see them since that side is the best to watch and the closest to them. We stayed one night and then headed back to BG by way of the Hartville Kitchen near Kent, Ohio, to have our eating meal treat. Leaving Niagara Falls and driving on, which seemed like, 25 lanes of highway at 80+ miles an hour, I didn't realize I was scaring Jeri – I thought she was just sleeping. I said driving long distance is for the birds. Jeri quickly agreed.

Reunion 8   2000 September Amtrak Arlington & DC

This train trip from Toledo to DC and back consisted of two planned projects for Jeri and me which took 18 days to do. The first was our 8th reunion meeting in Arlington, Virginia. The second project was to get to the archives in College Park, Maryland to continue our research on our ASA history book. This second project involved subway rides and is told within the section **SUBWAYS.**

One highlight for the reunion was that we had invited two prominent Army historians to our reunion to show them what we had been working on. One was able to come and spent several hours enjoying his visit with us. Jeri and I had met both of them before at Fort Belvoir, Virginia where they had a meeting with us discussing our plans to write our own ASA history book. They both had supported our book and helped guide us a lot. We sent a free copy of our book to them when we were finished. We enjoyed the reunion and seeing so many great people. This was really our social life.

After Jeri and I were finished playing soldier and WAC at the archives, we found a home in the Smithsonian History Museum in their Ice Cream Parlor–an old fashion ice cream soda fountain – great chicken noodle soup with a great vanilla soda finished off with a great great banana split. We went to that one several times. We decided if we ever came back to DC, this was to be our first stop.

Note: We kept our promise. Two years later we went back to DC and headed for our Ice Cream Parlor. It wasn't there. A favorite snack bar was in its place. Only the old ice cream floor tiles remained. Why didn't we just accept their answer and eat at the new snack bar? After a two year wait? No thank you. We traced down where the one in charge was and asked, the best nice way we could, where was our Ice Cream Parlor? They apologized and said it simply did not draw enough patrons. Our jinx was still working against us!

Back to our reunion, it was now time to head home. On our train trip back to Toledo – we left DC at 4 pm with three engines pulling us. It wasn't long before two of them gave. We crept along until we got to Pittsburgh where they had an engine waiting for us.

We arrived at Toledo at 8 am, three hours late - our jinx again? Nah, couldn't be.

Reunion 9 2001 September Ft. Mitchell, Kentucky – the first reunion Jeri and I missed – we went AWOL to our Churchill, Canada.

Reunion 10 2002 September Bus & Amtrak Ft. Mitchell, Kentucky and then on to DC.

To get to this reunion in Kentucky and a first class tour of the Capital Building in DC was a display of characteristics (and/or peculiarities) that should have told us "stay home and enjoy yourself." This trip was for Jeri and Jack – a bus ride (see story in the section **BUSSES),** a cab to the reunion where we stayed three nights and a cab to the Amtrak station in Cincinnati to be there when the train was scheduled to leave for DC at 5:39 am on Sunday 9/22/02. We arrived pretty early but had to wait outside of this large museum (the station had a small rental section for their one train three times a week) before someone opened the doors. The museum had originally been a beautiful large train station. The station with its small waiting room was for buying tickets and sitting. I guess if you missed the train, you knew there would be another in a couple of days. Actually quite a few passengers got on with us. It headed for DC through a steady downpour all the way. The scenery you could not see. We were looking forward to stopping at White Sulphur Springs, West Virginia where the luxury hotel Greenbrier (since 1778) was located. (Jeri and our family had spent a day there once in our car but did not stay. The cost per night was beyond us). Our train did stop briefly at White Sulphur Springs where there was an old small station, where people could wait for the train. We were not able to get off.

We arrived in DC Sunday 9/22/02 at 7:35 pm and settled in at our hotel for a seven night stay. A visit and tour to the capital building arranged by our congressman was early in our schedule. We took a taxi to meet our congressman's staff assistant, Kelley, whom we had met before, who took us through an underground tunnel, that connected congressional members' offices to the capital, on a two hour tour of the capital – no waiting in line. We visited the Capitol Rotunda which is a large room underneath the dome and has no specific functions except for ceremonial services and contains many statues and pictures centered around past presidents.

When you are in this Capitol Rotunda room and stand in one specific spot the acoustics make it so that if someone else is standing in another specific spot they can hear what you say even if you whisper. Rumor was that this originally was how some congressmen would know what others were talking about and

planning. "Kind" of like eavesdropping but each area was on the other side of this large room. If the others on the other end were not aware of being listened to, then I guess it was "working for someone." The two spots are marked on the floor and are pointed out during tours.

Meanwhile back at our hotel we were alerted to an international meeting that was to be hosted by the City of Washington DC beginning Friday September 27, 2002. This meeting was expecting some unusual activities from protesters. The hotel issued some tips during our stay such as:

When leaving the hotel, have an ID picture and room key with you. To get your vehicle may take longer than usual. Several streets were listed to be closed. Barricades would be erected at several locations including Pennsylvania Avenue. A final suggestion was visit the website for update information.

The DC transit authority was not planning any closures but suggested:

Allow extra time in travel plans.

Avoid traveling during certain peak hours.

Keep eyes and ears open for unusual behavior and report it.

The hotel gave us a map of the DC protests.

I suppose this was nice of the hotel to give us this information but as we tried to follow all of this, we kind of hit the streets that looked safe. We had plans to do research for our Army book at the national archives in College Park, which we did by way of a small bus that was provided for researches going to College Park. Jeri and I were allowed to ride this bus if there was room. No problem. We used it several times, no charge. They were able to lift Jeri into the bus and each trip was a sightseeing trip for us right through a section of DC we had never seen. It took about forty minutes to get to the archives.

We also had plans to continue our Army book research at Ft. McNair. This was a little trickier. We had to make our own way on this one. First a subway ride south to a waterfront exit, then a six block walk south to where the fort was located at the end of the "peninsula" we were walking on. We found Fort McNair. However, we were there but not in it "yet." An

Army guard at the entrance stopped us and wasn't impressed enough to let us through. Fortunately, I knew a civilian that worked there and asked the guard if he could call this person. A few minutes and our lady friend showed and took us to her office. Her office had a lot of Army documents. She knew we were working on an Army book but didn't think they had anything about ASA. But wait. She said we do have a thick book on Army citations issued in the past. That would do it. It was Jeri's and my one of our best "finds" ever. We found a number of citations awarded to ASA including our ASA headquarters in Japan. Can we make copies of ours, we asked since it was not classified? She replied, "I'll help you make copies of what you want." We were finished when I asked her if we could take her picture. She said we were not allowed to take pictures here but that she would walk us to the gate and we could take a picture outside the fence. This we did.

By now, Jeri was intrigued with all of our travel, her computers and so many other activities we had her involved in. She loved them all. What MS? She was definitely a "real trooper."

Before we checked out of DC and our hotel, we managed to question our coffee in the hotel's dining room. Why can't we just walk away? It must be our jinx to sometimes lose and sometimes win. This one was a tie.

After a week of dodging protesters, several trips to the archives, one comfortable tour of the Capitol by one nice congressional staff assistant and a subway trip to Ft. McNair, we thought we deserved a refreshing evening light meal in our hotel dining room. This was a nice clean, a bit expensive but good, way to relax. So Jeri and I ordered something to eat and both to have coffee. There were only two or three tables being used besides ours and they seemed to be having fun which was fine. Having finished a cup of coffee, we waited patiently for a fill up. The lone waiter seemed to be taking good care of the other tables. We were in no hurry but our coffee was cold and gone after about 20 minutes waiting and not being able to attract the lone waiter to bring us some more expensive coffee, we about gave up. But wait, I'll get his attention somehow. Finally, he came over to see what we wanted. Our bill, not yet. I decided to be polite to him and maybe joke a bit. I asked him if we qualified for extra coffee since we were not offered any more. He responded nicely by saying, of course you can have more and brought the coffee to us. Well we drank our second round and got up to leave. We did tip him with a normal tip. No problems. We thought no more of this. The next morning when we were checking out, the manager came over to us and said he heard we had a problem last night. This surprised us. I said there was no problem, just a little late on getting more coffee. The manager was really concerned that we may have been mistreated. He asked us if we were treated ok and would we come back again. We told him we would be glad to come back again. He was so relieved, you could feel it.

Our latest adventure over, we arrived safe and sound in Toledo the next morning at 4:55 am with Jeri ready for our next trip. No rest for the bad guys (Jack). Let me check. It was to be on VIA Rail back to Churchill for the third time.

Reunion 11 2003 September Ft. Mitchell, Kentucky – the second reunion Jeri and I missed – we went AWOL to our Churchill, Canada again.

Reunion 12 2004 September Car Ft. Mitchell, Kentucky

Jodi drove her three girls, Jeri and I on Friday afternoon; Jami, Craig, Dylan and Chloe came later that evening on September 17.

Our highlight: Being located in Tokyo, Japan, our alumni group was acquainted with the language. At five tables of men and women, exciting conversations were taking place when the noise dropped to zero. Music of Japan was suddenly heard out of nowhere. Our two granddaughters (Katie and Jenny) were singing a favorite Japanese song called "Moshi, Moshi, Anone." Since several Japanese members were part of our group (with one or two present), they were especially thrilled. The audience loved it, applauded the girls and made them sing it again.

At this reunion, our history book was approved for us to proceed to publish it

Reunion 13 2005 September Car Ft. Mitchell, Kentucky

Our highlights: Now, this was a reunion — 66 people there. Well Jeri and I did bring eight guests with us. At the reunion, our family besides Jeri and me consisted of Jami and her family (Craig, Dylan, Chloe) and Jodi and part of her family (Katie, Jenny, Kelly). While Jeri, Jami and I attended the business meeting, a raffle, an auction and the closing banquet, the rest of our "guests" went swimming.

Remember, listening to the many same "war" stories at each reunion with many memories getting a little older and each time the stories probably longer, humor our fine ASAers and listen. Wives and spouses, by now, knew the true stories and the not so true stories. I know Jeri enjoyed all of this. That's good enough for me.

Reunion 14 2006 Sept/Oct Car Ft. Mitchell, Kentucky

Jodi, with her three girls, drove Jeri and me to the reunion. At the time especially since Jeri was doing so good in traveling and everything, we never imagined that this would be her last ASA reunion.

ASAPAC HQ
Tokyo/Oji, Japan 1946 - 1952
Alumni Association
2006 Reunion

JERI
SCHROEDER

FOR JACK AND JERI REUNION 14 WAS OUR LAST ASA REUNION TOGETHER.

WELCOME TO CANADA – HOME OF CANADA VIA RAIL – THE SECOND HOME TO JACK AND JERI – HEADING FOR OUR THIRD HOME OF "ULTIMATE CHURCHILL."

DESTINATIONS

CANADA VIA RAIL

Introductory.....VIA RAIL CANADA had a nice surprise awaiting us on our fourth trip with them. We don't know when they started requiring a passenger in need of personal help to have an attendant with them and in return the assisting passenger would ride free.

On our 2001 trip to Churchill, in presenting a signed doctor's need for Jeri needing help, I was allowed to ride free. How nice. On using sleepers, we were able to get a double room for the price of one. Any food including in the ticket included the same for the assistant. A prior doctor's written approval was always needed beforehand. This allowed Jeri and me to travel more. We continued getting approved updated signed medical letters to give to Via Rail. Our trips were then affordable. This "free" trip continued on every Canadian trip we took from then on. Funny, I mentioned this to a lot of people in wheelchairs. I never found anyone interested.

Attendants were just like the ones on Amtrak in many respects. After taking care of passengers after boarding, they often would mingle with the passengers to get to know them. Actually, they were very good entertaining people especially children. For something to say, I would jokingly tell them that I was a "free loader." Usually they would frown nicely and say "Yea, we know." Other times, I might ask them a question like "Why do you give Jeri all of your attention and not me?" This one, they would just laugh. I would always do this in front of Jeri so she too could enjoy our trips more. She did and actually the attendants did always give her a lot of attention. Good for them.

Trains are truly the place to meet strangers becoming friends – so to meet strangers, go to a station that has ticket sellers that will gladly "set you up properly." Alain Bertrand is a story in itself. Alain worked in a Via Rail station office in Moncton, Canada on the phone helping callers set up their trip. One early call we made happened to get Alain on the phone. After a few minutes talking to this Alain person, we knew we had one we could count on. We introduced ourselves as Jeri and Jack and told him we wanted to make a reservation but that ours was a little different because Jeri was in a wheelchair. He responded like "great I'm in one also!" We were no longer strangers. We were friends. Every trip thereafter we were able to get most of our trips through Alain. Sometimes he would call just to see how Jeri was doing even when we were not after a reservation. When we did call to set up a reservation and he didn't answer the phone, he told us to tell the operator to tell Alain "call Jeri back." It worked every time. After several trips, we three wondered how we would be able to meet in person. We worked this out easily. Alain said when we take the next train to Halifax we would be stopping briefly in Moncton. He would know the time the train would come and be out on the platform to meet us. This would actually happen later.

The "Canadian" was the class of all Via Rail Trains – This was a cross country three nights trip that we used several times including partial connections to other trains. The name "Canadian" applied to the whole train which was made up of "Silver and Blue" class (a first class sleeper section) and a coach section less expensive but still well taken care of. We traveled on both sections with "Silver and Blue" being by far the best train we were on. Later, we will tell about a new train they put on in the east, the best train yet, in our time.

LET OUR DESTINATION TRAINS BEGIN:

1995 May - HALIFAX & VANCOUVER – TWO DESTINATIONS FOR THE PRICE OF ONE.

Riding VIA Rail for the very first time, all we knew about it was that it was a train, it was in a different country and it used different currency. The train was no problem. The country was our neighbor. The money, in color, was a different story. This was to be our inaugural train ride in Canada.

Why then did we choose to buy a 15 day Canrailpass that could be used anywhere on Via Rail trains? We didn't even know where to go. Jeri and I laid it out allowing about two days each for every stop we made to RR (rest and recuperate) and see the sights. Our trip looked like and was this: Windsor-Toronto-Montreal-**Halifax**-Montreal-Toronto-**Vancouver**-Toronto-Windsor! It was from May 8, 1995 to May 22, 1995, exactly 15 days. Our fee was $422.65 for the two of us.
Jeri had been in her wheelchair now for ten years, so I guess you could say she was ready. So what did she say – "Let's."

Now we would probably have scheduled Halifax and Vancouver eventually, but not at the same time. Halifax is in Nova Scotia on the Atlantic coast and Vancouver is on the Pacific coast. It was off to our first destination, Halifax.

In Halifax, we found a dock we walked out on and Jeri threw a nickel into the Atlantic Ocean. Now she will have to do the same thing in the Pacific Ocean. We then took a ferry across the bay to Dartmouth. Halfway across a Navy submarine passed right in front of us, on the water, not under it. We
stayed awhile and then returned to downtown.

The hotel we stayed at was halfway up the hill. I could push Jeri on that one. We decided to visit a Fort Citadel on another hill way at the top of our street we were on. We asked the hotel doorman about going up to see it. He said it was difficult to walk up to with a wheelchair. I don't advise your trying. With that answer, we knew we would try it. The next day as we left the hotel to walk up to the fort, the same doorman said, let me know when you get back. This part of the hill was much steeper. I had to double gear me to get Jeri up. Inside the fort, the whole large area was nothing but cobblestones. No way could I get Jeri over them. She waited while I walked over to see the fort quarters. Not much to see if you have seen forts before. Going back to our hotel, another person helped me back Jeri down to our hotel. The same doorman said we made the trip to the fort in record time.

We weren't done yet in Halifax. Catching the same taxi that brought us to the hotel, the driver picked us up to take us back to the train station. While waiting for our train to Montreal, we wandered around a bit, even went outside on the platform to see other trains that were there. I don't think we were supposed to leave the station. There were about 20 cars or so on our train waiting to begin taking the passengers aboard. We knew which car we would be on so we started walking down the platform to see if we could find it. There was not a single other person on the platform. We found our car and were tempted to go ahead and get on. As we walked near it deciding whether to get on or not, we heard and saw someone by the station, about 50 yards from us, waving and screaming at us not to get on our car. As they ran closer to us, they pointed to the top of our car. There was a telephone pole flat across it. By now our runner caught up to us and said that pole has electricity, they are trying to get the electric cut off. A bulldozer on the other side of our train accidentally knocked it over.

So that was why all the passengers except two were in the station waiting for a telephone pole to be removed. We rejoined them. Now we can leave Halifax. We will be back.

On the way to Montreal to change trains, we were fed well and again on the train to Toronto. Hey this Canrailpass was A-ok.

Arriving in Toronto, we knew by now and forever on, we would be the last to be off the train. We had no problem agreeing with this because passengers were quick to get in line and get off. We knew we had to wait for the standard lift to be put in the car doorway for us to get on or off. This time they forgot us. We were in the doorway to get off, people outside were waiting to get on. Finally someone found a lift and pushed it towards our door. It would not fit. The train was located where a lift could not get to it. The train would have to be moved. I told one person near us to stand in front of the wheelchair. Do not try to lift Jeri, just hold the chair slightly and be ready if I should slip. I would walk the wheelchair down the steps. That was simple enough.

We were to stay overnight in Toronto before catching the "Canadian" train the next day. Rather than taking a taxi to our hotel, we took our luggage and with the help of Jeri and her wheelchair we made our way through a lot of 5 o'clock people traffic. We checked in with the hotel and found out that there was a "Skywalk" from the train station to our hotel! We would gladly use that way the next morning. Later that evening we took a walk and found the Skywalk. As we walked towards the Skydome a girl wanted to know if we wanted her to take our picture which she did. She said she worked for the Toronto Blue Jays as a telephone ticket seller.

It was now time to find the "Canadian" and a three night stay aboard. The "Canadian" train's first class section is called "Silver & Blue Class." This is what we had on this trip. This was 1st Class all the way. The "Park" car is a two level car, the upper part being an observation car and the lower part a lounge area and is usually the last car on the train. We thought it was the best train in the US and Canada. Actually, as someone explained to us, it was originally a train purchased from the US and refurnished into a splendid travel train. I think it was the train that we first ran into that had a note in the restrooms that read, "Do Not Flush While in a Station."

Now it was time to sit back, watch for animals, mountains, make many new relationships and enjoy a life time experience. But wait. Don't sit back yet. We learned that everyone in First Class was invited to the Park Car for a welcome aboard reception. Our train aisle was quickly filling up with passengers heading to the last car. I told Jeri I would check to see if we could get there. It was packed. It was exciting. I returned to Jeri and said there would be no way to get you there in a wheelchair. We certainly didn't want to cause a disturbance so we stayed in our sleeper with our door opened to watch what was going on. Within a few minutes, an attendant lady poked herself into our room, held up and waved champagne at us. She said, "I have brought you some." She looked at us. I said,

"No, I don't think so, thanks." Jeri meanwhile, behind me had other plans. She waved her head yes. She got the champagne, I had a slight taste. How quick she reacted to the offer and with the biggest smile yet. What MS?

On our sleeper that day our attendant talked us into eating lunch in the dining car. Since Jeri rarely was able to eat in a dining car, we took him up on it. The attendant brought the train's Washington Chair (a small wheelchair) to take Jeri two cars away to eat there. She was excited. So was the attendant. The dining car was crowded. The chef met us and saw that Jeri was in their small wheelchair. He was caught off guard and told us we would have to wait until he found out where and how he would seat us. Now this train was a one level train so space was difficult. We could see he was having trouble seating us. He found a table for us and we had an enjoyable lunch. Finishing to leave he thanked us for coming and asked how far we were going. We told him all the way to Vancouver. I quickly told him from now on we will have our meals brought to our room. He was so relieved. He said that he thought that was a good idea, that we would get good service. He again thanked us. We were glad he served Jeri once. That's all we needed.

The highlight of this trip was going through the Canadian Rockies. There seemed no end to them. Passengers were up and waiting for the many mountains to take pictures of. We took a lot also. Why do they all look about the same in the pictures we took?

Arriving in Vancouver on May 16, we took a taxi to our hotel and checked in to be on the 9th floor of the Blue Horizon on Robson Street overlooking the harbor.

Our first and most important project we had to do was having Jeri drop a nickel into the Pacific Ocean. We headed down Butte Street (close to our hotel) which took us right to the waterfront. We were so close to the water that we could almost throw a baseball in it. We had to get closer. We began walking following the shoreline as close to the water we could get, but not close enough yet. We were searching for a small boat dock that we could walk on. It seemed most were private with a chain across their dock entrance. Finally we found a wooden dock that we could walk on out far enough to be over water. We were almost there. We found a spot that Jeri could throw her coin. She threw it. It landed not in the water but on a wooden ledge sticking out below us. We will have to repeat her throw. I climbed down through the outer undercarriage to our nickel. I was right over the water picking our nickel up. One slip and we both go in the water. No problem. I climbed back up to Jeri and gave her the nickel to try again. She did it! So within a week, Jeri finished her little extra curriculum activity of throwing a nickel in the Atlantic Ocean and one in the Pacific Ocean. Not bad for a handicapped person. Is there any meaning here? I can think of a lot of meanings. When we told this story at home, one of our children said. "Why didn't you just use another nickel for Mom to throw into the ocean?" Now she tells me!

Our hotel eventually suggested we take a tour on a bus. We told them that they would not let us on because Jeri was in a wheelchair. The desk clerk called the tour bus company and said they have a resident that would like to take your tour but she is in a wheelchair. The clerk got back to us and said that the bus would pick us up the next day, that they can take you. Just be right out front and they will stop for you. The next morning, we still did not feel comfortable and asked the same clerk if she would call the bus company again and confirm us getting on. She did and, excitingly, said it is ok, they will be here shortly. The bus pulled up on the street and stopped. The driver opened the door and said come aboard. I said, "She can't walk." The driver then said, "I can't take her then" and pulled away. We really weren't surprise but the hotel clerk was shocked. We should have told the bus company that Jeri was "confined" to a wheelchair, in which case, they would have refused us on the first call by the hotel. We did not learn this until later when train personnel explained it to us.

Our desk clerk was disturbed about this and called a travel agency to report this. She later had me talk to them on the phone. Their agent "Bud" invited us to come see him. I didn't think we could but I asked him where he was. He answered, "I am right across the street from you. I can see you from my office window. Come on up." Surprised, I said we will be right up. We crossed the street and met him in his office. He thought that was not very good of the bus company not taking us. He suggested we go downtown and take a bus over to Granville Island to sightsee. We kept this in mind but meanwhile, we decided to walk downtown. Passing the huge Eaton Department Store, a window sign read "come in for afternoon tea."  They let me have coffee. Jeri took tea, of course. We had a delightful time. Who needs a tour bus.

The next day we did go to Granville Island. It turned out to involve two city busses, a bridge and a heap of fast moving cars.

A Handicap Bus That Would Not Let Jeri and Jack on.......... We had no problem getting a handicap bus

downtown. It took us out to this Granville area where we expected to spend a nice afternoon. We walked all around the "island" (actually it was a peninsula), had lunch with Jeri eating her favorite shrimp but found nothing that interested us. It was time to leave. Our train leaving Vancouver was scheduled to leave at 8 pm that night.

We walked to the area where our incoming bus dropped us off. It was the only place we saw a bus sign. Luck was with us, momentarily. The first bus coming our way, I could see a big handicap sign on it. It stopped for us. Well actually it was to tell us he could not take us. We were at the wrong corner. He quickly pointed to somewhere in the distance and said we have to go there. He pulled away. Go where, I asked Jeri? Forget it, we are near the bridge that the bus brought us over on, let's walk back that way. We reached the bridge, a very large busy one loaded with cars. People walking? We didn't see any. I only saw a sidewalk on the other side of us. So, cross the street and continue your walk. Not so fast. We had to cross a fast moving lane that was merging with the main lanes on the bridge. Ok so we wait for a break in traffic. No traffic lights but this never really bothered us as long as we could cross to where we were going. There were no breaks. I told Jeri we would move up as far as we could to the edge of our sidewalk and with the first decent break, we go for it. However, the first car to reach us slammed their brakes on and the screeching halt began not only with the first car but also with several speeding cars behind it and more coming. My golly, we'll going to cause a pile up. We didn't want them to stop. I said we better dash across quickly. I tried to wave a "thank you" to them but holding on to a fast moving wheelchair was no place to try. To top it off, the bridge sidewalk was pretty high and it took a few extra seconds to get out of the way. We made it. We later found out pedestrians had the "right of way!"

Now we knew we had to hurry up a little. We finished walking across the bridge (I believe it was the Granville Street Bridge) and kept walking to our hotel about one and a half more miles. We gathered our belongings, thanked them and took our scheduled taxi to the train station. We made it also.

Our story of Vancouver still had a few more words to tell us. Once on the train, we settled nicely in our sleeper and once again began watching the scenery as we headed towards our next stop Jasper, then Edmonton and then home. At Edmonton's 30 minute stop, I got off the train to see if I could buy an Edmonton Oilers hockey shirt for our Jeff. I found one, bought it and got back on the train. I tried not to get off the train very often because I'm sure Jeri was always glad to see me back on where I belonged, not the next train in two or three days.

The train pulled out but within a few minutes, stopped. It had hit someone on the tracks. The train now had to wait until this accident was cleared by proper authorities to move on. It took an hour. It moved again but a few minutes later, a large rock had been thrown at the train and smashed a window in the Park car, a couple of cars from us. This time, the police came. One more hour and we were given the go sign, but only after the crew had covered the broken window to their satisfaction.

Our train continued with a change in Toronto back to Windsor where our (seemed like) permanent chauffeur daughter Jodi, awaited our return.

This 13 day Via Rail trip Jeri and I took alone had a lot of surprises – ups and downs – but we had a great time. How did we do it? Let's put it this way. If Jeri had not gone, I would not have gone. What a tremendous companion to have. The trip covered 8,387 miles. We continued our trips under the same reasoning. We never had a bad trip. To top it off, after we had returned from this trip, we sent a list of VIA Rail employees who helped make our trip a little more up than down among other remarks about a great trip. Who did we send the letter to? The President of Via Rail! Not expecting any answer, he answered with a letter that the first line said it all.

Dear Mr. and Mrs. John Schroeder:
Your letter reached me on July 6, 1995 and I wish all the correspondence I handle at VIA could be so uplifting.
/s/ TW Ivany, President

1998 April Jeri and Jack – Only 30 miles from Alaska but had to settle for Prince Rupert

That's right only thirty miles. We were sure we had the trip arranged to go by ferry boat from Prince Rupert. Jeri and I were both excited. We would see if we could put our hotel at Prince Rupert aside for us for a couple of days. Next we checked the ferry boat schedule. Passage was ready for us the next day or so. Just sign up. This would work. We asked when the ferry would bring us back, a day or two. During the summer, yes but this was April. You would be brought back in a week from Juneau, the capital of Alaska. Oh no, another "down" for us. Our schedule would not allow us that much time. So we stayed in Prince Rupert, an excellent substitute.

Located by the Pacific Ocean in the far northwest of Canada, this was quite a bit like our traveling to Churchill – as far as you can go by train both areas being different from our other trips. We loved both

 places but could only make it to Rupert once. By the way, I didn't plan for Jeri to throw a nickel in the Pacific Ocean in Rupert. She had already

thrown one in the Pacific Ocean and one in the Atlantic Ocean which cost me two nickels.

We did not look for Prince Rupert – like Churchill later, looking at a map was to see what might interest us. Prince Rupert showed– just like Churchill. Both places were meant for us. Both were adventures. Just to get to them was an adventure, let alone in a wheelchair. Mileage wise it was a trip of 6,398.75 miles. If you don't believe me, count it yourself, but who counts miles. On a train, miles, breakdowns, weather etc are not your concern – but it does get interesting.

Being a long trip way up to northwest Canada to spend a week at Prince Rupert would leave most riders going the opposite way to go south. I mentioned that our MS doctor said we were the only couple he knew that went north for a vacation. He probably was correct. However once you meet Jeri, anything counts as long as it was traveling by train. Our greatest trips were the long times through wilderness, few towns, even snow and certainly a lot of delays. So be it. We did it Jeri's way – nothing stood in our way.

Now this trip was a little like Churchill – long, tiring, not too much to see, no beaches to swim but there were always animals to watch, wild clean rivers to cross and the smell of freshness everywhere. Both Prince Rupert and Churchill surprised us. We both wondered if we would be so disappointed that we would only say hello and Goodbye. Not on your favorite horse would we do that.

We did choose to ride the Canadian train and the really nice Silver and Blue Class sleeping car on this trip since it was long enough to make the trip a little easier for Jeri. Now the sleeper included meals and other extras, even a private shower. While we had two beds, one being near the ceiling, I didn't use the upper. I preferred staying with Jeri in the lower bed. Close quarters but more comfortable and no bumping my head on the ceiling. I also was able to turn Jeri during the night even though half of me was in the aisle. Putting suit cases etc under me solved that problem.

Starting in Toronto, let's skip BG to Toledo to Windsor to Winnipeg to Edmonton and get to the start of our real adventure with this trip, Jasper, Canada.

We had left Toronto Thursday April 16, 1998 and arrived in Jasper on April 18 and stayed at the Amethyst Lodge for one night. We liked the lodge, nothing fancy but close to downtown area and our train station. Leaving to go north the next day, we said we would be back in a week, mark us for a two nights stay.

In Jasper we changed trains and boarded the Skeena train to take us to Prince George. This train only ran three times a week and since it was April, it only had two passenger coach cars. In the summer, the train adds the Park Car with its scenic upstairs dome. This was fine with us. We enjoyed, for a change, only a few passengers whom we were able to meet easier and sort of had the train to ourselves and the crew. Add snow we ran into and you have everything you need for an adventure train trip.

When we arrived at Prince George, the train, the crew and our few passengers spent the night there. The train was locked up and the crew and passengers got off to spend the night in a hotel of their choosing. We passengers paid for a night at the Ramada Hotel right across the street from our parked train. Now that was what you call service. I don't know who paid for the train and crew.

It seemed very strange why we stopped there for an overnight stay. Prince George was a large city but we never visited it. We must have parked outside the city because it seemed isolated to what we could see and do. I think the crew stayed at the same hotel and they did tell us about a nice restaurant nearby for breakfast in the morning. Now that solved everything. I took Jeri to our room and, still feeling funny about why we would park a whole train for an overnight stay. I decided to look around. The hotel was a beautiful clean seemingly very new, but where were the people? There was no one there. Now I am surprised, maybe confused. I walked around more and still could not find anyone. It was so quiet I wondered if we were in the right hotel. I decided to go downstairs to the basement. Holy mackerel, it was a full-fledged casino and going wild! I'm out of here. It's back to Jeri for me!

We had breakfast at the suggested restaurant and made our way across the street to our almost private train which was waiting for Princess Jeri and her attendant Prince John, sometimes called Jack.

On our train heading for Prince Rupert, we were told to pull over onto a siding to let a freight train supposedly on its way to pass us but hadn't reached us yet. We were a big bit up north and on one track. We came to the siding we would have to switch over on. The switches were hand operated. Watching out our back window, we could watch to see how it was done. It looked like our attendant was the one to move a switch to get us over onto the siding. Having to do it manually, it took a few poundings on the handle to turn the switch. It looked like he was using a sledge hammer. So we pulled onto the siding to wait for the freight train to pass. But before the freight train could pass us, the switch had to be turned again, back to the way it was. After the train passed us, the crew member now had to move the switch back to where we could get from the siding to the main track. Our crew member wasn't done yet. After we moved out onto the main track, he had to reverse the switch back to its original position to let the next train go straight through on the main track. Now you know the whole story. Do not try it with the way I just wrote it. I may have missed one switch change.

Now one reading this may not find it amusing or interesting, but trains in the far north are what one should want and expect. It's a different adventure. This is why Jeri, especially, loved these trips. How else would she be able to do such adventures?

Let me cite a few other instances which to us were almost unbelievable in this day of living. I think these happened on our trip to Prince Rupert but no matter, they would pop up anywhere on northern trains. In every case, we were present to watch.

Riding along enjoying the scenery and eating, of course, the train we were on stopped in the middle of nowhere. Why? Then we watched an attendant from our train window walking fast, carrying something, into the far woods. Then we saw a house among the trees. He was delivering a package to them! Back to the train and the train moved on.

This next one we liked a lot. Cruising along in a train where everyone seems equal and enjoying free surprises keeps you wondering what is next? Again Jeri rarely slept on the train especially during the day and on such adventure trains that we were taking.

Our train was slowing down, again in the middle of nothing, mostly trees and a few animals. This time we saw a person walking along the train tracks. He looked like he was just out taking a walk. The train stopped, he got on. Jeri was watching. I told her I was going to walk up to the car he got on just to see who this was. He was sitting there with a couple of the crew having coffee. I wasn't sure he was the one that came aboard. I asked an attendant if they had picked someone up. The new passenger spoke up himself and said, "I'm the one they picked up." I asked him how was he able to stop the train? Did you get in front of it? He said, "Oh, no, you don't want to do that. If you want them to stop, just hold both hands up with your fingers pointing to yourself. This meant stop for me." Later, talking to an attendant, I asked what if he had no money to pay. The attendant kind of shook his shoulders like "Oh well."

Arriving in Prince Rupert at 8 pm on a dark Monday and unable to see much, we still felt we came to the right place. Checking in at our Crest Motor Hotel after a walk from our train station and up a fairly good size hill, we loved the place right away. This was going to be a nice week in Rupert. The walking and hill to the hotel was going to become an everyday trek. Add a side door entrance for us to get in the hotel easier because of Jeri and her wheelchair, we felt at home. Our view from this island hotel overlooked the Pacific Ocean and the cruise and other ships that kept coming and going. We spent a lot of time just watching the ships and activity going on. Were we in on it? Well, not really but we sure felt part of it. To see Jeri enjoying this from our front seat high up view was joy in itself. Wow, we don't do these things staying home.

Every day we found our way down this hill and became familiar with anything or anyone that looked interesting. I even took Jeri's picture taken with a Royal Canadian Mounted Policeman who got out of his police car (not off a horse) to meet and pose with Jeri. One of the first stores we entered was a toy store. We visited that one about every day. The owner was so nice we desperately looked for a game or toy to buy. No success. Eventually we learned he was the mayor of Prince Rupert.

Our days were rarely planned ahead of time. Each day was a new day. One morning dressing Jeri in slacks, a white jacket with brown shoes, putting her sunglasses on her and sitting her in her "beloved" green wheelchair, we were ready to tackle the waterfront. Cow Bay was our unplanned objective. It was an inlet connected to the ocean and had a board walk for walking. Our brochure told us it was a historical area. That's all it read. Well the wooden walkway with an ancient wooden fence did seem a little historical. Now the next step surprised me. Jeri decided to throw a quarter into Cow Bay. Now we're getting somewhere, even updating my contribution from nickels to quarters. Way to go Jeri - she never ran out of ideas. Her "Let's" do it was so descriptive of herself, it never failed.

Besides roaming around the downtown area and even finding a fairly large mall, we met, what turned out to be a lovely, Japanese family visiting Prince Rupert. This brought a few memories back to me. They quickly liked Jeri and Jeri really enjoyed meeting this family because she had heard a lot about Japan from me. We met them again on our train to Toronto. Their oldest daughter was with them on leave from, I think, the United States Naval Academy, and was to become an officer.

Saturday was to be our last day in Prince Rupert. Our family practices often were that on the last day of a vacation, we would have a pleasant family dinner wherever you are. We decided to have our last day dinner at our hotel which has been so good with us. But first, we would attend Mass at the Catholic Church up on a hill. Now this meant dressing nice for a night out. We made dinner arrangements for two with our hotel chef for that evening. We were all set.

It started to rain early in the afternoon. It did not look good. I dressed Jeri and myself very nicely for "our evening out." The pour down continued but let up before evening. We went to Mass but the rain started again worse than before. Leaving church, what to do? Wait or run for it. I decided we would run for it. I knew Jeri wouldn't care — rain doesn't stop her. Just then another couple saw us and said they would take us back to our hotel in their car. This was hard to explain to them but we said, we appreciated their concern, but we are use to this and it would be difficult to get Jeri and her wheelchair into a car, that we would be soaked by then and would make your car very wet. Since we are not that far from our hotel, we can probably get there faster than trying to get into a car. We talked them into agreeing and began trotting downhill from the church and uphill to our hotel. We made it but it did take about 30 minutes in the dark and the rain never stopped. Soaked and exhausted, we decided we would not enjoy a formal dinner now and we cancelled it. We enjoyed just staying in our hotel that night. Our day was not spoiled at all. It was just another adventure, part of traveling. The next day, we left Prince Rupert and headed for, guess who, Prince George! (Note: there is little additional story about our visit to Prince Rupert under **"A LITTLE TOUCH OF RELIGION" – then under "This was one of Jeri's and my favorites…"**

We left Rupert Sunday April 26 at 8 am and soon ran into a snow storm blowing and beginning to cover the area. Ah. Now we have entered our first snow of our trip. This is what we came for – to ride through the snow watching the tracks ahead becoming covered with snow and only their steel rails showing and our train slowly and quietly making its way forward. No real problem to be concerned with because there are trains with snow plows attached to the front of the engine to keep the tracks plowed free. We needed no rescue this time. We were on our own. It doesn't get any better. It was exciting and beautiful. I am so glad Jeri was there to share this with me. Of course, if she were not there, I would not be there either.

We arrived at Prince George at 8:10 pm. Of course we had to stay overnight again. I showed Jeri the casino this time – don't remember if we played any "games" or not. Our train parked at the same place again. It seemed like we brought the train along with us instead of the other way around.

So it was Goodbye again George and hello again Jasper. We never said our usual "we'll be back." Strange, we did not come back, yet it was one of our favorite trips.

Arriving in Jasper April 27, Jeri and I made our way to talk with the Station Manager. We were scheduled to catch the Canadian "Silver & Blue Class" sleeper on April 29. We introduced ourselves to a very friendly lady Station Manager who knew we had just arrived by the train from Prince Rupert. She also was aware that Jeri was in a wheelchair and to which sleeper we were assigned to. Knowing that a Room F was larger than other rooms and at no higher charge, we asked her if there could be any way to be moved to a sleeper that was a "Room F" with a few more feet of width which would help us with the wheelchair. She said, "Here's what I want you to do. Check back with me Wednesday an hour or so before the train comes. I'll see what I can do by then." This sounded good enough to us. We shall wait and see. We thought if there were a vacant Room F on the train, we would get our change request. Meanwhile, here we were in Jasper to stay two nights this time, a week later, no less.

We checked in one more time at the Amethyst Lodge which was downtown right on the main street right by the sidewalk, an easy way in and out of the hotel for us. The very next morning as Jeri and I were eating by the window of our restaurant a herd of Elk went right by our window. Later we found the herd having a picnic in the city park. I counted six Elk.

Of course, Jeri roamed the stores in downtown Jasper. She found a Royal Canadian Mounted Police store with a lot of merchandise reference the RCMP. It was a bit expensive. As Jeri admired the RCMP pins, a girl employee came over and presented Jeri with a RCMP pin, no charge. Once more Jeri is excited either  with compliments or seemingly very nice gifts she receives so often traveling.

We had one more surprise that day as we went back to our hotel's very nice dining room and, dressed as we were, sat down at a table to celebrate. It was April 28. It was Jeri's 57th birthday.

Wednesday, April 29, 1998 — it was time to leave Jasper and head east on the Canadian. We walked to the station ahead of time to find out if we were able to get the larger sleeper. The girl who had waited on us was there and told us to wait outside for the train. When it came, two attendants in uniform approached us and asked if we were Jack and Jeri. They then explained that our sleeper was on the train that just pulled in and that it was getting cleaned for us and should be ready shortly. One attendant introduced himself and said he would come back to take us aboard. When the room was ready, the attendant came and helped take our luggage to our sleeper. It was a "Room F" sleeper. We were excited. Now the long trip to Toronto will be more comfortable. But wait. As the attendant took us aboard, we stared at our room. They had opened the partition between two sleepers and we were given both sleepers. Wow! The attendant explained that both rooms became available with no one scheduled to use either one – they were ours for the whole trip back to Toronto. One more surprise came as the train pulled out and on its way. Champagne was being served  in the Park Car as a welcome reception. They brought two glasses half filled to us in our room. This was stunning. To have some proof, I had the crew take pictures of us drinking the champagne.

Starting in Jasper, let's skip Edmonton to Winnipeg and arrive safely in Toronto since we are on our way home. Since we were enjoying our two room sleeper, no use stopping at Edmonton and if we went through Winnipeg, it could be another Jeri holding up the train. Arriving in Toronto at 9:35 pm, we left the train and headed for our hotel Crowne Plaza. This time we stayed away from going by sidewalk and found the "tunnel" connecting us to the hotel. In the morning we were back on the train for Windsor arriving at l6:19. Our exciting 17 day trip was over. But we were not done yet. Several more train trips were planned. Will they be better? We shall see.

A SECOND TRIP TO HALIFAX WAS A TWO-REASON CALL FOR JULY 2002, A 13 DAY TRIP.

One call was to see: The live stage production called The Nova Scotia International Tattoo.

The second call was that on our way home, we had to stop in Toronto to pick up our family of seven to take them home with us.

Before getting to this second trip to Halifax, I want to show some supporting activities we did to get to this second trip:

To begin three (2002, 2004, 2006) of our trips to Canada, we would have Jodi drive us to Windsor the night before the train was scheduled to leave at six in the morning. Jodi would always have her three young girls (one at a time) with her and we would always stay at Day's Inn the night before to make sure we were at the train station with our luggage on time. We would repeat our own nightly ritual in this manner. Jeri would stay with one child in the hotel room looking out to watch one or two of the children with me crossing the street to the Pizza store and bring back the Pizza. As each child grew, they took turns going with me for Pizza while Jeri plus one watched us from the hotel. In the morning, Day's Inn would have donuts etc. Being very early in the morning, Jodi arranged with the clerk that she and the children would be taking Jeri and me to the train station but they would return to their "room" to finish their sleeping and then getting up for donuts etc. The clerk said that was fine with her.

To get to Windsor when we did not have to stay overnight, we usually took the tunnel under the river from Detroit in which I, of course, had to pay the toll. On one trip when Jeri and I boarded the train and Jodi helped us get seated ok, the attendant was a bit concerned about Jeri in a wheelchair and that Jeri and I were traveling alone. Jodi spoke up and said, don't worry about my parents, they can handle themselves they won't be a bother to you. The train was ready to move out as Jodi quickly got off. I suddenly remembered that we were in Canada, that Jodi didn't have any money with her especially Canadian. How would she get back through the tunnel or bridge? I yelled at her as the train began to move and went to a train doorway where she saw me throw money out at her.

Now train riding can be like riding a horse. I never knew for sure what type train we were on. If it was without a handicapped car, we would be seated in a first class coach and receive all the trimmings that came with it - free meals. One trip out of Windsor, we were the only ones on the first class coach. Our personal attendant took such good care of us with too much food we had to tell him we were ok.

Sometimes this train from Windsor was scheduled to go all the way to Montreal. We were allowed to stay where we were in first class EXCEPT in Toronto once, they were overloaded and said we would have to move up to the regular coach seat. OK so we moved up, our attendant did help us. Later another attendant told us that they never should have made us move like that. They could have offered any one giving up their seats would be allowed to move up to the observation seating for the rest of their trip. He said people liked that idea.

Now to talk about this current trip, this was to be our second trip to Halifax. We wondered if the train preference points she was getting each trip was enough to help pay for our trip. We found out she had enough points, now a big question. Since I was receiving a free ride with her MS, it seemed unlikely that we could use both free rides on the same trip. I called the Via Rail Preference Office and asked if we would be able to use both on one trip. The answer was, "I don't see why not." We used both approvals on this train. The trip cost me $12.00 for food. See, we do have a lot of "ups" to go with our "downs."

Another interesting thing happened just before this trip. I had told you how our well **our friend, Alain, would set up our Via Rail trips for us and how we came to like him** without meeting him, at least not yet. He being in a wheelchair himself made our trips feel more comfortable. Anyway, Alain had set our next Halifax trip up knowing exactly where we would be and when. On a trip ahead of us, Alain took his only son on their train trip and went to Halifax. He must have mentioned Jeri often because in Halifax up on the hill where we were to stay, Alain told his son, "Do you see that hotel there? That's where Jeri and Jack are going to stay." He told us this little story before we left. To Jeri and me, it was precious. We have to meet Alain.

It's now time to get going on our free train ride but wait we found we had a surprise third reason for taking this trip. Alain was going to try to meet us in person on the trip he had just set up. He tried this once before but we were unable to make a timely connection. We shall try again. Since Alain was assigned to Moncton Station which was about 300 km (186 miles) away from Halifax, he said he was scheduled to work the day that the train would stop for 20 minutes at the Moncton station, that he would be able to meet Jeri then. It was becoming interesting and exciting. 20 minutes? We can do it. We alerted our attendant to this possible meeting. All the attendants knew Alain and soon found out about this "secret" meeting. Soon all the passengers in our car learned about it. I would have never guessed at the excitement that was suddenly taking place. The attendants explained how they would work this, given only a 20 minute stop. There would not be enough time to get Jeri off the train so they would open a regular door near us (all doors are not opened at all stops) and move Jeri right to the door entrance so she could meet Alain. So now everyone knew the train's stopping schedule at Moncton including a first time meeting between a Via Rail regular and a Via Rail employee. The train arrived as the passengers all looked outside to watch for Alain. We then learned Alain did not work that day. A couple of minutes passed and pumping as fast as he could in his wheelchair, Alain came roaring in straight to the open door where

 Jeri and everyone else were watching. A relieved crowd became a cheering one. It was simply exciting to watch all of this. I jumped off the

train to take a picture and meet Alain. Jeri and Alain needed no introduction, they were both excited. So Alain did the talking and Jeri did the listening, smiling and nodding her head. They both looked very nice. I had dressed Jeri earlier in a red dress. Alain coming all the way from his home himself and moving his wheelchair was a bit worn out. Then the train announced "all aboard" by way of all the step stools being put back in the train. The train started to move and so did Alain, once again pumping as fast as he could to keep up with the train and watching Jeri for a few more minutes in her doorway. The attendants, all knowing Alain, started cheering him to "pump faster." So he did for several minutes until the train outran him. What a delightful twenty minutes. As promised, we finally met Alain. We were not a least bit disappointed. I don't think our passengers were either and I'm sure Alain wasn't. (NOTE: Later, perhaps several years, Alain had an odd accident in his home. He had pushed himself under the counter which was built for him, to do something. Somehow the counter came down on his knees and broke them. He was no longer able to work and we never saw him again.)

July 2, 2002 at four in the afternoon was kind of a welcome home as we began to remember Halifax and our earlier pleasantries. A very old city which kept its age mixed with modern times. Its downtown where we had shopped before never seemed to change. It was waiting for our return in which we did do a lot of Christmas shopping to take back to BG with us.

A taxi took us to our Cambridge Suites Hotel on top of "our steep" hill we recognized – 9 blocks up and away from Halifax Harbor. Right above our hotel, another steep walk up another hill called Citadel Hill we had climbed in1995. The 19th century British Fort was still there. We saw no need to reclaim it. Let someone else climb that hill.

Our prime reason for coming this year to Halifax was to see the Nova Scotia International Tattoo show, a combination of military and civilian performers from around the world. Seating nearly 10,000 in the Halifax Metro Centre which also served as an ice arena, it was a perfect place to be. We had no idea what to expect. Who reads programs? About half through the first half, an unforgettable program began centered around our USA 9/11 catastrophe by having two different performers singing America the Beautiful and another song. It seemed most of the bands present took part with music ever so loud. When this part of the tribute was over, a huge American flag was carried by many people as was a huge Canadian flag as they entered the stadium together before a loud clapping standing ovation. There was more. I don't know how they did this but the two different flags were then matched when one on top opened and the other one underneath opened. The holders then quickly opened both flags together side by side wide opened and flat. I think the noise doubled.

This was concluded with the MC telling everyone whoever wore the uniform of their country to stand up. Next to Jeri and me were a Canadian man and wife – he was a POW in World War II and she was in the Canadian army women corps. Of course, I stood up. Very emotional - It doesn't get any better than this. I was so glad Jeri was able to experience this. We saw this show three times that week.

Not sure how this next situation came about but we found in our travel "archives" two pins. One pin was with a RCMP on it marked Canada. The other showed a dog on a RCMP pin with a "Police Service Dog" engraved under it. In this same package was a large picture of a dog encircled by "RCMP POLICE DOG SERVICE and underneath the picture it read "GRC SERVICE DES CHIENS POLICIERS." This small collection showed my writing to be "From Tattoo 2002."

Finding our way to the Metro Center before the show, we had stopped at a couple of offices of the Tattoo show just for something to do. We met a girl who was in charge of mailing their magazine Tattoo Times. Introducing Jeri, I told the girl that Jeri had MS. All of a sudden Jeri and the girl became instant friends. The girl's mother had MS also. We met this girl again when we returned other years to see this show.

During the time they were in Halifax, the Tattoo performers were often seen around town and would meet the people. Some would always stop and talk to Jeri which allowed us to take some pictures.

Jeri seemed to be part of the activities the way she was treated. We would often eat hot dogs or whatever in the park area near us where the activity was going on.

We also ate at our hotel at a discount and where we were getting to know those who worked there. One day we walked into the dining room bar and asked for two Tom Collins. The girl would not let us pay. Did she give us the two? Yes.

Another stop out from our near the top of the world was seeing if we could find "The Halifax Highland Games & Scottish Festival" somewhere on the same level of the hill we were on. There would be no walking down. There would be no walking up. There would be a one mile going and one mile back to and from the games and festival. This sounded good to us. We began our walk. We arrived pretty well. Jeri was tired of riding and I was tired of walking on a hot afternoon. A ten dollar admission charge seemed worthwhile. We roamed around for several hours watching the games, people dancing (this kind of hurt since Jeri could no longer do it) and all wearing Scottish clothing. We enjoyed it but were not meeting anyone. Well so we were wearing the wrong clothes. We noticed there were about twenty tents set up with crowds in each one. We walked by them. Each was marked with a Clan name. I was not aware if Jeri or I belonged to any clan. We both decided it was time to get on our way. Where we entered, we left. I think they refunded our admission. They knew we were not enjoying ourselves too well. Actually we were glad we went and did enjoy it even though we couldn't really take part. We thanked them and began our mile return to our hotel.

We were far from done on this trip. We were just getting started. I once told Jeri that sooner or later, one of us was going to have to quit these trips we are on. However, "I'll be darn if I'm going to let some helpless cripple beat me!" Jeri looked at me and smiled. I knew what that meant. It read, "Don't look at me." It turned out we both won — we both kept going. Neither one quit. We were just too busy.

So it was on with our schedule. This next stop was to visit St. Mary's Basilica high on a hill, of course. We visited the church and Jeri lit a candle with me holding her shaking hand. I always allowed her to light a candle but kept three eyes on her — ok to light a candle but not the church. This was the first time we were in this church but a church is safe isn't it? Well we came in the church, walked down the aisle on the right and walked back on the aisle on our left — our tour. Half way down the left aisle in a darkened church but still looking around at this very old church, I held the wheelchair with both hands pushing Jeri and did not see a step down as I caught Jeri ready to go down with the step. WOW, what gives here? Apparently when they built this church on a very uneven steep hill, they found out one side was a foot lower than the other. A little carpentry by building a step would help somewhat in solving a problem. They certainly would not tear up half the church to level it out. How did we solve it. This first time made me a bit more alert in this church — I always remembered which aisle to use — the right one.

We happened to meet the Priest in charge, Very Rev John Williams, who took to Jeri quickly. Before we left Halifax, he had become good friends.

In between going and coming from seeing Tattoo two more times, a couple of minor interruptions happened. First our suction machine went dead and second Jeri's feeding tube came out. As for the suction machine, we would plug it into our room socket and run it the best we could until the power gave out. The feeding tube was out all the way. I was able to push it back in slightly and then taped it in using a lot of tape. It held until we got home. So was I able to feed Jeri until we got home? I think so! Meanwhile back at our hilltop palace, we were having a fun time at our hotel and eating very good food with a 20% discount.

Shopping was a beautiful pitfall. Between the "main" street stores and the ones in the newer section, it was good we had a credit card along. Of course we had to go down the hills to get to the stores. Of several stores we got to know, one was the "Plaid Place." Having already been to Tattoo and the

"Scottish Festival" the Plaid Place interested us the most. It was a very expensive store, dealing only in Scottish clothing and what went with it. We actually became good friends with the lady owner and started buying from her. She gave us a 15% discount every time we purchased something (including three sets of matching  Scottish blouses and skirts for Jami's daughter Chloe and Jodi's Katie, Jenny and Kelly) and every time we returned. She was a lasting friend. Sometimes in our return to see her, we would walk into her store quietly. It was always busy. We would shop around ignoring her and even ask her a clothing question. She would look up and almost faint when she realized it was us back again. Meanwhile, Jeri was at her best shopping, buying and looking. I was usually good for one hour. Jeri loved doing it forever.

Another store up on our hill we liked and got to know the owner slightly, at least enough to buy something from him because he seemed to appreciate Jeri and me stopping in. He handled only copper and told us how difficult it was to find any to use in his jewelry. He said the only place he could find any copper was India and he had to go after it himself. Jeri? She loved all this meeting people and of course shopping. She did buy a copper bracelet.

Some of the items we carried with us to Halifax for Jeri included:

Slacks, shorts, tops, swimsuit, sweater, skirts, coat, hairbrush, Ensure, prune juice, other juice, snack packs, Tylenol, baby food.

Also: Canadian money, one wheelchair, one smile all for Jeri.

Leaving Halifax Wednesday, July 10, 2002 we had one more order to carry out, stopping at Toronto to pick up some of our family. We arrived in Toronto July 11 staying two nights at the Hotel Delta Chelsea. Funny, in our taxi with Jeri, when we arrived at our hotel, I asked the driver what was our fare? He answered, "Whatever we thought was fair." I gave him $10.00. When you traveled with Jeri, strange things happened.

While we had taken a taxi from Union Station to Chelsea, Jodi had the rest of our group follow her with their luggage rather than pay for a taxi. I suspect it was a mile walk but they made it.

The Chelsea was noted for having activities for children like swimming, large areas to paste, draw, games etc, with attendants helping, a really nice safe place to stay, including a large outside (or inside) garden to eat. We stayed there several times especially when we had the kids. Jeri and I especially did like the garden area with a lot of tables in which you could order food of your choice inside and take it out to your tables and spend an evening there.

The next day we gathered up our family of seven (three adults and four children) and arrived in Windsor Saturday, July 13, 2002.

Ending train trips should not be allowed. OK, so our seven person group was tired arriving back from Jeri's and mine second Halifax trip. If the kids are too tired, Jeri and I will return to Halifax ourselves. In fact our plans will be arranged for our third trip back in July of 2003.

OUR ONE YEAR WAIT TO RETURN TO HALIFAX JULY 2003 HAD A BIG SURPRISE FOR US – WE WOULD NOT BE GOING.

Were we kidding? I would guess it was shortly after Christmas that we began working on this next trip back to Halifax to primarily see the Tattoo show and revisit our new found several friends. The trip was booked with paid train tickets, hotel reservations at Day's Inn, Windsor, at Halifax, Westin Nova Scotian and Toronto Strathcona Hotel. That wasn't all. We had received our Tattoo tickets for Thursday July 3 @ 7:30 & Sunday July 6, 2003 @ 2 pm. There was one other surprise. Our train 70 in Windsor was to become train 60 in Toronto which meant we would not have to change trains until Montreal. How's that for planning ahead of time? Now Jeri and I could sit back and think about this trip. We had these trips so figured that we could relax and enjoy the upcoming trip and begin packing about two weeks before leaving. It worked every time. Well almost.

Then it happened. A SARS outbreak (whatever that was) hit Toronto early and quickly. Oh Oh. This surely can't affect us. We kept an eye on SARS watching on TV as it continued to spread. VIA Rail kept us personally updated by phone. We thought SARS was cleared in Toronto until our last weekend in which we had to decide to go or not. With Jeri's MS, it made no sense to take the trip. We called VIA Rail and all our hotels and cancelled the trip. There was no problem with the hotels (no charges), VIA Rail gave us a full refund but four tickets to TATTOO could not refund any tickets, which is normal with theatres.

We decided to send our Tattoo tickets to Fr. John Williams at St. Mary's Basilica, Halifax. We wrote a letter to Fr Williams and enclosed the tickets suggesting he use them. We had intended to visit the Basilica but perhaps this was our visit anyway. We said we hoped to see him the following year.

OK, so what's our next trip we have to schedule yet?

OUR JULY 2004 TRIP TO HALIFAX BECAME OUR THIRD.

This trip seemed to be made just for Jeri while my part was to get Jeri to Halifax in a nice and easy way. To make it nice and easy for her highness, I not only purchased a regular seat ticket for us, I also bought a special ticket for us which cost $25.00 more which was called a Comfort Plus which allowed us to ride a special coach car that included different amenities such as food, coffee at any time in a newer coach for privacy. This was good for the train from Montreal to Halifax.

We were now ready for a nice trip to Halifax. Let's head for the train station by way of pro Jodi and her crew driving us to Windsor and later meeting us in Toronto by also riding the train from Windsor to Toronto. Note: This is kind of a difficult trip to write in order but also trying to keep up with where our children and grandchildren were — sort of a "who's running this outfit." Sometimes our clan met Jeri and me in Windsor and more often, they liked to scare us by popping up in Toronto.

Meanwhile back at the train station we learned that Via Rail had cancelled their Comfort Plus cars. Oh well, we still have our regular tickets. We never received our $25 back but that was no real concern. We were on our way finally.

From Windsor to Toronto took four hours, then a hour or so wait in Toronto and finally arriving at Montreal at about five in the evening. It seemed that Montreal had no elevators to move passengers up a floor to wait for their next train. How did we get Jeri upstairs? A Red Cap made it look easy. He took Jeri in a rush to the escalator put her and her wheelchair on the escalator holding the wheelchair by its arms and followed the escalator upstairs. I never tried that. Maybe going down to our next train in a couple of hours I could try it. I don't think Jeri liked my idea, another call for a Red Cap.

With tickets for our coach car in hand, we found our car and got on ourselves. The platform was even with the train so we needed no help. Good grief, did I put us on the wrong train? It was all white and blue inside. It was a beautiful new train. It was shocking. With our attendant's help, we moved Jeri to our new double white seat which was about a foot above the aisle. This was a sudden disappointment. I could not lift her into this high seat which I was so use to and never had to ask attendants to help me. This time the attendant and I lifted Jeri up into the seat. She could see out much better. What a train! We were not done yet. I had to step up also to get into our seat. The train started moving and was very quiet and being a bit higher off the rails, the noise was hardly noticeable.

As we settled in nicely in our coach seat for an overnight ride to Halifax, a girl attendant came along and said, "I think you are in the wrong seats. You are supposed to be in a sleeper." I answered, "No, I don't think so." She asked, "Didn't you buy a Comfort Plus ticket?" This I remembered and said, "Yes, but that was cancelled because they don't do that anymore." Her answer was, "That's right but because they cancelled that ticket, they upgraded your regular tickets to a sleeper." "They did?" Well Jeri was listening to all of this – I was glad she was not asleep yet. We both had an awakening even before we slept. The attendant said, "Come on, I'll help take Jeri and you and your luggage up to your sleeper." We carried everything and the girl pushed Jeri through several coach cars to our car. Each car connection was made so well that you could walk between cars without knowing you were doing so. Our car was "out of this world." It was next to its own outside door and it was divided into two rooms well furnished with bathroom, tables, beds etc and was called an "Accessible Suite" for handicapped persons. The entire floor was a soft rubbery floor obviously to protect someone who might fall. The train itself was called the "Renaissance."

What an unbelievable surprise for Jeri and me. Did I call her "her highness" earlier in this story?

STAYING AT THE TRAIN STATION HOTEL WE GOT OFF AT IN HALIFAX was a new interesting experience.

On an earlier trip to Halifax, we had learned that the train station was connected to and part of the Westin Nova Scotia hotel. We thought this was a great convenience idea and on this trip we decided to stay at this connecting hotel. It saved moving our luggage and not needing a taxi both ways to another hotel. It was also convenient to the boardwalk.

Of course, something would happen early. Arriving at four in the afternoon, we took our time checking into the hotel as we carried what we had to our room and set up a little housekeeping before I went after the rest of our luggage. No need to hurry. Our luggage was safe in the station. After a bit of getting settled in, I still was not in a hurry to claim our luggage from our connecting station but we soon needed our clothing etc. I went down stairs to the lobby and by way of a large ramp I came to the door to the station. It was locked. Checking with the hotel, I was told the station was closed for the night and that they had no way of getting in. You will have to wait until morning. I could not find anyone connected with the train that might let me get to our luggage. Oh well. We'll just have to wait. This was no surprise to Jeri. She didn't even bother to give me a surprise look when I told her. In the morning we reclaimed our luggage. Now I could shave and change Jeri with a clean brief.

The first evening there exploring the boardwalk was an easy wheelchair ride about two blocks away from our hotel and about a mile long. There was no activity going on at this end of the boardwalk. As we walked towards the other end there was little going on there also. It was obvious that our end of the boardwalk had made its way to this other end where business was. Isn't anything going on this night? It was night time and business was well closed. We were starved but found nothing worthwhile. An ice cream cone was not exactly what we had in mind. We walked back towards our hotel. Just as we were about to go in, we noticed a restaurant across the street with a couple of lights on yet. "Let's" was our hungry cry. We entered but found little activity, only two other tables were being used. It was about eight at night when the owner said they were still open. It was just what we wanted – a spaghetti restaurant.

Being waited on, I asked the owner if we "could split one dinner." "Of course" he answered. With it I ordered coffee. Jeri ordered wine. I should have joined Jeri at least this once to socialize with her. I think I took a sip or two. There was so much spaghetti brought to us, I could have ordered it as a single half and split that in half! It  was delicious. By now there was only one other table being used and this by a man and lady. We were not watching but the lady came over to us and "asked Jeri if we would care to join them?" "Jeri smiled with a yes." We carried our food over to their table and introduced ourselves and thanking them. "They said they were from North Carolina and were traveling north." "We said we were from Ohio." We never got around to telling them Jeri had MS. I don't think they cared. They were having a bored dinner and Jeri looked nice enough to get together with them. Pretty soon the owner came over, talked a little and sat down with us. It was perfect. "He was funny and we all were having a great dinner that lasted until midnight." They were staying at the same hotel as us and we walked over together. We never saw them again but we made each couple a night to remember, probably our spaghetti guy also.

The next surprise was the next day when we decided to begin our usual exploring to see where we were and what we would do for a few days. This was during the day when activity was on. This was more like it. There were shops, entertainment, food and a few other things to do downtown. The one far part of the boardwalk became crowded with the same, shops, eating places etc. We found a nice reasonable good food place where you carried your food to a table yourself. This was great. We sat outside eating and watching the Atlantic Ocean. We soon found a toy workshop that made trains etc, actually got to know the owner and even met him again on our next trip to Halifax. We became a good customer of his.

The train hotel was a rather old hotel still needed for trains as other newer activities made their way to the other end. It, however, was still close to a dock where a large cruise ship docked when we were there and went to see it. There were probably 20 little outside shops set up selling souvenirs. This ship was large with a lot of passengers getting off. Because we were so close to the gang plank where the passengers were getting off, I think they thought Jeri and I were residents and were there to greet them. We enjoyed just watching them get off. Jeri and I never had any desire to vacation on one. We took a lot of pictures there probably because we knew we would never get any closer to a cruise ship.

We then spent most of our days in this area shopping and watching people, a favorite pastime. Once as we were walking along the boardwalk, I couldn't resist doing the next trick. As I pushed Jeri along, we came to a young man sitting a bit high in his "rickshaw" waiting for a passenger to pull around the boardwalk. He seemed bored waiting. I pushed Jeri right up alongside of him, looked up at him and said, "Wanna

race?" He looked down, didn't know what to say and finally, realizing we were joking, laughed. That startled him briefly. He allowed me to take his picture looking down at Jeri. Relaxing, fun "stunts" are rather important, I think, for Jeri and me. So we can't run, dance and many other normal activities, we shall create our own entertainments. What MS?

It was now time to get ready for you know who — TATTOO. We had brought out tickets with us to see an afternoon show at 2:00 pm Sunday, July 4 for our handicapped admission price of $28 each for our special seating. We changed to our Sunday best and climbed — no, wait, I think we took a taxi to the show. Once — again, we enjoyed the show which was very different from our first time since many different countries come for their first time to show what best they can do.

When we left Metro Centre after Tattoo, we came out of the entrance near the top of the hill. Looking towards the Bay, we had in front of us a long but fast ride down the several blocks before leveling off. As we started down hill, at the very next entrance to the Metro was one of the RC mounted policeman from the show standing outside meeting people leaving. He had taken off his red jacket but still had the rest of his uniform on. When "Jeri" pulled up to him to pass, he stopped us. To give us a speeding ticket? Naw he wouldn't do that to Jeri. He grabbed the handles of her wheelchair and said, "I'll help you down the hill." So he did. We went several blocks and I told him we could handle the rest of the way (because the blocks were not as steep) and we thanked him. But wait a second. I wanted to take his picture with Jeri. He said I have a better idea. He looked across this

busy intersection and saw a young fellow across the street waiting to cross downhill. Our RCMP friend yelled over to him and motioned him to come over to us. I think the chap thought he did something wrong

and looked a little concerned as he followed directions to come to us. Our officer asked him to take a picture of the three of us. That was easy and everyone smiled for the picture even the fellow taking it. Was this one way of our being entertained? You "bet chum."

Seeing Tattoo again reminded us that it was time to pay Fr. Williams a visit at the Basilica. He was the one we sent Tattoo tickets to a year ago when we could not come. He was home and I think he recognized Jeri even though it was two years ago when we met. He then said, "Oh, you were the ones who sent me the Tattoo tickets." He then seemed surprised because he probably never expected to find out who really sent the tickets. So again we had a nice visit with him.find out who really sent the tickets. So again we had a nice visit with him.

Walking back to downtown and the busy boardwalk, we made a new decision. There was a deluxe hotel about a three minute walk from where we were entertaining ourselves with all that was going on. Next time in Halifax, this is the hotel where we will stay, taxi and all.

As we begin once again heading home by way Toronto, we had a reservation to stay at the Royal York one night and then on to Windsor to meet Jodi and family at the train station. As we got off the elevator in Toronto, a family was standing right by the elevator door as it opened. "What are you doing here? We are to meet you in Windsor." It was Jodi and her three girls. They wanted to stay at the Chelsea hotel. It was about five pm, a little late to cancel our Royal York reservation but we called and they cancelled it.

This time, Jodi picked a cab to take them to the Chelsea Hotel. Jeri and I beat them to the hotel and were waiting for them at the entrance. They arrived but as soon as they unloaded and met us at the entrance to the hotel, Jodi realized her wallet had dropped out somewhere. Her taxi had already left to go back to the train station. Another taxi was unloading and Jodi quickly got in, told the driver she thought her wallet was in the other taxi, to take her back to the train station, which he did. Jodi arrived back about 30 minutes later, said she found the other taxi, checked the back seat and there was her wallet. WOW.

The next day it was taxis to the train station and our train back to Windsor and another book closing to another successful train trip.

Just to give an example of what we had taken extra for Jeri on this trip besides a suction machine included: Tylenol – 2 bottles, some pills – Jeri could swallow pills easily, quickly, no water and no choking – she always took any needed pills this way!

Extra feeding tube

Ensure – 6 cans

Prune juice – 5 cans

Cranberry juice – 4 cans

FRIDAY JUNE 30, 2006 @ 0600 Jeri and Jack boarded their train in Windsor for their last train ride together. It took them to Toronto, Montreal, Halifax and back to Windsor where they debarked their train for their last train ride together.

This trip was a splendid unexpected but happy trip to match possibly our best train trip ever.

The happy story:

We arrived first in Toronto to change trains to Montreal to change trains to Halifax for a five nights stay.

When we left Montreal and were settled in our coach seats for a long overnight destination to Halifax, an interesting event took place. The train we were on was the daily one to Halifax, a very crowded train of probably 25 cars and probably over 400 passengers. Now unlike the "Conductor" head in Amtrak, VIA Rail called their train's head person "Sevice Manager."

Not knowing anyone but Jeri aboard, I helped Jeri get comfortable in her seat next to her window. I was picking out clothes we needed behind her in our luggage. Bent down, I looked up and there were two uniformed "attendants" watching me. I said, "Oh, are you our attendants?" The one person spoke saying, **"I** am the Service Manager." **WOW!** I stood up and told him I wanted him to meet Jeri. Excited, I told Jeri, this person is the Service Manager!

In a slow but effective tone of voice with a half way apology of not succeeding, he said to us, **"I wanted to tell you that I met with my crew about seeing if there would be more we could do for Jeri."**

I was stunned! What a surprise. I know Jeri was too. I finally said, "That was really nice of you to do, but actually we were fine but really appreciated your coming to us like that."

I think it was the BEST comment to Jeri we ever had.

WE AIN'T DONE YET! There's more to do and Jeri and I had more plans yet. Heck, Jeri did Avon for over 25 years and it is still being done by our family under Jeri's name. I guess if we had a family banner, we could say our banner is still flying.

Back to business at large - As we said in our previous trip to Halifax, we found another hotel near the waterfront near the activities going on. We checked into this hotel, Halifax Marriott Harbourfront for five nights. It was a very good choice. I think there was a casino nearby but we never found it nor were we looking for it.

The hotel was connected by several enclosed walkways which were clean and in turn had several other walkways connecting to other sections like over the streets, other shopping and food restaurants, including a spaghetti restaurant etc. These were interesting and we used them a lot. I thought I knew our way after a day or two but after leaving the hotel into a walkway and looking for our Scottish store location, I became hopelessly lost in the walkways. I finally asked someone to tell us how to get back to our hotel. We went back to the hotel and started over. We finally found our favorite Scottish shop where we had met the owner before and had become friends with, one of only a few we did get to know in Halifax. We had eaten at the spaghetti restaurant among all of these closed walkways but never found it again. The "maze" kind of overwhelmed me. We had more to do then play you go that way, I'll go this way. Come to think of it, we couldn't do it that way either.

We liked this hotel because of its location – minutes to the boardwalk and or downtown shopping, food etc. We found also that they had a morning breakfast that sounded good primarily because they would provide room service of our choice and time. Jeri's "let's" sounded and we checked it out. Since Jeri and I always only needed one meal at a time, we ordered one meal with our choices. It was the right choice. We had plenty to eat and drink and it was convenient for us. We ordered this meal four days in a row, the price ranging from $16-25 each day. It was excellent and the right amount of food. It also allowed us to go straight to the boardwalk or downtown to start the day – no walkway to go through.

Now we had tickets for Tattoo for Sunday, July 2, afternoon at 2:30 pm. Our hotel being near the bay meant we walk or get a taxi straight up from our hotel to the eight or so blocks to the show at Metro Centre. Someone on another trip had told us that we could ride elevators up all the way from the Bay to Metro Centre. This sounded great and we decided to look into it. The person telling us did say, each floor has an elevator you ride one by one up to the Centre. However the stores may close their elevator off when they close their store and you may find yourself locked in. This sounded exactly what we learned on this trip, that there is a walkway direct to Metro Centre. A walkway? We decided to play it straight. I will push Jeri to Metro Centre. We will make it or else. We made it. There was an unfortunate way Jeri had to watch the show – from her wheelchair. There were no practical chairs to move her to. So for several hours Jeri had no choice but she sure didn't let it bother her.

After the shows would be over, many of the performers would return to the Centre to meet people. We could never make it to get downstairs in time after the show to meet them. They would all be gone. This time we put our wheelchair on high speed. We will meet the Northwest Mounted Police! When we reached the main floor, the only performers left were two Mounted Policemen. That was enough. We introduced ourselves and they did likewise. We asked if they had ever been stationed in Churchill. "One lit up surprised by our question said he was stationed there!" Automatically we became friends. Jeri was enjoying all of this even the speed to get to meet these fellows. She was excited and they seemed excited to meet her especially when they learned we liked Churchill in our visits there.

Strange, here Jeri is in a wheelchair, over a thousand miles from home talking to a Northwest Mounted Policeman in a strange city, telling him we knew Churchill well and were glad to meet someone else from Churchill. I think this is almost unreal. Who is this person I'm married to?

I believe it was July 4 when a fireworks display was to take place in the bay that evening. It was real close to our hotel so we walked over to be on the boardwalk and "claim" our spot to watch thanks to another person sitting there and invited us to sit by them. Waiting for over an hour and still seeing the bay well, we felt we had the right spot. As the fireworks were about to begin, we found many people right in front of us. Oh well. We could see the ones going off up in the air but not the flat ones on the water. Actually, we didn't think much of them anyway.

Before leaving Halifax, we, I should say Her Highness (or her other nickname we used long ago, Watashi) had shopping in mind. This time it was more for the children. We were close to the main shopping street. Between that and the boardwalk area, we did pretty well. This time I think I forgot myself and I bought a lot "out of my money." Now that statement is not true. It was **OUR** money. I think Jeri may have used MORE of OUR money.

We also climbed the hill to the Basilica for a visit and to see our friend the Rector Fr. John Williams. Not finding Fr John we stopped at the rectory. The housemother answered the door and recognized us right away. She invited us in but said, "Fr Williams had been transferred and was no longer there." We were disappointed but were introduced to the new Rector. It is never the same.

We started back down to ground level by way of going backwards - remember, Jeri is still in her wheelchair and I am still responsible and I still remembered the hot pepper.

To spend our last day in Halifax, we checked what we might have missed. We took a picture of our Scottish girl in her store, took one of our wooden train maker in his store and a picture of the decorated tug boat that they would not let Jeri ride on because they thought it was too  dangerous. So we took Jeri's picture with the boat. The only boat we seemed to be allowed on was the ferry boat. We rode it twice. Enough was enough.

The next morning we took a taxi to the train station. It was time to catch a train. Jodi and her mighty three may be waiting in Toronto. We have a two night engagement there at Delta Chelsea before Windsor and Bowling Green.

Not knowing this was to be our last visit to Halifax, I think we had perhaps our best visit primarily because of the comment our Service Manager had made. We sent a letter to VIA Rail President Cote on July 21, 2006 about this "...special complimentary comment by your Service Manager Des Lewin reference my wife Jeri, was really appreciated. He said they had wished they could have done more for Jeri."

We also mentioned several other names and that the crew was great, plus a few more comments like: traveling by wheelchair is an adventure itself; we have never had need to send in a complaint letter etc. We signed it Jack and Jeri Schroeder.

August 15, 2006 from President Cote: (abbreviated) "I have indeed received your letter. It is a pleasure to encounter a letter such as yours. Your comments have been forwarded to the manager responsible who will be pleased to congratulate our staff for such an outstanding performance. Again, thank you for writing. It would be our pleasure to serve you again.... Sincerely, (signed) Paul Cote, President and CEO."

Jodi and her crew were waiting for us in Toronto. We had another good time at the Delta Chelsea play area and out in the back large garden. Watching Jeri enjoying this so much with family a long way from home and seemingly a long way from MS surprised us how well she seemed. Even on a four hour train

 trip back to Windsor was very relaxing for her as the grandchildren would sit with her, even feed her.

Jeri's and my last train trip together? That is what the opening statement said. Repeating this introductory statement that read:

"FRIDAY JUNE 30, 2006 @ 0600 Jeri and Jack boarded their train in Windsor for their last train ride together...."

Now this statement was correct but our next trip was already established and we reversed our June 30, 2006 to record that it actually was our last train ride together, per:

Dated January 4, 2007, we had already arranged for Trip #5 to Churchill. We had our Via Rail train tickets, our hotel reservations and Jeri and I were ready to leave Friday August 24, 2007. No problems with Jeri. She was ready! On March 10, 2007 is when Jeri had a choking problem which took her to the hospital.

We had no choice but to cancel all of our reservations. However this may have been best. We could have had this happen somewhere in our travels. We still had Jeri – that was what was important.

BACK IN TIME NOW TO HEAD FOR OUR LAST TRAVELING SECTION WHICH SEEMED UNREAL BUT WAS SO AMAZINGLY TRUE. THIS SECTION IS MADE UP OF FOUR SEGMENTS IN ORDER. WE WANTED THIS TO BE THE LAST SECTION TO BE THE ULTIMATE SURPRISE AS IT ACCIDENTALY ENTERED OUR TRAVELING BECAUSE WE COULD FIND NO OTHER PLACE THAT IMPRESSED US. IT WAS JERI'S "LET'S TRY IT."

ULTIMATE CHURCHILL

ULTIMATE CHURCHILL TRIP #1 1999

WHY CHURCHILL... Jeri and I were running out of trains in the US and Canada. We took out the VIA Rail Canadian train map and began searching. We seemed to have covered both countries well with nothing else interesting showing. Way up near the Arctic Circle on the Hudson Bay showed a town marked Churchill. I said to Jeri, "This looks interesting." "Let's," said Jeri. Churchill it was. We began to work on reservations with "Alain" at Via Rail the very person we talked about earlier. We knew nothing about Churchill. We did not even realize it was bear country. Now that was a surprise when we got there.

The day before we were to leave, I was checking Churchill on the computer. Some of the mail did not speak well of it. One said their flying insects were very bad, that to go there, you better have good insect spray and a mask to wear over your head and face. They named the insect spray you would need. Wow. This didn't sound good. No way should I be exposing Jeri to such a condition. We maybe should cancel our trip. I showed Jeri the message. We decided not to cancel the trip but to see if we could buy the insect spray they referred to. We called two drug stores which did not seem to know what it was and that they did not have it anyway. We had a lot of Avon insect spray on hand – that'll do it. We loaded all we had in our luggage which by now was five large pieces. To get to Churchill was to take us four days and three different trains, a round trip of about 5000 miles. Since the train to Churchill only went there times a week, we scheduled our time which allowed us eight days in Churchill, which would mean a 17 day trip.

Not knowing what to expect, we carried mostly winter clothes, gloves, boots and even some food. People had asked us what we were going to do in Churchill. We said we didn't know but we would know when we got there.

One change we made in our traveling was we had a new blue travel wheelchair for Jeri to use. This was an expensive chair but we were excited about it because it seemed to be more up to date than the green one we were using.

We were on our way, leaving Windsor, Canada Saturday August 7, 1999 by 1st class and made our first train change in Toronto leaving there at 11 am on the Canadian in the Economy Class (no sleeper), arriving at Winnipeg the next day at 5 pm. At 10 pm, it was raining pretty hard as we left the downstairs waiting room in a large freight elevator heading up one flight to the platform joining a few other passengers boarding our escape to Churchill. We had reserved a sleeper for two nights and as Jeri and I were taken outside up in our manual lift to our car entrance, I started pushing Jeri in her wheelchair towards the entrance, slipped on the wet metal floor entrance and went sliding a bit. Not falling down, there was no problem. However our attendant watching me asked if I would make a written report on my sliding. I said there was no cause to write such a report but he put it in such a way, it would protect him from any questioning. So be it. I did so the next day. I could see their point in wanting a report.

So for one day and two nights of watching our wild country from a fast and slow train and enjoying this forest of many trees, a few animals and meeting the crew of perhaps five or six, our adventure had begun. Our train consisted of one coach, one sleeper and one cafe car. I think we only had about 10 people heading for Churchill. Now this was nice as we got to know crew and all and there were only a few stops in between. We entered the area of Churchill which we could see in the daylight distance. This scene was always a beautiful sight as Churchill became larger as we pulled up to the station. This happened on our four trips to Churchill, as it eventually became like a second home.

It was raining when we arrived in Churchill Tuesday August 10 at 7:30 am, no sun and it was cold. We were picked up by our "Hotel Churchill" car in which they welcomed us to Churchill, our first ever visit. The people there checked us in, nothing fancy but clean and, considering where we were, very adequate, comfortable and on one floor. We asked if there was some place we could get breakfast? They pointed us to a door that led to their very nice restaurant. The breakfast was delicious and inexpensive.

I told Jeri to take a rest while I took a walk to see what there was to see and do. Still raining, I walked around the area. About 15 minutes later, I had found nothing interesting. What will we do here? I can't expect Jeri to stay in a room for a week watching TV, which had little to watch (it improved later in our trips). I'm going to tell her we should catch the next train leaving. By the time I reached Jeri, I decided that we made a commitment to come here, we will stay.

Our new found land quickly became our favorite as we began our adventure in Churchill. I think our first pleasant surprise was Jeri had no sidewalks to wheel on and no curbs to go up and down on. There were none. Most roads were dirt but well kept except for the many dirt roads way out in real bear country. There were few cars and trucks. You could not drive into Churchill. The only ways were fly or by train. If you wanted your car there, it would cost you about $700 one way on the train. There were also a few beware of polar bears signs posted around including even behind the school building near the bay.

We learned that the year around population was about 700 and that the elevation was 15 feet.

We made our way around which eventually became "our" town to see what it was all about and to see if we could begin meeting people who lived there. We knew the residents knew we were tourists. That was easy for them. We acted like we had never been there before, which was correct, had money to spend and kept a fast pace to see everything. Having a person in a wheelchair surprised them by watching Jeri and wondering if this was a one day visit to see bears and leave Churchill that night. Jeri was not an average tourist.

One of the first persons we met was Mark, who ran a tour business there. He became an early friend and would help us later as we found out. He had a rather old school bus that he used to take visitors around town and fully explain Churchill. We went with him on one of his tours of town and area but found no bears. Later, we heard that one tour did find bear as the tourists came back excited to tell us about finding the bear. Gee, we hoped we would be able to do the same.

We had lunch at Gypsy's where we would meet owners Tony and Helen and they soon become one of our favorite places to eat and, more important, very good friends. Finished eating, I couldn't find the men's room and asked an employee where it was. He pointed to the door to the outside!

It was still a wet and dreary day but we were not disturbed because this was one reason we came to see how others lived and how we would like it.

Getting late in the day, we decided to go back to our hotel and have dinner there and also get rested from the long train ride. So far, so great - we will continue our exploring in the morning. We already liked being here. It had already been a true adventure from the time we left BG.

The next day, the sun was out in full and the weather, while jacket weather, was beautiful. From here on, it was all "down-hill," no pushing Jeri up-hills, there were none, just friends to meet and things to do. We were never disappointed.

We had a delicious breakfast again at our hotel – they got use to us in the morning by having "our" table waiting for us. This morning as we were finishing our coffee, Marian, the manager, sat down with us. We had something to give her. It was a white Churchill cap. Not their Churchill but rather our grocery store we used in BG named Churchill. We brought a few of these caps with us to pass out. Marion was surprised and laughing as Jeri sat next to her and looked up at the cap Marion had now put on.

As we went outside into the sun, we still had to wear jackets and learn the manners of being on their roads with a wheelchair. The main street was a nicely paved two lane road that went from one end of town to the other, probably about five or so miles. The roads stayed nice because the weather does not freeze off and on to break up the road during the long winter. Everyone seemed to own a four wheeler but were not allowed on the paved road, only to cross the road if need be. Our wheelchair -- well we knew of no regulations and I usually kept Jeri on the edge of the paved road unless the traffic was busy which I don't remember it ever being too busy.

When walking and you passed someone, 4 wheeler, car or themselves walking, you would always speak or wave to them, no matter who they were or if you knew them or not.

There were other two lane roads in town and outside areas, mostly just dirt. I do not remember seeing any speed signs, no signs for that matter, just a few identifying certain locations. There were few cars and few trucks and two adequate gas and repair stations hardly noticeable. There were no established roads into Churchill. We did hear that it was possible to use different dirt roads if you knew which to use to go to Churchill but because of bears, they were not for everyone to try. Better you fly or take the train.

After crossing the street safely with Jeri, right across from where we stayed was the Arctic Trading Company where we met the owner Penny and her staff for the first time. This was a true trading post – we were told that if we came in at the right time, we would find traders back from gathering furs to trade. Penny's fantastic old but well kept shop was indeed one that had many native made items that put us in the right feeling that we were indeed in this wild north. It was packed with mostly Canadian items from furs and endless clothing items, gifts etc, many being made right there and kept displayed in the show rooms, even hanging on the ceiling to be sold. Their sales were sent worldwide. The employees had individual nicely kept rooms to do their sewing etc. We were happy they let us watch. One of the girls was making pictures out of fur, another one held up a very large sheet of fur from which they would cut to make pictures with. Another girl was shown making Eskimo moccasins. Over our four trips we probably bought 15-20 moccasins and probably 10-20 framed pictures plus many other items. These girls were always friendly and nice to talk with plus they kept their working areas pretty neat. Now Penny's office was ......oh well, she knows. As long as she had coffee nearby like her office for certain friends, she was A-ok. If during the day, Jeri and I had spare time to see what was going on, we would usually go back to Penny's "place" to go through all the aisles to see what we missed. We missed a lot but continued searching all the little items on display and crowded together. We also expected coffee each time, talking about getting spoiled! Jeri really loved visiting there and also searching the aisles for whatever interested her. Penny always made time to sit with us — between her ongoing business telephone calls. We had quite a few things made for us during each trip. Even after we went home, we would send requests to Penny, sometimes even drawing ideas up for them to make and especially put individual names sewed on and placed in autographed beautiful frames.

One day we were visiting Penny who had just sold a very expensive rug which was kept up in the ceiling rafters for protection. Jeri and I watched the staff very carefully taking this item down. They were rushing this because the customer said they would buy this if they could get it ready before the train left that night. They beat the train.

Penny showed us a thank you document from a government office that congratulated her hiring these people to do meaningful hand work projects. The workers were very good at this.

We became very close to Penny and were sorry to learn that her husband had died a few years earlier taking several clergy in his airplane to a northern Catholic settlement when it crashed.

We then decided we wanted to go bear hunting (with our camera) and called Mark. He was busy but sent someone else to take us out in which we had to pay $50 each. Jeri wanted to go again that afternoon and wanted Mark to take us. Mark not only took us, he was with us all afternoon and said he enjoyed it. He would not accept any payment. We did see bear that day. Two were swimming in the bay while another was stretched out on the rocks taking a sun bath. So we did see our first bear. Now we were satisfied.

Our next required stop daily, was the Gypsy Restaurant and bakery to see Tony and Helen and also to eat there. Tony's hamburgers and French fries were the best anywhere we ever visited. Their meals also were excellent and their homemade bakery cooking was tops. We would take baking items to our hotel room for later eating about every day.

I don't know how they did this but Jeri and I were watching TV in the morning when an announcement appeared on the screen which listed names and a message which read, "So and so, your order has arrived. Please pick it up as soon as you can." Later in the day when we went to eat at Gypsy's, sitting on the floor were about 15 boxes of fresh food and supplies individually addressed that came in on the train that day. Now we know the TV was used for more them just everyday bingo. We thought this was pretty neat. Now that is "communications." By the way, we never played the bingo. We never knew how and our presence here was to get outside, whatever the weather was.

Our next visit – the POST OFFICE -- Now who takes a vacation to visit a Post Office? I certainly don't think we ever did except maybe to deliver vacation post cards to be mailed home.

Finally a visit to their Post Office and we eventually met the girls who worked there (Fay, Janet, Heather, Corrina, Adilia, Chavon). Fay, we were to get to know well and still keep in touch with. Anyway, now we knew we found the place we "belonged" Churchill! We would meet these girls as often as we could when here. They loved Jeri to come (I suppose that meant me also) and would stop working to talk with us. They were our required persons to stop to see them. We did every trip.

Within the Post Office were individual mail boxes where incoming mail would be put and not delivered. The residents would pick up their mail, no delivery service. This method created a central community area for people to see each other when mailing or picking up their mail or buying stamps etc, just like any big city would do. Jeri and I really liked stopping to see these girls. We would stay to talk with them but had to watch the time – they were working girls. We would be back.

Close to the Post Office was the RCMP – now surely everyone knows the Royal Canadian Mounted Police! On Wednesday, August 11, 1999, we made our presence known. They gave Jeri one of their pins and also drew up the identity of each part of the pin for us to see:

-the crown represents the queen

-the buffalo represents their food & clothing

-the 12 maple leafs represent our 10 provinces and 12 territories

-maintiens le droit means maintain the right of peace.

Time to take on a Tundra Buggy! A What?

Whatever it was, we were gamed to take it on. We signed up for a ride and then were driven to an area where we would get on. It was a reconstructed school bus with tires about five feet high. Well too late to change. I took Jeri on and we were given a front seat right across from the driver. I transferred Jeri to her seat, sat next to her and already began holding her from going forward. No safety belts. Hey, we are in adventure country. Other passengers got on and our lady driver took control. "Is everyone ready?" "Yes."

The buggy could only travel about five miles an hour as we headed for the tundra, a treeless marshy area apparently well known in arctic North America. Our mission was to look for bears or just explore the area. Our group did both. At first our ride was smooth and becoming interesting. Soon we hit the area not so smooth but bumpy enough to think we were in an amusement park. I clung to Jeri and could barely keep her seated. If I let go, she's on the floor. We were both bouncing around as we followed a road path and soon saw us heading straight to one of the cleanest large ponds you never see. Oops, we're not

stopping. We are going to go through the water which was about 3 or 4 feet deep. Now we knew what the high wheels were for. Our driver was hanging on to the steering wheel with both arms and hands. Looking closely, we could see through the water – there was a car path under water that we were on and following. WOW. That was worth coming. After about at least a mile "under" water we pulled up the other side and stayed on our same path and once again on land. We could see why the buggy had to stay on a used path. It would probably sink right into the ground otherwise.

As our driver kept moving along with us, I noticed something was wrong. I said to her, "You have a flat tire don't you." Her answer was, "I think so

 but hope not" as she stopped and looked. "Yes we have a flat tire." She found a spot where she could pull over.

It was now, everybody off but don't roam too far less a bear comes. So we are stranded with a huge flat tire that

needed replaced. But we weren't stranded after all. Our driver called back to town and asked for another bus to come out for us. We were probably at least an hour from their garage. We waited, wandered outside watching for bears and exploring our area of the Tundra. Finally in the distance we saw our rescue buggy coming - at five miles an hour. Forty-five minutes later we were together. The new buggy pulled up right behind ours and connected us where we could walk right onto our replacement. As we prepared to head back, I had watched our original bus and I saw the new driver walking into the area and finding what they needed, a very large rock which they carried and placed it under the bus near the flat tire. I was surprised no one was helping them change the tire. I couldn't see the finish but apparently they didn't need help. After changing to our rescue buggy, we headed towards Hudson Bay and then on our way back to town, we took a different way which led through a beautiful forest of pine trees. Our buggy, being so wide, could barely stay on the small path. As we were driving through very close to the trees, we clipped part of a tree limb off of one and it came right in  through Jeri's open window and landed on her. She was allowed to keep the limb.

When we got back to town, we thanked our driver for the ride and the free entertainment. Now that was fun even without bears. Also, I never let go of Jeri the whole ride. It was not easy!

As for Tundra Buggies, they could attached each buggy to each other and form a "train" in which there were sleeping quarters and mess services, the end intention was the train would be set up out on the Tundra for overnight stays to watch the bears come right up to the train. We didn't have time to do this but were tempted.

We still had several days left in our first trip to Churchill. One was where we met Bill assigned to us by Mark to take us bear hunting. Bill quickly became another of Jeri's friends. If anyone looked like they belonged to Churchill in this northern area, it was Bill. He could fit any northern woodsman type person in a movie.

As Bill picked us up in a van, we had something for him, one of our new Churchill hats. He was surprised and couldn't understand that we had a Churchill hat. Of course, it was a BG Churchill grocery hat.

Going for bear with Bill, I think this was one of the bears that we found fairly close, thirty yards away. It had popped out of the rocks and stared at us, in our car of course. This bear appeared to be brown! A guide later told us the bear had probably been playing in the dirt. After a minute or so, it turned and ran the opposite direction running fast. I didn't have time to take a picture. Now to keep truths correct, our bear hunting was by camera and binoculars, no guns. Bears were reported to be able to go 45 miles an hour, with or without cameras. We were also warned that if a bear reached you, lie down and do not move, play dead. I don't think I would have been playing.

A couple of other things we drove to on this our first visit included seeing where a large transport airplane had crashed in the 80s landing on a rock area, was badly damaged and was never used again. There was also a freighter that was still standing in the bay about fifty yards from shore that had sunk but was still standing in the water where people could walk to it.

Bill took us to see Huskies (dogs) being trained at two locations outside of town. At one location the Huskies were kept outside year round and were chained together about twenty yards apart. There were about 70 of them being located around the water ponds where they were also fed. Bill petted one and invited me. I wasn't quite trusting Bill yet or was it the husky? The other training location had what looked like a wooden obstacle course set up where we could see many Huskies being trained.

One of the most interesting stories we took back with us to BG was about the bears. It wasn't about where they lived, how they ate, how they played (which they did) or how they liked to chase visitors carrying food in their pockets a mile away. So, what was left out in our story? The question is what happens if the bear gets arrested? The answer: They were sent to the **bear prison!**

Now this is a nice and comfortable warm metal building where each bear has its own cell. Water is served but no food. Now this was all explained to Jeri and me one day. It sounded more like they were explaining people to us rather than animals. Anyway we enjoyed talking to this person about all of this including more. It was explained that water was sufficient for the bears, that they would lose a pound a day without harm. If the prison became overcrowded and they needed more cells, they would release any available bear qualifying for good behavior. No visitors were allowed to visit.

What brought all this about? The bears were waiting for Hudson Bay to freeze so they could go out on and under the ice to get seals for food. The problem was, a freeze had no date. Early bears ran into food problems and often would come into Churchill searching for food. If they became unruly, security would have to capture them, by knocking them out, and putting them in round metal cages to haul them to their prison, five miles outside town. When the bay finally froze the bears could get on the ice. When this happened, many visitors came to Churchill to see bears heading for the bay including those being released from prison. This was done by helicopters carrying the bears about 30 miles out and turning them loose.

Our visiting and bear hunting continued until Sunday when things quieted down. This took us back maybe 30 years (or was it 100 years) when Sundays were considered days of rest, attending church etc as stores would be closed that day. That's about the way it was here in Churchill. It was kind of nice.

As we prepared to eat breakfast, we found our hotel restaurant closed for the day. There were only three churches in Churchill, an Alliance, an Anglican and a Catholic. It was Sunday August 5, 1999 so we decided to walk to the Catholic Church, a nice well kept small church where one priest was present and a Bishop also was assigned there. By Catholic history, if a Bishop is assigned to a church in a diocese, the church becomes a cathedral. This meant that Churchill's Catholic Church was a cathedral, not bad for a small out of the way church. I wonder how many visitors realized that. We also learned that their diocese was actually called, "Diocese of Churchill-Hudson Bay." It covered one-third of Canada and had nearly 25,000 people in all communities with five priests helping the Bishop. We stayed for Mass and found out something else. Their Sunday bulletin read that the collection for a couple of Sundays before was $119.00 "for which we thank you very much as usual!" To add to this, we read the Sunday bulletin again two years later which read "THANK YOU for your donations of $97.00."

After Mass, we still had not eaten. Do we call for help? Do we ask the next person we see? What next person. It was Sunday. We were on our own. So we decided to explore the outer sides of Churchill and headed north on an empty main street, Kelsey Boulevard. At the edge of town we found a restaurant opened. As we entered we saw only two other people eating there. They quickly asked us to join them and we introduced each other. The man was Bro. Georges while his friend was a Lay Apostle named Fabiinne. We not only enjoyed having breakfast with them but we became good friends before we left Churchill which was only two days away.

Jeri and I continued our exploring and soon came to railroad tracks with a small work train just a few yards away from us. I couldn't resist this. I parked Jeri right on the tracks just ahead of the stopped engine and stepped back and took her smiling picture. Train or no train, it didn't bother her as she was laughing at me. OK so the train didn't come. I knew that, I think. It made a pretty picture. By the way, this train engine was closed for the day and no one was in it.

Continuing on our way, we came across the factory where the Tundra Buggies were assembled and built. They were closed except for one employee who came over to meet us. People in Churchill loved to meet and talk to people. This fellow told us all about the Tundra Buggies and that they would buy old school busses and rebuild them into their buggies. Now some of these buggies were the large train-like ones for people to sleep, eat and watch the bears come to them out on the tundra. Jeri and I enjoyed this and listened to him for a couple of hours. Our whole Churchill stay seemed like a private learning experience with no ending.

Not sure where we ate dinner but after a little more exploring in a residential district near the Churchill River where we saw no one, we headed back to our hotel to get ready to go to a movie. Actually we learned later that being near the Churchill River just walking around was not a very safe idea. We forgot that we were in bear country and even a wheelchair can't go 45 miles an hour. Watch the bear signs or you will have a beautiful hungry bear wanting a handout from you.

We had decided earlier to go to the only movie theatre in Churchill that evening to watch a pretty good movie called, I forget. We dressed for the night out at their only theatre if we could find it and hope it would be open. It was over two blocks from us and held on the third floor of Town Centre their large indoor building where the schools, library etc were. This being Sunday everything seemed to be closed except the theatre for one showing. Different floor levels being connected by large ramps made it easy to go up and down and was great for Jeri in her wheelchair but a little extra heavy pushing for me, which didn't bother me as long as we didn't go all the way to the top wherever that was. I knew the theatre was in this building somewhere but after a few ups and downs on the ramps, I couldn't find it. I bet people going to the movie had fun watching us and probably thought we were just exploring the building. I finally exposed myself to being another tourist and asked someone, "Where is the theatre?" They kind of laughed and said to follow them. I think it was on the third floor well hidden.

There were about 40-50 people at the theatre watching the movie. I told Jeri that when the movie was over, we will try to go out with the crowd because of bears. Well the crowd not only beat us out, they disappeared. Nary a one was in sight. It was dark and here we were in a deserted corner near a deserted building facing two blocks of walking, running, riding and looking for bears behind each dark passageway. We were off and I did keep my eye out for bears. I thought I saw several and ran a little faster with Jeri. We beat the shadows to our room just in time. There were no bears. So ends our night out. We never did see another movie on our four trips here, but we had fun every day with no time for a movie.

As our first trip kept getting better for us and more comfortable, we did find one thing wrong. We had mentioned at the beginning of this trip that we had Jeri's new blue wheelchair to take with us instead of the older green chair we had been using for years. This tells you how important it is to choose the correct wheelchair because after using this new one on our first trip to Churchill, we found it simply did not work well for Jeri. When we got back home, we eventually switched back to our old green wheelchair which worked much better and we never used the new blue one again. Our new blue wheelchair had cost us $1,796 out of pocket expense and since we had decided not to use it, we donated it to a welfare company. Sometimes you win sometimes you lose. We expected our blue chair to be given to someone who needed it. I hope we were a winner.

Monday was to be our last full day in Churchill. We were prepared. We spent most of the time with another bear hunt and also with our new friends, Bro. Georges and Fabiinne. For the first time we decided to visit the Eskimo Museum next to our church. But there were many steps to get into the museum. There were several construction workers next door laying a pipe line, who saw Jeri, and came right over and carried her and the wheelchair up the steps. They made it look easy. This museum was indeed a surprise cleanly kept with a large bear welcoming people coming in. We would visit this every time we came and would buy some of their books and gifts every time. Incidentally, this was owned by the Catholic Church, another surprise. Also this is where the Bishop had his office and also where church affairs were held. In Churchill, nothing really surprised you, at least after one day's experience.

Day 8, the fun was over. It's back to working on the railroad. We were in no hurry to leave but we had a daughter and Baby Katie scheduled to meet us in Windsor in five days. We met ok but we took a funny way to get there. This "funny way" started at 8 am in the morning of Tuesday, August 17.

We were up and getting ready to pack for our long train trip home that night and wanted to say Goodbye and that we would be back to everyone we had met. Our housekeeper was making beds in the rooms when I told her she did not have to make ours because we were leaving by train that evening. She spoke up and said, "You're not leaving today on any train. Haven't you heard? There's been a derailment and your train cannot get into Churchill." Now this was surprise news to hear. We better get ready and find out what's going on. Our friend Mark called and explained that another train ahead of ours did have a derailment and that our train would not get into Churchill today. It is now stopped in Thompson, 12 hours from us and is to remain there. Mark then said he had talked with Via Rail that said they would have an airplane come for us to take us and the other passengers to Thompson to get on the train. Mark said he explained to Via Rail that Jeri was in a wheelchair and that this might be a little more difficult for her. Via Rail agreed and said they would have a different airplane to pick Jeri up and take her straight to Winnipeg. Mark then told us about all of this and that Jeri and I should be ready at 6 pm when he would take us to the airport outside town.

How fast things change. It was kind of exciting because to us it was a little bit like being in a movie and an airplane had to come and get us out of where we were.

We packed and then had plenty of time to say Goodbye to everyone we knew and to tell them we would be back, our favorite saying no matter where we were. Our first stop was the Post Office. As we walked into their office, one person spoke up quickly and said, "We already know you are leaving by plane!" I asked, "How did you know". She said, "We know everything that goes on here."

Finishing our "Goodbyes" and "we'll be back" we went back to our hotel room, moved our luggage outside and waited for Mark to pick us up and take us to the airport.

We had only seen this airport once as someone had taken us around in a car showing us different military abandoned buildings etc. They also showed us the airport and explained that SAC (Strategic Air Command) had used this field for B-29s. We also learned that, now this was 1999, this field was now one of five alternate landing fields for our space shuttle in an emergency.

Mark came and to the airport we went. There was a large airplane there which we were hoping was ours but it took off as we approached. We only saw dust flying. Then where was ours? We looked, we found, we fainted – no not really. It was ours, a one motor, eight-seater airplane. Well traveling beggars can't be choosy, what did we expect for nothing. As we pulled up to ours, the only plane now at the airport, the pilot was already there with the side back door opened and Jeri's seat taken out and put on the ground. He was putting luggage etc in the plane. Mark and I got out of our car to help with the loading. I wanted to help but did not do to well. The pilot did ask me to go inside the plane to help from the inside with the luggage. When he said to do this, I was standing by the door facing him with the left wing behind me. As he spoke I turned around quickly to do what he wanted and bumped right into the wing. He yelled and asked me, "Are you trying to wreck my airplane?"

Finished loading, they put Jeri's seat back in and with Mark helping, lifted Jeri into the plane and then into her seat. I thanked Mark for taking us here and helping Jeri. He said, "I'm going with you to Winnipeg to make sure they take care of Jeri." I was put into a seat across from Jeri while Mark was in a seat right behind the pilot and co-pilot. Apparently at the last minute, a man arrived and got on the plane plus a young lady arrived with a tiny baby.

As we took off with a bright sun coming through our right windows, I took a picture of Churchill and then watching Jeri to see if she was scared, I started making sun figure drawings on Jeri's side for her to watch. Jeri scared? No sign of any, as she watched my stupid pictures.

Looking out the window, it seemed we were up pretty high, with only a lot of swamp below us with no place to land if need be. I asked the pilot how high we were. 26,000 feet he answered.

Along about then, Mark opened up a snack bag and passed it around. Three hours, 1,000 miles later the sun was gone and we were about to land. Jeri had flown before but had never landed at night. I told her to watch as we landed how pretty with all the lights all over Winnipeg. It was beautiful. As we landed we had another surprise waiting for us. When we got near the administration building, we stopped. Waiting for us was a taxi to take us downtown to our reserved hotel suite. Mark carried Jeri out of the car and into the taxi. He then directed the driver where to take us. Mark had now accomplished what he wanted to do and wished Jeri well. We definitely would see Mark again.

As we headed downtown, Jeri and I were alone again not believing all of this was happening. There was still a little more to it.

Our taxi ride, which had been paid also, took us to the Place Louis Riel Hotel, a very deluxe hotel, which already had us registered and our stay already paid for two nights. We were assigned to room 1702, on the 19th floor. The clerk told us there would be no need for us to check out when the time came.

After being in Winnipeg one day, the next day, our train day, we decided to try something. It almost got us arrested! Again! We were on our own expense account now, no more free loading. Here goes: We were three blocks from the train station, had with us from the airplane our Churchill luggage to carry onto our next train. This could cost us some money to do this by taxi. We had a cheaper and better way. I would take our luggage myself to the train station where they would hold it for us until the train came later today. It would take several trips to get our stuff there. I would leave Jeri in our room, take her wheelchair and stack it with luggage and wheel it to the station from our 19th floor room. This we did and it took several trips to do. Now meanwhile, I was being watched and didn't realize it until the person watching seemed to be in a different location in the lobby each of my trips. I realized I was suspicious looking and probably looked like I would eventually go up stairs, put Jeri back in the wheelchair and walk out of the hotel. He would be convinced unless I stopped to check out at the desk. Remember, we were told we did not have to check out. When I had one more trip to the train station to make, I decided, as I passed our spy, to suddenly stop and beat him to the punch by saying nicely, I know you must think I'm trying to sneak out of the hotel and I admit I do look suspicious. I had caught him by surprise and he gave me a big smile. I explained we were trying to save a taxi fee, that we had been brought here through Via Rail's approval and who paid our bill because of a train wreck and that the desk clerk said we did not have to check out. He was really pleased to hear this especially when I introduced him to Jeri. All three of us laughed together. He felt relieved and we became unexpected friends. He did admit he was suspicious.

We were now "safe" to walk out of the hotel and head for the train station.

We left Winnipeg Thursday August 19, 1999 at 1:50 pm on the Canadian but in Economy Class.
We didn't mind this class too much because it was cheaper and you met more people compared to a sleeper car because Jeri was too confined in a sleeper. It worked well for us for this one night trip but when a trip took two nights, it was a bit hard.

Arriving Friday, August 20, at Toronto, we were about seven hours late checking into the Royal York Hotel around three in the morning. Our two night rooms were still held but I think they only charged us for a one night stay. We left Toronto Sunday August 22 and arrived at Windsor by 1st class at around four in the afternoon to be met by Jodi and baby Katie. Our first and successful Churchill trip was history. We will be back.

As stated just above, Jeri and I did leave Toronto Sunday August 22, 1999 at 12:30 pm and we arrived at Windsor, Sunday August 22, 1999 at 4:26 pm give or take the four minutes short of the 4 hours needed. It was in between the time we left Toronto and the time we laughed ourselves into Windsor that we had one heck of a laughing party of seven plus all the train passengers in our car being entertained by our group who had met for the first time.

This started with passengers getting on at Toronto in our coach and trying to find an empty seat in our packed car. Our seat was made up of two seats facing two seats with Jeri using one to place her legs on and be all set for the four hours of a pretty fast bumpy train ride to Windsor. Usually when the attendants would seat us this way, it was to give Jeri more room. This time was no exception. We liked the idea and no one ever bothered us to sit at Jeri's extra seat she would be using.

Now it became interesting. We watched two nicely dressed fellows coming down the aisle looking for two seats. They wouldn't dare try to sit by Jeri and make her move her legs off of the second seat she was using. Ah, but they saw the two seats and Jeri stretched out on them. "Do you mind if we sit there," they asked Jeri. "Of course not", Jeri would tell them, "you can sit there." I moved her legs and sat her up straight. There was not much room then between the fellows and us. It could be a long four hours. Now why didn't they ask me first? I stayed out of that one and figured it was not my problem. I wanted to watch to see if the three of them could actually make this work and if the two men realized Jeri was in a wheelchair and then they would get up and leave. Nothing doing. What wheelchair, what MS? Jeri's well done smile did it again. The two men not only stayed, they became the train entertainment professionals.

I don't think we ever introduced each other. Three girls were sitting in their double seat across the aisle from us. They were watching us and smiling at what was happening. The remarks began. The guys would make a remark the girls would return a better one. This simply grew into a laughing matter. It never stopped for the whole trip. We were entertaining everyone. I even managed to slip a couple of remarks in and brought a few remarks back. I never saw Jeri laughing so much, she was having a great time watching and listening. This went on the whole trip with no winners and no losers but it was a lot of fun. Arriving in Windsor and exchanging Goodbyes, one of the men said, "The two of us have taken this ride often but this was the first time we ever enjoyed it. It was our best ever." All of this simply because Jeri moved her legs off a seat and sat back to watch and laugh. I knew Jeri would say yes to them for the same reasons she would say "Let's." We never saw our group again.

P.S. Below is a copy of a letter we sent to Churchill:

August 25, 1999

Churchill Chamber of Commerce
P.O. Box 176
Churchill, MB, Canada ROB OEO

People of Churchill,

My wife, Jeri, and I just spent 8 great days in your community and we want to thank you for allowing us to live with you for even a short period.

Perhaps you saw us roaming (actually exploring) your town – Jeri in a blue wheelchair and some cluck (me) pushing her. We really had a delightful time and, while we never got all the names of so many nice people, we would like to thank all of you and mention some names we do remember.

We loved your town, your 4 wheelers, the stores, and no sidewalks with curbs! With a wheelchair, sidewalks and curbs are difficult – you made it easy for us.

Thanks to the girls at the post office; thanks to Mark, Bill, Jodi (North Star); the friendly mechanic at the

Tundra Buggy Shop; Helen and crew (Gypsy bakery); RCMP office; your bank; the Eskimo Museum and the people and construction workers who carried Jeri up the steps to go in; the Arctic Trading Post (s/b Arctic Trading Company) and the girls helping us shop and showing us their work areas; Brother Georges; the two drivers driving our Tundra Buggy tour (and not charging us extra for the flat tire); the people we passed walking who always spoke or waved; Marion and her staff at the Churchill Hotel and the restaurant; yes, even to your very impressive health center where someone told us about it there; and thanks to all the drivers who got out of our way (they obviously knew of my reputation as a reckless driver) and still waved to us. And finally, as we were leaving, thanks to the 2 unknown girls who said they had been observing us and wanted to tell us they enjoyed watching us around town.

We have concluded that there is no town like Churchill.

Thanks for a great ride.

Jack and Jeri Schroeder
123 Summerfield Blvd.
Bowling Green, Ohio 43402
USA

(Chloe)

P.S.2   Whatever happened to all of our Avon insect spray we loaded into our luggage bag that we, at the last second, took with us as a must item? Answer: We carried it to Churchill, we carried it home.

A final climax to our first trip to Churchill happened when we arrived home. I asked Jeri, "Were you scared when you saw that one motor airplane we got on?" Her answer: **"Nobody asked me!"**

ULTIMATE CHURCHILL TRIP #2 2001

Buying our train tickets months ahead of time (in this case, it was June 29, 2001) was always our intention so we had something to look forward to and leisurely review our thoughts with some new ideas to go along with our new adventure. This obviously was more fun than trying to figure MS out. We will work on MS another day.

Planning ahead to trip #2, we had July and August to talk about going back to Churchill and how excited we felt. I watched Jeri a lot to see her reactions to make sure she really was excited. She surely was. Our three children were busy with their own family with schools etc so we never asked them to go. All we needed from them was to be taken to the train station and to pick us up when we returned. Now I knew our children were not overjoyed in letting us go alone but they did know how this would help Jeri with forgetting her MS. Years later, Jami told me she worried about us the whole time we were gone on every trip. One other thing to remember is that we planned each trip one at a time, never expecting when it would end.

So it was on to Churchill by way of overnight in Windsor (Day's Inn), leaving Wednesday September 5, 2001 for an overnight stay in Toronto (Royal York) and then a long trip to Winnipeg in a sleeper that was a "double-F" (meaning two people/more room/same price/if available).

I think only the Canadian had upper tourist domes for the free use of passengers to use. On previous trips, I would tell Jeri I was going up in the dome for a while. It never occurred to me to take Jeri up with me or ask for help to do so. In putting this book together, I came across a picture of someone sitting up in the dome car all by herself. My goodness, it was Jeri. I must have asked someone to help me take Jeri up to the dorm car on this second trip to Churchill. Why did I wait so long to let her go up? So then I remembered and here is how we did it.

While on this trip to Winnipeg we asked an attendant if there was a way to take Jeri upstairs to sit in the dome car. We knew the narrow winding stairway upstairs would be difficult to carry her up. The attendant said, "I'll be right back and as soon as I find another attendant, we will get Jeri upstairs." This they did. Now we were using a sleeper on this trip but this going upstairs in the dome was pudding on the ice cream or whatever you want to call it. Jeri was thrilled. It was hard to carry her up the stairs and it did take two to do it. At their directions, I stayed out of the way. I joined them upstairs and did help them move Jeri in near the window. We were now sitting together. Now we were on a real train going on a real vacation. What we could see was over our train cars ahead of us, the scenery better and even the "traffic" signals along the track for the engineer to see. Of course, red meant stop, green meant go. Until you get use to this, it is fascinating. Other passengers joined us upstairs and cameras were a necessity.

We were so thrilled with this that we missed our dinner. Our attendant came up to see if we wanted to go back down to our car for dinner. We said no that we would rather stay here for now and evening and forget dinner. The attendant came back a little later and said he had just put some deserts in the refrigerator downstairs for us. When you are ready, "I can bring it up to you." This he did. Finally, it was getting dark, time to get our attendants to carry Jeri back down and to our sleeper. Even doing this carrying Jeri was difficult. Our sleeper was two or three cars from the dome car and two of us would have to carry her back. Their "Washington" chair was most difficult to use especially through the narrow walkway and turns in the sleeper car. We used two methods to carry her. Two attendants would carry her or more often I would carry Jeri with one attendant helping. We did it!

Amtrak once used these dome cars but switched to a different kind of car where people could sit sideways etc and see through the overhead windows. We were told that Via Rail had purchased these cars from Amtrak and rebuilt the cars completely. We could tell that except we found out that our sleeper car "restroom" toilet was the same size and not redone. It did make a difference because to take Jeri to our sleeper restroom was next to impossible. Somehow I pushed her in her wheelchair to the opened restroom door, then carried, more like dragged, her the rest of the way, which was about five feet. OK, whatever works! Now this old restroom did not have a sign that read "do not flush while in a station" which I mentioned before. If someone took that sign down, I wonder why they could not have modernized the restroom. Never mind, I got her in every time.

By the way, we did go back using our old green light weight wheelchair. This chair lasted over 9 years piling up a ton of miles without anything breaking. I cannot say it was Jeri's favorite traveling chair. I don't think it is polite to ask anyone which is their favorite wheelchair. No wheelchair is idolized.

Arriving in Winnipeg Friday September 7 around 4 pm we chose the Place Louis Riel Hotel for our two nights. I think we forgot that we had stayed there two years ago when we were brought from Churchill all the way to Winnipeg by air. So what to do here? We had traveled through Winnipeg several times. Now we have two days here before our train to Churchill.

After checking in to our hotel (this time Via Rail did not pay), the next day we took a taxi to the riverfront where we boarded a large paddle wheel river boat for a cruise. This was a nice pleasant ride that took us through the downtown area and beyond. The Captain of the boat came over and introduced himself to us. He asked where we were from. We told him where and also that we were on our way to Churchill. He almost fainted he was so surprised and excited. "I lived there for many years, he said, and loved it." We then talked for a while before he got back taking care of his boat. He asked if we would do something for him. He wrote his name and "Hi Mark" on our boat ticket to give to Mark in Churchill. We did.

When we got off the boat where we got on, we decided to walk back to our hotel, a pleasant two mile hike. Hey, no taxi fee. The next day we would prepare to catch our train to Churchill. This time we did not walk out with our luggage on the wheelchair. This was Jeri's turn to use her wheelchair. We paid our bill and – now I don't remember if we took a taxi or not. I think we walked again. No matter, we were excited because our next stop would be Churchill.

As we approached the Churchill area two and a half days later, we began looking for the Churchill skyline which indicated we had about twenty miles yet to its station. This was two years later – were we concerned we might be disappointed? Would it be the same as we left it, the people we knew and the fun we had? We never gave it a thought. We said we would be back. Unlike our first time, we did not bring any insect spray.

It turned out we had two new situations to face when we got to Churchill. One we knew ahead of time, which was good while another one we did not know until we arrived at Churchill which was not good.

The first situation that pleased us was that we had three letters we carried with us to Churchill:

Feel free to laugh at our new idea. We recalled how we had read about people many years ago who traveled from their country to another country, they would take a "Letter of Introduction" from the ruler of their country to the ruler of the country they wished to visit. Just to do something different, Jeri and I asked ourselves why we don't do this as we go from the US to Canada? But where would such a letter come from. Well, we had not met the Bishop of Churchill yet but perhaps we will on this second trip. Jeri was all smiles and said, "Let's."

We knew the Bishop of Wheeling WV and wrote a letter to him asking if he could write a "Letter of Introduction" for us to take to the Bishop of Churchill. He said "he would be delighted to." Our local priest, hearing this, said, for Jeri and me, he would ask the Bishop of Toledo to do the same. The Bishop said he liked the idea and sent us a "Letter of Introduction" also. Next our local priest said "he too liked the idea and would write a letter to take to the local priest in Churchill." Jeri and I were really surprised at being able to do this. I know Jeri really felt good about the response we had. MS will wait.

Our three letters had to wait as we arrived in Churchill. Our second situation was not so good.

The time was 0830 September 11, 2001. The next scene was an about face as we quickly were being told what was happening in the US.

As we checked into our Churchill Hotel, several people were watching TV and when they saw us, yelled out to us that the US was being attacked, that several airplanes were diving into buildings, that all planes still flying were to land in Canada. WOW! We began watching this with them in disbelief. It was eventually known as 9/11. Here Jeri and I are getting off into another country and wondering what affect all of this would have on us being from the US. We kept watch on this during the day but still managed to do our purpose of coming back which was to renew our friendships of two years prior and meet new people this time around.

We began our routine with breakfast at our hotel at our "reserved" table of two years ago and then began our walk around town. Now whenever I say "our walk" I'm referring to Jeri riding and me walking. I would rather say "us walking" but it has the same effect and almost as enjoyable since Jeri was right there with me.

Our next several days kept us concerned about 9/11 but also allowed us to do what we came for.

Our second visit to Churchill found the Bishop there. This was our first time to meet him.

When we stopped at his residence next to the church, there was no answer. We had seen pictures of him which helped when a car pulled up near us, a man dressed in "jeans" got out. He said, "Can I help you?" I started to say we were looking for.....then I stopped and said, "You're the one we're looking for." I recognized him as the Bishop. We told him we would like to talk with him. He said to go to his office in the Eskimo Museum, "I will meet you there." This we did and delivered to him our three introduction letters. He was surprised and pleased. From that point on we, especially Jeri, were able to meet him several times. He became a special friend with Jeri.

Since we hadn't seen anyone here for two years and we did not tell them we were coming, our immediate intention was to check to see if everyone we knew were still here. They were and we received some nice greetings. I think maybe it was once a Churchiller always a Churchiller. Now these people we were interrupting were actually working. They all took time for us, especially Jeri. Being two years ago when we were in Churchill, it seemed impossible to be back. It felt like one week ago. People would come up to us and say they remembered us. Now we knew we were at our second home. We felt a lot more comfortable being here, we were not strange tourists anymore. So it was to Penny at the Arctic Trading Company for shopping, new stories and a free cup of coffee. Penny was always very busy but she always made room for us. Again Jeri and I loved to search their primitive fully stocked shelves and all the little spaces in their Arctic Trading Company for many hidden items lost among larger articles. Every trip we were there, we would come back with fur hats, polar bear jewelry, even craft supplies to make some articles ourselves. One item they had a lot of was "ivory" whether on jewelry or large handmade articles. We would be able to buy the ivory articles but we would not be allowed to take them across the border so we did not buy any item with ivory.

Their prices were fairly high but then they were excellent articles handmade right there in their work areas. Their prices went from five cents up to thousands of dollars. I liked to tease Penny by asking her what country did some of her inventory come from? She would say all from Canada. She was right, it took me a long time to find something not made in Canada and when I did find one article, I think she was ready to throw me and the article out.

We then continued renewing our friendships with our other neighbors. By the way, Penny's store was just across the street from our hotel so whenever we had spare time, we would often end up in her Arctic Trading Company, pretending we wanted to buy more gifts, only Jeri wasn't pretending. She loved it there.

Our return to Churchill felt like, "We came as tourists now we are visitors. We wondered what we would be if we came back again?"

Because Churchill's buildings etc were all within walking distance or short rides, it allowed us to see much more than we expected to see and do, even to get out of the cold.

This time out we reentered Town Centre to see the high school. For whatever reason, there were no students to be seen but we were able to talk to a caretaker. Our one question was a normal question. "How many students do you have?" Our gentleman was delighted and proud to answer this one. He said, "We had four graduates this year." Jeri and I thought this was great and told him so. It was great because we never expected to see such regular schools this far north. They had a high school hockey team (in cold Churchill it did not surprise us) and we watched them practicing in their ice arena. However, they did not have enough players for two teams.

Exploring more we found this Town Centre to be built with wide ramps connecting different size floors which were wheelchair friendly. Now I said "wheelchair friendly" — not for the wheelchair pusher who was on his own ups and downs. Actually it was better for me because it was better than elevators. This building was a well kept clean practical building. We had never seen one built like this anywhere.

We thought we had better get to Penny again (for coffee?), the post office girls, of course, and the Gypsy for lunch and bakery including night time snacks to take back to our hotel.

Later that week, we continued our Town Centre tour and enjoying this unique building which was probably built this way because of the cold and snow to come for months at a time. We especially liked the children's play area and would have gone in to see it more but we did not pass the height maximum size to get by a large standing bear at the entrance to go in. Wait a second, perhaps Jeri did qualify. Gee, I didn't even ask her. To continue, we also saw the connecting indoor route to their elementary school but that would wait for another day or another trip. We had already met the elementary school principal's secretary and were anxious to meet the principal. We would be back.

What else did they have for us? Well another nearby building contained a regular bank. We were able to exchange our AAA travel checks into Canadian money which gave us about 20% more than US money. At Toronto, the bank there would not cash my travel checks even though they were AAA. It didn't take long but we soon learned that travel checks were becoming obsolete and travelers began carrying more cash and credit cards. This "bank" building also had offices and a store selling "booze" or whatever it's called in Canada.

Now some of our walking tours by ourselves were often nicely interrupted by Mark or someone to get us back out on the "range" to find bears or different areas where visitors would come to learn more about birds etc. We did see one Fox go right by us once. Another time, I found Jeri talking to a girl in a four wheeler. Now what was that all about? She was asking Jeri to let her take us up in her helicopter where they could fly around to find a bear for us. A helicopter? Why not? A very good idea! We liked it. Before Jeri had a chance to say, "Let's" I asked about the cost. The girl said about $500. I think we will stay searching on the ground. I think if she had said $200, we would have gone with her.

When we weren't visiting or looking for wild animals called White Polar Bears we would cruise our town which was well kept, quiet and interesting — just covering the streets they had and where they led. We found and went into the food+ store. It was a "Northern Store" (which I found to be from a long time Canada source of stores) which had whatever you needed. We were surprised how fresh the food was. Bananas in the cold of winter? Other fruit? It was all there. One interesting thing about groceries was that you could buy different cereals but your choice came in one size only. No giant boxes etc. You buy what they had or go somewhere else, wherever somewhere else might be. We liked the idea. No choices to make. The same with all the other merchandise they had as we toured the building. You want a new couch? There it was. The best thing about this was it seemed to work well and made sense. Jeri loved this shopping seeing Churchill first hand and all that went with it.

The service and people buying at the Northern — how were they? Well I was using the store about every day for groceries for us. One day I went over to the store (it was only across the street from us) and bought a large orange juice and some cranberry juice for Jeri (they only had one size, surprise). As I waited in line behind only one other person, the fellow turned around and said, "You go ahead of me, I have more than you." Well he did have three grocery items. Now I call that being "very polite." Was Jeri and I in the right town?

Finishing our own visiting of a few more stops, like the Eskimo Museum to see what souvenirs they carried and which we did buy several books etc, we headed back to our room for our Gypsy baking snacks. One night as we returned to our hotel, we headed for the kitchen. The dining room was closed. No matter, I asked the one person still there, "Is there any way of getting a milkshake?" She answered, "Of course, I will make you one." Now I knew Jeri and I were getting spoiled here. Why couldn't the waitress just say "No" to me. It was a very good milkshake.

The next day we were able to get one of Mark's busses to take us out for more searching and also to see the northern part of Churchill where the ocean port was. The driver took us all through that area including back to the tundra. That was an interesting port to see and a little about how they served the ocean freighters coming in, unloading and then reload with what Canada had to ship out. More about this in our fourth trip in 2005.

Friday we began with breakfast at our own table. Remember, everyday our routine included not only getting up but also dressing two people. Jeri was so pleasant and smiling when I tried to dress her nicely every day. She was always ready to roam Churchill whether by wheelchair, car or bus. We used all three since some of tours were by car.

Let the day's adventure begin. We started with a long walk down Kelsey Boulevard not sure what we were going to see that day. Actually our interest started early as we headed south to see what street we wanted to turn on. Strange, we expected to see people along the way. It was a beautiful sunny day but wait, there was nothing on the road or area. No people, cars, trucks, four wheelers – no one as far as we could see. I took a picture of this and came up with a nice quiet pretty street area with no one in sight. We continued our walk. I think this was the day we walked on LaVerendrye Ave for the first time and came across a building named Carbou Hall. Apparently it was where activities would be decided. It seems to me we saw a sign there that read Girl Scouts, which would have interested Jeri. At the time it looked like the building was closed so we did not try to go in.

We were now satisfied to head to our Gypsy restaurant for an afternoon lunch. Probably Helen was the one who took our picture sitting there and eating. According to the picture, it seemed I had a hamburger and coffee, Jeri had what looked like a sandwich and tea and a third person was squeezing in between Jeri and me. What third person? We came in with the two of us. Who was the mystery guest smiling? Why it was our waiter friend from Montreal, the person who directed me to the outside when I asked him, on our first visit here, where the men's room was. Jeri was smiling too so I guess we let him stay. Actually we enjoyed his company.

Sunday Jeri and I headed for Church. We knew the Bishop was there for Mass. After church, we met Penny and other people we knew. Mark had left Churchill and didn't get back until Tuesday, the day we left. So in the meantime we did hire a taxi for two days in a row to take us hunting. We never saw a bear. The driver was nice and felt bad but we still had a good time seeing the area. The way they would drive over some of these large rocks was something to feel. I guess this is what they called "real polar bear hunting." Unbelievable but it didn't bother Jeri at all. She became a very personable person to our drivers and seemed to make their day every time.

When we say seeing the area in a car or bus, the rides are free amusement park rides in themselves with the rough roads. Looking for bear meant seeking unused roads, rocks to drive over, dead ends and probably a little damage to the car. The natural habitat of bears seems to be the warm months in which they can pop out at you and tell you to stay in your car or else. You are in their personal living grounds. We learned that the bears seem to know that there are no animals here bigger than them and therefore they are not afraid. Interesting, we found out they like to play with dogs and vice versa.

Monday, it was our last full day to be here. If I recall correctly, we had our regular breakfast, coffee at Penny's plus more shopping there and then to "where?"

Now this "where" leads me to how we never made schedules ahead of more than one when Jeri and I traveled alone. We learned from our stays in Churchill not to plan ahead or too much planning. We were comfortable traveling our way. In wheelchairs, one cannot just get up and do or go etc. It can be difficult to keep schedules etc. Doing it our way meant no pressure for Jack and no worry for Jack by Jeri. Take our time we will do things as we meet them. This is why we would be seen and why we "roamed" around town by ourselves. (We did this in many cities). A good example is when we took the tundra buggy ride our first trip here. There was no advanced reservation needed. Walking, we came across this tundra ride and stopped to see what it was. Within minutes we were out on the tundra, one of our favorite rides.

Tuesday September 23 we made our own tour around town. A stop at the Gypsy to eat we found Helen had cooked her own recipe of egg mixed with several items of her own choosing. We liked it and asked her if she could write the recipe for us. She said yes and wrote one for us on scrap paper. I later remembered that it was not polite to ask someone for their created recipe. I mentioned this to Helen and she said, "No problem." We still have it.

Leaving Churchill was difficult. It was so different, interesting and seemingly happy. Of course when the snows came it was probably a little different. In fact we learned that a few places close for a period during winter.

We were able to take one more ride looking for bears. We did see several bears during this trip which was nice but we were mostly glad of being part of Churchill. We had to be at the train station that evening, courtesy of our hotel so no problems there and getting our five+ "barracks" bags ready for another train ride was easy from experience.

As we took our last walk around town, all we could say was, "We had a great time. We will be back."

It was time to leave on train 692. We found out later that our attendants would keep Jeri very occupied. I would go for coffee and come back and find them entertaining Jeri. She was always laughing at or with them. This is why we always enjoyed our train trips. Every train we were on the attendants, men and women, seemed to like to visit Jeri. No airplane this time. We're on our own. Do we miss the airplane ride back? Actually no, a one thousand mile trip in a one motor airplane was great adventure. Twice, who needs it? We belong on a train and on this coach trip back, we had a sleeper waiting for us in Winnipeg.

A handwritten message left with us signed by four members of the crew read:

For: Jack and Jeri Schroeder

It was fun for one. It was fun for all. Thank you for riding on train 692 (with a smiling face).

Arriving in Winnipeg, we were to change trains and ride the Canadian by sleeper to Toronto. Sitting in the station waiting for our train, we looked up and saw our attendant from the train we had just left. He stopped and immediately spoke to Jeri and said, "I have a pair of earrings I bought for my girl friend but I want you to have them!" Jeri was speechless but smiling, gladly accepted them. It was a beautiful scene. We still have them.

After boarding the Canadian and getting settled in our sleeper which was to be an overnight trip we soon found out that a couple next to us were in a seat section that would be converted to beds at night. They seemed to stay in their seats during the day instead of meeting other people etc. After a while, as I walked by them still in their seats, I introduced myself as their neighbor. They seemed to light up, smiled and introduced themselves. Talking to them, they said they had been to Vancouver and even took a cruise to Alaska. Wow. It still seemed like they were not meeting people. To continue my visit with them, I said we are right around the corner from you and that my wife Jeri has MS and is in our sleeper right now. She would be delighted to meet you. Now I didn't mean right now but sometime during the day. Well, they kind of got up real fast and said, we want to meet her. Entering our sleeper, I told Jeri we have neighbors who came to see you. Jeri gave her big smile. They were an older couple and seemed very elated to meet her. As the couple's husband went right over to Jeri to talk with her, his wife stayed with me. In a little while, the husband pulled out of his pocket a silver chain of some sort and handed it to Jeri. I told him that wasn't necessary. His wife spoke up and said, "Leave him alone, he wants to do it."

The husband left his card with us which we did not read until we got home. It listed his name and that he was "President and C.E.O." of a large company! We did get a Christmas card from them.

I soon asked Jeri if she wanted to sit upstairs. Of course. We asked our attendant if he and another attendant could carry Jeri upstairs. He was excited and said he would find someone to help him but had to get approval from someone first. He came back shortly looking quite sad. My boss said we could not do this for safety reasons. Our attendant really felt bad and told us so. I had told him it had been done before on another train but he still could not get approval. I told our attendant that we know he wanted to do it and felt bad but since we had it done before with approval, we might have to break our record of never filing a complaint and send a letter to Via Rail. Now the attendant really felt bad. Our little discussion here was taking place in our room with the door open. As we talked, the Service Manager was walking by, saw us talking and asked if there was a problem. I told him we were trying to see if Jeri could be carried upstairs to sit and watch there for a while. That's all I said, nothing else. The Service Manager responded quickly and said, "Of course we can take her up. He told our attendant sitting there to go find another attendant and take Jeri upstairs!" It was so done. Our attendant was really relieved to be able to do this. Later as we reached Toronto, our attendant gave us a preprinted large card titled Canada's Classic Train Journey which also read, "In commemoration of your journey aboard Canada's legendary transcontinental train, the Canadian." It was dated September 21, 2001 and signed by Gordon Peck, Service Manager. On the back was a handwritten note written by Jeri's attendant still disturbed by his not being able to get approval until he actually did get approval. His message read:

Dear Jack & Jeri, Congratulations on your perfect "track" record. I wish you many more wonderful memories. Good Luck! Gilles Noel
P.S. Thank you for being such friendly folks.

Coming back on the train to Toronto from our second trip to Churchill, a stranger came into our sleeper and said to Jeri, "I watched you on the train to Winnipeg from Toronto a week ago and now I'm watching you again on a train going back to Toronto. Watching you both ways, I wanted to let you know that you have become my role model." She gave us her card with her picture and address on it and left.

When we got home we sent her a letter thanking her for complimenting Jeri. We said we didn't think Jeri would ever forget. In our letter to this girl, Patricia, we also told her, "We have told many people here at home about a surprise visit paid by a stranger – they have enjoyed our story immensely. Our Parish Priest couldn't believe it! He was overwhelmed by it."

The letter was returned by the post office as undeliverable. We never heard from her again.

On Friday, September 21, we arrived in Toronto at eight pm for a holiday of rest at The Royal York for two nights. Arriving late, we enjoyed the stay for two days there, even eating there and exploring this beautiful hotel. On a picture I took of Jeri, she was in our living room (our Royal York suite) on a couch out of her wheelchair with legs stretched out on a table liked she owned the place. Actually we had two old but beautiful large rooms. On Sunday, a bellhop came to take our five+ pieces of luggage and us across the avenue to

Union Station where he turned us over to a Red Cap. We gave him a fairly easy $20 tip. When you're "uptown" act like it.

One more comment about our special hotel, Royal York: Using this hotel several times, I remember our first trip with them. It was difficult to wheel Jeri into the lobby through the front doorway. We had to use a ramp and then a regular door got us through. Eventually, the door man said, we have a rather hidden side door that might work better for you. We tried it. There was nothing fancy like the front entrance, but it became our easy entrance leading to the main lobby. There was one more advantage, there was no doorman to tip.

A four hour train ride to Windsor took us right to Jodi and two girls, this time, named Katie and newest arrival, Jenny. When we arrived home in Bowling Green there was a sign on an outside wall that read:

Welcome Home Pap Pap & Gram! We missed you! Jenny, Katie, Dylan, Chloe, Sierra.

SAYONARA to our 19 day train adventure. We shall return.

ULTIMATE CHURCHILL TRIP #3 2003........
or "the 3rd time's our charm." Now this is the trip that broke, not the camel's back, but Jack's back with Jeri's help! It was also our first official dog sled ride!

Getting ready for our third trip to Churchill, I was reading a Churchill map which, like all maps, wrote the names and locations of places like restaurants. There was one marked "Polar Bear Cafeteria" shown on the outskirts of Churchill. I said to Jeri, "I don't think we ever ate at that one, let's plan on eating there." I didn't see how we missed that restaurant. Later before leaving for Churchill, I reread this map. Now I see why we didn't eat there. It was referring to where the bears ate which was the town garbage pit!

When we arrived in Windsor to start a train trip and to know which direction we were heading depended then whether we stayed overnight in Windsor or not. Going north, we stayed overnight in Windsor. Going west, we stayed overnight in Toronto. We left this up to Jodi, our "official" free boarding guide. This time Friday, September 12, 2003, we chose west to head eventually north. Jodi also had another new passenger, Kelly. They (Jodi, Katie, Jenny, Kelly) drove us to Windsor and helped load us aboard the train with the five large luggage bags plus a couple of small packages and sent us on a seventeen day trip back to Churchill via Toronto and Winnipeg.

We stayed at the Strathcona Hotel for one night in Toronto which was across from the train station where we also received the same Red Cap service with luggage service. With MS and in a wheelchair, we always had a lot of luggage with us and usually needed a Red Cap. In our case here, when the Red Cap reached our hotel across the street, I reached to give him a tip. I had planned to give him a twenty dollar bill. I usually would have my tips ready ahead of time, but we were tired and rushed to get in the hotel on this one. I gave him the tip and he looked and with a smile said, "Do you want to give me this much?" I said that it was fine and yes. He really appreciated my tip.

The next morning we checked into the train station where we were taking the "Canadian," (Silver and Blue) train to as far as Winnipeg. When the VIA Rail employee was checking people in and when he found out we were going to Churchill by way of Winnipeg, he introduced himself and said he would be on that train to Churchill also and would see us then.

The next day it was on to Winnipeg by sleeper in our "double-F" room.

Sitting nicely in our sleeper room, I was checking my Canadian money. I said to Jeri, "You're not going to believe this. I'm missing a fifty dollar bill. I gave the wrong color money bill to our Red Cap by mistake. It was a fifty dollar tip!" I thought I was giving him a twenty dollar bill. Because there was nothing we could do, we began laughing about it. We must have really "made" the Red Cap's day. Perhaps he really needed it.

We arrived at Winnipeg Sunday, September 14 around three pm. Since we had a five hour wait for our Churchill train, we decided to spend it in the nearby park we knew so well. The benches were all filled but another couple moved over for us to sit down. They asked where we were from and told us that they had retired as a bus driver and moved to the US, but then they had to move back to Canada because it was too expensive in the US.

It seemed that if Jeri did two things traveling, she was always well accepted and did not "scare" people away from not knowing her and why she was in a wheelchair. The two things for her to do: dress nicely and smile. She easily did both.

We then decided to walk through the park's building complex for eating, shopping etc which we were familiar with since we had been there before. At a fudge store inside, we could not pass it up and stopped for some homemade fudge to eat on the train. The fudge cost us $19.02. How's that for memory (actually I still have the receipt). The owner was the only one there when we stopped and found he was very nice especially to Jeri. I asked him if he could come out from behind his counter so we could take a picture. He left his apron on and stepped out for my camera to take our picture. I said, "No, I want to take a picture of you with Jeri." He was surprised and a bit excited. I took their picture together. He stood right by Jeri putting his arm on the wheelchair just above her. He seemed honored to be asked to do this and gave a nice smile for the picture. Jeri joined him in also giving a nice smile. There's a little more to this story, but it happened two years later when we returned to Winnipeg. Look for it then.

By now it was time to head back to our station. This is the one we had to use their large freight elevator every time we came and also in which they took care of our luggage without putting it in some locker or whatever. We left our luggage with this downstairs group many times. They never once charged us storage. One more way we were able to know them was this trip we were now on. As we arrived back at the station and went downstairs to their ticket windows and waiting lobby, we found only one employee at the ticket window and nobody in the waiting room. We were the only passengers waiting for the "Hudson Bay" train to take us to Churchill. Well, we were a little early. The train was to leave for Churchill around eight pm. There were still no other passengers at about seven pm. Finally we had company. A couple came in and went to the ticket window and came into the seating area, a little surprise to see only us. Introducing each other, the girl was a nurse and said she would be glad to help Jeri. They were going to Churchill also.

Now not so fast, another problem facing the train brought three attendants at 10 pm Sunday night to Jeri and me in the waiting room downstairs with their problem. Their problem? Now what trouble are we in? They marched right to us. The train was scheduled to leave at 2045 pm (8:45 pm). The three attendants had planned on getting Jeri on the train when they found the car door they were to get her on was blocked by the train parking too close to a pole or something. They could not get the lift to work there for Jeri's boarding. We could see their concern because the train was already late. They asked us if we had any suggestions.

Yes we do. We think our new wheelchair (our adult stroller travel wheelchair) will go through the coach car because it did work on another train. But they said, "That was a new train. This train had old cars." Continuing we said we could back Jeri up to the steps in another car, lift her up in her wheelchair to then go through the train to our seats in the car blocked. They didn't think it would work but we said try it because it will work. Reluctantly, they agreed. They did say rather than carrying Jeri up the steps, they would use the lift to get her in this other car. Two of the men went ahead to get Jeri's seat ready. It worked pushing Jeri through the train aisle that was barely large enough to get the wheelchair through. The two who went ahead to Jeri's seat could not believe it when they saw Jeri being pushed right down the aisle in her wheelchair to where they were. We were rewarded by the attendants by arranging two double seats to face each other plus one seat behind us for our luggage. Good job.

At that point, several other people got on the train with us so we all had coach or sleepers.

With Jeri in her new wheelchair we could get her easily into the Café Car which served limited meals because there would be fewer passengers on board. We liked this car. We were getting good meals and enjoying our few passengers aboard. I think we only had three or four train cars attached. We began to meet the other passengers plus our train crew of two engineers and three service people. This was our car. Welcome.

One more comment about Winnipeg station's employees which I had mentioned earlier how much they helped us and how we always met up with one employee who we saw just about every time we were there and how we waved to him and vice versa. We had never really met him but he looked so much like our nephew Bruce Lucki that we almost mistook him for such. We never learned his name until this trip to Churchill when we did meet him by name (Christian Duval) and mentioned to him that he looked like our nephew. Later at home we prepared a list of eight names to send to Via Rail which included Christian. Karl Coffen, Senior Director (Via Rail), wrote us a letter which included, "It is a pleasure to encounter a letter such as yours, expressing appreciation for services rendered...................Again, thank you for writing and for your generous comments. It would be our pleasure to serve you again soon."

On our train to Churchill, the Service Manager (and chief cook) was the person who had checked us in at Toronto. He came to greet us and welcomed us aboard. He now told us he was the Service Manager on that train. It was after midnight so there were no evening meals served. The next morning we found out that we were right next to the Cafe car which meant we could get Jeri there in her wheelchair. This was a real break – Jeri could enjoy all our meals there and further more have our Service Manager serve us.

For something to say after we finished eating and were talking with him, I told him about our (MY) tipping the Red Cap fifty dollars by not watching which color money I was using. We were laughing about it because by now we felt it was funny. He said, "Didn't he ask if you made a mistake? He must have known it was too much and should have told you so." I said the fellow tried to say it was too much but I said that it was ok, still thinking it was twenty dollars. Our Service Manager then said to Jeri and me that he wanted to do something for us. "I am treating both of you to supper tonight." We said no, that we were just telling a funny story. He insisted. Finally, we said ok but only one meal that we would split. We thanked him and Jeri and I had a very nice meal later. One complete dinner was more than enough for us. What a nice gesture out of nowhere. This was another fantastic train trip. I know Jeri made the Service Manager's days on that one.

During the day, because we had a coach seat, we could watch out our back window and take pictures. This idea came to a close when we stopped in Thompson a city 12 hours from Churchill. Three freight cars were attached to our car with supplies for Churchill. So much for our back window. As far as the three freight cars hooked up with us, I can remember the day when passenger trains were never allowed to have freight cars attached. Obviously up north needed this to be done.

Arriving near Churchill we again began looking in the distance for the low tops of Churchill to be seen. In the coach seat, Jeri could see much better. Getting Jeri off the train since they had no lift at the station was no problem. Either the train or station crew quickly took care of Jeri. As we waited for our transportation to our hotel, we saw Tony from the Gypsy unloading their supplies. From a distance, he managed to recognize us and waved. We recognized him also and waved back.

As we made it to Churchill again in our third trip here, we found our hotel's van waiting at the station for us. They would take our luggage back while we preferred just to walk back. It was at least two blocks away! We found our "own" hotel had our nice large room with places to keep food etc, waiting for us. I think they were the only ones knowing we were coming. And yes, our table was also waiting for us.

After getting settled in our room, we did find energy and time to go across the street to our base hangout, Penny's worldwide Arctic Trading Company. Later the next day, Wednesday, after we got settled in our hotel, we went to the Gypsy to see Tony and Helen. When we entered their restaurant, Helen asked where we had been, "they had expected us yesterday." Helen explained that when Tony came home after seeing us get off the train, he was excited saying, "Guess who is in town, Jeri and Jack!" This remark of remembrance really surprised us, as if we were celebrities. Jeri and I appreciated this and never forgot it.

Early on our first trips to Churchill, there seemed to be quite a few passengers getting off the train. Of course, it was the last stop, the end of the line. There also seemed that quite a few Churchill residents were waiting there to meet the train. Our friend Mark was usually there with his well used old bus to take visitors around Churchill. He was good at this and gave some good stories as he toured the town and outskirts. We learned later to ride his bus for the tour. Actually this ancient bus of his, fit right in with Churchill visitors. Tourists would climb into the bus right off the train and seemed to like it as they expected it would be going to Churchill. I know we liked Churchill getting off in the cold and rain. We would have been disappointed any other way. On the other side, we also found out our Churchill also had a beautiful sun.

Jeri and I soon learned something else about Churchill. The train would come three times a week. Why so many residents waiting? Why, because these were exciting "train days." Would you believe, Jeri and I, when we knew a train was coming in that day, we would walk to meet it. It really was train day. I'm sure many passengers thought we were residents. I'm sure also that at home when people asked us what we did, we would tell them. They could not understand "train days" and that we had such good times there, even in a wheelchair!

I hope we have the right time and facts on some of our activities that took place here but no matter, they did take place. My secretary and wife, Jeri, "decided" to take a wheelchair and let someone else keep track of our trips. She was our volunteer for all of our trips. I found many of our pre MS trips written up in her own shorthand but now she was not able to do so and really missed doing this. It was one more thing she loved to do that was taken from her. Now, she was here for a vacation. No she wasn't. She was here because she belonged here and enjoyed every minute of it. I was now secretary among other assignments by Jeri. We soon had Mark taking us out bear hunting and seeing the area. When he couldn't go, he would have someone else take us including Bill, who became a close friend as we got to know him better.

On one of our free tours in a car by our friend Mark, he stopped his car among scattered bushes and growth and had Jeri and I get out. He had a shovel and began looking around. Apparently he found what he was looking for because he began digging a hole wide enough to stick your arm in and deep enough to explore what was in it besides dirt and water. He then told me to stick my arm in it. I did so and about 16 inches down, I found it — ICE! I took this to mean the ice layer and that we were out on the tundra, still learning, of course. Jeri watched closely to what we were doing. This was a new one on her and a surprise. I'm sure she would have liked to stick her arm in it also. Mark filled the hole back up and we did some more traveling for whatever else we could find, especially a bear. We thanked Mark and also told him if he didn't let us pay on these trips, we would not go with him anymore. He mumbled, "We'll see" and changed the subject.

As time went on that day, we managed a stop in the Post Office where Fae, Janet and Corrina were on duty. We would always take pictures there, especially with Jeri and the crew. I think they allowed me to be on one picture.

Since the RCMP was next door to the Post Office, we made a second visit to say hello to them. They seemed to like our first visit so why not another. Entering their station, a large brown dog was sitting on their counter but never moved a bit when we came in. The lone policeman began telling us about their job including their biggest job was to find lost tourists. We noticed they had a number of patches from other police departments. We told him we knew a policeman well at home in which he said he would give us one of their patches to give to the one we knew and would we be able to get one of their patches in exchange. We did this.

Another favorite stop we made several times and were soon recognized was the town's Royal Bank, usually to sell them our travel checks as we needed cash. Today's trip was one of those visits. Our checks today were for $100.00 US which became $134.68 CAN. Amazingly, I mentioned that Toronto banks would not accept our checks, but here tiny Churchill gave us no problems at all. Interesting, when I went to the bank, I had to leave Jeri parked near the street away from the bank building. The area around this building was all gravel and no walkway from the street to this building. People going into this building would offer to help get Jeri in but we explained that she was fine where we left her. Did Jeri complain? Of course not! Again we didn't have to remind ourselves where we were. All of the cold, mud puddles, rain were all part of our adventure. We actually got use to it.

Back to Gypsy's for lunch, Mark came in and so did Bill. Besides living in his cabin outside Churchill, driving busses and cars for tourists, Bill was also a Customs Agent. More on Bill later. Helen had seen Cindy (secretary at elementary school) and told her we were here. Cindy came to Gypsy's where everyone made a big fuss over Jeri. We talked to Mark about more bear rides but also asked him about Jeri and me taking a dog sled ride! Talking to Helen, we asked her how her winters had been. She had something to say on that one: "One night we were asleep upstairs when we heard a bear trying to break our front window. We called the department that handled the bears to come get it." I then asked Helen if she was scared. She said, "OF COURSE!"

Later, we asked Bill (Jeri's special friend) a similar question we asked Helen, how his winters had been. We knew he lived outside Churchill in a log cabin. We'll let him answer our question. "One night when I was asleep I heard this bear at my door, which was locked and had a bar closing it also. The bear came right through the door! I had no choice but to shoot it, which I hated to do."

That same day, we received a call from the person that handled dog sled rides. He said, "He could arrange this for the next day, Thursday if we wanted to go." We said YES. He said be ready by a certain time and he would pick us up. Oh happy day. Or was it to be that way. Jeri was all for it. I was almost all for it!

It was then time to get ready for tomorrow's Wild West ride with six Huskies and a carriage.

In our room, we had an unexpected slide by Jeri, right out of her wheelchair! I was lifting her to get her into bed when she started sliding. Once in a slide, it is hard to stop someone who can't stop themselves. I had to guide her to the floor to land softly which worked. What didn't work was when I tried to lift her back on her chair, half way up, I felt a "muscle pull" and had to let her back down on the floor. I was able to get someone from the kitchen to help me lift her. No problem at all. We lifted her right into her bed. This "minor" "muscle pull" was not going to stop us. While it hurt a bit that night and next day, I had no good reason to stop. The next day the dog trainer knocked on our door. We were ready. Thinking he was going to take us to the dogs, he said, "The dogs are waiting for you right outside your door." Sure enough, the dogs and sled were out there waiting for us. The dogs were anxious to get going. The trainer lifted Jeri into a wooden seat with me next to her to hold her in. There were no safety belts. I think maybe we are in the wild west. Our "carriage" had wheels with the trainer standing right behind us with his hands on the ropes guiding each dog by their name as to where to go or where to stay with the other dogs. Of course, they

were tied together and to our riding seat. The dogs were in their glory jumping, running and going through water their way, they thought. The trainer continuously yelled at them. Meanwhile we were taking all of this in, watching the dogs and me hanging on to Jeri, not to hold only Jeri but rather both of us. It was a wonder we didn't bounce right out of our seat. We were also entertaining people on the streets or, because they were watching us but not cheering, they maybe were trying to get out of our way, as if we had any control over this. So we and the dogs had a delightful trip around Churchill and near the Bay. We actually had fun, an experience not done too often. It was then back to our "stall" at our front door. JERI, WE DID IT!

Well, yes we did it, first and last time, but we did it!

Well, the story wasn't quite over yet. It took four years before the FINALE. This ending happened in a hospital emergency room in Bowling Green. I had gone there for a kidney stone test. They decided to take an X-Ray. A doctor came in holding an X-Ray up high with both hands acting a bit nervous and saying to me, "You have a broken back!"

"I do?" I hesitated a few seconds. "Oh, I know what that is. It happened up in Churchill, Canada. The night before Jeri and I were scheduled to take a Dog Sled Ride, Jeri slid out of her chair onto the floor. When I tried to lift her back on the wheelchair, half way up I thought I had pulled a muscle and had to put her back down. So that's what it was and not a muscle pull!" Hesitation and to the doctor, "Don't do anything, no surgery, nothing. It's fine. Leave it alone." End of a neat FINALE!

We still had several days left in Churchill with nothing to do! Us with nothing to do, I don't think so. We had several visits to make in any order we wanted over Friday to Tuesday, our train day to leave. Putting them in some kind of order, let's start with visiting Cindy at the elementary school. On our way by way of the connecting walk that took us to the elementary school, we almost had a severe accident. This walk to get to the school had walks on both sides of this area. On the side we were walking and about half way to the school, there was a step at that point that I did not see until the very last second and stopped Jeri in time from going down the step. This step surprised me. Apparently it was to even the walks up. No harm done but a little scary for me, the driver without a license. I don't like to criticize such unimportant topics like this but I do hope people in wheelchairs or their "drivers" learn how dangerous wheelchairs can be and how important it is for drivers to pay attention when a wheelchair is in their hands. I keep learning this from our accidents.

Back to the good part. We found Cindy's office by walking through a covered overpass (Laverendrye Ave) into a different building. The first thing we saw was a bushel of fresh beautiful apples, not fake, but real sitting on Cindy's desk. She told us how she was using the apples. As each student made an appearance, she gave them an apple! But so much for that. It was obvious that Cindy was enjoying her part in education as we could tell talking to her. We were glad also to meet the principal, another fine person. We appreciated both of them for seeing Jeri and me. We were very impressed again because they were so far north, who would believe what they were doing so well unless you saw them. I should say we visited with them partially – Cindy was kept quite busy answering student questions and giving out apples. We saw more of Cindy later at church with a very nice husband whom we met.

When we left Cindy, we noticed a lot of stones and rocks around the building across the street from where we were. We walked to them and realized that they were from this area. They didn't look precious but, as we had done in many travel trips, we picked up a few stones and rocks to take home. To identify them later as being found in the area near the Arctic Circle became another souvenir for us. We probably still have them somewhere!

Another first stop we met here in meeting people was to visit the Town Government Offices in the Town Centre Complex. As we found where they were in this building, we quietly opened their office door and stopped at a counter. We explained to the only person there, a very pleasant lady, who we were and we just wanted to meet the people working there. "She said she knew who we were, that she had seen us around town." After a little talk, this girl said wait a minute and walked over to a filing cabinet and brought something back for us, two pins that read "The Town of Churchill 3 YEARS SERVICE." What a splendid surprise for Jeri and me! Somehow she even knew this was our third time in Churchill. We still have the pins.

From this visit, we headed to Gypsy's once again to have dinner there. Outside the restaurant was a rather large sailboat with the name GYPSY'S underlined on the sail. The name even appeared on the front of the boat. Now where did they get this boat and where would you find a place to sail it in Churchill? We asked the next person coming out of Gypsy's to take Jeri's and my picture in the front of the boat. Anyway, interesting things happen in Churchill – that's why we liked being there. Churchill was a great diversion for Jeri's ignoring MS!

On a Saturday evening we decided to take Penny up on inviting us trying out her restaurant in the downstairs under the main floor of the Arctic Trading Company. We didn't know she even had one. This turned into a little mystery walk for us. Entering through the main floor which was closed we heard a lot of noise downstairs. We found no Penny but did find the way downstairs. How with Jeri? I have no idea. It's a mystery to me also. But we did it. We heard a lot of laughter. Were we sure there was something down there for us? Trusting Penny, we were trying to please her anxiety to get us to try it. The laughing was a party going on loud and cheerful. It was an all girls affair including "our" Post Office gang. Were real drinks available? If so, I'm sure Jeri had something when we sat down at a vacant table. We enjoyed watching their fun time, our having an excellent meal and one drink for Jeri, wine, and coffee for our little boy Jack. Did this dining crew recognize us? They sure did and did not hide their party. We were glad we came. So this is what a group of girls do on a Saturday night in Churchill. Good for them.

Sunday Jeri and I headed for Church. We knew the Bishop was up north visiting church "settlements" and Churchill was without a parish priest at the time, in which case they had no one to say Mass that Sunday. So this Sunday with the Bishop gone, was probably the one we found Cindy on the altar saying "Mass." Well, part of the Mass because one part the "consecration" was not allowed for her to do. Other than that, Cindy did a beautiful "Mass". Afterwards, I complimented her with saying, "You're making a believer out of me in that maybe women should be allowed to do this more."

After Mass, we were personally invited to have coffee with everyone. Now we knew for sure we were among friends.

To us, we liked this Church, our little Cathedral, very much. The size was just right for the number of people attending. It was perfect even though they had no heat or air condition. I know we told people about sitting in "handicapped" sections which we usually disliked and avoided them to choose where we wanted to be in church. We always felt it was our choice. Jeri had more than enough "privileges" taken from her.

Now we had been in this one in Churchill on other trips but this time we did a little checking. Going up the isle on the right side, the second pew had an open area, obviously for wheelchairs. What we liked about it was NO Handicapped sign was put on it. We chose to sit there like anyone else in church. It may sound being stubborn but try it and see what you can do but not allowed to do in places like a church (theatres and such need such sections) which should be the delight of doing or not doing, your choice. To make our church visit complete, our guitar player again welcomed us for the third time.

Not sure what exactly we did the rest of that day but we did not go back to our hotel. This being a Sunday, we would visit whoever was available although residents seemed to stick to their homes that day. We would continue our hiking around and I think we went back to the Town Centre to explore that facility again including using a bay window facing Hudson Bay to relax and watch for bears. It was back there that a sign was posted to beware of the bears. It was also the area that our six Huskies took us.

We still had one more building we wanted to see before we left. This one will knock you out. It was the hospital connected to the Centre. As we walked in, well Jeri rode in, which perhaps the one man (doctor?) thought Jeri was an injured casualty I was bringing in. He greeted us and seemed to know us. He, too, had seen us around. Actually this hospital was rather large and up to date. He showed us around and said that they did do minor surgery there but for major cases, they would fly the patient back to Winnipeg. Strange but again it was an interesting tour for us.

Jeri and I had heard about the military being stationed in Churchill years ago. In fact there were still buildings there scattered around that we would see looking for bears. Their age showed and looked abandoned for a long time. We learned a few stories about these buildings and that one was being used currently for a Northern Studies Center. One story we heard was when a large Canadian military force was stationed for several years and when they left, a lot of valuable property was left behind.

Another story was about the military being stationed here. It went like this. A group of the military was to be transferred to Churchill. Apparently a small group was to explore ahead of time as to selecting a good location to build a permanent camp. They met with a Churchill "executive" about the land they chose and asked this executive in charge different questions. They liked his answers and bought it and built the camp needed. After this unit came in total and moved in, they had, to them, a serious problem. They arranged to meet with the person that transferred the property to them and were quite upset. What was the problem? "The officer in charge asked why they sold him this property, that they didn't know there were bears here, and that the bears were a real nuisance and dangerous. Why didn't you tell us you had bears here?" The person from Churchill simply said, "You didn't ask me."

An important comment here about the above and other stories: For what we knew, such stories were always accurate and brought interesting stories to a party involved in listening and enjoying such stories. They were printed here in this book not to "show off" but to help a very important lady we knew to be Jeri. It worked and did wonders. Try it yourself to help those without.

VISITING "OUR NEW" TRAIN STATION

Renovating the train station in Churchill was a little different as one would find in other areas. There were few renovations being done here in Churchill, sort of one by one. When we returned to Churchill every two years, we would usually see something was renovated, maybe one maybe none. The train station's renovation began before we arrived this trip. A lot had been done. We thought we would see the finished product. As we were getting ready to head home, we asked the workmen if the station would be finished before we left. Our answer came from one of the few workers who said, "No, you will just have to come back." We came back!

While watching the renovation taking place, we noticed something had been added to the station. A Parks Canada small museum was a transfer from the bank building to the train station. We wondered what had happened to it because we had gone through it before. This museum was built with the history area in mind with local exhibits etc. When we visited this museum before this trip, Jeri and I were asked to sign in at their entrance as to where we were from. To sign the registry, they handed us a foot long feather attached to a long pen to sign their registry. Now it seemed like a native museum from long ago. They let us keep the pen and feather. It is now connected on our living room wall to a Churchill picture. I don't think any visitor ever saw it. Oh well, so much for our only Churchill history museum.

As time turned to Tuesday, we turned a little disappointed. Like it or not, our train leaves tonight. We must be on it or wait for the next train which would be Thursday. If we didn't have train and hotel reservations for our trip home, I'm sure we would have stayed. To play it safe, I did not ask Jeri. Her "let's" would have committed me to a lot of travel adjustments.

We did make one more stop before leaving. We needed some more Canadian money. So it was off to the Royal Bank. By now we seemed to be recognized by the bank meaning we had no problem cashing checks. We would wait in line like everyone else. We cashed TRAVELLERS CHEQUE(S) in the amount of $200.00 in U.S. dollars for Canadian dollars. No fee was charged by the bank and they issued us at the exchange rate a total of $267.44 in Canadian money. Not bad for two poor visitors from Ohio learning and having fun!

Leaving Churchill: I would guess that we traveled five miles walking each day whether it was cold, raining (no snow yet) or a little sunlight and heat. They were indeed adventure days, perhaps never to happen again. Now whose idea was this anyway? If you say Jeri, I'm going to make her walk from here on. Actually, she would love it.

The same couple we came to Churchill with showed up to get on the same train we were on going back to Winnipeg. This we never expected and were glad to see them again.

We had also mentioned that strange things happened on, at least, our trains, every one of them. Well nothing new will happen on this one we were about to get on. We've had enough strange things happening on our trips – the odds are now on our side.

We were to leave at ten pm. It was now near midnight. Here we go again. Now what happened?

As we waited, all of a sudden a group of at least 20 high school students came into our train waiting room laughing, cutting up, having fun while we held our waiting room seat before they take it. Now this was no normal group of boys and you would not see this except in this wild area of hungry bears. They were dressed completely in hockey uniforms, helmets, flag poles (or were they hockey sticks), carrying ice skates and making themselves at home. Why were they doing this? They were on their way to play another school in hockey! Train was the only way they could get to their game. That was really a good answer. It was their only way to play hockey games with others.

We actually enjoyed this and watching all these students this far north having a great time by their own doing.

We moved in to our coach seat where it was quiet. The hockey team must have had their own car. We never saw where they were playing or getting off.

Going home was just a reverse of how we came, including Jeri causing problems with the engineer in Winnipeg. Actually, she never caused any problems on this Churchill train because Winnipeg was the end of the line. The train coming from Vancouver for us would likely be the lucky one to stop by a pole and block Jeri's wheelchair from boarding their train. Naw no problem. They probably knew it was Jeri again. An example of this is written in more detail under the section **"JERI HOLDING UP TRAINS."** It was repeated several times as we passed through or boarded at Winnipeg.

We arrived in Toronto Friday, September 26 and took a nice two days "off" at the Strathcona Hotel. After leaving Toronto on a 1st Class car and heading for Windsor, we soon looked out our back door. By golly, it was an Amtrak train following us right behind us. As we stopped, it stopped, almost touching us. Now Amtrak had trains on the west coast and east coast but none in this area. How did they do that? "I don't know!" and "We don't care." Waiting in Windsor was our Jodi, Katie, Jenny and Kelly.

From home to home was our 17 days latest adventure. We lost no luggage, no wheelchair and no Jeri. That is what is called a "safe and happy trip."

ULTIMATE CHURCHILL TRIP #4 2005 came to be not our last trip (we were in Halifax in 2006) but it was **our last trip to Churchill**.

We rarely mentioned what we took on our train trips. We did mention a little about how many pieces of luggage we took, anywhere from four pieces to six not counting small pieces of necessary carryon bags to have nearby at all times. Our last 17 day trip to Churchill in the far north required special attention to the cold we would face – to be happy! I would think that any person that has traveled or would like to travel and is a bit handicapped would know a minimum amount of baggage not wanted but needed. Here's a partial list of Jeri's donkey (Jack) of what we took with us – all Jeri's needs, we would hope:

Slacks	6 heavy, 7 light
Shorts	3 (green, red, yellow)
Tops	16 mixed with long/short sleeves
Dresses	2 (green and blue)
Briefs	68 pairs
Shoes	3 pairs
Socks	15 pairs (heavy, light)
Sweaters	4 (one w/hood, 1 heavy, 2 dress)
Boots	No room
Gloves, hat	1 of each
Jackets	1 (a heavy BGSU)

12 cans Ensure
8 cans prune juice
6 cans baby food
6 bottles cranberry juice

Topped with a 10 pound suction machine we never used.

It was Friday August 26, 2005 at two pm when we left Windsor, arriving four hours later to stay at the Strathcona Hotel once again in Toronto. Our trip from here was our usual routine – sleeper to Winnipeg, economy (coach) to Churchill and we are at our destination, a period of four days and three trains to get to Churchill.

On our sleeper to Winnipeg, we eloped up stairs to the dome which was empty. Well not quite. Someone took our picture. I had my arm around Jeri and was holding a straw in her mouth to drink I don't know what. Probably wine! She had a funny look about her and raised her eyes in her well known surprise look when "whoever" was taking our picture.

The only idea we had planned took place when we stopped at Winnipeg. Before leaving Bowling Green, I told Jeri, wouldn't it be funny if we found the picture of our fudge owner in Winnipeg and surprised him with his picture that was taken two years ago. Jeri liked the idea. We found the picture and took it with us. We realized we would probably never find him at the fudge counter even if it was still there. Well, he was at his fudge counter! We stopped and looked at the fudge he had and to see if he would recognize us. He did not recognize us. I handed him "his" picture. He stared, looked odd and did not recognize the picture except he knew it seemed to be him. He then realized that it was him and began laughing with us. That had to be his surprise of the day. He knew it was him but how could this be? How did we get his picture? I think he then realized that he did remember us and that we took his picture. So many people remembered Jeri but I know being in a wheelchair helped. Add a smile and people remembered. I don't think bears paid any attention to Jeri, wheelchair or not. They were always after three things – seals, sleeping and playing with the dogs.

In Winnipeg we went downstairs in our favorite freight elevator to wait for our Churchill train. We were the only ones there. Two attendants approached us looking a little sad. Now what happened? They asked us "if we were aware that there was no lift at Churchill to get Jeri off." Relieved to ourselves and the attendants, we told them we were well aware of no lift but never had any problems there getting Jeri off the train, thanks anyway. It's nice to learn about traveling and nicer when you can use your experience like we did on this trip.

Probably the only worthwhile discussion on our train to Churchill was a train stop at "The Pas" which we never heard of and weren't interested anyway. Now each time we would go to Churchill and return, the train would stop here for about an hour. All we could see was the small train station, forests and nothing else. It eventually caught our interest because on every trip each way, at least a hundred passengers in a loud and joyful manner came out of nowhere and, loaded down with baggage, would board the train, find a seat and put their belongings somewhere. When this happened at night, we would be asleep and seemed to wake up in some kind of panic going on. The train used their whole hour to settle everyone down to a nice evening of a little bit of quite. It worked. We later learned that at the Pas, there was a very attractive summer area for camping, living etc to be found after a long walk from the train.

So what did we have planned for Churchill? Actually, nothing. We were hoping they had something small planned for us even if were just "hello." Well that would not work because only the hotel and Penny knew we were coming. So they could "spread" the word that the Schroeders were coming. That doesn't work either. They are a busy place with lots of visitors this time of year. The Schroeders can wait on themselves.

The day before Churchill, we had someone take our picture in the dining car which showed Jeri with a pretty large plate with a pretty large selection of pretty good looking food. What MS? It looked like I had a hamburger. It was so pleasant for Jeri and me to be able to get her to the dining car because of her new wheelchair. We could now enjoy our food, other passengers, the crew (even the cook) and especially for Jeri just being one's self to feel you belong on the train.

The train dining cars were the most relaxing place to be three times a day. Having meals brought to your room or seat was not very comfortable but sometimes one would have no choice. It worked but not quite as well. I remembered, and I'm sure Jeri did too, watching passengers going through the cars (including sleepers) on their way to "train call," always meeting others going the same way, in an unbelievable "mood" of smiling, talking etc. and sitting with other passengers to dine with they never knew. Now that is train traveling.

As mentioned before in other trips to Churchill, we were always excited seeing the flat lands, some pine trees, large lakes surrounding the area and then the low skyline of Churchill appearing to the right of our train. It would look like we were still in the US except there were no high buildings to see and no car/trucks etc to mingle with on your way in and, better still, only a few vehicles in town. Gee, why didn't we bring a four wheeler with us or a snow mobile for the snow soon to come. We then could have stayed longer. Jeri would have agreed to that! Well, we did have a wheelchair with us. By the way, speaking of wheelchairs, in our four trips there we only saw ONE other wheelchair there. It was used by a man staying in our hotel. We only saw him once from a distance and never again. This surprised us because Churchill seemed like a good place to visit in a wheelchair.

Arriving in Churchill and with the crew carrying Jeri off the train, we were immediately met by "our" Penny. A bit excited, she quickly welcomed us and said, "You must come to a reception we are having for the Bishop Saturday." We said we would be there. Jeri was really excited now. No planning was needed. I later asked Penny if they were taking up a collection to buy something for the Bishop. She said they talked about it but decided they would all bring food and set up tables etc at the Eskimo Museum in a large room. Meanwhile, we would stay out of their way so they could get things ready for Saturday knowing there was no way we could cook or help. We did have one idea that we were able to do after the reception was well underway. We will come back to this unexpected surprise later in the week. Meanwhile, what did we find to do?

Let us interrupt this after arriving by train to Churchill for the fourth time with a challenge question that bothered me on each train trip there. When we would leave this train with all its cars intact, their pulling engine was always first. When we would see the train later, the pulling engine would be first on the other end of their train on the same track they came in on. How did they do this when only one track at Churchill was for Via Rail? The other tracks apparently were used for the Port's Sea North Dock. I later found a map with a siding about three miles outside Churchill in which they could turn the train around using several switches and by backing and forwarding to maneuver the engine upfront again. I'm glad you "enjoyed" this little story. Now you know one more way of entertaining yourself on a train ride! A similar story about train switching was written in our trip to Prince Rupert, 1998.

After we checked into our hotel and headed for our breakfast dining room, we found a little renovation had been done which was very nice. We even found a lighted candle on our table. In any case, we felt at home once more.

Coming here on Tuesday, August 30, we began to face some colder days here beginning Thursday September I. We were not bothered. We just dressed a little warmer and continued our fourth visit to Churchill. We still went bear hunting and we also did more traveling in the busses south and north of Churchill. Of course we couldn't very well go east because of a "small" Hudson Bay and we couldn't very well go west because of the Churchill River. Add a lot of marshes and ponds and you become restricted. Top all of this and be ready to spot a beautiful white bear who might just be watching you. This was his/her homeland, so be careful who you talk with and don't "carry sandwiches in your pockets!" The bears were not interested in playing catch with you. Maybe a bit of running and finding food but nothing more exciting. They were king of this area and were present to prove it.

In addition to buying things from Penny and her fantastic living museum and the Eskimo Museum, we found some good printed signs at Gypsy's to take home which read **"POLAR BEAR ALERT** (a large footprint of a bear) **STOP DON'T WALK IN THIS AREA."**

We were now ready to get a tour bus to go happy hunting for many things we had not seen yet plus some we had seen. We always rode in these buses up next to the driver where the wheelchair was placed for Jeri to see out the side and front and where I would sit in the front seat near her. It worked well. On this trip, as usual, we were the only passengers. Included were visits to historical sites such as Cape Merry where we met the two ladies from the train we came on. We had to leave Jeri in the bus because the trail of rocks to get to the Cape was too difficult to get Jeri to it.

This was the second time we covered the northern end of the peninsula slowly and interesting. It was incredible. We had taken a brief tour of this area and the Port in Churchill Trip #2. Coming into this section there were many large storage oil and gasoline tanks. At a distance from the tanks were the facilities of the Port of Churchill, a sea port that apparently was considered the second largest in Canada. A seaport in the middle of Canada, I don't think so. But there it was, better take a few pictures. I roughly checked a map to see where it was really located – it looked like it was straight up north from Minnesota which put it half way across the US. As we rode around all of this, it didn't seem possible - all of this in an isolated section of the country, near the Arctic Circle. It indeed was worth seeing. We understood we could take a tour of the very large grain elevator but we learned this too late as our trip was about over. Also included here were four "berths" of unloading and loading trains for receiving and exporting goods from ocean vessels in and out of this port. Now we know why there was another train track along side of the one we used.

Our bus driver finished this part of our tour by way of heading back to other sites on our way back to "town." This including driving past the Bear Prison (nothing exciting going on there, at least outside the prison) and also along the Bay area where we again saw this freighter abandoned off shore, but still dug in. This was explained a little earlier but as said we could see people walking out to it probably because of the tide. We couldn't take Jeri out because of the wheelchair. In normal times, she and I would certainly have walked out to it. On this trip which included looking for bears we did not find any.

It should be remembered that bears are hard to find this time of year. Now when you do find one, then you did it. You found a bear. You can go home bragging. Visitors are very disappointed when they have to leave without seeing one. After Jeri and I found our first bear we were very glad. The pressure to find at least one was all you needed. Now you can relax and see all the goodies of Churchill.

On one cold afternoon when we left Gypsy, we were undecided where to go next. We found ourselves under a street sign that pointed to the Eskimo Museum. I asked Jeri if she wanted to go back there for a while. Jeri and her "let's" sometimes would get me in trouble! There is a slight hill from where we were and a long couple of blocks to the museum. It was one of our coldest days ever being in Churchill and very windy. I said to Jeri, "We can make it there." I will push faster in the street because we were the only ones there. When we got to the museum, the wind and cold was devastating. I said, "The heck with the museum, we're heading for our hotel ROOM." Now we were about one mile from our hotel. Absolutely no one was in sight. One mile it was. We will make it. Jeri was so covered with warm clothes I could barely see her eyes. Was she still in there? Strange, we were not too concern, we knew our way. No help needed! This "walk" did happen but remember this was one reason for us to go to Churchill. Go south to Florida? No adventure there (to us). Anyone can do that. Jeri in a wheelchair helpless did what we wanted to do and we did it.

Saturday became the day of celebrating the Bishop's reception plus a choice of brunch you would not

 believe provided by those attending, no speeches, a nicely dressed group of about 40 people many of whom we had never met until now – a real pleasure of enjoyment for all and taking place in, of all places, an Eskimo Museum. This was probably the nicest of all our invites anywhere we went.

To me seeing Jeri sitting next to the Bishop of Churchill enjoying the feast was simply unreal. Come to think of it, after getting Jeri her delicious choice of food and helping her by feeding her, I had forgotten to get any for myself. Well, I could care less about that.

I had never seen such a nice get together with everyone, including a few children, enjoying each other. I knew what to do then. I took out my camera.

We had to have pictures of all of this. However, I was a little too uneasy to go around each table and taking their pictures. Ah, Cindy, my favorite woman handling a school and helping say Mass was my answer. "Cindy, would you mind taking my camera and taking pictures of each table?" "Of course not, I would love to do that." I don't think any other pictures were taken, probably because I saw no cameras. After our celebration was pretty well over, I thanked Cindy and told her when we get home I will have the pictures developed and send you a copy of each to pass out to everyone here.

We had prints made and sent them to Cindy. She returned a letter to us, "saying everyone was so delighted to get pictures of our reception." So thankfully, our little idea did allow us to get involved in this reception.

Sunday became another separate day with more happenings. It would be our last Sunday ever in Churchill which, of course, we did not know. For some reason, it was an extra special adventure that day beginning with us getting out of bed, having breakfast (wait a second, they were closed on Sundays), walking the mile to Church and being surprised to meet the new pastor named Fr Albert. Needless to say, Jeri became his "idol" the way he took to Jeri starting with when we came out of Church and it was pouring down rain. Waiting for it to stop, Fr Albert said to Jeri, "Wait right here." He ran swiftly to get an umbrella. He could not find one. He did find a large piece of plastic and he came running back to cover Jeri and then wanted to get a car to take her back to the hotel. We said, we can get there faster than trying to get Jeri in a car. Later that day, it was dry and we walked back to the Bishop's home to return Fr's handmade umbrella. He came out to talk with Jeri, her in a wheelchair and he sitting on the ground next to her. He even took his "baseball" cap off to do so. Making this up? I don't think so. I have a picture to prove it. Hopefully it will be in this book.

The afternoon was beautiful, sunny, a bit chilly but no snow nor rain. It was time to find Mark or his crew to take us on another land cruise. A large white bus came to pick us up. Again there were no other passengers but a pleasant driver, who would spend several hours with us. First was to cover the northern peninsula to watch the whales. Our bus took us right to the shore of Hudson Bay where the beluga white whales, hundreds of them, were swarming in the Churchill River and the Hudson Bay constantly going high in the air and back under water, some even coming closer to the shore. This was the time of year the whales would come to migrate near the river. Jeri and I watched from the shore and took pictures. Now Jeri and I had seen whales other places but white ones? Never! As we watched from the shore, they were beautiful sights to watch – the whiteness of the whales made a difference. Why didn't we pay for a boat ride out to see them closer? We had understood that on a boat being used, they had a way of entering something in the water to listen to the whales! Wow!

After the whales, we went closely around the dock area again. As we were getting to explore this area better, our driver received an alert call on her telephone from another bus that was touring people. A bear was sighted on the southern end of Churchill. We were able to listen to this call and told our driver to get to the bear before it leaves. We were about five miles away and could not tell the bear to wait for us. Even Jeri's not that good. It certainly woke both of us up quickly and excited. When we spotted another white bus, we were almost there and slowly and quietly moved closer to the other stopped bus trying not to scare the bear if there was one. There was one in the distance coming towards us about a hundred yards away. The bear stopped moving. Both busses waited about 30 minutes but then had to move on. So Jeri and I had another chance to watch a bear for a while. We did take some pictures.

A rather interesting happening is when white bears mingle around white rocks on flat grounds like we were watching, it is very hard to identify which rock is a bear, if any. You actually wait until a bear moves and begins slowly walking away from the rocks. If nothing moves, then there's no bear or a sleeping one. Both the rocks and bears looked the same until one walked!

We continued our bussing and came along one of "our" Husky's training grounds. This time Jeri wanted me to get out and pet one. Sez who? Sez Jeri, ok then. I went up to the nearest dog, got behind him, bent over and held my hand under his chin which was facing right up to me and seemed to say "Thank you." The driver took my picture to make sure I would not make it up.

MONDAY, SEPTEMBER 5, 2005 a beginning of saying "Goodbye" to so many good people and leaving so many friendships behind. Four trips of 8 days stays each over a period of seven years going north to near the Arctic Circle in a wheelchair will never be understood. It was the favorite of all of our trips, unrehearsed, unplanned, unbelievable and never forgotten. How could this be?

It was time to try and enjoy our leavings and perhaps tack on a few more surprises. We had to take another of Mark's bus trips around these "forsaken sacred polar bear grounds" not to say Goodbye but just to see if we could see one more bear. We saw none. We did take a picture of Jeri with her last tour driver provided by Mark. We had lunch at Gypsy's where Tony and Helen posed behind us sitting at our table eating and where someone took our picture. I think we made two pretty good looking couples. I was even smiling! There were three post office employees on duty when we stopped to see them and of course had our picture taken with them by someone. Then came our Bill into the post office and Jeri smiling the best I ever saw her do. Bill's beginning hugging Jeri left Jeri not missing a smile. He was hugging her like he wasn't going to let her get away. I was taking pictures at this time and I told him to go ahead, it is ok, kiss Jeri. He did and a picture was taken. I wonder if Jeri and Bill were playing Post Office! Naw, probably neither one knew that "game." On second thought, they seemed to know what they were doing. Unlike Jeri, she did not turn her head. WOW. I'm jealous. I'll talk to her later. Bill had been driving tourists around the whole time we were there. As he left Jeri he told her, "When you come back the next time I will drive you around." He was quite a guy.

As the next day was Tuesday, train day, we refused to just go away. We had a few other things to do besides packing and catching a train.

We spent time with Penny at the Arctic Trading Company as I posed with her and Jeri. Two nicest people (Penny and Jeri) we would never forget. But then, everyone in Churchill seemed to be that way as we got to know them.

Jeri decided to see if we still could take the boat ride to see the whales. Great idea! We shall try. We headed right to the home of the boat owner who did his business out of his home. He was not there when his wife answered the door. We asked her. She said, "Of course there is time and you would go with my husband on the boat before you leave. She said it would cost $50 each." No problem. We were so glad we could do this since we heard so much about it. I paid her the $100 dollars and she said meet us here at three o'clock this afternoon. We thanked her and walked away like we were walking on air, excited. Well Jeri still had to stay with her wheelchair but no matter we were going to end this with a wild visit to the whales.

We were back at three, the husband answered the door but was not smiling. Oh oh! Now what did we do wrong? He said, "He was really sorry but he felt he should not take Jeri out on the boat that day, the waves were too high and dangerous. Since we have no way of protecting Jeri and did not want her to get hurt, it would be better not to take her today." We could understand and appreciate what he was saying. I was kind of proud of him because a lot of people would have taken Jeri out without considering any danger for Jeri. He handed our $100 dollars back. I give him credit once more because in Churchill, I'm sure this money would have meant a lot to this family. So there are many people who do good things in spite of personal need.

The zero hour approached us. Were we packed and ready to take a train ride? We were always ready to take a train ride but this one leaving Churchill was not too exciting. Our hotel took our luggage to the station while we enjoyed our last long walk to "all aboard," the traditional announcement that the train was ready and you better get aboard.

I wheeled Jeri to our economy (coach) seats and found we had two seats we could use – one double seat facing the other double seat. This was a big help for a two night stay. Well, while Jeri had only a half smile, she looked very comfortable stretched out to put her legs on the seat facing her, had her shoes off, was wearing my warm sweater and wearing her sun glasses. At eleven o'clock at night, wearing sun glasses!

Just before the train pulled out, we had a visitor, a real surprise visitor. Our Penny came to see us leave. That one put a smile on Jeri and me. She sat with us for a while until it was time for her to leave. So now it was time to head back to Winnipeg where we would transfer to a sleeper on its way to Toronto. We were glad to know Jodi and her three girls (Katie, Jenny and Kelly) would meet us in Toronto where we would spend two nights in the Delta Chelsea Hotel which was the one with excellent facilities for children. So now there were six of us boarding the train to Windsor.

Another surprise happened on our train to Windsor.

Train back to Windsor and Jenny... On a train from Toronto back to Windsor with Jodi and her three daughters with us – they use to take us to the station and then pick us up when we returned – this time they were with us on the train. Jenny was sitting on my lap as we neared Windsor. I said to Jenny, "Oh. Let's look out to see if Jenny is waiting for us." I leaned over with her to look ahead of the train. Jenny very seriously looked at me, pointed to herself and said, "I'm right here grand pap." (Jenny)

A FITTING MEASUREMENT OF FOUR TRIPS TO CHURCHILL BY TWO UNAUTHORIZED ADVENTURERS WHO DIDN'T KNOW THE DIFFERENCE BETWEEN A "POLAR BEAR CAFETERIA" AND A "GARBAGE PIT" should not be the ones to explain their experience of getting to love Churchill. I shall speak for Jeri as how we became Churchill "pioneers" to join the Town of Churchill as we saw it.

Our first year, we came as **"TOURISTS"**
Our second year, we were **"VISITORS"**
Our third year, we were **"FRIENDS"**
Our fourth year, we were treated as
"PART TIME RESIDENTS"

We had one more way of looking at Churchill:
"What took us so long to decide to go to Churchill" and **"Why didn't we stay longer?"**

UNTITLED -- A LAST AND A BEGINNING

JERI'S DOWN BUT NOT OUT

An unexpected emergency to get Jeri to our local hospital and a transfer to a Rehab...............

On March 10, 2007, we had a family dinner at a restaurant. I had just given Jeri some coffee and apple sauce when Jodi noticed something wrong. Jeri seemed to be choking but could not talk. An ambulance came and took her to our local hospital. She was choking. They found apple sauce in her lungs. It was later decided that she should be put on a ventilator, at least temporary. I wasn't too keen on this until one of the nurses at the hospital said, "Don't put Jeri through this again." Jeri recovered pretty well but was kept on the ventilator. It was recommended that we have Jeri enter a Rehab that was very good at weaning patients off of the ventilator. Reluctantly we agreed when we understood that this was the best way to go to get Jeri off of the ventilator. Her next stop was 3/23/07 and began a period of recovery at a Rehab. At first we thought it was working and we thought we made a good decision. Several weeks later, we were not pleased with their trying to wean Jeri off her vent. Several times when I arrived to visit Jeri, she was on a regular vent "numbering system" and not weaning her off at all. Several times then, when I came to visit Jeri, I would ask the nurse why Jeri wasn't on the system to help wean her off. They would say, "Oh, do you want her on that, I'll put her on it right away." I thought that was what she was there for. Jeri was not acting herself, was putting too much weight on and simply was not herself. Jami and I driving home one evening decided we would take her home. The next day we told her. She instantly became Jeri. The great part was, she was still with us and still smiling.

After deciding to leave Rehab, bringing Jeri home brought some new equipment to learn .... including a ventilator.

Before bringing Jeri home, we were given classes and practice on the vent. Difficult but we did good enough to "pass." Jami and Jodi did great. I came in third. This did bring along some new problems but so what? The Rehab doctor commented "if any family can do it, I think you can." He gave the approval that we could take her home. It was 5-15-07 and we were thrilled to have Jeri with us again. We were told we could continue the weaning at home.

I'm adding a new section **WHAT WENT RIGHT – AMBULANCE STYLE**..........needing an ambulance every time just to visit a doctor or whatever, sounds unexciting.

When Jeri was brought home in an ambulance from Rehab with a ventilator attached, this was a new MS game for us. We wanted her home. To be home, and have to go in an ambulance, just to see a doctor? Jeri showed no signs of anxiety. She had to be concerned but in these cases she would wait and see. Jeri's wait produced some unexpected results.

Our first call for a private (not emergency) ambulance brought us a crew that quickly eliminated any bad concerns. They were great. They did everything well, moving Jeri in and out of the ambulance, taking her right to the doctor's office and staying with her. One visit they even helped the doctor changing her trach. We were able to get this crew several times. Other crews were good too. Jeri seemed very relieved. They would kid her, talk to her and were very careful in taking her and when returning, carefully transferring her back to where she wanted to go. One visit and we were all relieved.

Jami and sometimes a nurse would go with us to the doctor's office. One visit required her to go to her dentist. This was beautiful, believe it or not. She was really fond of her dentist and he was always glad she wanted him to be her dentist. He let Jeri stay in her ambulance bed while they treated her.

They allowed me to ride in the front seat of the ambulance. On a return trip going home, I started talking to the driver about Jeri, not to her face because all I knew she was in the back somewhere. Talking more to the driver, I said, "I don't think Jeri is listening to me. She can't hear me, can she?" The driver said, "She's right behind you listening and laughing."

After leaving Rehab with Jeri, we assumed we would get helpful assistance from the company with the ventilator.

At home, we were told we could call the company involved if we ran into a problem. This didn't work as well as expected. We felt we were on our own.

One time Jodi was present when the vent let out a message that read it was on an empty battery. She called the company but was told to ignore it, that it doesn't really mean it's empty just that it's not full, that it's like a cell phone battery. Let it run out to test it so you can see how much time it really holds. It should hold about 30 minutes. Jodi tested the battery - it ran out in 6 minutes.

We were able to have Jeri off the ventilator 15 hours with no problems except for worrying about our 24 hours attempt to get her off. She seemed comfortable and alert. The fear was because the ventilator was giving a few warnings off and on over the period we used it.

It was an evening Jeri and I were alone and we were about to go through some of our kept items in a metal box when suddenly she seemed and looked different. Within seconds and with her eyes open half ways, she gave me a half smile and was gone. It was Sayonara. I think Jeri reached a point when she felt she could no longer do any more, that she had one cross too many the evening of January 10, 2009.

NOTE: Many of the medical and other stories we used "up front" of this book were taken from this above "hereafter" section after bringing Jeri home for the first time since March 10, 2007. She rejoined her family where she belonged, reinventing her smile and becoming Jeri again.

APPENDIX

(From: "**2001-02 Family of the Year Application**")

When my sister told me we were nominated for family of the year, I fell on the ground laughing! Us? Family of the year? Oh golly ned...that's all we need! My family is so simple and un-spotlighting that this would be the furthest thing from our minds.

We're not special, we're just us. I remember my parents reading a book called "And now We Are a Family." My sister and brother were adopted and this book was about adopted families; as dad put it, we all adopted each other including him and Mom.

When we were young, Dad worked 9-5, walking to and from work and home for lunch, he played tennis and taught us all to swim. He used to walk us kids to school and he'd take funny steps. (skips or double steps or things like that) to make the walk fun. I still walk fast to this day because of trying to keep up with him!

There was a family vacation (or more) every year and he would drive all night; perhaps to save money on a hotel but more likely to just to drive while the kids slept so that we wouldn't have to endure hours in the car. I still remember waiting to find a Howard Johnson's for an ice cream soda (vanilla!)-for a middle of the night break"

Mom was a homemaker to a tee. She taught us to sew and crochet and knew every fun craft thing to do (who could forget bunnies made out of egg cartons and animal bookmarks made from felt as birthday party flavors). She was a leader of three Girl Scout troops at once because no one else would do it. She taught mini-courses at our school and took us camping (including tent camping in the middle of winter with outdoor latrines).

Mom has always been there for us: bringing forgotten lunches or homework to school, playing the piano for our dance lessons, getting us up for school and now (even though she has a very hard time talking) she's always smiling and willing (no, wanting) to listen to everything we have to say.

Mom and Dad have always made sure we were a family. I remember Mom telling me (in so many words) that if there were only one apple, she'd want us kids to share it...we would have then and still would today! Mom and Dad always wanted us to enjoy being together and even on each other's birthday's we would each get a little gift.

When we moved to Bowling Green, Dad and Jami and Jeff came here in the fall while Mom and I stayed in Kent (to sell the house), by January Dad decided that we would all move to Bowling Green (even though the house didn't sell for another year) because he wanted the family all together.

Now Mom and Dad have harder adventures (probably one of their favorite words)-Dad can't drive anymore due to his eyesight and mom has multiple sclerosis, but they don't let that stop them.   They travel everywhere by train now (rather than car) and Dad still walks-although now its pushing Mom (in a wheelchair) up and down the hills of Vancouver or other places that their vacations take them to, or they walk to Wood County Hospital for lunch (leave it to our parents to think Hospital food is good).

After one trip across Canada, they told the story of how Mom had a tossed a coin into the Atlantic Ocean at Halifax and then when they got to Vancouver they went down to the waterfront (amidst construction mind you) just so she could toss a coin into the Pacific Ocean! Now what comes to mind is: why? But we've learned over the years not to ask why, just go along with them; and you know what? We have the best times because of it!

Only our parents would go to Churchill, Canada-Polar Bear Capital of the world-because "it's as far north as the train goes;" not once but twice.

We took a cross-country train trip and what an adventure that was, I was 25, Jami was 20, and Jeff was 17; you can imagine how "thrilled" we were with the thought of a train trip with our parents was at those ages, but we had a terrific trip.   And (another indication of how Mom and Dad are) two friends of our family (mother and daughter) came with us because we thought of them as family too.

Just a couple of years ago we all (grandkids and in-laws) went to Sea World and camped out. Mom and Dad stayed in a hotel but on the last night they decided to stay with us at the campground, sleeping on the ground in a tent!

We've never had a bad vacation-even when problems happened Dad would make them adventures (once our transmission went out on the first day and we just found a hotel-with a pool-and waited while our car was fixed). Knowing now about expenses and thinks like that, I'm sure Dad wasn't too thrilled with the added cost but he sure didn't change his mood with us kinds...the vacation goes on!

They also have a way of making every day special. Now that we kids are all grown and have families, holidays can be tricky with different families trying to get together on the same days but Dad simply says (and Mom will smile in agreement): "it's just another day. Whenever we get together is special, not just one or two days a year." So we tend to celebrate the "holidays" on non-traditional days; as Dad says, it's not the day that's special, it's the fact that we're together that's special.

Getting together is special to us but it's also very common to us. While Jeff and Jami and their families live in BG, my family and I live in Michigan, but I still bring my two girls down on the weekends. All the grandkids feel as much at home at Mom and Dad's as they do at home.

I think the reason we have such a great family is that Mom and Dad always put family first (or maybe more correctly, they put us kids first). Now that I have children of my own I realize exactly what that means. I don't remember Dad and Mom watching what they wanted on T.V. —rather we played games or played outside. I remember so many nights when all the neighborhood kids would be at our house playing because our Dad was the only one outside playing, and you could always count on Mom for homemade popsicles. And all the kids called them Mom and Dad.

I don't remember Mom and Dad doing what they wanted on the weekends but we sure went swimming or camping and sled-riding a lot-or then again, maybe that's what they wanted to do too and that's why it was so great?!

As far as the rest of our family, I don't think we're any more "family-of-the-year-ish" than Mom and Dad. We just do what we do because it's the family-thing to do.

Jami lives in Bowling Green and helps Mom and Dad the most. She's terrific and helps Mom and Dad with their errands without complaint. She takes them grocery shopping, out to eat, helps with Avon (Mom's an Avon rep) and just keeps an eye on them in general. She's married to Craig and they have two wonderful children, Dylan and Chloe.

Jeff also lives in BG and is always up for helping with big jobs, to watch the football game with Dad or to organize the annual family Christmas tree-cutting outing. And leave it to Jeff to start a cannonball contest in the pool. Jeff is married to Niki and Sierra is their terrific daughter.

I try to help out when I can, on the weekends or by driving Mom and Dad on mini-vacations; to their favorite Amish restaurant, to West Virginia to visit family, or to the train station for one of their trips. Bob and I and our two super little girls, Katie and Jenny live in Michigan.

All things considered I guess I do consider us very special-not because of what we do or have, but because of who we are-we are a family!

If you asked Mom and Dad "words to live by," I know family and adventure would be at the top of their list. I only hope I can be as special to my children and grandchildren as Mom and Dad are to us.

Jodi Anne (Schroeder) Engler, daughter

We are touched and honored that those who know our family took the time to think of us for this unique tribute. Initially, we questioned whether or not to participate in "Family of the Year." Our parents are quite modest and have passed that quality along to us as well. We, as a family have always known that we are blessed and special in our own way. However, we don't see ourselves as being extraordinary. We thought, "There must be other families more deserving than us, many others who are making a difference." What people see us doing with and for our parents is just a reflection of what they have always done for us. We are a family, but above all a family that begins with two amazing parents. Ultimately, we agreed to submit this as a tribute to our parents, Jack and Jeri because we feel they are the ones who deserve recognition. They are an inspiration to us and others and their story has touched the lives of many. They face obstacles and challenges every day, but they never give up. At the end of each day whether good or bad, they still have each other and they always find something to chuckle about! When asked about our parents, people who know them would probably tell you that our father is a dedicated husband, a storyteller, and a man who lives life with a sense of humor. If he isn't seen taking a walk with our mother, he is probably holding one of his grandchildren. He has an amazing memory and is currently writing a military history book. People see our mother as a beautiful woman inside and out. Her strength, courage, and positive attitude are an inspiration to many. But it is her radiant smile "that can light up a room" that people remember most about her. Despite her MS, she looks forward to traveling and is learning to use the computer. Growing up, we did everything together. We ate together, prayed together, and played together. We planned and took vacations together and created "Schroeder Family" traditions together. Our parents treasured every moment with us. They helped us become who we are today. We are not perfect, but we know what is important in life. Our parents taught us the meaning of family – something we treasure every moment together.

Jami Sharon (Schroeder) Baker, daughter

When Dad asked me to write something about Mom I had no idea where to start. After all, telling stories isn't my thing; I leave that for my Dad. I thought about talking about how she always supported my music or how she got the biggest smile on her face every time I came to visit. I thought about playing games with her growing up or the long talks we used to have when I was in high-school when she could still talk to me about things. Then I thought about how I truly believe she managed to hold on just long enough to see her last granddaughter born before she decided it was time to go; almost like she knew. When it comes down to it there is just too much to tell and trying to pick one special moment or memory in time was going to be impossible for me to do. Then I thought about Mom and Dad and how truly special both of them are. You see, while Mom is the strongest woman I have ever known, my Dad is as equally strong and truly is the most amazing and loving man I have ever known. The unconditional love that both of them have for one another is truly special. It is this love that allowed them to look past the bad things that life had thrown at them and live life to its fullest. So, while I know my Dad wanted me to pick one special memory of Mom, I would rather take this moment to say thank you to both of them for everything. Thank you for showing me what is important in life and how to live life to its fullest. You both mean the world to me. I love you both very much!

Jeffrey John Schroeder, son

Jeri's grandchildren loved Jeri not only for her smile but because she would listen to them. Each of the grandchildren has a place in her book with pictures.

Dylan   **Sierra**   **Chloe**

Katie   **Jenny**   **Kelly**

Sophia

ASAPAC Reunions

On Way to Churchill

Arrive

Raining

Our Quarters

Our Guide

Trading Company

Kelsey Boulevard

A Few Pictures from Churchill

1999

Bear Prison   **Huskies**

Hotel   **Train**   **Home**

2001 Heading Home

2003 Jeri found a friend in the Trading Co.

2005 Treats in Bed

POLAR BEAR
ALERT

STOP
DON'T WALK
IN THIS AREA

Leaving Toronto for Train Home

US TRAVEL
Kent

DC

NY City　　　　## Boston　　　　## San Francisco

Las Vegas

WV

Gatlinburg

Pipestem

GS Pipestem

GS Everywhere

Disneyland

Christmas

Detroit Tigers

Cedar Point

Lake Placid

Lake Erie

Niagara Falls

Sledding

Lake George

Atwood Lake

Cape Cod

Home + A Round Up
Our Family

Our Travels

Jeri's Relaxing Time

More Relaxing Time

Our Train

Jeri's Other Activities

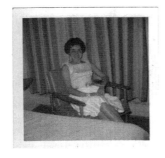

Canada – Travel

Toronto

Halifax

Winnipeg

Jasper

Vancouver

Prince Rupert